WOMEN AND GENOCIDE

WOMEN

AND

GENOCIDE

SURVIVORS, VICTIMS, PERPETRATORS

Edited by
Elissa Bemporad and
Joyce W. Warren

INDIANA UNIVERSITY PRESS

This book is a publication of

Indiana University Press
Office of Scholarly Publishing
Herman B Wells Library 350
1320 East 10th Street
Bloomington, Indiana 47405, US

iupress.indiana.edu

The paper used in this publication meets
the minimum requirements of the
American National Standard for
Information Sciences—Permanence of
Paper for Printed Library Materials, ANSI
Z39.48-1992.

*Manufactured in the
United States of America*

Cataloging information is available from
the Library of Congress.

ISBN 978-0-253-03276-8 (cloth)
ISBN 978-0-253-03381-9 (paperback)
ISBN 978-0-253-03383-3 (ebook)

1 2 3 4 5   23 22 21 20 19 18

To Joyce, who believed in the
power of education and in the empowerment of women

CONTENTS

PREFACE

SOME OF the genocides described in this book will be familiar to readers, while others will be relatively unfamiliar stories. But even the most familiar stories will appear unfamiliar for most readers because of their emphasis on women. Conventional narratives have not pointed out, or in some cases even mentioned, the separate ways in which women have functioned during genocidal actions, either as actors or as victims. In some of the instances of genocide discussed in this book, women were among the perpetrators. But women were primarily victims of genocide, and were subjected to gender-specific treatment which often was sexually violent and particularly brutal. The master narratives have focused on the horrors of the mass murders of marginalized groups, but what the chapters in this book bring to light is the way women were specifically targeted during many genocides. In some instances, the sexual maltreatment was a deliberate and often official strategy of the perpetrators as a way of exterminating a culture and an ethnicity. A mass assault on women's reproductive abilities was seen as an effective means of destroying a people, their culture, and their posterity.

That women were specifically targeted in so many of the genocides suggests that there is a significant thread of misogyny underlying the actions. One explanation for gender-specific violence is that in all cultures there has existed—and continues to exist—a hostility toward females, ranging from the brutality witnessed in genocides, to the hostility that today manifests itself on the internet and in social media, which abound with violent sexual insults and threats directed at women. Of course, cyberattacks are not only directed at women; they also attack people for their race, sexual orientation, religion, and ethnicity or because of personal animosity. However, only women seem to receive sexually violent attacks and threats. Women have been verbally attacked, humiliated, and in some cases, destroyed virtually by the hate-filled sexual violence of internet trolls. Even a relatively benign figure like Emma Watson, known and beloved by many as Hermione in the Harry Potter films, was the victim of attacks directed at women. After she spoke at the UN in September 2014, she not only received messages of support for her feminist HeForShe speech, but also hate-filled insults, including threats to reveal nude photos of her on the internet.[1] If women are seen as intruding on male turf, the attacks can become particularly ugly. When Anita Sarkeesian and other women spoke out against the misogyny in the male-dominated gaming culture, they were harassed and threatened with sexual violence and death. The attackers discovered their addresses and phone numbers, and so stalked, harassed, and threatened them that, in some cases, they had to leave their homes. Sarkeesian's life became a nightmare, with constant death and sexual threats made against her and her parents. A video game was even created in which the viewer could punch her face until it was bloodied or looked as if it had had acid thrown on it.[2] Similarly, sports fans who disagree with female sports reporters have attacked these women on social media, threatening sexual violence and death. Recently, male sports reporters were asked to read aloud the Twitter messages the women received; they were shocked. Some said the threats were so horrendous that they refused to read them aloud; the men said that although they had been criticized, they had never been subjected to anything like sexually violent attacks.[3]

However, gender-specific violence is not confined to verbal or virtual attacks. According to Department of Justice calculations, a woman is beaten or sexually assaulted every ninety seconds in the United States.[4] The FBI (Federal Bureau of Investigation) does not keep a record of hate crimes against women, although it keeps tabs on crimes against other targeted groups.[5] And there have been few recorded cases of crimes against women that are officially labeled as hate crimes. If a person is killed or beaten because of hatred of identity (the person's race, religion, ethnicity, sexual orientation), the crime is labeled a hate crime. But if a woman is beaten or killed—as occurs daily—even if the perpetrator is heard to spew gender-specific hatred during the attack, the crime is seldom labeled a hate crime.

In 2006 an armed killer invaded an Amish elementary school. He forced the girls to come to the front of the room, and then he shot them all. The media was outraged at this crime against "school children." Most people did not even notice that the murdered children were all girls. As Bob Herbert wrote in the *New York Times*, "Imagine if a gunman had gone into a school, separated the kids up on the basis of race or religion, and then shot only the black kids. Or only the white kids. Or only the Jews. There would have been thunderous outrage.... The attack would have been seen for what it really was: a hate crime. None of that occurred because *these were just girls* [italics added], and we have become so accustomed to living in a society saturated with misogyny that violence against females is more or less to be expected."[6]

For the most part, history has written of genocidal mass killings in the same way—speaking generically of the horror of mass murder, but not taking note of the gender-specific nature of much of the horror. With this book, we hope to start a conversation about why women and girls are targeted as objects of hatred, a conversation that we hope will lead to a better understanding of misogyny, not only in the past or in other parts of the globe, but today and in our own culture now.

The ubiquitous nature of misogyny in American culture was emphatically brought to light during the 2016 presidential election campaign. Anti-woman campaign merchandise was openly sold at the Republican National Convention and at Trump rallies (T-shirts and buttons that read, for example, "Life's a Bitch. Don't Vote for One"). At the same time, anti-woman hate groups have been proliferating on the internet. In 2012, the Southern Poverty Law Center published a list of some of the groups, and the editor commented that he was "completely astounded" at the findings, stating, "I had no idea that there was this dark world of women hatred. A whole universe of these people was quite shocking." He noted that within the radical right in recent years there has been increasing evidence of misogyny.[7] Within this background, perhaps, it is not surprising that it was so easy for her opponents to demonize Hillary Clinton, with a tumult created over her use of a private server for some of her government email—despite people hardly noticing when male politicians committed irregularities with their emails.[8] Donald Trump labeled her "crooked Hillary," and used that dubious epithet to elicit anti-Hillary venom from his raucous crowds. "Lock her up," Trump supporters chanted.[9] "She lies," they insisted—despite independent fact checkers rating her as one of the most honest of politicians, and Trump as one of the least.[10] Even more damning was the way in which people were willing to believe even the most outrageous fake news about Clinton, for example, that she was the head of a trafficking ring that held children in sexual slavery.[11] (This about a woman who had dedicated her adult life to helping children.)[12] At the same time, when Donald Trump was caught on video tape bragging about how he could sexually harass and assault women with impunity, even grabbing them by their genitals,[13] the most common reaction was to shrug. As one man said, all it proves is that he is a "healthy heterosexual." And many women who voted for him excused his behavior with the explanation that this is just the way men are.[14] He was like their husbands, they said. They seemed to have internalized the misogyny and accepted it as part of the culture.

Sexist comments might annoy some, but the tendency is often simply to shrug them off as stupid, or perhaps as innocent culturalisms. The term "bitch" as a demeaning insult appears in popular songs, in movies, and in ordinary speech, and many just accept it as evidence that "boys will be boys." But the stories in this book stand as evidence of how far such attitudes can carry people, and the horrific results of gender-specific hatred apparent in so many genocides are nothing to shrug off.

JOYCE W. WARREN is Professor of English and Director of Women and Gender Studies at Queens College of the City University of New York. Her books include *Women, Money, and the Law*, *Fanny Fern: An Independent Woman*, and *The American Narcissus: Individualism and Women in Nineteenth-Century American Fiction*. Among her edited books is *Feminism and Multiculturalism*.

NOTES

1. The threat to reveal nude photos later proved to be a hoax, designed to humiliate and discredit Watson.
2. See, e.g., Nick Wingfield, "Feminist Critics of Video Games Facing Threats," *New York Times*, October 16, 2014, A1. In 2012 Sarkeesian had started a Kickstarter campaign to fund a video on *Tropes vs. Women in Video Games*, which critiqued the treatment of women in games. In addition to cyberattacks, the attackers also sought to

prevent her from speaking. When she was scheduled to speak at the University of Utah, for example, the university received a threat of the "deadliest school shooting in American history," and the email message was signed with the name Marc Lépine, the man who in 1989 systematically went from class to class killing women at the École Polytechnique in Montreal, who claimed that he was "fighting feminism." Sarkeesian's talk was cancelled because the university could not provide sufficient protection for the students in the audience. Other women who were also viciously attacked for speaking out on gaming include Zoë Quinn and Brianna Wu.

3. See, e.g., Julie DiCaro, "Threats. Vitriol. Hate. Ugly Truth about Women in Sports and Social Media," *Sports Illustrated*, The Cauldron, September 27, 2015, www.si.com /cauldron/twitter-threats-vile-remarks-women-sports-journalists. The website *Just Not Sports* made the video "#MoreThanMean," in which male sports reporters read aloud the tweets that DiCaro and Sarah Spain had received.

4. See the 2012 Bureau of Justice Statistics, US Department of Justice. The figures are calculated from the US Department of Justice National Crime Victimization Survey, 2009–13.

5. According to FBI statistics, of the 113,000 hate crimes since 1991, 55% were based on race, 17% on religion, 14% on sexual orientation, 14% on ethnicity, and 1% on disability. See, e.g., Jim Abrams, "House Passes Expanded Hate Crime Bill," *Washington Post,* May 3, 2007. The 2009 Matthew Shepard and James Byrd Jr., National Hate Crimes Act was drawn up as a response to the torture and murder of two men—Shepard for his sexual orientation, Byrd because of race. For the first time, gender and sexual orientation were included as categories of hate crimes. For information on the 2009 Hate Crimes Act, see the Civil Rights Division, US Department of Justice, accessed May 27, 2016, https://www .justice.gov/crt/matthew-shepard-and-james-byrd-jr-hate-crimes-prevention-act-2009-0.

6. Bob Herbert, "Why Aren't We Shocked?" *New York Times*, October 16, 2006, A19. Italics mine.

7. Southern Poverty Law Center, *Intelligence Report* (Spring 2012). See also, Ginia Bellafante, "Reanimating Misogyny," *New York Times*, October 16, 2016, MB1. Also relevant is the 2013 case of Gilberto Valle, the "cannibal cop," which revealed a subset of internet anti-woman websites that indulged in male fantasies of tying up women, raping them, slashing their throats, and in some cases, eating them.

8. As many have noted, the Bush administration illegally erased millions of emails; Mitt Romney wiped servers, sold government hard drives to his closest aides, and destroyed his administration's emails; and Colin Powell used his Blackberry to deliberately bypass federal law.

9. For example, the editorial board of the *New York Times* describes in "An Even Stranger Donald Trump," August 12, 2016, how Donald Trump at his rallies told his supporters (falsely) that President Obama was the founder of ISIS and "crooked Hillary" was the co-founder. As soon as he mentioned the words "crooked Hillary," "the crowd erupted into cheers and chants of 'Lock her up,'" https://www.nytimes.com/2016/08/12 /opinion/an-even-stranger-donald-trump.html.

10. During the 2016 campaign, the independent fact-checking organization, PolitiFact, rated the two candidates on its "truth-o-meter." Based on their public statements, Hillary Clinton rated a 72 for true statements, while Donald Trump rated a 4. His false statements were 164, while hers amounted to 31. Politifact.com,

"Comparing Hillary Clinton, Donald Trump on the Truth-O-Meter," accessed
February 5, 2017, http://www.politifact.com/truth-o-meter/article/2016/nov/01
/truth-check-clinton-and-trump-truth-o-meter-1-week/.

11. The pizza parlor in Washington, DC, that the fake story named as the headquarters
for the ring, as well as other businesses on the block, received constant hate calls and
death threats. One man was so convinced of the truth of the story that he armed himself
and drove from Salisbury, North Carolina to Washington to, as he said, "rescue the
children." When he found no children, he fired his weapon anyway and was arrested.
For information about the fake news story, see, e.g., Sarah Lee, "Armed Man Enters D.C.
Pizza Parlor, Inspired by Fake News," *Washington Post*, December 4, 2016; and Marc
Fisher, John Woodrow Cox, and Peter Hermann, "Pizzagate: From Rumor, to Hashtag, to
Gunfire in D.C.," *Washington Post*, December 6, 2016.

12. See, for example, her work with the Children's Defense Fund, which in November
2016 honored her for her lifelong advocacy for children; her bipartisan work to pass the
Children's Health Insurance Program (CHIP); her work in the Senate on legislation to
improve children's education and to protect children's safety from wrongful medication;
and her work as Secretary of State against sex trafficking and the exploitation of children
around the world.

13. For a transcript of the tape, see, "Transcript: Donald Trump's Taped
Comments about Women," *New York Times* (October 8, 2016), https://www.nytimes
.com/2016/10/08/us/donald-trump-tape-transcript.html.

14. See, e.g., Irin Carmon, "Low Expectations for Husbands and Presidents," *New York
Times*, December 11, 2016, SR1.

ACKNOWLEDGMENTS

WE ARE grateful to Queens College of the City University of New York for help and encouragement with this important project, particularly the Women and Gender Studies program, and the late Virginia Frese Palmer for funding and support. The catalyst for this book was a conference on Women and Genocide at Queens College on March 17, 2014, without which there would have been no book. We also thank Peter Ryan for providing an accurate and conscientious transcription of the complex proceedings. Finally, we are indebted to the Andrew W. Mellon Foundation for its support.

WOMEN AND GENOCIDE

Memory, Body, and Power

Women and the Study of Genocide

Elissa Bemporad

WHILE GATHERING material for her first book, titled *The Unwomanly Face of War* (1985), Belarusian writer and Nobel Prize laureate Svetlana Alexievich conducted interviews with Soviet women to chronicle and evoke their experiences during World War II. Alexievich explained her focus on women and her quest to find out "how a woman feels" by asserting that "women tell things in more interesting ways. They live with more feeling. They observe themselves and their lives. Men are more impressed with action. For them, the sequence of events is more important."[1] In capturing the intricacies of the gendered nature of memory,[2] and in hinting that gender could determine the predilection for emotional information, Alexievich's words also remind us of the significance of viewing war, violence, and genocide through the eyes and experiences of women. Historical narratives have downplayed the emotional landscape of war and genocide. It is through the space occupied by women in this history that we can access and discuss emotion as a determinative factor in how this history unfolds.

The intersectionality of gender, ethnicity, and class plays a crucial role in the way women experience genocide. It may also determine the greater focus on the self and the emotional sphere as opposed to the "sequence of events" described by Alexievich.[3] The experience of women intersects with multiple factors, including ethnicity, race, religion, and class, thus shaping the ways in which they live through—or die from—conflict and genocide. In other words, in the context of war and genocide, oppression intensifies because two or more oppressed identities are occupied at the same time; it creates a marginalization that cannot be corrected by any single act of inclusion. To fully grasp the reality of war and genocide, we must closely consider "intersectionality."[4]

The experience—and memory—of war and genocide is inseparable from the notion of the body and power structures in society. The biological nature of female bodies, including their ability to carry life, consistently turns women into targets for sexualized violence during war and genocide. Mass rape often becomes the first stage for the annihilation of the enemy group.[5] Women's bodies are turned into the space where the genocidal project of eradicating the "social pollution" produced by the alleged enemy group is implemented. By breaking down moral order and kinship structure, mass rape serves as an instrument of ethnic cleansing. According to Debra Bergoffen, it precipitates and legitimizes genocide as it creates a community of perpetrators who bond together through rape. Disgust and shame turn the victims into "whores," and the raped women are often accused of being accomplices of the rape itself.[6]

Women in religiously conservative, patriarchal, or fascist cultures, which often place them in inferior social roles, face greater risk for abuse. Nevertheless, brutality against women can persist within an ideology rooted in the Marxist principle of equality of the sexes. Even in the context of some of the most revolutionary systems ostensibly committed to women's emancipation, the alleged female enemy becomes sexualized and targeted for rape. Such was the case of the counterrevolutionary, bourgeois, or kulak women in the Stalinist Gulag, or female prisoners of the Khmer rouge, who were viewed as women first and thus subjected to sexualized violence.[7]

The power structures of a specific society and culture largely determine the position held by women. As a result, these are the same power structures that women might choose to contest and actively challenge as they take advantage of the collapse of civil society produced by genocide. In the midst of conflict, in a society ravaged by war and violence, new possibilities for women's upward mobility and increased visibility in social life take shape.[8] These dynamics of empowerment and agency took place during the Rwandan genocide, when a number of Hutu women actively participated in the violence as leaders, authority figures, and perpetrators.[9] Similarly, the restoration of civil society following the genocide in Rwanda brought many Tutsi women to occupy prominent positions in public life and politics.

If the memory of trauma is gendered, then exploring the experience of genocide cannot be complete without including the voices and perspectives of women. However, women's perspectives must be seen not simply as an appendix to the exploration of events, but rather the epicenter of a scholarly reexamination and thus enhancement of our understanding of the dynamics that emerge in the context of genocidal violence. By studying the multifaceted roles women played as victims and perpetrators in different genocidal and postgenocidal societies, this volume sheds new light on the genocide of the Native peoples in the Americas, of the Herero, Armenian, and Roma peoples; genocides in Bangladesh, Bosnia, Cambodia, Darfur, Guatemala, Iraq, Rwanda, and Syria; and the *Holodomor* and Holocaust. By placing women at center stage, the contributors to this volume attempt to better grasp the nexus between misogyny and genocidal violence in societies where genocide erupts. In addition, this volume brings to the forefront the unexpected and often exceptional intersection between women's empowerment and genocide.

Scholarship on women and gender in the context of genocide studies has generated new research.[10] Over the past twenty years, scholars in genocide have incorporated the experience of women and gendered perspectives in their studies of the Holocaust and more recent genocides. However, we still have more to do to uncover the totality of genocide as a social engineering project,[11] a project that coerces the breakdown of old norms and hierarchies while creating new ones in every aspect of life and for every member of a given society. To understand both the full spectrum of responses of those targeted for annihilation and the range of roles fulfilled by those who promote and participate in violence, we must study the totality of women's experiences. More specifically, we must explore the voices of female victims, female perpetrators, and female actors within the blurred boundaries of the so-called gray zone, the space that separates the victims from the perpetrators.[12] The contributions included in this volume represent an essential stride in this direction, and intend to inform future discussions of genocide.

A DIFFERENT STORY

In his daring efforts to chronicle the life and death of Polish Jewry within the walls of the Warsaw ghetto, the largest ghetto in Eastern Europe, historian Emanuel Ringelblum fully grasped that the experience of women in the midst of genocidal violence was different from that of men, and should be studied as such. Ringelblum secretly created the *Oyneg Shabes* archive, an extraordinary collection of diaries, statistics, excerpts from the underground press, essays, photographs, and witness accounts that captured Polish Jews' multilayered responses to persecution and violence in the face of extermination. In his work, Ringelblum made the study of women in the ghetto a top priority.[13] He saw that women's socioeconomic status, biological identity, and the power structures and cultural constructs around them counted immensely, and that overlooking them would prevent future generations from gaining a full insight into genocide as a social phenomenon. In his *Notes from the Warsaw Ghetto*, the journal he kept from September 1939 until the eve of the destruction of the ghetto in April 1943, Ringelblum singled out women for praise. He was quick to note that "the future historian will have to devote much attention ... to the role of the Jewish woman in the war. She will receive an honored place in Jewish history because of her courage and powers of endurance, which enable thousands of families to survive this bitter time.... the story of the Jewish women will be a glorious page in the history of Jewry during the present war. And Jewish women will be the leading figures in this story."[14] Ringelblum believed that women showed a remarkable ability to adjust to the changing circumstances, the collapse of civil society, established gender relations, and traditional family structures. He pointed out their resourcefulness as they filled roles formerly assigned to Jewish men, who had been rendered powerless and unable to protect their families.[15] For example, Ringelblum noted "the toughness of women. The chief earners. The men don't go out. When they—the Germans—catch a man for labor, the wife is not afraid. She runs along, yells, screams. She's not afraid of the soldiers. She stands in long lines for food."[16] A few months before his capture by the Gestapo, writing from his underground bunker, Ringelblum made one more comment about the bravery of Jewish women in war, which he had personally witnessed during the battles of the Warsaw ghetto: "[Their] courage, ingenuity, and combat skills left the men far behind."[17]

Despite this call for recognition of Jewish women and their gendered responses to destruction, Holocaust scholars did little or nothing about the subject for decades. Why not? Part of the answer can be found in the poignant words of Ruth Kluger, Holocaust survivor, writer, and scholar in the field of German literature. Born in Vienna in 1931, Kluger was deported to the Theresienstadt concentration camp at the age of eleven and later survived the Auschwitz-Birkenau, and Christianstadt labor camps. Many years later, as a professor emerita of German at the University of California, she wrote in her memoirs that, "wars, and hence the memories of wars, are owned by the male of the species. And fascism is a decidedly male property, whether you were for or against it."[18] Thus, according to Kluger, the history and memory of war and violence, as well as the ideologies that facilitate and trigger genocide, become male property whether women are victims or perpetrators. However, this gendered appropriation of the memory of violence defies reality. The biological differences and social status of women do not make them immune to theories and ideas of violence, whether these stem from religion, fascism, nationalism, or communism. Like men, women can be swayed by genocidal ideologies, and can act as criminals and perpetrators in a genocidal society, as revealed by this volume's chapters on Cambodia, Nazi Germany, and Soviet Ukraine.

Women are not merely helpless victims: they can take advantage of the new power structures generated by genocidal regimes and engage in rituals of violence. The anti-Jewish violence unleashed during the Russian Civil War of 1918–21 resulted in approximately two hundred thousand deaths, three hundred thousand orphans, massive destruction and looting of property, and extensive rape. This mostly forgotten instance of genocidal violence, overshadowed by the events of the Holocaust that took place in the same territories some twenty years later, sees women actively participating in ethnic violence.[19] The wives of some of the atamans, the leaders of the Cossack armies during the Russian Civil War, were eager to seize the property looted by their husbands during the attacks on the Jewish settlements, and thus encouraged them to engage in violence and murder.[20] During one of the anti-Jewish pogroms that took place in Kiev from October 4 to 7, 1919, and resulted in the death and rape of dozens of Jews, a notice appeared throughout the streets of the city specifically appealing to Russian and Ukrainian women, inciting them to play an active role in the ethnic cleansing of the local Jewish population. The notice read as follows: "Women! It is your turn to do something for the sake of our suffering Russia, boycott everything that is Jewish, and spread this idea as much and as far as you can. Remember—this will be for them worse than all other pogroms, and they will leave Russia. Do not buy from or sell to the Jews ... Boycott the Jews!"[21]

Because of the gender-neutral policy of murder in most genocidal contexts, the research about the complexities and multifaceted responses to destruction by women is still incomplete, as is the examination of sexual violence perpetrated against them.[22] Furthermore, even fewer studies address the question of women's empowerment and advancement in the midst of, and following, persecution. For example, we know very little about the women who served in the Jewish Police, auxiliary units organized in the ghettos of Eastern Europe under the authority of the German occupiers during the Holocaust.[23] Similarly, no study has yet discussed the role of women in the Judenrat, the administrative agency created by the Germans to control the Jewish population in the occupied territories.[24] The propensity to forget these roles played by women stems also from the position of power they occupied in the very structures that, forced to cooperate with the Germans, facilitated the annihilation of the Jews. The gendered memory of violence tends to ascribe to women the role of subdued victims only.[25]

STRUCTURE OF THE BOOK

By bringing together some of the most prominent scholars in the field of genocide studies, this volume examines instances of twentieth- and twenty-first-century genocide through the experience, memory, and trauma of women. It places women at the foreground, examining the dynamics of violence unleashed in genocidal societies, as well as the role that gendered memory of violence plays in postgenocidal societies. This book strives to accomplish two intertwined goals. First, it focuses on the intersectionality of women's experiences in genocidal and postgenocidal societies. Second, it explores the multifaceted roles that women came to play in different genocidal contexts, as well as the roles they play in the struggle for justice in contemporary postgenocidal contexts. This book is about women as survivors, victims, and perpetrators of genocide.

Gender mattered and continues to matter: whether women are victims, perpetrators, or agents in the "gray zone," their gender identity determines their experience. Being female and Herero, female and Roma, female and Tutsi, female and "bourgeois", or female and "counter-revolutionary" creates a double burden in the context of war and geno-cide.[26] Moreover, whether they are rooted in racism, nationalism, or communism, genocidal ideologies almost always intersect with sexism and build on preexisting foundations of cultural misogyny. Even without the mass rape of the female members of the targeted enemy group, shame and disgust are still applied to the "other" woman who becomes a "whore" and is treated as such. To take a single prominent example, an account of an incident during the Russian war in Chechnya by journalist Anna Politkovskaya tellingly captures the intersections between misogyny and violence. In the process of destroying a Chechen village in December 2001, the Russian soldiers turned to elderly Chechen women with the words "'Bitch! Whore!' ... [But] 'How am I a "bitch"?' one of them ... cries out ... 'I told them, "shame on you, boys! ... What if someone called your grandmother a bitch?'" and the soldier says 'They wouldn't, because she's Russian.'"[27]

Violence intersects with questions of gender, always. One of the ways to better grasp genocide as a total social project is through a careful study of the interplay between sexism and racism. This volume provides insight into the congruity of gender in the study of genocide. Whether women become victims of rape employed as an instrument of genocide, or, enthralled by a specific genocidal ideology, they become actors and participants in violence, using it to empower themselves and reject existing power structures, their status is marked by their gender identity. These outcomes can be fully understood through the analysis of the unique geographic, historical, and social dimensions of violence unleashed in the different instances of genocide covered in this volume.

Structured chronologically, and including detailed historical contexts for each specific genocide discussed, the volume begins by focusing on indigenous genocides and their gendered logics. In the first chapter, Andrea Smith explores the legacy of the indigenous genocide, and the gender violence that was an integral strategy of the Native American genocide. Moving beyond the direct extermination of Native peoples, Smith analyzes the dynamics between the colonial settler society and the Native peoples in contemporary American and Canadian contexts, showing, in particular, the effects that these have on the lives of Native women. Emphasizing the tension between addressing issues of sexual and domestic violence in Native communities and the work for the survival of the group and its identity, Smith exposes the gendered genocidal logics that are manifest in US and Canadian contemporary policies.

In the second chapter, Elisa von Joeden-Forgey examines the neglected history of women during the Herero genocide of 1904–07 in German South West Africa and demonstrates that gendered power structures that had characterized German domination before 1904 directly influenced the experiences of Herero women during the genocide. Von Joeden-Forgey explores the sexualized violence and gendered patterns in the genocide in German South West Africa, emphasizing the many similarities this genocide shared with other cases of genocide in colonial and national contexts. As an example, she shows how German propagandists superimposed images of a hypersexual Herero woman and a manically cruel Herero male soldier on the enemy group and used these stereotypes to brutalize them. Finally, von Joeden-Forgey discusses the different survival strategies practiced by Herero women as they faced sexualized violence and mass rape in the concentration camps.

By exploring the events and memory of the Armenian genocide through the life of survivor Aurora Mardiganian, a briefly famous actress who starred in a film about the genocide, the third chapter studies the gendered experience of the group destruction and the gendered politics of memory. Donna-Lee Frieze looks at how the violence against women portrayed in the film illuminates the genocidal biological absorption practices committed at the time of the defeat and dissolution of the Ottoman

Empire. She also discusses Mardiganian's experiences of stardom and exploitation in Hollywood and her personal experience as a female victim of genocide. Frieze argues that recent scholarly and artistic attempts to resurrect Mardiganian's muted narrative voice encourage new knowledge about gender-specific destruction as crucial to understanding genocide.

The contribution by Olga Bertelsen is one of the first scholarly attempts to study the *Holodomor*, the state-engineered famine promoted by Stalin in the Ukrainian Soviet Socialist Republic in 1932–33, through the experiences of Ukrainian women. Drawing from the fields of anthropology, psychology, biology, and medicine, Bertelsen analyzes new archival material to shed light on the gendered aspects of the *Holodomor* and examine women's responses to the famine that took the lives of more than four million people. She shows that the collective experience of starvation not only destroyed women's support networks, so prominent in traditional peasant society, but also inhibited their abilities to advance themselves physically, morally, and intellectually, forcing them into isolation and delusion.

In chapter 5, Marion Kaplan measures the importance of employing gender as a research tool in the field of Holocaust studies. Focusing on German Jewry, Kaplan reminds us that gender made a sharp difference in the destiny of Jews and in the survival strategies that women and men adopted in the context of violence. Kaplan also considers the mechanisms of gender role reversals: women taking on traditionally male roles both in private and public and transforming their own female identities in times of crisis. Finally, exploring the relationship between gender and memory in a rich body of memoirs, diaries, and letters, Kaplan argues that gender plays a role in how the Nazi era is remembered. Gender informs the memory of violence and the destinies and decisions made by those targeted for annihilation.

In chapter 6, Wendy Lower focuses on German women in the Nazi East, examining their background, behavior and identity, participation in the terror promoted by the Third Reich, and their choice to actively support Nazi fascism. By analyzing the different roles played by German female perpetrators—some of them mothers, wives, and daughters—Lower shows how these women became an integral component of the SS-led machinery of destruction, in particular in the killing fields in the imperial setting of the eastern territories. While German women may not have obtained formal positions of power at the highest levels of the Third

Reich, they ultimately promoted Nazi racial policies in Germany and the occupied territories and shared with men in the task of mass murder.

In chapter 7, Michelle Kelso examines the experiences of Romani girls in Romanian-controlled Transnistria during World War II. Showing that the intersections of ethnicity, gender, and age played a crucial role in the way Romani girls experienced the genocide, this study is one of the first scholarly attempts to reveal the forgotten experiences of Romani girls and women sent to perish in Transnistria in 1942. Based on extensive interviews with Romani survivors, Kelso's analysis of the girls' resistance strategies and their struggles to survive and make sense of their experiences in the midst of destruction and trauma brings to life the silenced voices of a marginalized ethnic group. This original study opens the possibility for a deeper understanding of the still largely neglected Romani genocide.

Based on primary research carried out in the International Crimes Tribunal of Rwanda (ICTR), International Crimes Tribunal (Bangladesh) (ICT of Bangladesh), and the International Criminal Court (ICC), Bina D'Costa's contribution to this volume examines women's experiences of sexual violence and torture in the Bangladesh Liberation War of 1971, when more than two hundred thousand women were raped and tortured. She focuses in particular on the process of silencing rape victims and suppressing their memories of sexual and gender-based violence by awarding women who were raped in wartime and after independence with the title of *birangona*, or war heroine. In the final part of the chapter, D'Costa examines the broader contexts of women's advocacy in the region in redressing rape and sexual violence. Here she discusses the gendered politics of memory and the ways in which women's narratives about the war crimes of 1971 have been excluded from the official construction of a national history and of a masculine Bengali identity. By suppressing women's experiences of sexual violence during the war, their bodies have again been taken by force, this time in the interest of the nation and the construction of a triumphant historical narrative in postgenocidal society.

In her analysis of the roles of women in the Khmer Rouge communist regime that took hold of Cambodia from 1975 to 1978, Trude Jacobsen shows how many female party members were attracted to the new system and its ideology by the promise of empowerment, advancement, and equality with their male counterparts. However, as Jacobsen shows, there were clear limitations to the ostensibly gender-neutral approach to the creation of a new revolutionary society. Ingrained cultural perspectives on gender roles and female sexuality from previous eras affected the status of women, even of those who held positions of power. Khmer Rouge men used their political status to sexually exploit and abuse women in their power. Jacobsen's research reveals widespread breaches of "revolutionary morality," which forbade sexual interaction between men and women of the Khmer Rouge at all levels. These breaches included the "rewarding" of men with young women, localized practices of polygamy, the expected submission of wives to their husbands, the control of female sexuality, and the use of rape and torture specifically applied to women as a tool of oppression.

Chapter 10 explores sexual violence against women and its legacy during the Guatemalan genocide, which took the lives of 200,000 civilians, annihilated 626 villages, and displaced 1.5 million people. As Victoria Sanford, Sofia Duyos Alvarez-Arenas, and Kathleen Dill remind us, the data on the number of women and girls who were raped, abducted, and forced into sexual slavery is at best incomplete. Despite developments in international law, little progress has been made in prosecuting the crimes of systematic rape and torture to which Mayan women were subjected during the genocide. As the authors of this study show, rape became a military strategy to terrorize the Mayan population, destabilize their reproductive roles, provide soldiers with land and spoils of war, and confirm the historic colonial power relations between Euro-American elites and Mayan communities.

Chapter 11 explores the struggle to rebuild society and integrate women in postgenocidal Rwanda. In her contribution, Georgina Holmes examines the complex dynamics of gender, genocide, and the military in postconflict Rwandan society. In particular, she studies the attempts of the current government, led by the Rwandan Patriotic Front, to recruit women into the national armed forces. Based on extensive personal interviews with female military personnel, senior leaders, and government policymakers, Holmes shows how new societal perceptions about military women have emerged out of the 1994 civil war and genocide. She also argues that integrating women into the national armed forces facilitates regime survival, and is used to demonstrate that the Rwandan Defense Force is a cohesive yet diverse force that is helping society move toward reconciliation. The paradox, of course, is that the intended outcome of the gender program is to support the government's policies and strengthen the legitimacy of the authoritarian state. If gender-based violence played a prominent role during the 1994 genocide, the status of women is still an essential contributing factor to the paradoxical nature of postconflict development in Rwandan society today.

By focusing on the voices of female survivors of Srebrenica, a small town in Bosnia that in the summer of 1995 became the epicenter of the worse genocidal violence perpetrated in Europe since World War II, Selma Leydesdorff explores the dynamics of silenced memories of suffering. The memories of survivors, most of them socially and economically displaced women, contrast sharply with the public reports and official analyses of the genocide, which generally fail to mention their experiences. Based on extensive personal interviews with female survivors, the chapter discusses the legacy of a silenced genocide and silenced experience of trauma in contemporary Bosnia, where most families have only one parent, where women are unable to provide adequate role models for the young men who were children during the war, and where crime and unemployment are rampant. As Leyesdorff argues, "The way in which the women of Srebrenica have been isolated and denied recognition is an expression of the world's inability to recognize its own failure to keep a promise."

In chapter 13, Samuel Totten examines sexual violence against black African women and girls committed during the Darfur genocide of 2003–09 by the troops of the Government of Sudan and their allied militia, the *Janjaweed*. By discussing the hostile response to the victims of sexual violence, who in postgenocidal society are vilified and marginalized by local authorities, and ostracized by their families, Totten reveals the painful legacy of this genocide for its female victims in particular, who were singled out for systematic rape. Many women and girls refused to inform about sexual abuse, or even to seek medical assistance following the attacks, fearing that members of their family and community would treat them as pariahs for having been raped. As Totten argues at the end of his chapter, scholars and journalists should discontinue the use of such terms as "unspeakable" and "unimaginable" to describe the sexual assaults suffered by women and girls in Darfur. As in other genocidal contexts, the perpetrators did not perceive such crimes as unspeakable nor unimaginable; similarly, the assaults were neither unimaginable nor unbelievable for the victims. To fully comprehend—and thus prosecute those responsible—these crimes should become both "conceivable" and "imaginable."

Chapter 14 is based on the work carried out by MADRE, an international women's organization that partners with community-based women's groups worldwide facing war and genocide to advance women's human rights and peace. By discussing the role of grassroots women's groups in responding to gender-based violence in Colombia, Guatemala, Iraq, and Syria, Lisa Davis and Cassandra Atlas describe and analyze MADRE's approach. MADRE provides replicable tactics for advocates in other contexts wrought by war and its aftermath, as they struggle to empower women in the specific genocidal and postgenocidal settings. The chapter examines the gendered politics of genocide adopted by ISIS, the Islamic State of Iraq and Syria, which imposes its fundamentalist agenda directly on the bodies of women. As in the case of the assault on the Yazidi ethno-religious minority by ISIS, women's bodies become the frontline for genocide. In the second part of the chapter, Davis and Atlas show how MADRE, by building on the robust foundations laid in the realm of women's human rights, is embarking on follow-up programs with grassroots women's groups in Colombia and Guatemala to cultivate peace and justice at the community level. They argue that in postgenocidal societies, peace built with women's leadership from the ground up can provide a stronger foundation for sustainability and redress in the long term.

A selected bibliography of further readings focuses on the question of women and gender in each genocidal and postgenocidal society examined in the volume. Compiled by the authors of the case studies included in the book, these readings serves as an important resource for scholars and students who wish to further investigate women's experiences and the gendered nature of memory and trauma in genocides perpetrated in the twentieth and twenty-first centuries.

ELISSA BEMPORAD is the Jerry and William Ungar Chair in East European Jewish History and the Holocaust and Associate Professor of History at Queens College of the City University of New York and the CUNY Graduate Center. She is author of *Becoming Soviet Jews: The Bolshevik Experiment in Minsk* (IUP 2013).

NOTES

1. Masha Gessen, "The Memory Keeper: The Oral Histories of Belarus's New Nobel Laureate," *New Yorker*, October 26, 2015. https://www.newyorker.com/magazine /2015/10/26/the-memory-keeper. For the English-language version of Svetlana Alexievich's account, see *The Unwomanly Face of War: An Oral History of Women in World War II* (New York: Penguin Random House, 2017, translate by Richard Pevear & Larissa Volokhonsky).

2. See, for example, Selma Leydesdorff, Luisa Passerini, and Paul Richard Thompson, eds., *Gender and Memory* (Oxford: Oxford University Press, 1996); and Sarah R. Horowitz, "Gender, Genocide, and Jewish Memory," *Prooftexts* 20 (2000): 158–90.

3. On the intersection of race, gender, and class see, for example, Patricia J. Williams, *The Alchemy of Race and Rights* (Cambridge, MA: Harvard University Press, 1991); Kimberlé W. Crenshaw, "Mapping the Margins: Intersectionality, Identity Politics, and Violence Against Women of Color," in *The Public Nature of Public Violence*, ed. Martha Albertson Fineman and Rixanne Mykitiuk (New York, NY: Routledge, 1994): 93–118; and Bell Hooks, *Feminism is for Everybody: Passionate Politics* (New York: Routledge, 2015); see, in particular, chapter 2.

4. See Kimberlé W. Crenshaw, "From Private Violence to Mass Incarceration: Thinking Intersectionally About Women, Race, and Social Control," *UCLA Law Review* 59 (2012): 1418–71.

5. One of the earliest and most powerful accounts by a woman on her journey through Auschwitz-Birkenau is told through the experiences of the female body, the destruction of femininity, and maternity. The author of this memoir, entitled *Questo Povero Corpo* (This poor body) and first published in 1946 in Italian, is Giuliana Tedeschi. While this book is not available in English, see, by the same author, *There Is A Place on Earth: A Woman in Birkenau*, trans. Tim Parks (New York, NY: Pantheon Books, 1992).

6. Debra Bergoffen writes as follows: "Here the genocidal rapes served two functions: the widely noted function of destroying a people from within, and the little noticed function of legitimating the genocide in the eyes of the perpetrators. In the first case, the shame of rape transforms women's birthing bodies from the source of their people's biological future into a mark of their death. As polluted, the women's role as nurturers of the next generation and anchors of their people's moral dignity is ruined." Debra Bergoffen, "The Genocidal Politics of Rape, Shame and Disgust" (paper presented at the conference "War and Sexual Violence," CUNY Graduate Center, April 28–9, 2016). On the intersectionality of genocidal rape, see Sherrie L. Russell-Brown, "Rape as an Act of Genocide," *Berkeley Journal of International Law* 21 (2003): 350–74.

7. On rape and sexual exploitation of women in the Gulag see, for example, Anne Applebaum, *Gulag: A History* (New York: Doubleday, 2003); see, in particular, chapter fifteen. For sexual violence against women in the Soviet labor system see also Katryna Coak, "A Day in the Life Of... Women of the Soviet Gulag," in *The View East: Central and Eastern Europe*, https://thevieweast.wordpress.com/2012/06/19/a-day-in-the-life -of-women-of-the-soviet-gulag/ accessed December 1, 2016.

8. See, for example, Oksana Kiss, "National Femininity Used and Contested: Women's Participation in the Nationalist Underground in Western Ukraine in the 1940s–50s," *East–West: Journal of Ukrainian Studies* II (2015): 53–82.

9. On women as perpetrators in the genocide in Rwanda see, for example, Donna J. Maier, "Women Leaders in the Rwandan Genocide: When Women Choose to Kill," *Universitas* 8 (2013): 1–20; and Nicole Hogg, "Women's Participation in the Rwandan Genocide: Mothers or Monsters?," *International Review of the Red Cross* 877 (March 2010): 69–102.

10. See, for example, Amy E. Randall, ed., *Genocide and Gender in the Twentieth Century: A Comparative Study* (London: Bloomsbury Academic, 2015); Adam Jones, ed., *Gendercide and Genocide* (Nashville, TN: Vanderbilt University Press, 2004); Samuel Totten, ed., *Plight and Fate of Women During and Following Genocide* (New Brunswick, NJ: Transaction Publishers, 2009); Andrea Smith, *Conquest: Sexual Violence and American Indian Genocide* (Durham, NC: Duke University Press, 2015); Anika Walke, *Pioneers and Partisans: An Oral History of Nazi Genocide in Belorussia* (New York Oxford University Press, 2015). On the intersection between the security of women and the security of the state and its incidence of conflict and war, see Valerie M. Hudson, Bonnie Ballif-Spanvill, Mary Caprioli, Chad F. Emmett, *Sex and World Peace* (New York: Columbia University Press, 2012).

11. Daniel Feierstein, *Genocide as Social Practice: Reorganizing Society under the Nazis and Argentina's Military Juntas* (New Brunswick, NJ: Rutgers University Press, 2014).

12. I am referring here to Primo Levi's definition of the "grey zone," or the realm with "ill-defined outlines which both separate and join the two camps of masters and servants." On the "grey zone," see, for example, Adam Brown, *Judging 'Privileged' Jews: Holocaust Ethics, Representation and the 'Grey Zone'* (New York: Berghahn Books, 2013).

13. Quoted in Samuel D. Kassow, *Who Will Write Our History? Emanuel Ringelblum, the Warsaw Ghetto, and the Oyneg Shabes Archive* (Bloomington: Indiana University Press, 2007), 122. See also, Jacob Sloan ed., *Notes from the Warsaw Ghetto: The Journal of Emanuel Ringelblum* (New York: Schocken Books, 1974).

14. Kassow, *Who Will Write Our History?*, 239.

15. See, for example, Dalia Ofer and Lenore Weitzman eds., *Women in the Holocaust* (New Haven, CT: Yale University Press, 1998); and Judith Tydor Baumel, *Double Jeopardy: Gender and the Holocaust* (London: Vallentine Mitchell, 1998).

16. Kassow, *Who Will Write Our History?*, 241.

17. Ibid., 251.

18. Ruth Kluger, *Still Alive: A Holocaust Girlhood Remembered* (New York: Feminist Press at the City University Press, 2003).

19. On the anti-Jewish violence perpetrated during the Russian Civil War see, for example, Henry Abramson, *A Prayer for the Government: Ukrainians and Jews in Revolutionary Times, 1917–1920* (Cambridge, MA: Harvard University Press, 1999); Peter Kenez "Pogroms and White Ideology in the Russian Civil War," in *Pogroms: Anti-Jewish Violence in Modern Russian History*, eds. John D. Klier and Shlomo Lambroza (Cambridge: Cambridge University Press, 1992), 293–313; and Oleg Budnitskii, *Russian Jews Between the Reds and the Whites, 1917–1920*, trans. Timothy J. Portice (Philadelphia: University of Pennsylvania Press, 2011).

20. Elias Tcherikower Collection, RG 80, folder 450, folio 7, YIVO Archives.

21. Elias Tcherikower Collection, RG 80, folder 409, folio 34, YIVO Archives.

22. See Sonja M. Hedgepeth and Rochelle G. Saidel, *Sexual Violence against Jewish Women During the Holocaust* (Waltham, MA: Brandeis University Press, 2010).

23. For example, we know that several Jewish women served in the Jewish Police force in the ghettos of Lodz, Warsaw, and Vilna. I thank Sam Kassow for sharing this information with me.

24. In one of the ghettos in Slovakia, Gisi Fleischman became an important member of the Judenrat; in Wieliczka, near Krakow, and in Zaglembie, women became members of the local Judenrat, helping to run the ghetto by taking on secretarial positions; in Lodz, the charismatic Dora Fuchs served as the personal secretary of the authoritarian head of the Judenrat, Mordechai Rumkowski, and was involved with all aspects of ghetto administration.

25. On the trope of the good woman in Holocaust representation, see Sarah Horowitz, "The Gender of Good and Evil: Women and Holocaust Memory," in *Grey Zones: Ambiguity and Compromise in the Holocaust and Its Aftermath*, eds. Jonathan Petropoulos and John K. Roth (New York: Berghahn Books, 2005): 165–71.

26. See Marion Kaplan, *The Making of the Jewish Middle Class: Women, Family and Identity in Imperial Germany* (Oxford: Oxford University Press, 1991), viii–ix.

27. Anna Politkovskaya, *A Small Corner of Hell: Dispatches from Chechnya* (Chicago: University of Chicago Press, 2003), 93. While the violence carried out by the Russian government during the first and second wars in Chechnya has not been recognized as genocidal, in some circumscribed instances it can be defined as such. Politkovskaya, who was murdered for writing the truth about wars and politics, referred to the violence perpetrated by Russians in Chechnya as genocide.

1

The Gendered Logics of Indigenous Genocide

Andrea Smith

enocide and Native[1] studies scholars have debated whether
Native peoples in the Americas suffered genocide. Such discussions focus on what counts as genocide. Is intentionality required on the
part of those who inflict it? Does it require a complete lack of agency from
those who suffer from it? Does it count as genocide if many of the deaths
resulted from disease? The debate continues. Critical ethnic studies and
Native feminist scholars, however, have shifted the focus from defining genocide to analyzing the genocidal logics at play. As Ruth Wilson
Gilmore and Dylan Rodriguez's work suggests, if we understand racialization as the process by which "people are subject to premature death," then
racialization and genocide cannot be so sharply separated. Genocide is
less a politics of the extreme or the exception, and instead a foundational
logic on which white supremacy is based. In addition, as Maile Arvin
notes, Native peoples are not simply subject to mass extermination, but
to the logic of being in a perpetual state of disappearance that enables the
settlers to imagine themselves as the rightful heir to all that is indigenous.
As Arvin argues,

> I find it important to articulate the ways in which settler colonial practices
> of elimination and replacement are continuously deferred—they are

not, and cannot ever be, complete ... the permanent partial state of the Indigenous subject being inhabited (being known and produced) by a settler society ... [provides] ... a promised consanguinity between settler and native that is often eclipsed in formulations that focus only on settler colonial "vanishing" and "extinction." This consanguinity enables constant (sexual, economic, juridical) exploitation, by producing the image of a future universal "raceless" race just over the settler colonial horizon.[2]

Thus, expanding our framework for articulating genocide enables us to see what Michelle Raheja terms "the everyday forms of genocide"[3] to which Native peoples are subject. This shift then reframes how Native feminists in particular have organized against the logics of genocidal gender violence.

HISTORICAL CONTEXT

As I have argued elsewhere, Native genocide operates through a gendered logic in a number of ways.[4] Sexual violence was routinely used in the conquest of Native peoples. Massacres were always accompanied by rape and sexual mutilation as these examples illustrate:

> I saw the body of White Antelope with the privates cut off, and I heard a soldier say he was going to make a tobacco-pouch out of them.[5]

> Each of the braves was shot down and scalped by the wild volunteers, who out with their knives and cutting two parallel gashes down their backs would strip the skin from the quivering flesh to make razor straps of.[6]

> Two of the best looking of the squaws were lying in such a position, and from the appearance of the genital organs and of their wounds, there can be no doubt that they were first ravished and then shot dead. Nearly all of the dead were mutilated.[7]

> One woman, big with child rushed into the church, clasping the altar and crying for mercy for herself and unborn babe. She was followed, and fell pierced with a dozen lances ... the child was torn alive from the yet palpitating body of its mother, first plunged into the holy water to be baptized, and immediately its brains were dashed out against a wall.[8]

Sexual violence was a strategy used to justify raping Native peoples, and by extension, invading their lands and extracting their resources. Colonizers did not just kill Native peoples; they destroyed Native peoples' sense of even being people. Native studies scholar Luana Ross notes that Native genocide (and the sexual violence central to it) was never against the law; in fact, it was sanctioned by the law.[9]

Gender violence was also an important strategy in instilling patriarchy in Native communities. When colonists first came to this land they saw the necessity of instilling patriarchy in Native communities because they realized that Indigenous peoples would not accept colonial domination if their own indigenous societies were not structured on social hierarchy. Patriarchy in turns rests on a gender-binary system; hence, it is not a coincidence that colonizers also targeted indigenous peoples who did not fit within this binary model.[10]

Gender violence was largely introduced into Native communities through the boarding school system. During the nineteenth century and into the twentieth century, Native children were taken from their homes to attend Christian and US government-run boarding schools as a matter of state policy. The boarding school system became more formalized under President Grant's Peace Policy of 1869/1870. The goal of this policy was to turn over the administration of Indian reservations to Christian denominations. As part of this policy, Congress set aside funds to erect school facilities to be run by churches and missionary societies. Although they were under the direct control of church administrators, the churches were acting under the auspices of the state. These facilities were a combination of day and boarding schools erected on Indian reservations.

Then, in 1879, the first off-reservation boarding school, Carlisle, was founded by Richard Pratt in Pennsylvania. Pratt argued that as long as boarding schools were primarily situated on reservations, then (1) it was too easy for children to run away from school, and (2) the efforts to assimilate Indian children into boarding schools would be reversed when children went back home to their families during the summer. He proposed a policy in which children would be taken far from their homes at an early age and not returned to their homes until they were young adults. By 1909, there were 25 off-reservation boarding schools, 157 on-reservation boarding schools, and 307 day schools in operation. The stated rationale of the policy was to "Kill the Indian and save the man." Children in these schools were not allowed to speak Native languages or practice Native traditions.

Physical, sexual, and emotional abuse were rampant. Children were given inadequate education that only prepared them for manual labor. They were often forced to do grueling work to maintain the schools and to raise monies for the schools and salaries for the teachers and administrators. They were given inadequate food and medical care, and overcrowding contributed to the spread of epidemics. As a result, children routinely died in mass numbers of starvation or disease.[11]

In general, while other settler states such as Canada have at least acknowledged their histories of boarding school abuse, there has been no such acknowledgement in the United States. A number of human rights violations have occurred and continue to occur in these schools. US officials have provided no recompense for victims of boarding schools, nor have they attended to the continuing effects of human rights violations. The Boarding School Healing Coalition began to document some of these abuses in South Dakota and interviewed boarding school survivors in South Dakota. Some of the findings are included in these interviews described below.[12]

RELIGIOUS/CULTURAL SUPPRESSION

Native children were generally not allowed to speak their Native languages or practice their spiritual traditions. As a result, many Native peoples can no longer speak their Native languages. Survivors widely report being punished severely if they spoke Native languages. A survivor of boarding schools in South Dakota testified to the following abuses: "You weren't allowed to speak Lakota. If children were caught speaking, they were punished. Well, some of them had their mouths washed out with soap. Some of their hands slapped with a ruler. One of the ladies tells about how they jerked her hair, jerked her by the hair to move her head back to say "no" and up and down to say "yes." I never spoke the language again in public."

The continuing effect of this human rights abuse is that of the approximately 155 Indigenous languages still spoken, it is estimated that 90 percent will be extinct in ten years. By 2050, there will be only twenty languages left, of which 90 percent will be facing extinction by 2060.[13]

INADEQUATE MEDICAL CARE

Survivors report that they received inadequate medical care.

> There was a time when my little brother was sickly and he was in the hospital with a cold and I don't know what else was wrong. But they had the high beds in the hospital and he was little. And he fell out of bed during the night and got a nosebleed. He told them that he had a nosebleed, but they didn't believe him because the thought was that everybody, Indians, had TB [tuberculosis]. So they sent him to Toledo, Ohio to a TB sanatorium, where he spent about a year doing tests to see if he had TB. And he didn't have TB, but it took a year to find out that he didn't have TB. That was a whole year that he was sent away because they wouldn't believe him when he had nosebleeds.

> I just suspect, you know, that he must have been sick and had appendicitis. And he was thrown over the hood of a bed, the metal bedstead. And he was thrown over that and whipped. And he must have been sick. And so whatever it was, he wasn't doing or he got punished for it and got whipped and then he got sick and died from it. He had a ruptured appendix.

They also report that when they were sent to infirmaries, they were often sexually abused there. Besides the effects that continued to arise from the lack of proper medical treatment in the boarding schools, survivors reported a reluctance to seek medical attention after they left given the treatment they received.

PHYSICAL ABUSES

Children reported widespread physical abuse in boarding schools. They also reported that administrators forced older children to physically and sexually abuse younger children. Children were not protected from the abuse by administrators or other children, as shown in the following report:

> If somebody left some food out and you beat the other one to it, they would be waiting for you. So there was a lot of fighting going on, a lot of the kids fighting with each other, especially the bigger kids fighting the little ones. That is what you learned.

They used to send the boys through a whipping line. And we were not too far from there and the boys lined up, I don't know how many, in a line, and they all wore leather belts. They had to take off their leather belts and as the boy ran through, they had to whip them.

SEXUAL ABUSE

Sexual, physical, and emotional abuse was rampant. Many survivors report being sexually abused by multiple perpetrators in these schools. However, boarding schools refused to investigate, even when students publicly accused their teachers. One former BIA (Bureau of Indian Affairs) school administrator in Arizona stated the following: "I will say this ... child molestation at BIA schools is a dirty little secret and has been for years. I can't speak for other reservations, but I have talked to a lot of other BIA administrators who make the same kind of charges."[14]

Despite the epidemic of sexual abuse in boarding schools, the Bureau of Indian Affairs did not issue a policy on reporting sexual abuse until 1987, and did not issue a policy to strengthen the background checks of potential teachers until 1989. In 1990, the Indian Child Protection Act was passed to provide a registry for sexual offenders in Native country, mandate a reporting system, provide rigid guidelines for background checks for prospective BIA and IHS (Indian Health Services) employees, and provide education to parents, school officials, and law enforcement on how to recognize sexual abuse. However, this law was never sufficiently funded or implemented, and child sexual abuse rates are dramatically increasing in Native country while they are remaining stable for the general population.[15]

Survivors testify to the following:

There was the priest or one of the brothers that was molesting those boys and those girls.

It seems like it was happening to the little ones. The real little ones. And that ... I know that guy that they were accusing of that would always be around the little ones ... the little kids ... the little boys.

One of the girls, who was nine, nine or ten, jumped out the sixth floor window. The older girls were saying the nuns and the priests would take advantage of her and finally one of them explained to us younger ones what it was. And she finally killed herself. That was the most overt case that I can remember. They have been others that I have made myself forget because that one was so awful.

As a result of all this abuse, Native communities are now suffering continuing effects of increased physical and sexual violence that is believed to have been largely absent prior to colonization. Consequently, Native women are the women most likely to suffer domestic and sexual violence in the United States.

DEATHS IN SCHOOLS

Thousands of children have died in these schools, through beatings, medical neglect, and malnutrition. The cemetery at Haskell Indian School alone has 102 student graves, and at least 500 students died and were buried elsewhere. These deaths continue today. On December 6, 2004, Cindy Sohappy was found dead in a holding cell in Chemawa Boarding School (Oregon) where she had been placed after she became intoxicated. Someone was supposed to check on her every fifteen minutes, but for over three hours no one did so. When checked on, she was found not breathing, and was declared dead a few minutes later. The US Attorney declined to charge the staff with involuntary manslaughter. Sohappy's mother is planning to sue the school. A videotape showed that no one checked on her when she started convulsing or stopped moving. The school has received warnings for the past fifteen years from federal health officials in Indian Health Services about the dangers of holding cells, but they ignored these warnings. Particularly troubling was that Sohappy and other young women who had histories of sexual assault, abuse, and suicide attempts were put in these cells in solitary confinement.[16]

Two paraphrased testimonies from survivors regarding the death of Native children in boarding schools provide further details of conditions:

Two children died in school, and the administrators took the bodies home. However, the parents weren't there, so the administrators dumped the bodies on the parents' house floor with no note as to what happened to them.

I used to hear babies crying in my school. Years later, the school was torn down, and they found the skeletons of babies in the walls.

United States boarding school policies would appear to be a direct violation of the United Nations Genocide Convention, which, in article II, defines genocide to include "forcibly transferring children of the group to another group." Furthermore, as discussed previously, the stated intention of this policy was explicitly genocidal: "to kill the Indian" through the forced transfer of children into boarding schools. This genocidal policy was constructed through a logic of gender violence in which cultural genocide would be accomplished through the imposition of patriarchy onto Native communities.

THE LOGICS OF GENOCIDE

As mentioned previously, our analysis of Indigenous genocide cannot be limited to the direct extermination of Native peoples. Rather, settler colonial society operates through genocidal logics in which Native peoples must continue to disappear in order to minimize the threat they pose for the legitimacy of settler society. These genocidal logics continue to inform US policies as they directed against Native peoples. Reproductive health policies illustrate these logics of disappearance. The Genocide Convention specifically name "imposing measures intended to prevent births within the group" as an aspect of genocide because genocide must ultimately stop a targeted group's ability to reproduce the next generation. Native women have been no exception to this general rule.

In 1972, a Native woman entered the office of Dr. Connie Uri, a Cherokee/Choctaw doctor, and asked to have a womb implant. Dr. Uri discovered that the woman had been given a hysterectomy for sterilization purposes and had been told that the surgery was reversible. Dr. Uri began to investigate. Her work prompted Senator James Abourezk to request a study on IHS sterilization policies. The General Accounting Office released a study in November 1976, indicating that, in violation of federal guidelines, Native women were being sterilized.[17] These investigations led Dr. Uri to estimate that 25 percent of all Native women of childbearing age had been sterilized without their informed consent, with sterilization rates as high as 80 percent on some reservations.[18]

While sterilization abuse has been curbed somewhat with the institution of informed consent policies, it has reappeared in the form of Norplant and Depo-Provera. These extremely risky forms of long-acting hormonal contraceptives have been pushed on Indian women.[19] Depo-Provera, a known carcinogen that has been condemned as an inappropriate form of birth control by several national women's health organizations,[20] was routinely used on Indian women through IHS before it was approved by the FDA (Federal Drug Administration) in 1992.[21] There are no studies on the long-term effects of Norplant, the side effects of which include constant bleeding (sometimes for over ninety days), tumors, kidney problems, strokes, heart attacks, and sterility. These side effects are so extreme that approximately 30 percent of women on Norplant want it taken out in the first year,[22] with the majority requesting within two years to have it taken out, even though it is supposed to remain implanted in a woman's arm for five years. The Native American Women's Health Education Resource Center conducted a survey of Norplant and Depo-Provera policies of IHS and found that Native women were not given adequate counseling regarding the side effects and contraindications.[23]

It is difficult to ascertain the accuracy of statistics. But what is of importance, as Dorothy Roberts notes, is not simply the number of Native women affected, or its effect on the population of Native peoples, but the genocidal logic that informs these policies and practices.[24] The ability of Native women to reproduce the future of Native peoples becomes so threatening to the colonial imagination that curbing this ability to reproduce becomes part of US policy.

Another example of how these gendered genocidal logics are manifest in US policy is in environmental policy. Native lands are disproportionally affected by environmental destruction. Almost all uranium production takes place on or near Indian land.[25] To date, over fifty Native reservations have been targeted for waste dumps.[26] In addition, military and nuclear testing also occurs almost exclusively on Native lands. For instance, there have already been at least 650 nuclear explosions on Western Shoshone land at the Nevada test site. Fifty percent of these underground tests have leaked radiation into the atmospheres.[27]

Katsi Cook, a Mohawk midwife, argues that this attack on nature is yet another attack on Native women's bodies because the effects of toxic and radiation poisoning are most apparent in their effect on women's reproductive systems.[28] In the areas where there is uranium mining, such as in Four Corners and the Black Hills, Native people face skyrocketing rates of cancer, miscarriage, and birth defects. Children growing up in Four Corners are developing ovarian and testicular cancers at fifteen times the national average.[29] Meanwhile, Native women on Pine Ridge experience a miscarriage rate six times higher than the national average.[30] Thus, environmental destruction becomes another form of sexual violence, inflicting destruction on Native women's bodily integrity.

The gendered logics of genocide are far-reaching, expanding beyond extermination to structuring colonial society in a manner that subjects indigenous peoples to a slow death. Such policies must be seen as examples not just of racism, or colonialism, but also of genocide.

DECOLONIZATION

Native genocide is structured by a logic of gender violence. It is not simply that gender violence happens in the course of genocide, but that gender violence is the integral foundation for genocide. At the same time, in detailing how gender violence is inextricably linked to genocide, it is important to also present the ways in which Native peoples have been organizing against the gendered policies of genocide. To neglect this organizing is to reinforce the notion that Native peoples are indeed vanishing and this vanishing can never be reversed. By contrast, Native women continue to resist genocide and insist on the creation of new futures for Native peoples.

Native peoples have been resisting genocide since 1492. But the emergence of the contemporary movement to address the links between gender violence and genocide began in the 1970s. In 1977, the White Buffalo Calf Women's Shelter was founded on the Rosebud Indian reservation in South Dakota, one of the first domestic violence shelters in the country. Tillie Black Bear, one of its cofounders, attended a national meeting on domestic violence, where she networked with other anti-violence advocates, and helped found the National Coalition Against Domestic Violence. In 1978, she, along with other Native activists, such as Karen Artichoker, helped to found the South Dakota Coalition Against Domestic Violence. Thus, while the mainstream anti-violence movement marginalized Native peoples, Native activists were central to its formation.[31]

This movement developed in the midst of numerous challenges. Even twenty years ago, there was a deafening silence around the issues of gender violence within Native communities. To discuss gender violence resulted in being told you were airing dirty laundry, or being divisive. At the same time, as Kimberley Robertson's work demonstrates, Native women were key organizers of the anti-violence movement and helped spawn the National Coalition Against Domestic Violence and the South Dakota Coalition Against Domestic Violence. However, despite the key leadership role played by Native women, Robertson argues Native women did not participate in significant numbers in the mainstream movement.[32] Thus, anti-violence advocates had to organize creatively under challenging circumstances. In Minnesota, Native women organized by advertising events through matchbooks at bowling alleys. In Chicago, activists distributed anti-violence brochures while offering free blood-pressure testing at Native flea markets. A central problem faced by many Native feminist organizers was that gender violence was seen as secondary to Native genocide. Such an understanding presupposes that we could actually address Native genocide without addressing sexism, which ignores the fact that it has been precisely through gender violence that Native genocidal practices were enacted.

Despite the fact that the gender violence was an integral strategy of Native genocide, it was common to hear in Native organizing contexts that Native peoples do not have time to address sexual/domestic violence in our communities because we have to work on "survival" issues first. However, Native women suffer death rates twice as high as any other women in this country because of domestic violence.[33] They are clearly not surviving as long as issues of gender violence go unaddressed.

When the Native anti-violence movement developed, it did not articulate gender violence as separate from genocide. Movement activists argued that violence was not traditional but was the result of colonial imposition of gender hierarchies through massacres, boarding school policies, and so forth. The anti-violence movement that developed then simultaneously organized against genocide and colonialism.

As this analysis developed, it became increasingly apparent that it was not simply that gender violence happens in the course of genocide, but that genocide is structured by a logic of sexual violence. Now, it is commonplace for Native organizers to make these connections. Leanne Simpson argues:

> What the colonizers have always been trying to figure out is "How do you extract natural resources from the land when the peoples whose territory you're on believe that those plant, animal and minerals have both spirit and therefore agency?" ... [They] answer: You use gender violence to remove Indigenous peoples and their descendants from the land, you remove agency from the plant and animal worlds and you reposition aki (the land) as "natural resources" for the use and betterment of white people.[34]

Winona LaDuke and her organization, Honor The Earth, similarly organize around the links between gender violence and environmental violence. "We are in a time of extreme extraction, as we grasp desperately for the last remaining deposits of fossil fuels to satisfy our addiction. This means extreme violence against Mother Earth, exploding her bedrock, pumping lethal chemicals into the water, removing entire mountaintops, and destroying our own habitat. This violence affects Indigenous communities the most, especially women. Violence against the land has always been violence against women."[35]

At the same time, however, it has not always been that simple to tackle gender violence through a framework that addresses genocide and colonization simultaneously. This difficulty is evidenced in the growing prominence of the Native anti-violence movement. In the United States and Canada, the public visibility of the Indigenous anti-violence movement has grown significantly in recent years. In 2004, Amnesty International issued a report titled *Stolen Sisters* that detailed the lack of law enforcement response to the hundreds of missing and murdered women in Canada.[36] In 2007, Amnesty International published *Maze of Injustice,* a report detailing the epidemic of sexual violence in Native communities in the United States, as well as the jurisdictional gap that allowed perpetrators of sexual violence against Native women to act with impunity.[37] The public outcry from these reports contributed to some government action. In Canada, the federal government offered an apology for Canada's residential school system, which Native children were forced to attend and where they were systematically abused. After a plethora of lawsuits, the federal government agreed to a settlement that included the establishment of a Truth and Reconciliation Commission to document this history of abuse. In the United States, Congress passed the Tribal Law and Order Act of 2010, which facilitated the ability of tribes to exercise jurisdiction over perpetrators. This Act was followed by the passage of the 2012 Reauthorization of the Violence Against Women Act (VAWA), which provided limited tribal jurisdiction for non-Native offenders. Previously, the US Supreme Court had ruled in *Oliphant v. Suquamish* (1978) that tribal governments could exercise no criminal jurisdiction over non-Native peoples on tribal lands, which allowed non-Native offenders to perpetrate violence with impunity. VAWA provided some limited corrective to this decision.

These hard-won victories were the result of many years of organizing without support, resources, or recognition. Eventually, however, this organizing gained strength, and helped pave the way for the passage of the Violence Against Women Act in 1994, which provided tribal set-aside funds for domestic and sexual violence programs on Native reservations. With this increased funding, the number of anti-violence programs on Native lands began to proliferate As Kimberly Robertson notes, urban Native women were largely excluded from these services, but were supposed to seek support from mainstream anti-violence programs (even if they did not do so). In addition, these programs largely focused on domestic violence in isolation from sexual violence. It was often easier to gain traction on domestic violence because it could be framed as a "family" issue whereas sexual violence necessarily entailed a critique of patriarchy.

In response to this exclusion, some anti-violence activists began to focus on sexual violence. It was many of these activists, in collaboration with Amnesty International, who coalesced to produce the *Maze of Injustice*, which detailed the systemic lack of accountability for perpetrators of sexual violence against Native women. One of the leading coordinators of that project, Sarah Deer, also worked with the Tribal Law and Police Institute to assist tribes in developing sexual assault codes. This work so increased the public visibility of this issue that both Democratic Party candidates incorporated it into their political platforms in the 2008 Presidential elections.

Similarly, in Canada, Native women collaborated with Amnesty International to publish *Stolen Sisters* in 2004, which detailed the hundreds of murdered and missing Indigenous women in Canada as well as the lack of police response to investigate these deaths. In response, Canada provided funding to the Native Women's Association of Canada (NWAC) in 2005 for a Sisters in Spirit campaign that did educational work and maintained a database of missing and murdered women.[38]

The Indigenous anti-violence movement has achieved great successes in terms of gaining greater state recognition and public visibility. At the same time, this success has ironically also placed this movement in danger. To quote from the work of Beth Richie on the black anti-violence movement, the question is, Will it win the mainstream only to lose the movement?[39] In particular, will this movement be able to center gender violence as a key strategy of decolonization within the context of state recognition? Thus, these questions have given rise to new theoretical directions for how the anti-violence movement should proceed.

As many scholars and activists have noted, anti-violence activists often organize within a context where they are primarily funded by the federal and state governments. This funding does provide needed resources for survivors of violence. At the same time, it becomes difficult for these groups to organize around state violence without risking the loss of funding. Many shelters and programs also must abide by funding mandates to receive services, which can include, for instance, reporting undocumented survivors or those with arrest warrants to the authorities. The previously described Sisters in Spirit campaign in Canada discovered that state funding is not always a secure source of support. In 2010, funding ended for this program and the families that had mobilized under this program had to form Families of Sisters in Spirit (FSIS) and continue their work without funding. Based on this experience, FSIS has insisted on doing its work beyond the "nonprofit industrial complex."[40]

Dian Million's groundbreaking *Therapeutic Nations* articulates how the state co-opts Native feminist organizing so that work against gender violence actually continues rather than disrupts the logics of genocide. In particular, state funding begins to support Native feminist healing movements in order to mark Native peoples as national wounds requiring healing rather than as nations requiring decolonization. At the same time, Million does not dismiss the importance of these movements. Rather, she details their complex genealogies, including their subversive potentials as well as their tendencies toward being domesticated into settler state imperatives. In particular, she argues that the settler state centers indigenous suffering and genocide as a spectacle that, while inducing sympathy, is also predicated on the assumption that suffering can never end.[41] Indigenous peoples are to suffer in perpetuity so that the state can continue to administer to this suffering. This spectacle substitutes as a movement to dismantle the structures that create this suffering. The state, which actually creates the suffering, is now supposed to be the impartial body that will minister to this pain.

Some scholars have contended that it is possible to organize beyond an "either/or" approach to violence. For instance, Sarah Deer has advocated a two-fold strategy: (1) The short-term strategy of holding the federal government accountable for prosecuting rape cases, and, (2) encouraging tribes themselves to hold perpetrators accountable so that they will eventually not need to rely on federal interference. This approach can be misread as a simple formula for reform. However, it is important to remember that decolonization is a positive rather than a negative project. The goal is not to tell survivors that they can never call the police or engage the criminal justice system. The question is not, should a survivor call the police? The question is, why have we given survivors no other option but to call the police? Similarly, Deer is suggesting that it is not inconsistent to reform federal justice systems while building tribal infrastructures for accountability that will eventually replace the federal system.

This strategy was apparent in the Amnesty International report, *Maze of Injustice*. Amnesty's work on violence against women has almost solely targeted states with the responsibility to act with "due diligence" in prosecuting offenders. The problem with this approach is that conservative law-and-order advocates co-opt it to support repressive anti-crime agendas that negatively affect Indigenous peoples. For instance, the heralded Violence Against Women Act was attached to the repressive Violent Crime Control and Law Enforcement Act, which increased the use of the death penalty, added over fifty federal offenses—many of which criminalized youth of color, eliminated Pell Grants for prisoners, and expanded the prison industrial complex by $9.7 billion. This expansion of federal criminalization disproportionately affects Native communities since Indian reservations are subject to federal jurisdiction.

At the same time, it is also true that federal and state officials were refusing to prosecute offenders, rendering the rape of Native women legal. In response, Deer shifted Amnesty's focus to calling for the federal government to discontinue policies that interfere with the ability of tribes to prosecute offenders. In particular, the report called for a legislative repeal of *Oliphant v. Suquamish* (which prevents tribes from prosecuting non-Native offenders on Native reservations) and the repeal of Public Law 280 (which grants states criminal jurisdiction over some tribes). As a result, the Obama administration passed the Tribal Law and Order Act of 2010. Unfortunately, some components of this act increase federal presence in Indian country. However, other components of this act redress some of the problems of *Oliphant*, by increasing cross-deputization between state and tribal police, allowing tribal police to arrest non-Native offenders. This is important because, unlike most other ethnic groups, Native women are most likely to be raped by non-Native offenders. Consequently, this type of approach attempts to attend to the immediate needs of survivors while simultaneously building autonomous Native structures for accountability.

Other organizations, adopting an explicit "Indigenous feminist" analytic, have focused less on working in partnership with the states and have moved on to developing community-based approaches. One such organization is the Native Youth Sexual Health Network (NYSHN). Jessica Danforth, of NYSHN, builds on the work of Beth Richie, critiques the mainstream anti-violence movement for its investment in legitimacy.[42] Danforth argues that we tend to narrate histories of movement success based on when they gain political legitimacy.[43] Consequently, the history of success becomes conflated with the history of accommodation to the colonial state. Rather, argues Danforth, we should consider narrating movement histories through the spaces that remained illegitimate and illegal. First, if we center our analyses in these places, we will have a different assessment of our successes. For instance, the success of the anti-violence movement in addressing gender violence looks much less successful if we center the experiences of sex workers. In addition, if we build movements based on these places, then we are more likely to build movements that address the intersecting forms of violence people face. This does not mean that one cannot also organize around short-term legal strategies. NYSHN was active in organizing around the 2012 VAWA reauthorization. But in this work, the longer term vision of decolonization more dramatically frames the short-term legal advocacy.

Chris Finley has also countered this tendency to portray Native peoples solely as perpetual sufferers by declaring, "We are alive, we are sexy, and some of us are queer."[44] Danforth similarly argues that the response of Native communities to their histories of desexualization has been to suppress sexuality and internalize heteronormativity.[45] As has been circulating recently in social media, "Indigenous feminists are too sexy for your heteropatriarchal settler colonialism." Thus, this organizing reflects a faith in Indigenous futures beyond genocide that depend on the simultaneous eradication of heteropatriarchy and settler colonialism.

CONCLUSION

As the Indigenous anti-violence movement has gained strength and legitimacy within United States and Canadian contexts, these structures of legitimation have also forced this movement to a crossroads. Should organization efforts focus on greater collaboration with law enforcement and professional health authorities? Or, should they somehow return to their grassroots beginnings? What are the costs involved in each direction? And how can we strategically move forward while navigating all the political possibilities? In this chapter, I have traced those strands that are not necessarily abandoning short term legal and political involvement, but are focusing on building grassroots movements for decolonization that center gender justice as central to that struggle. These strands suggest that ending gender violence in Native communities will not happen simply through a government-funded program. Rather, it will happen through a political organizing that transforms the conditions that enable genocide through gender violence in the first place.

ANDREA SMITH is Associate Professor in Ethnic Studies at University of California, Riverside. Her books include *Native Americans and the Christian Right: The Gendered Politics of Unlikely Alliances* and *Conquest: Sexual Violence and American Indian Genocide*. She is also editor of *The Revolution Will Not Be Funded: Beyond the Nonprofit Industrial Complex*, and coeditor of *The Color of Violence, The Incite! Anthology*.

NOTES

1. I use the term "Native" rather than Native American to highlight the fact that Native peoples precede the creation of "America" as well as to highlight the connections between Native peoples in the United States with indigenous peoples across the globe.

2. Arvin Maile, "Pacifically Possessed," *Ethnic Studies* (La Jolla, CA: UC San Diego, 2013).

3. Michelle Raheja, Critical Ethnic Studies Plenary Address, UC Riverside, February 2008.

4. Andrea Smith, *Conquest: Sexual Violence and American Indian Genocide* (Cambridge, MA: South End Press, 2005).

5. David Wrone and Russell Nelson, eds., *Who's the Savage?* (Malabar, FL: Robert Krieger Publishing, 1982), 113.

6. Ibid., 90.

7. Ibid., 123.

8. Ibid., 97.

9. Luana Ross, *Inventing the Savage: The Social Construction of Native American Criminality* (Austin TX: University of Texas Press, 1998).

10. Scott Lauria Morgensen, "Settler Homonationalism Theorizing Settler Colonialism within Queer Modernities," *GLQ: A Journal of Lesbian and Gay Studies* 16 (2010): 1–2.

11. Smith, *Conquest: Sexual Violence.*

12. All of the references for this information can be found on the website of the Boarding School Healing Project at *www.un.org/esa/socdev/unpfii/documents /IPS_Boarding_Schools.pdf.*

13. Michael Krauss, "The World's Languages in Crisis," *Language* 68, no. 1 (1992): 4–10.

14. Jeff Hinkle, "A Law's Hidden Failure," *American Indian Report* XIX, 1 (2003): 12–14.

15. Ibid.

16. Suzan Harjo, "A Native Child Left Behind," *Indian Country Today,* July 2, 2004.

17. General Accounting Office, "Investigation of Allegations Concerning Indian Health Services B-164031(5); Hrd-77-3" (Washington, DC: General Accounting Office, 1976).

18. See "The Threat of Life," *WARN Report,* 13–16 (available through WARN, 4511 N. Hermitage, Chicago, IL 60640); Brint Dillingham, "Indian Women and IHS Sterilization Practices" *American Indian Journal* 3, no. 2 (January 1977): 27–28; Brint Dillingham, "Sterilization of Native Americans," *American Indian Journal* 3, no. 7 (July 1977): 16–19; Pat Bellanger, "Native American Women, Forced Sterilization, and the Family," in *Every Woman Has a Story,* ed. Gaya Wadnizak Ellis (Minneapolis, MN: Midwest Villages & Voices, 1982), 30–35; "Oklahoma: Sterilization of Native Women Charged to I.H.S.," *Akwesasne Notes* (Mid-Winter 1989), 30.

19. For a description of the hazards of Depo-Provera, see Stephen Minkin, "Depo-Provera: A Critical Analysis," (San Francisco: Institute for Food and Development, n.d.).

20. For a statement on Depo-Provera from the National Black Women's Health Project, National Latina Health Organization, the Native American Women's Health Education Resource Center, the National Women's Health Network, and Women's Economic Agenda Project, contact NAWHERC, PO Box 572, Lake Andes, South Dakota 57356-0572.

21. Mike Masterson and Patricia Guthrie, "Taking the Shot," *Arizona Republic,* 1986.

22. Debra Hanania-Freeman, "Norplant: Freedom of Choice or a Plan for Genocide?," *EIR* 20, no. 19 (May 14, 1993), 20.

23. *A Study of the Use of Depo-Provera and Norplant by the Indian Health Services*, Native American Women's Health Education Resource Center, South Dakota, 1993.

24. Dorothy Roberts, *Killing the Black Body* (New York: Pantheon Books, 1997).

25. Winona LaDuke, "A Society Based on Conquest Cannot Be Sustained," in *Toxic Struggles*, ed. Richard Hofricher. (Philadelphia, PA: New Society Publishers, 1993), 99; Conger Beasley Jr., "Dances with Garbage," *E Magazine* (November/December 1991); Valerie Tallman, "Tribes Speak Out on Toxic Assault," *Lakota Times*, December 18, 1991.

26. Ibid.

27. Valerie Tallman, "Toxic Waste of Indian Lives," *Covert Action* 17 (Spring 1992).

28. Lecture at Indigenous Women's Network conference at White Earth reservation, September 17, 1994.

29. Tallman, "Toxic Waste of Indian Lives."

30. Lakota Harden, *Black Hills PAHA SAPA Report*, (August–September 1980), 15.

31. Kimberly Robertson, "Rerighting the Historical Record: Violence against Native Women and the South Dakota Coalition against Domestic Violence and Sexual Assault," *Wicazo Sa Review* 27 (Fall 2012).

32. Ibid.

33. Rennison, Callie. "Violent Victimization and Race 1993-1998." Washington, D.C.: Bureau of Justice Statistics, 2001.

34. https://www.leannesimpson.ca/writings/not-murdered-not-missing-rebelling -against-colonial-gender-violence

35. Honor The Earth, "Fossil Fuel Extraction Dangers: Native American and Women's Organizations Request UN Help on Sexual Violence," Indian Country Today, accessed February 22, 2016, http://indiancountrytodaymedianetwork.com/2015/05/12/fossil-fuel -extraction-dangers-native-american-and-womens-organizations-request-un-help.

36. https://www.amnesty.org/download/Documents/92000/amr200012004en.pdf and https://www.amnesty.ca/sites/amnesty/files/amr200032004enstolensisters.pdf.

37. Amnesty International, *Maze of Injustice: The Failure to Protect Indigenous Women from Sexual Violence in the USA* (New York: Amnesty International Publications, 2007).

38. Martha Trojan, "Sisters in Spirit? NWAC Hit by Division, Funding Crunch," Indigena, accessed February 22, 2016, http://www.mediaindigena.com/martha-troian /issues-and-politics/sisters-in-spirit-nwac-hit-by-division-funding-crunch.

39. Beth Richie, *Arrested Justice* (New York: NYU Press, 2012).

40. Incite! Women of Color Against Violence, ed., *The Revolution Will Not Be Funded: Beyond the Non-Profit Industrial Complex* (Cambridge, MA: South End Press, 2007).

41. Dian Million, *Therapeutic Nations: Healing in an Age of Indigenous Human Rights* (Phoenix: University of Arizona Press, 2013).

42. Richie, *Arrested Justice*.

43. Jessica Danforth, "Decolonizing Activist Practices," (Evening Plenary, Critical Ethnic Studies Association, Chicago, IL, September 20, 2013).

44. Chris Finley, "Decolonizing the Queer Native Body (and Recovering the Native Bull-Dyke): Bringing 'Sexy Back' and out of the Native Studies Closet," *Queer Indigenous Studies*, ed. Qwo-Li Driskill, et al. (Tucson, AZ: University of Arizona Press, 2011).

45. Jessica Yee to First Peoples Blog, September 24, 2010, accessed February 22, 2016, http://www.firstpeoplesnewdirections.org/blog/?p=1881.

2

Women and the Herero Genocide

Elisa von Joeden-Forgey

The genocide committed by the German Empire against the Herero and Nama peoples in the colony of German South West Africa (present-day Namibia) from 1904 to 1908 was the first genocide of the twentieth century and took the lives of an estimated 80 percent of the Herero and 50 percent of the Nama peoples. Despite the comprehensive nature of the genocide, it is still a little-known event in human history, dwarfed by what came after—the Armenian Genocide in World War I and the Holocaust in World War II. In the past twenty years, both scholars and the wider public have begun to recognize the Herero genocide. There is a growing scholarly literature on the genocide, and the Herero people have maintained a steady pressure on Germany to both recognize the genocide and offer reparations. Still neglected, however, is the history of women during the genocide. Herero women's experiences are rarely included in studies of gender and genocide, with the notable exception of the pathbreaking work of Gesine Krüger.[1] The absence of a gendered frame of reference in most works on the genocide is a pity, since the Herero genocide is an instructive case study of gender and genocide. In this case, the leadership of both sides instrumentalized the treatment of women as part of their explicit communication with one another about their war aims. This chapter will examine the secondary literature on women and the Herero genocide, and argue that a gendered concept of power, constructed through the process of colonization, greatly facilitated the choice among German authorities to turn to a policy of genocide.

The relative erasure of the Herero genocide from history after 1945 can be explained by several factors, including official German efforts at denial after the genocide, a tradition carried on by some scholars today.[2] Moreover, the effectiveness of the genocide in undermining Herero collective life and the fact that the genocide occurred in a European colony in Africa, especially one that was administered by South Africa after World War I—a state that actively sought to suppress all memory of the genocide—helped ensure that there was no powerful institutional mechanism for remembrance. Germany's loss of its colonies in World War I and the enormity of the Holocaust also led, over time, to a collective amnesia about the violence of German colonization and made the colonial era appear insignificant to postwar West German historians. In Namibia, ethnic politics after independence may also have limited the ability of the Herero to press Germany for recognition. Only in the past two decades have historians and the German public begun to appreciate the impact of the German colonial era on Germany and its colonies. As a result of this recognition, the study of the Herero genocide has also expanded.[3]

Despite its long-term historical silencing, the Herero genocide was very well known in Germany as it was occurring. Debates in the news, in the public sphere, and in parliament resulted in a full-fledged political crisis for the imperial German state.[4] During and after the First World War, the Herero genocide was used by the Entente Powers as evidence of a particular German brutality that made the country unfit for overseas colonization. An important British government *Blue Book*, originally published in 1918 and recently reissued and edited by Jeremy Silvester and Jan-Bart Gewald,[5] is still one of the few collections of survivor testimonials in existence. The genocide was of course also integrated into Herero oral tradition and became a core focus of collective memory among survivors and their descendants.[6]

BACKGROUND

As gender scholarship on colonialism has shown, European empires were as much constructed through gender categories as through race and class. Women's experiences of colonialism are thus very telling when it comes to the colonial process. The ways in which women's experiences of colonialism intersect with their experiences of genocide help us understand both processes better. In the Herero case, we see the colonial conflict between competing gendered politics of patriarchal power that resulted, on the German side, in a root-and-branch genocide pursued with the aim of shoring up German masculine authority.

The experiences of Herero and Nama women during the genocide were directly influenced by the gendered structures of power that had characterized German domination up to 1904. German South West Africa (Deutsch-Südwest Afrika, or DSWA) had the greatest number of German settlers in the German Empire, making it Germany's largest settler colony when measured by German population.[7] Unlike Germany's tropical colonies, DSWA was free of the diseases that exacted such a high toll on Europeans. It was rich in arable land and already had a thriving cattle culture before Germans arrived. It is the only colony that the central state in Berlin ever identified as suitable for mass emigration and settlement by Germans. The state planned to use DSWA to solve the emigration crisis of the mid- to late nineteenth century, when Germans were leaving the country in large numbers. DSWA was thus viewed as an integral part of the future of the metropole, a place where Germans could return to the simpler life of the preindustrial era. These plans set the stage for conflict and eventual genocide.

As in other settler colonies at the turn of the century, the early years of colonial domination were characterized by a German imperial patriarchy in which unequal power between the colonizer and the colonized coexisted with multilateral diplomatic relationships and the possibility of horizontal exchange. Herero leaders represented themselves as analogous to German aristocrats and conducted themselves accordingly.[8] The early German colonists, who were mostly administrators, officers, soldiers, and missionaries, relied on local culture to survive and were deeply embedded in local politics and commerce.[9] Their labor force was supplied to them by Herero leaders and, in the early years of the colony, these leaders saw it as a matter of pride to offer their daughters to work in German households. Of course, the presence of young Herero women in the homes of German male settlers frequently led to sexual relationships, both consensual and coerced. At this time, things like sexual relations between German men and African women, as well as formalized marriages between the two, were not met with the same hostility as they later came to be; indeed, in these early years, they were both accepted and the norm. There was in fact a relatively high level of intermarriage, and the benefits of this practice for European men were well recognized.[10]

Although no comprehensive study of women in Herero society exists for the period before the genocide, it does appear that women enjoyed significant social power in patriarchal Herero society. The Herero practice a bilateral descent system according to which children trace their heritage through both their father's and their mother's lineages. Inheritance of land and cattle is also traced bilaterally. As in other southern African societies, Herero families were often polygamous, with men heading the homestead and women comprising separate households within it. While the leadership position of the homestead was usually conferred to male family members, women could also inherit these powerful positions. Traditionally, cattle raising and trading were seen as men's work, while women were responsible for milking cattle, taking care of the households, and trading in other goods.[11] Before the genocide, German men commented on the "helpfulness and obedience" of African women in comparison with "spoiled and demanding" German women.[12] Nevertheless, Europeans also commented on what they believed to be the relatively high status of Herero women in Herero society, basing this assessment on the fact that women were not involved in the backbreaking agricultural work as seen elsewhere in Africa.[13]

Companionate marriage between German men and African women, including Hereros, was widespread in the early years of German imperial rule in DSWA. German men often married into prominent African families in order to gain status, land, cattle, and trading connections.[14] They spoke local trade languages, used local farming techniques and commercial norms, and founded families. However, once the colonial administration began to formalize its rule, and the settler population began to grow, these sorts of liaisons came under scrutiny. "Race mixing" became

a central preoccupation in Germany's colonies as well as in pro-colonial
circles in the metropole. So-called mixed marriages were believed to
undermine the position of whites in the colonies and lead to politically
destabilizing and racially inferior mixed-race children. DSWA was the
first colony to ban mixed marriages—during the Herero genocide—and
the citizenship status of the children of these marriages was constantly
called into question.[15] Lora Wildenthal views the obsession with race
mixing and mixed marriages as part of a transition between two forms of
colonial masculinity: "imperial patriarchy," on the one hand, and on the
other, the "liberal nationalism" that superseded it as the guiding principal
of colonial governance.[16]

Although imperial patriarchy left room for negotiations, marriages,
and consensual sexual liaisons between Germans and Africans, it also
expressed itself as a belief in the colonizer's right of access to native wom-
en's bodies. This did not change in practice once the marriage ban was in
place. Among the most widely publicized colonial scandals in Germany
were those involving sexualized violence against colonized women. One
case, which occurred in the German West African colony of Cameroon,
involved the flogging and mass rape of the wives of the colony's African
police force, ordered by the interim governor Karl Theodor Heinrich
Leist.[17] In another case, this one in German East Africa, the famous adven-
turer and colonial administrator Carl Peters, out of jealousy, had his sex
slave and her lover hanged, and their villages destroyed, an atrocity that,
once it became known, ended his government career.[18] Both of these scandals in Cameroon and German East Africa resulted in uprisings against the
German colonizers.

In German South West Africa, sexualized violence was widespread.
Settlers even had special terms for it, such as Verkafferung (going native)
and Schmutzwirtschaft (dirty trade).[19] As these terms indicate, no distinction was made in colonial discourse between consensual and forced
sex. Indeed, sexual relations between European men and African women
were described with reference to the race hierarchy that governed the
German social order. The will of African women was completely irrel-
evant to naming. To wit, in May 1904, Governor Leutwein, in a letter to the
Colonial Department of the Foreign Office, completely conflates rape and
sexual relations: "Throughout the years I have spent in the Protectorate,

not a single case of rape has been brought to the notice of the authorities, although it cannot be denied that sexual relations between whites and natives are common."[20]

As was the case with the scandals in German East Africa and Cameroon, the Social Democratic Party publicized incidents of rape in DSWA. The Social Democratic paper, *Berliner Tagwacht*, for example, published the description of the gang rape of an African woman by three German settlers as follows:

> The overseer of the kraal, a German, and two of his cronies had locked themselves in with the wife of a native, probably after having administered a heavy dose of schnapps to her. Her husband, who had got wind of the matter, rushed to their house, hammering at the door and demanding the release of his wife. Thereupon one of these heroes came out to give the black man a good hiding, a practice which, albeit forbidden, is fairly commonplace here. However, the black man offered resistance and, after having himself struck a blow, fled into his hut. The whites, blazing with anger, dragged him out and maltreated him, subsequently bundling him off to the police station where he was given fifty lashes into the bargain for having assaulted a white man.[21]

Subsequent reports on the incident by the District Office and the Imperial Railway Authority at Swakopmund confirmed the details of the case, but, independently of one another, remarked that such goings-on were so commonplace that they did not deem the case worthy of note.[22]

Rape and sexual violence played a role in creating the conditions for the outbreak of the Herero anticolonial rebellion in 1904. One case that was particularly offensive to the Herero was the attempted rape and murder of the wife of the son of Herero Chief Zacharias in 1903. A German trader, who was traveling with the family, had attempted to rape her at night when everyone was sleeping; when she protested, he shot her, killing her and injuring her newborn. The German was acquitted of charges of manslaughter and subsequently, on appeal, sentenced to three years imprisonment. Such violent and disrespectful treatment of Herero of high standing is cited alongside loss of land and cattle as a contributor to the Herero decision to revolt.[23]

Herero survivors of the genocide were still speaking of these degradations, including the specific case of Chief Zacharias' daughter-in-law, when the British gathered testimony for their blue book during World War I.

Samuel Kariko (son of Subchief Daniel Kariko) told the interviewers: "Our people were shot and murdered [before the outbreak of the revolt]; our women were ill-treated; and those who did this were not punished. Our chiefs consulted and we decided that a war could not be worse than what we were undergoing.... We all knew what risks we ran ... yet we decided on war, as the chiefs said we would be better off even if we were all dead."[24]

WOMEN IN THE WAR AND GENOCIDE

As Gesine Krüger has pointed out, men, women, and children were intentionally killed during the Herero genocide. Neither sex nor age determined Herero chances of survival. Women and children were directly targeted by the German military, which aimed to destroy the social body of the Herero in its totality. The German military made no distinction between combatants and noncombatants.[25] Like men, women and children died from dehydration, starvation, disease; they were killed in battle, shot as prisoners, and worked to death in concentration camps.[26] According to eyewitnesses, women and children were also hanged, bayonetted, burned alive, and mutilated. Nevertheless, despite the gender-neutral outcome of the genocide in terms of lives lost, we do see gendered patterns within the genocidal process in DSWA that are similar to other cases of genocide, both in imperial and national contexts.

The genocide against the Herero occurred in the context of a German counterinsurgency campaign against what they believed had been a Herero revolt. Most scholars now view the outbreak of war to have been the result of a series of misunderstandings, driven by a national security paranoia on the part of German settlers and administrators, who were constantly afraid of a Herero rebellion.[27] The Germans mistook a meeting of Herero chiefs regarding inheritance issues as a sign of imminent attack. The panicked German response led the Herero to believe that the Germans planned to kill their paramount chief, Samuel Maherero. In response, on January 14, 1904, a small group of Hereros revolted, murdering 123 white Germans, including 3 women.[28]

> After this, the rest of the Herero were forced into war by the strong German military response. Samuel Maherero issued a letter to Herero chiefs in which he delineated legitimate and illegitimate targets, saying,

"I have issued an order, a straight word, meant for all my people, that they should *no longer* lay their hands on the following: namely Englishmen, Basters, Bergdamaras, Namas, Boers; we do not lay hands on these. Do not do this. I have sworn an oath to this, that this case does not become open, also not to the missionaries. Enough."[29]

In a similar fashion, Maherero also guaranteed the safety of German women and children.[30] Subchief Daniel Kariko reported that "[a]t our clandestine meetings our chiefs decided to spare the lives of all German women and children.... Only German men were regarded as our enemies."[31] There are examples of Herero soldiers escorting German women and children to safety at great personal risk. Governor Leutwein favorably noted Maherero's policy toward women and children after the war: "It seems to have been the definite intention of the Herero leaders to protect all women and children. When, in spite of this, some were murdered, this to be ascribed to the fact that everywhere inhuman people are to be found who do not confine themselves to such limits."[32] In point of fact, no more than four women and one child total were ever killed by Herero forces during the war. Many German women described their good treatment by Herero soldiers for the full period of the war, up to the German defeat of the Herero at Waterberg on August 11, 1904.

Despite this humane treatment of women and children by Herero soldiers, atrocity stories ran rampant among settlers and especially in pro-colonial circles in Germany. They contributed to the overall sense of national security emergency in Berlin as well as the redefinition of what was a very a limited colonial conflict as a "race war." Propaganda described rapes, eviscerations, breast mutilations and murders of German women by Herero soldiers.[33] Equally destructive were propaganda images of Herero women as "castrating Amazons."[34] In fact, colonial authorities named Herero women as the most ferocious and cruel of all fighters, despite the lack of evidence that women participated as soldiers.[35] Instead, as was the case across Africa, Herero women followed behind their male family members in battle, singing songs of support and taking care of the logistics of feeding and caring for the troops.[36]

German women in South West Africa embraced the concept of the race war with few known exceptions. According to Lore Wildenthal, German women's memoirs "retell colonial experiences such as the Southwest

African War of 1904–1907 or confrontations with African servants, in often formulaic ways. They embrace the 'race war' interpretation of colonial war: Africans had inexplicably turned on German men and women using duplicitous, unconventional methods and were never again to be trusted with any notable measure of liberty. It is predictable that the women authors like other colonists who had experienced the war at first hand, blamed Africans and reflected little on the role of the Germans in provoking the conflict."[37] German women who arrived after the end of the genocide were even more racist, as they "took up the race war thesis and applied it to peacetime life."[38] The memoirs' inveterate support of General Lothar von Trotha's measures against the Herero (and later the Nama) can be interpreted as the consequence of German women's reliance on a strict colonial race hierarchy for their position of relative power vis-à-vis African populations and especially African women. Such formulaic approaches to the genocide were also in keeping with the literary conventions that had emerged around German colonial wars.

For the most part, the atrocity stories circulating among German settlers must be seen as fabrications. Even at the time, missionaries sought to disabuse Germans in the metropole of their false—and radicalizing—impressions.[39] However, some instances of mutilation may have occurred. One missionary wrote in the Social Democratic paper *Der Reichsbote*: "Certain newspapers report that appalling atrocities have been perpetrated by the Herero, alleging that they have massacred the wives of settlers and also castrated a number of men. As far at the latter assertion is concerned, they have indeed done so in the case of whites who have raped their womenfolk in the most brutal manner."[40]

The German colonial military force (Schutztruppe), first under the command of Governor Leutwein and, after June 1904, under General von Trotha, responded to the initial Herero attack with typical colonial ferocity. Settlements were raided, the inhabitants murdered, and all structures burned. Because German soldiers would not distinguish between African groups, all African settlements were at risk, not just the Herero.[41] Such a response was not at all out of the ordinary in the German Empire. Germans pursued pacification of the Maji Maji rebellion in German East Africa in a similarly brutal fashion, for example. What is different, however, is the comprehensive nature of the orders that soldiers reported having received, even before reaching the colony. According to the memoirs of one marine who arrived in DSWA shortly after the start of the war, for example, he and his fellow soldiers had been told that men, women, and children were all to be slaughtered—no one was to be left alive.[42] While there does not appear to have been an overall order to this effect from Governor Leutwein or metropolitan authorities, localized orders like this one resulted in gender-neutral massacres on the ground even before the arrival of von Trotha.[43]

Throughout the first eight months of the war the Herero sought a negotiated settlement and were encouraged in their efforts by Governor Leutwein, who believed "[i]n colonial issues there must always be a diplomat standing next to a leader. The rebels must know that their route back is still open, one that does not always lead to death."[44] However, neither General von Trotha nor the authorities in Berlin had plans to negotiate. Von Trotha wished to destroy the Herero to the fullest extent possible—in his words, "the nation as such should be annihilated."[45] He embraced a view of the war as a "race war" and conducted the war accordingly. When he took over the war effort in June 1904, he switched to a new policy of annihilation, one that involved defeating the Herero militarily and forcing the entire population into the Omaheke desert, where all points of exit as well as the watering holes were to be sealed off and the Herero nation starved to death.

The document that is most often cited as evidence of genocidal intent, at least on the part of General von Trotha, is the extermination order of October 2, 1904. It was written two months after the Herero had been militarily defeated at Waterberg, when what was left of the nation was forced into the Omaheke desert. Von Trotha issued an order that read as follows:

> I the great General of the German troops send this letter to the Herero people. The Hereros are no longer German subjects.... All the Hereros must leave the land. If the people do not do this, then I will force them to do it with the great guns. Any Herero found within the German borders with or without a gun, with or without cattle, will be shot. I shall no longer receive women or children. I will drive them back to their people or I will shoot them. This is my decision for the Herero people.[46]

In a supplement for his officers, he added these instructions: "And the shooting of women and children is to be understood to mean that one can shoot over them to force them to run faster. I definitely mean that this order will be carried out and that no male prisoners will be taken, but it should not degenerate into killing women and children. This will be accomplished if one shoots over their heads a couple of times. The soldiers will remain conscious of the good reputation of German soldiers."

As Horst Dreschler and Dominick Schaller have pointed out, this addendum to the original extermination order was not designed to spare the lives of women and children—far from it.[47] Aware of criticism in Germany of the "take no prisoners" policy that had been followed up to that point—both within the central state and among colonial opposition parties in the Reichstag—von Trotha was publicly advocating genocide by attrition behind empty words about shooting above women and children "to make them run faster." As it turns out, the supplement was never adhered to in the first place, and women and children were directly murdered alongside men. All the testimonials collected by the British during World War I suggest that the German forces did not discriminate between men, women, and children. If they came upon women stragglers in the Omaheke, they murdered them without mercy.

Henrik Campbell, commander of the Rehoboth force that fought alongside the Germans at Waterberg, testified to Germany's gender-neutral policy of murder: "When the engagement was over, we discovered eight or nine sick Herero women who had been left behind. Some of them were blind. They had a supply of water and food. But the German soldiers burned them alive by setting fire to the hut in which they were lying."[48] A similar fate awaited a group of men, women, and children— all prisoners—who were confined in a small enclosure of thorn bushes. Kindling was heaped upon them and lit on fire.[49] In another instance, a group of fifty prisoners, again of mixed sex and age, were bayonetted to death.[50] Some young women were eviscerated by German troops.[51] A baby was impaled on a bayonet as soldiers let out "roars of laughter."[52]

A Griqua African who traveled with German troops reported that

> [t]he Germans took no prisoners. They killed thousands and thousands
> of women and children along the roadsides. They bayoneted them and hit
> them to death with the butt ends of their guns. Words cannot be found
> to relate what happened; it was too terrible. They were lying exhausted
> and harmless along the roads, and as the soldiers passed they simply

slaughtered them in cold blood. Mothers holding babies at their breasts, little boys and little girls; old people too old to fight and old grandmothers, none received mercy; they were killed, all of them, and left to lie and rot on the veld for the vultures and wild animals to eat.[53]

During the war, women and girls were also subjected to rape in what appears to be very high numbers. One African observer testified that "[o]ften, and especially at Waterberg, the young Herero women and girls were violated by the German soldiers before being killed. Two of my Hottentots [the witness was a chief] ... were invited by the German soldiers to join them in violating Herero girls. The two Hottentots refused to do so."[54]

The horror of the direct assault by German forces on defeated Herero soldiers and civilians was matched by the conditions they faced in the desert. Von Trotha made sure that the desert was sealed off and all means of escape barred. He then ordered the watering holes to be sealed and, in some instances, poisoned. At first, entire families and settlements retreated into the desert along with their possessions and their cattle to avoid German troops. An old German settler, who had taken part in the war, described the desert floor as being littered by "blankets, skins, ostrich feathers, household utensils, women's ornaments, cattle and men, dead and dying and staring blankly."[55] "I saw tracks of innumerable children's feet," he added, "and among them those of full-grown feet. Great troops of children, led by their mothers, had passed over the road here to the north-west." As time wore on, however, survivors were forced to discard their possessions and groups became less cohesive.

Women constructed makeshift huts from branches and leaves to shelter their children. They attempted to endure the freezing nights with small fires in these shelters as well as using them to find shade from the harsh sun of daytime. Families tried to stay together. In one instance, an emaciated married couple emerged from the desert together and approached German troops to surrender because they could no longer go on—the man's leg was badly wounded by a bullet and he was forced to lean on his wife's arm to walk. After having been given some provisions by a kindly transport driver, the couple was unceremoniously shot by German soldiers.[56] Even in the desert, Herero families were constantly threatened by German patrols, which would ambush and slaughter them down to the last child.

For over a year survivors attempted to remain alive in the desert. People tried to survive by digging for wild onions and for water. Families were torn apart as members died en route or could not keep up. Terrible decisions had to be made about who would drink and who would not when scarce water sources were discovered. Such "choiceless choices" show up in Herero oral tradition, which tells of grown men suckling from women's breasts instead of children and women lancing their own breasts to feed their children their own blood. Gesine Krüger has interpreted these traditions to refer not so much to actual events but rather to the terrible decisions that Herero women had to make as they tried to keep family members alive.[57] German patrols often came upon lone children and infants, whom they murdered. Herero oral traditions tell the stories of children who lost their mothers and of women who took care of orphans whom they found in the desert.[58] As in other cases of genocide, these stories of individual family tragedies carry the full weight of the sorrow of the crime of genocide committed against the larger group.

Eventually, the Imperial Government in Berlin, concerned about the economic impact of von Trotha's policy as well as the reputation of Germany as a colonial power, recalled von Trotha and installed Friedrich von Lindequist as Governor. Lindequist's orders were to coax the remaining Herero to surrender. A survivor described their condition on surrender in the following stark terms: "We then had no cattle left, and more than three-quarters of our people had perished, far more. There were only a few thousands of us left, and we were walking skeletons, with no flesh, only skin and bones."[59]

CONCENTRATION CAMPS

Surviving Herero were placed as forced laborers in concentration camps on and near the coast, and on white farms. In these camps thousands of Herero perished—they were murdered, worked to death, mistreated, and starved; unaccustomed to the damp climate, they also died from disease at very high rates. It is in the camps that we begin to see gender differentiation in the treatment of victims. All Herero men of fighting age and Herero leaders were "systematically sought out, tried in 'court-martials' and executed, usually by hanging."[60] Everyone else was subjected to hard labor. As had been the case throughout the war and genocide, women and girls were additionally raped in high numbers. Helmut Bley notes that rape in the camps reached "catastrophic proportions."[61] Women and girls as young as seven years old were raped not only by the military personnel who guarded the camps, but also by white civilians, who would come to the camps and take women and girls to be abused as sex slaves.[62] Starting in 1906 girls and women were also subject to humiliating internal exams, ostensibly to inhibit the further spread of sexually transmitted diseases, which had reached epidemic proportions. These exams, which were conducted by male doctors, were so humiliating that Herero women eventually openly protested.[63]

David Olusoga and Casper Erichsen point out that not only was rape common in the camps, but it was "actively celebrated." They describe a postcard that circulated at the time, one of many atrocity postcards that were popular among Germans, as depicting "a naked, adolescent Herero girl standing in a tiny shack, probably the interior of the guards' shelter.... Squeezed between the girl's thighs, in an unconscious effort to retain some semblance of dignity, are the torn remains of her dress that had been ripped from her body."[64]

Missionaries in the camps were completely powerless to protect Herero women from sexual exploitation. In fact, when faced with evidence of rampant sexualized violence, rather than lay responsibility for it on German soldiers and civilians, the missions instead blamed the victims. One missionary wrote, "I was appalled by what you reported on the disgusting activities of the Herero women. Of course one cannot really expect anything different from these people. Even if they have become Christians, we cannot allow ourselves to forget the deep immoral dirt out of which they have come, and again and again with our love and patience we must attempt to show them the disgusting and shameful aspects of their activities."[65]

Despite these attitudes, Herero prisoners in the camps were attracted to Christianity. Jan Bart Gewald argues that in addition to providing material resources and some protection, Christianity helped orient people who had lost everything and who were deprived of the opportunity to rebuild. Women, whose work in the camps included taking care of surviving children and other family members, may have been particularly attracted to the missions, which offered food, clothing, and basic health care. The missions also tried, with little success, to offer protection to families so that family members would not be separated and sent to separate camps. Husbands and wives who professed Christian beliefs could at least avail themselves of the help of missionaries in petitions to be able to stay together.[66]

Herero women, because they were not summarily executed like battle age men, were often left to do some of the most horrific of tasks related to genocide. For example, Erichsen and Olusoga cite evidence that women prisoners were forced to aid the research efforts of Eugen Fischer and other scientists. Among other things, they were put to work boiling the heads of dead inmates and scraping off remaining skin and eyes with shards of glass to prepare the heads for skull studies. As the authors note, these may have been the heads of the women's family and community members.[67]

The dream of one dying Herero woman, retold by Gewald, is indicative of the extent to which the struggles that women faced in the desert to keep family members alive and together followed them to the concentration camps. This prisoner told a missionary named Meier how she had seen in a dream two "spotlessly clean men" who asked her if she was ready to come with them to heaven. She told the men that she wanted to take her one-year-old child with her. Meier relates that as the woman told him about her dream, he "saw how her sunken face glowed with inner joy." Shortly afterward, her little daughter died; the woman followed within days.[68]

CONSEQUENCES

The death rates in the concentration camps were remarkably high. Estimates vary between 45 and 60 percent.[69] In the end, the Herero genocide took the lives of an estimated sixty-five thousand to eighty thousand Herero, between two-thirds and over three-fourths of the total population before the genocide. The Nama, who joined the war later, were also systematically murdered, resulting in a loss of 50 percent of their prewar population. Between 1905 and 1907 the authorities in DSWA also passed legislation that furthered the genocidal process. These "native regulations" forbade Herero and Nama from owning land or cattle, from settling in groups of more than ten families, and from traveling without permission of white employers. All adults had to have a labor contract or face criminal charges and all people over the age of eight had to carry identity cards.[70] The former self-standing nations had been destroyed, and the people reduced to a brutalized labor force.

The consequences of the genocide are felt up to this day in terms of continued dislocation from historical lands, long-term underdevelopment of affected communities, and memories of violence written deeply into family stories. Especially with cases of mass rape, the physical traces of genocide are present in daily reminders across many generations. Festus Muundjua, a descendant of Herero victims, for example, recently told the German newspaper *Deutsche Welle*, "I have to look at my great-grand-mother every day, she looks like a German, she has green eyes," Muundjua said. "It always come [sic] to my mind, how many times was [her mother] raped, how did she feel, did anyone come to her help?"[71]

In August 2004, the German state for the first time officially apologized for the actions of the German Empire during the war. The development aid minister, Heidemarie Wieczorek-Zeul, went so far as to admit that the state's actions would have qualified as genocide had the term and its current legal definition existed at the time. The use of the term genocide was reaffirmed by German parliamentary speaker Dr. Norbert Lammert during a visit to Namibia in 2015. In December 2016, Germany and Namibia began negotiations over how to address the past, and the German special envoy, Ruprecht Polenz, affirmed that Germany would describe the atrocities as genocide.[72] However, Germany continues to reject calls for it to pay reparations to Herero descendants of victims and survivors, preferring to meet its obligations with increased foreign aid to independent Namibia as a whole.[73]

CONCLUSION

The evidence we have for the experiences of Herero and other African women during the genocide in DSWA conforms to patterns we know from the total genocides of the twentieth century, in which men and women were killed in fairly equal numbers by perpetrators who saw them as cosmic "internal enemies." The period during which von Trotha's extermination order was in effect mirrors in this respect much larger genocides of the twentieth century, such as the Armenian genocide, the Holocaust, the Cambodian genocide, and the 1994 genocide of Rwandan Tutsis. Also like several of these larger scale genocides, the genocide of the Herero involved many different genocidal tactics, from direct killing, to starvation, to murder in concentration camps through hard labor and exposure. Once the extermination order had been lifted, however, the genocidal pattern reverted to a more common and gender-selective type, in which men and boys of battle age are killed outright, and women and children subjected to sexualized violence and genocide by attrition. Like all genocides, mass rape and other forms of sexualized violence existed throughout the entire process.

The colonial nature of the genocide cannot be overlooked. This is especially true because of the sexual transgressions committed by German men, which contributed directly to the environment in which war would break out and all but ensured that what could have been a limited conflict would devolve into catastrophe. A culture of impunity regarding rape of African women clearly links the genocide to the pregenocide era. German claims about Herero atrocities in 1904 were a mirror image of what they themselves had been committing and planned to commit. As is the case in many genocides, the genocidaires here—the people in the grips of a genocidal mentality—accused their victims of constituting sexual threats—as rapists and as castrators.[74] These rumors and stories helped create a sense of panic and national security crisis among Germans in DSWA and back in the metropole, and reaffirmed existing commitments to an all-out "race war."

Some aspects of German paranoia can be explained by the gendered nature of colonial relations of power. As Andrea Smith explains, "[n]ative peoples have become marked as inherently violable through a process of sexual colonization. By extension, their lands and territories have become marked as violable as well. The connection between the colonization of Native people's bodies—particularly Native women's bodies—and Native lands is not simply metaphorical."[75] Given that both imperial patriarchs and national liberals agreed on the goal of expropriating Herero land and cattle, and that all colonists claimed the right to African women's bodies, they ruled with a concept of power that rested on the tension between the "inherent violability" of Africans and inherent inviolability of Germans. Germans would therefore understand any African uprising—even the mere perception of one—to constitute a threat to their inviolability. Projecting their frameworks onto their enemies, Germans came up with specters of castrating Amazons and sexually fierce wild men who had to be dealt a deathblow. This helps explain why the genocidal process continued well past the recall of von Trotha from South West Africa in fall 1905 and into the First World War.

That these paranoid images stand in such contrast to the comportment of Herero troops during the war is striking. The Herero and the German leadership were in a literal conversation about war aims that captures the key difference between war and genocide. Using the bodies of women and children as symbols of their goals, Maherero and von Trotha pursued diametrically opposed courses.[76] Not only did the Herero decide to pursue a war against an armed force rather than civilians (much less a group as such), but also the very limits Samuel Maherero placed on soldiers' behavior made it possible for him to seek negotiations, albeit unsuccessfully. Maherero was pursuing political aims and a political solution, neither of which were defined as requiring an undermining of German life as such. Lothar von Trotha, on the other hand, was possessed with a metaphysical sense of cosmic threat and zero-sum power dynamics, according to which an enemy must be annihilated, women, children, male noncombatants, and disarmed soldiers included. This required not merely the use of extreme violence against Herero settlements and bodies as a means of retribution and "pacification," but also the destruction of the foundations of Herero life. Such devastation and genocidal war aims empowered German soldiers and civilians to proceed with maximum brutality against the Herero, both while the extermination order was in effect and afterward. Preoccupied with cosmic goals, von Trotha led a cosmic war in which no political solutions were possible. Indeed, a final political solution had to be imposed from without, in the form of the imperial government in Berlin (though this only resulted in a continuation of the genocide by other means).

The experiences of Herero and other African women during the genocide in DSWA deserve more research and deeper analysis, building on the hard work already done by Gesine Krüger in her book *Kriegsbewältigung und Geschichtsbesußtsein*. Such research will help integrate the Herero genocide into comparative studies of the gendered dimensions of genocidal processes. A greater sense of continuity and change in the position of women before, during, and after the genocide, as well as the effects of colonization and genocide on the gendered social body, is necessary if we are to begin to fully grasp both the enormity of this crime for the Herero and Nama of Namibia and the enduring responsibility of Germans in the former metropole.

ELISA VON JOEDEN-FORGEY is Associate Professor and Director of the Master of Arts in Holocaust and Genocide Studies Program at Stockton University as well as founding director of the Genocide Prevention Certificate Program.

NOTES

1. Gesine Krüger, *Kriegsbewältigung und Geschichtsbesußtsein: Realität, Deutung und Verarbeitung des deutschen Kolonialkriegs in Namibia 1904 bis 1907* (Göttingen, Germany: Vandenhoeck & Ruprecht, 1999).

2. For an overview and critique of revisionist positions in scholarship on the genocide, see Jeremy Sarkin, "Implementing the Genocide: Annihilating 'the African Tribes with Streams of Blood and Streams of Gold,'" chapter 2 in *Germany's Genocide of the Herero: Kaiser Wilhelm II, His General, His Settlers, His Soldiers* (Cape Town, South Africa: UCT Press, 2010), 102–54.

3. The classic studies of the Herero genocide are Horst Drechsler, *Südwestafrika unter deutscher Kolonialherrschaft* (Berlin: Akademie-Verlag, 1966) and Helmut Bley, *Kolonialherrschaft und Sozialstruktur in Detusch-Südwestafrika 1894–1914* (Hamburg, Germany: Leibnitz Verlag, 1968). In the 1990s new studies of the German colonial period in German South West Africa began to be published in fairly rapid succession, including Jan-Bart Gewald, *Herero Heroes: A Socio-Political History of the Herero of Namibia 1890–1923* (Oxford: James Currey, 1999); Krüger, *Kriegsbewältigung* (1999); Nils Ole Oermann, *Mission, Church and State Relations in South West Africa under German Rule (1884–1915)* (Stuttgart, Germany: Franz Steiner Verlag, 1999); Jürgen Zimmerer and Joachim Zeller, eds., *Völkermord in Deutsch-Südwestafrika: Der Kolonialkrieg (1904–1908) in Namibia und seine Folgen* (Berlin: Ch. Links Verlag, 2003); David Olusoga and Casper W. Erichsen, *The Kaiser's Holocaust: Germany's Forgotten Genocide and the Colonial Roots of Nazism* (London: Faber and Faber, 2010); Dag Henrichsen, *Herrschaft und Alltag im Vorkolonialen Zentralnamibia: Das Herero- und Damaraland im 19. Jahrhundert* (Basle, Switzerland: Basler Afrika Bibliographien, 2011); Jeremy Sarkin, *Germany's Genocide of the Herero: Kaiser Wilhelm II, His General, His Settlers, His Soldiers* (Cape Town, South Africa: UCT Press, 2011).

4. Helmut Walser Smith, "The Talk of Genocide, the Rhetoric of Miscegenation: Notes on Debates in the German Reichstag Concerning Southwest Africa, 1904–1914," in *The Imperialist Imagination: German Colonialism and its Legacy*, ed. Sara Friedrichsmeyer et al. (Ann Arbor, MI: University of Michigan Press, 1996), 107–23.

5. Jeremy Silvester and Jan-Bart Gewald, *Words Cannot Be Found: German Colonial Rule in Namibia, An Annotated Reprint of the 1918 Blue Book* (Leiden, Netherlands: Brill, 2003).

6. Gewald, *Herero Heroes*, 5.

7. Despite German South West Africa having the highest population of German settlers in the empire, the population was still very small relative to the size of the colony. In 1896, there were 2,000 Europeans (including German military forces); in 1903, the population was 4,700; in 1907, it was 8,000 (excluding German military forces); and in 1914, it was 14,000. These Europeans, and especially German settlers, constituted a ruling class that controlled a population of 500,000 Africans. See Helmut Bley, *Namibia Under German Rule* (Hamburg, Germany: LIT Verlag, 1996), 73–74. The female European population is estimated to have been 306 women in 1899 and 670 in 1903. See: Birthe Kundrus, *Moderne Imperialistin Das Kaiserreich im Spiegel seiner Kolonien* (Wien, Austria: Böhlau Verlag, 2003), 78n117.

8. Bley, *Namibia*, 88.

9. Ibid., 86–91.

10. Lora Wildenthal, *German Women for Empire, 1884–1945* (Durham, NC: Duke University Press, 2001), 80.

11. Gordon D. Gibson, "Double Descent and Its Correlates among the Herero of Ngamiland," *American Anthropologist* 58, no. 1 (1956), 109–39.

12. Wildenthal, *German Women*, 82.

13. Silvester and Gewald, *Words Cannot Be Found*, 63.

14. Wildenthal, *German Women*, 80.

15. Ibid., 92.

16. Ibid., 80–81.

17. Helmuth Stoecker, *Drang nach Afrika* (Berlin: Akademie Verlag, 1991), 59–60; L. H. Gann and Peter Duignan, *The Rulers of German Africa, 1884–1914* (Stanford, CA: Stanford University Press, 1977), 145–46.

18. Martin Reuss, "The Disgrace and Fall of Carl Peters: Morality, Politics, and Staatsräson in the Time of Wilhelm II," *Central European History* 14, no. 2 (June 1981), 110–41.

19. Sarkin, *Germany's Genocide*, 107.

20. Bundesarchiv-Berlin (BA), Reichskolonialamt (RKA) 1001 2115, Leutwein to the Colonial Department, May 17, 1904, cited in Horst Drechsler, *Let Us Die Fighting: The Struggle of the Herero and Nama against German Imperialism 1884–1915* (London: Zed Press, 1980 [1966]), 168n12.

21. *Berliner Tagwacht* 75, September 18, 1901, cited in Drechsler, *Let Us Die Fighting*, 133.

22. Drechsler, *Let Us Die Fighting*, 168.

23. Krüger, *Kriegsbewältigung*, 45; Benjamin Madley, "Patterns of Frontier Genocide 1803–1910: The Aboriginal Tasmanians, the Yuki of California, and the Herero of Namibia," *Journal of Genocide Research* 6, no. 2 (2004), 167–92. See also Silvester and Gewald, *Words Cannot Be Found*, 96.

24. Silvester and Gewald, *Words Cannot Be Found*, 95–6.

25. Sarkin, *Germany's Genocide*, 110.

26. Gesine Krüger, "Bestien und Opfer: Frauen im Kolonialkrieg," in *Völkermord in Deutsch-Südwest Afrika: Der Kolonialkrieg (1904–1908) in Namibia und seine Folgen*, eds. Jürgen Zimmerer und Joachim Zeller (Berlin: Ch. Lnks Verlag, 2003), 144.

27. Gewald, *Herero Heroes*, 142–56; Dominick Schaller, "Herero and Nama in German South-West Africa," in *Centuries of Genocide*, 4th ed., ed. Samuel Totten and William S. Parsons (New York: Routledge, 1997), 89–114, 91.

28. Dreschler, *Let Us Die*, 150. The plaque at the foot of the *Reiter* statue in Namibia, which was erected in 1914 to memorialize the 1,633 Germans who died during the war, cites four German women and one child killed; Silvester and Gewald, *Words Cannot Be Found*, 101n104.

29. Gewald, *Herero Heroes*, 157.

30. Krüger, "Bestien," 148.

31. Dreschler, *Let Us Die*, 144.

32. Silvester and Gewald, *Words Cannot Be Found*, 101.

33. Krüger, "Bestien," 148. Krüger points out that it stands to reason that Herero soldiers, similar to their European counterparts, probably viewed enemy women as booty and could therefore have committed wartime rape. However, there is no evidence of widespread rape of European women by Herero during the war and, despite contemporaneous German narratives to the contrary, there seem to be no documented cases of the rape of German women by Herero soldiers at all. Whether this has to do with women's unwillingness to come forward with their stories or the comportment of Herero troops is unknown.

34. Krüger, *Kriegsbewältigung*, 149.

35. BA-Berlin, RKA 2089, Chief of the Army General Staff von Schlieffen to Chancellor von Bülow, December 16, 1904, cited in Dreschler, *Let Us Die*, 174n113.

36. Krüger, *Kriegsbewältigung*, 116–22.

37. Wildenthal, *German Women*, 152–53.

38. Ibid., 154.

39. Dreschler, *Let Us Die*, 146.

40. *Der Reichsbote* 69 (March 22, 1904), cited in Dreschler, *Let Us Die*, 146.

41. Dreschler, *Let Us Die*, 159.

42. G. Auer, *In Südwestafrika gegen die Hereros: Nach den Kriegs-Tagebüchern des Obermatrosen G. Auer*, bearbeitet von M. Unterbeck, 2nd ed. (Berlin 1911), 30, cited in Gewald, *Herero Heroes*, 164.

43. Dreschler, *Let Us Die*, 152; Jürgen Zimmermann, "Rassenkrieg und Völkermord: Der Kolonialkrieg in Deutsch-Südwestafrika und die Globalgeschichte des Genozids," in *Genozid und Gedenken: Namibisch-deutsche Geschichte und Gegenwart*, ed. Hennig Melber (Frankfurt, Germany: Brandes & Apsel, 2005), 23–48. For a discussion of the various orders that German soldiers may have received at different moments in the war, see: Isabel Hull, *Absolute Destruction: Military Culture and the Practices of War in Imperial Germany* (Ithaca, NY: Cornell University Press, 2005), 28.

44. Gewald, *Herero Heroes*, 168.

45. Sarkin, *Germany's Genocide*, 112.

46. This extermination order is reproduced in most studies of the genocide. For this translation, see Schaller, "Genocide of the Herero," 89. For a discussion of the original text, see Sarkin, *Germany's Genocide*, 110–12.

47. Dreschler, *Let Us Die*, 157; Schaller, "Genocide of the Herero," 89–90.

48. Dreschler, *Let Us Die*, 158.

49. Schaller, "Genocide of the Herero," 106.

50. Ibid.

51. Ibid., 107.

52. Ibid., 104.

53. Silvester and Gewald, *Words Cannot Be Found*, 117.

54. Ibid.

55. Ibid., 112.

56. Schaller, "Genocide of the Hereros," 105.

57. Krüger, "Bestien," 156.

58. Ibid., 155.

59. Silvester and Gewald, *Words Cannot Be Found*, 177.

60. Gewald, *Herero Heroes*, 197.

61. Helmuth Bley, "German South West Africa after the Conquest 1904–1914," in *South West Africa: Travesty of Trust*, ed. R. Segal and R. First (London: Andre Deutsch, 1967), 35–53. Cited in Sarkin, *Germany's Genocide*, 122.

62. Krüger, "Bestien," 154–55.

63. Marion Wallace, "'A Person Is Never Angry for Nothing,' Women, VD and Windhoek," in *Namibia under South African Rule: Mobility and Containment 1915–1946*, ed. Patricia Hayes et al. (Oxford: James Currey, 1998), 77–94.

64. Olusoga and Erichsen, *Kaiser's Holocaust*, 213.

65. Gewald, *Herero Heroes*, 201.

66. Ibid., 200–1.

67. Olusoga and Erichsen, *Kaiser's Holocaust*, 224.

68. Gewald, *Herero Heroes*, 197.

69. Dreschler, *Let Us Die*, 213.

70. Bley, *Namibia*, 170–3; Wildenthal, *German Women*, 95.

71. Renate Rengurash, "Is Germany Moving Closer to Paying Reparations for Namibian Genocide?" *Deutsche Welle*, October 8, 2015, http://www.dw.com/en/is-germany-moving-closer-to-paying-reparations-for-namibian-genoicide/a-18769503.

72. Norimitsu Onishi, "Germany Grapples with Its African Genocide," *New York Times*, December 29, 2016, https://www.nytimes.com/2016/12/29/world/africa/germany-genocide-namibia-holocaust.html?_r=0.

73. Alan D. Cooper, "Reparations for the Herero Genocide: Defining the Limits of International Litigation," *African Affairs* 106, no. 422 (January 2007), 113–26.

74. Elisa von Joeden-Forgey, "Gender, Sexualized Violence, and the Prevention of Genocide," in *Reconstructing Atrocity Prevention*, eds. Sheri P. Rosenberg, Tibi Galis, and Alex Zucker (New York: Cambridge University Press, 2016), 125–50.

75. Andrea Smith, *Conquest: Sexual Violence and American Indian Genocide* (Cambridge, MA: South End Press, 2005), 55.

76. For a similar discussion, see Katharina von Hammerstein, "The Herero: Witnessing Germany's 'Other Genocide,'" *Contemporary French and Francophone Studies* 20, no. 2 (2016): 267–86.

3

Arshaluys Mardigian/Aurora Mardiganian

Absorption, Stardom, Exploitation, and Empowerment

Donna-Lee Frieze

INTRODUCTION

This chapter explores the question of women and the Armenian genocide through Aurora Mardiganian, a survivor of the Armenian genocide (1915–23) and a briefly famed film actress, who arrived in New York in 1917, and who was coerced into starring in a 1919 Hollywood movie about her experiences in the genocide. After touring the world, the film, like most silent movies of the era, was lost, and much like the Armenian genocide, forgotten. Mardiganian, whose birth name was Arshaluys Mardigian, was born in Chmshgatsak in 1901.[1] She became a recluse after the film, despite being a globally important symbol for the recognition of the Armenian genocide. She died in obscurity in 1994. It was in this same year that reels of the 1919 film in which she starred, *Ravished Armenia*, resurfaced in Armenia. However, only about twenty minutes of footage were found, which is all that remains of the film today.[2] Following the discovery of the film in Yerevan in 1994 by Eduardo Kozanlian, the twenty-minute segment was incorporated into two new films (although both used the same footage), one by filmmaker Zareh Tjeknavorian, and the other by Richard Kloian, founder of the Armenian Genocide Resource Center in Northern California.

Attitudes toward Mardiganian are complex: she is at the same time a revered figure (called the Joan of Arc or the Anne Frank of the Armenian genocide) and yet is a neglected one as well. The reasons for these complex attitudes are bound in the tropes of genocide, and in this particular case, in the gendered experience of group destruction. This chapter seeks to accomplish several things. It will briefly put into context the Armenian genocide with Turkey's ongoing campaign of denial. It will look at how acts committed against women in *Ravished Armenia* illuminate the genocidal biological absorption practices at the end of the Ottoman empire. It will discuss Mardiganian's experiences of stardom and exploitation, and her experience as a female victim of genocide and of Hollywood. Finally, it examines the recent scholarly and artistic attempts to resurrect her genocidal narrative from her muted Hollywood voice.

CONTEXTUALIZING THE ARMENIAN GENOCIDE

The disintegration of Ottoman rule in the late-nineteenth and early-twentieth centuries coincided with the emergence of Turkish nationalism and discrimination against "the non-Muslim subjects of the empire," who "rendered that empire ripe for perennial conflicts."[3] The Ottoman authorities, the Committee of Union and Progress (CUP)—a political organization that began as a revolutionary party—were preparing the "ground for a radical solution" against the background of the allied invasion of the Dardanelles Peninsula in 1915.[4] According to Jay Winter, the British Allied landing at Gallipoli on April 25, 1915, "clearly aimed to knock Turkey out of the war ... and precipitated elements of the genocide, evidently planned before the assault on the peninsula."[5] The genocide was ordered by the CUP, and perpetrated by ex-convicts and the military, the so-called Special Organization.[6] From April 1915, the Armenian population was subjected to forced deportations without food, water, or shelter, and mass killings; many women experienced sexual torture, rape, sexual slavery, and mandatory conversion to Islam. Women and children were the principal victims of these genocidal methods, since most of the men had already been murdered. In short, the Ottomans committed intended

group destruction of the Armenians, a deft description of what was later
to be termed "genocide."

The genocide commenced on April 24, 1915, in Constantinople, when
the CUP rounded up approximately 250 prominent Armenian intellectuals, professionals, and political and cultural figures, and executed them.
As the genocide developed, the targeting of important Armenian cultural leaders (mainly men) became a pattern throughout Ottoman Turkey.
Such executions are common in most genocidal contexts, as perpetrators
believe it will be harder to organize a revolt without leadership. Moreover,
these acts may demonstrate intent to destroy the remainder of the group,
and hence can be a warning of genocidal action.[7] Shortly after their arrest,
Armenian men in the Ottoman army were disarmed and then executed
in order to destabilize the remaining Armenian population in Ottoman
Turkey.[8] In addition, sexual abuse of women was used "to intimidate the
Armenian leadership and dampen its will to resist."[9] Ostensibly, the CUP
was punishing the Armenians (who numbered approximately two million) living in Ottoman Turkey for colluding with the Russians against
the Ottomans during the First World War, even though the Armenians
had been a persecuted Christian minority living loyally under Ottoman
rule for hundreds of years.

The genocide occurred all over Ottoman Turkey, intensifying in 1915
when over one million Armenians were massacred. After grueling death
marches into the northern part of the Syrian Desert in 1916, Armenians
were again massacred. The genocide continued with less intensity until
1923. It is estimated that 1.5 million Armenians were killed.[10] Once the
genocide was over, it became "clear that the majority of the survivors
were infants, girls, and women, a significant number of them held by
Muslims."[11]

DENIAL AND GENOCIDE

To this day, the Turkish government denies the Armenian genocide,
even though Raphael Lemkin formed the concept of the term "genocide"
partly based on the massacres and deportations of the Armenians.[12]
The denialists claim that the genocide was part of the war, although the

Armenian genocide was not a consequence of the war; the CUP used the war to justify the genocide. Despite this claim, many missionaries, allied and axis troops, and ambassadors witnessed the genocide. Perhaps the most reliable eyewitness in the English–speaking world was Henry Morgenthau Sr., the American ambassador to the Ottoman Empire beginning in 1913. Because the United States was still neutral in the war, Morgenthau held his post until 1916, and thus witnessed massacres and tortures, which he described in detail in his memoir.[13]

The Ottoman regime had disintegrated by the time Mustafa Kemal (Atatürk)—with his "master-narrative of modern Turkish history"[14]— became modern-day Turkey's first president in 1923. Atatürk's desire to court the European world coincided with his eagerness to forget and deny the past, accentuating his "master-narrative" of Ottoman history and Turkish nationalism. Historian Taner Akçam claims that Atatürk may have displayed contrition regarding the treatment of the Armenians—calling the events "a shameful act."[15] However, there is stronger historical evidence suggesting that Atatürk combined "the myth of 'murderous Armenians'" with the victimization narrative of the Turks "as an 'oppressed nation,'"[16] versions of history that would establish official Turkish nationalism and ideology. While the vicious and ongoing denial campaign in Turkey focuses on the massacres and deportations, acts of biological and cultural absorption are often overlooked as evidence of a genocide.

BIOLOGICAL AND CULTURAL ABSORPTION

While it is well known that rape is carried out during war and during genocide, genocidal rape is a specific crime that is part of the intentional destruction process of the "out" group as outlined in international criminal law. The Convention on the Prevention and Punishment of the Crime of Genocide (CPPCG) lists four groups targeted for destruction by perpetrators: racial, religious, national, and ethnic groups, excluding gendered groups. However, as Katherine Derderian rightly points out, the CPPCG describes "the character of genocide as an act of physical and cultural aggression and as an attack on the social and biological reproduction of the victims, including the prevention of births or the assimilation of children. In addition, the institutionalized marginalization of the victim group before genocide strongly suggests analogies with the institutionalized differentiation between the genders."[17]

Biological absorption was one of the key acts of intended destruction committed on Armenian women during the genocide: many were forced into Islamic conversion and raped, ensuring the children born of the enslavement would be absorbed into the Turkification process.[18] It is important to separate the terms "assimilation" and "absorption" when discussing genocidal acts. Cultural assimilation is voluntary and has occurred throughout history as a consequence of migration. Biological absorption is where the "out" group is destroyed (or there is the attempt at destruction) organically and forcefully through the reproductive component of a group. Even the term "biological assimilation" assumes *blending* into a community, not *disappearing* from one.[19] Not all genocides use biological absorption as a tool; since genocide connotes destruction, acts can be committed through absorption and/or sometimes through extermination. The Nazis would have found biological absorption abhorrent as a tool of genocide as this would "poison" the blood of Aryans. The Nazis did not want Jews to infiltrate German society (or German blood), but rather, carried out the destruction process by extermination.[20] Similarly, there is evidence that Interior Minister of the CUP Talaat Pasha, after hearing of intermarriage five months after the genocide began, forbade the marriage of Turkish men with Armenian women.[21] As the chaos of war and genocide collided, the CUP orders were obviously ignored by militia in the provinces as the blood "of Armenian women and young children was seen to be devoid of the capacity to pollute the Muslim nation because it had no agency or consequence."[22]

The perpetrators of the Armenian genocide performed acts of sexual assault, specifically targeting women, because women "embody its [a group's] genetic and cultural community."[23] Thousands of Armenian women were sold to harems, and women who were pregnant from choice (from their Armenian husbands) were often killed through mutilation of the belly.[24] Rape and forced marriage were part of the absorption process. Enslaved women often endured permanent facial tattoos, representing "a new belonging and a marked change in their life,"[25] but also a permanent and public reminder of their violated selves.

As Vahé Tachjian observes, women who are raped and enslaved in genocides (recent examples include Bosnia and Herzegovina and Darfur) harbor guilt despite their inability to prevent the crimes and thus are too ashamed to return to their families. In keeping with the "traditional perception of [Turkish] men as the sole bearers of ethnicity,"[26] the children raised by Armenian women would, in turn, be Turkish. During the Armenian genocide, many women were forced into prostitution and "were the targets of accusations by their compatriots and were laboring under deeply guilty feelings." As a consequence, many Armenian women stayed with their Turkish "husbands," denying a connection with their Armenian national identity.[27] In particular, women who gave birth to children as a result of rape were often "rejected by the ... [woman's] family." Likewise, the Armenian family would sometimes reject the half-Turkish child. A woman either had to "return to her real family alone or stay with her rejected child, and distance herself from her national community."[28] It was common for women who had experienced rape to give away, neglect, or abandon their babies.[29] On the other hand, abortion and infanticide were discouraged among some Armenian patriarchal circles, in order to invigorate the nationalist agenda expressed in *"Mayr Hayasdan* (Mother Armenia)."[30] Such life-shattering choices were probably made in isolation, and forced on many women.

Biological absorption does not cease when the killings stop. It continues into the national psyche, and "the ultimate result was a genocidal pattern of loss of women and children to the Armenian ethnos."[31] In addition, while adult men were not required to convert to Islam, many women and children, male and female, were forced to renounce their religion and thus, their culture. This continued generational absorption sustained and prolonged the genocide long after the killings, deportations, and rapes ended.

Although the acts committed against Armenians were not considered genocide until the crime was ratified under international law in 1951, they were publicized through the film *Ravished Armenia,* considered to be the first film that represented women's experience of the genocide.

STARDOM AND EXPLOITATION: ARSHALUYS
MARDIGIAN BECOMES AURORA MARDIGANIAN

Ravished Armenia was an eight-reel, eighty-five-minute, silent dramatized film first screened in New York City in 1919, primarily for the purposes of raising funds for Armenian orphans of the genocide. Aurora Mardiganian, a survivor of the Armenian genocide, played the lead role in this film. With no homeland to return to (Armenia became a short-lived republic from 1918 to 1920), survivors of the genocide spread into the diaspora, which emerged as a consequence of the genocide, from the Middle East to the United States. Mardiganian, an orphaned survivor of the genocide, found her way to the United States, arriving on November 5, 1917.[32] The film was the creation of the American Committee for Armenian and Syrian Relief (ACASR), a missionary organization developed in 1915 to help the victims of the Armenian genocide. Proceeds from the film, which eventually reached $30 million, provided food and shelter for thousands of Armenian orphans through the ACASR.[33]

Film historian Anthony Slide is credited with bringing Mardiganian's story and surviving intertitles from the original film to print, allowing a historical investigation into *Ravished Armenia*.[34] According to Slide, Mardiganian's adopted Armenian-American parents placed advertisements in the paper searching for her lost brother, and only surviving family member. The notifications caught the eye of newspaper journalists, who interviewed her regarding her experiences of the genocide. Screenwriter Harvey Gates and his wife saw these interviews and were quick to see the commercial potential of Mardiganian's story; eventually the Gates family became her legal guardians. Mardiganian wrote her memoir in Armenian in 1918, which Gates rewrote into English through a translator.[35] Because Mardiganian's English was poor when she arrived in New York City, she had no means of verifying Gates's reconstruction of her story. Shushan Avagyan points to Lawrence Venuti's theory of translation, that "every translation submits the foreign text to a *domestic* interpretation, based on some kind of reconstruction, be it lexicographical, textual, or ideological, that answers to the needs of a particular interpretive occasion."[36] The translation of Mardiganian's retelling of her experiences in the genocide are textually and ideologically in the vein of a Hollywood narrative, with a clear beginning, middle, and an end; evil versus innocence, and issues that have to be resolved and conquered, result in resolution and closure. A Hollywood version of Mardiganian's genocidal narrative was the perfect vehicle to capture the imagination and sympathy of an American audience who knew about the Armenian massacres through newspapers and missionary reports. While the notion of the starving Armenian orphans was well known in the US, the details of the genocide, including the rape and forced slavery of women, were less publicized. However, because *Ravished Armenia* was based on Mardiganian's experiences in the genocide, the film explored gender issues relating to genocidal rape.

In 1919, at the prompting of Gates, Mardiganian signed papers authorizing her to appear in a "picture," which she understood to mean a still photograph. He changed Arshaluys Mardigian's Armenian name to an only slightly less Armenian sounding name, and then rushed her to Los Angeles to star in the film about her experiences in the genocide.[37] The film, which was based on Gates's book (also titled *Ravished Armenia*), was screened in the United States, South America, Europe, Australia, and Canada.[38] The book was published in many languages.[39] Because of her experiences in the genocide, Mardiganian became a Hollywood star. The journey from genocidal rape victim to Hollywood superstar rape victim was a favorable outcome for everyone—everyone, that is, except Mardiganian. It marked the beginning of Aurora and the "erasure of Arshaluys."[40]

CHRISTIAN, "WHITE," YOUNG, AND FEMALE

Ravished Armenia was an "eyewitness report ... presented as popular entertainment for the masses ... of an oppressed minority—a minority that just happened to be white and Christian and with which most Americans could empathize."[41] In other words, the film claimed to dramatize documentary truth, to seek missionary aims through aid to orphaned Armenian children, and to have a fair dose of cynicism behind it.[42] As displayed in the posters advertising the film, Mardiganian was portrayed as a white, young, and innocent female, making her recognizable for a

Christian, American audience. Mardiganian could be appropriated as a white, youthful Christian specifically because she was female.

Ravished Armenia was a sensation, not because it was highly crafted—indeed, it received only a few lukewarm reviews[43]—but because the publicity focused on rape, redemption, religion, and race. As Meg McLagan points out, Ravished Armenia "was a coproduction of commercial and quasi-Christian-quasi-humanitarian human rights interests."[44] More than Mardiganian's narrative of the genocide, the film represents the navigation between human rights movements in the early twentieth century and the interplay between "affect-intensive images and narratives."[45] The emphasis on the sexual violence against women in the film cannot be overlooked, particularly as a normative understanding of this genocide is most widely associated with its deportations, as gas chambers are associated with the Holocaust. Vartan Matiossian rightly argues that Ravished Armenia "mixed stardom and exploitation."[46] The exposure of sexual violence in the film was in reality a "transgression that objectified women and girls, thus downplaying the gravity of the committed crimes."[47] The rape of Armenians is common in eyewitness testimony, with some victims as young as twelve and many others raped in public view of deportees and villagers.[48]

The poster for the New York City opening insisted that this film would make "the blood of American women boil," and the advertising for the film enticed audiences to see "girls impaled on soldiers' swords,"[49] promising that "Ravished Armenia ... [will] show real harems."[50] The representation of Mardiganian's experiences in the genocide was either exploitative or enticing. Gates often used euphemisms in the book Ravished Armenia, "to signal acts of rape or other forms of sexual violence against Armenian girls and women during the genocide,"[51] and even though the film sensationalized the acts of sexual and biological violation, the book "tried to sanitize the brutalities."[52] Mardiganian was portrayed on the one hand as a sex slave and on the other as a purified and redeemed young girl.

It was not only Hollywood and American society in general who held these ideals of purification. Writing in 1917, Vahan Malezian (an Armenian writer living in Egypt) exclaimed, "It is the Armenian woman who has preserved our national existence, clinging to all the sacred relics left to the nation by our forefathers: religion and language, family, and morals.... It will once again be the Armenian woman who will pit herself against ruins and tombs with her two supreme virtues–fertility and purity."[53]

Slide also argues that Mardiganian was exploited by the missionary relief fund, ACASR, saying, "Because they were using this film to raise money and to their credit, they raised hundreds of millions of dollars for Armenian relief, but they didn't seem to realize how to treat this young girl. She was just an object, really, to be used."[54]

The purification illustrated by Mardiganian's Hollywood persona meant more than raising funds for orphaned survivors: for the ACASR, it was a trope of Armenian national reconstruction, as shown in the following quote: "The image of the martyr-nation is sacralised, and the victims are transfigured and become subjects of admiration or even veneration. In this work of sanctification, the victims of the crime be they those killed or the survivors, are draped in the martyrs' unique, immaculate and innocent mantle."[55]

While the specific incidents of Mardiganian's experience of the genocide are in the book and the film, her narrative voice exploring the deep trauma transforms into a sentimental story about a white Christian girl, who was brutalized by dark-skinned men, and was eventually saved by white Christian Americans. The turn of the century immigration and racial laws in America deemed Armenians as white and therefore Westernized.[56] However, according to Slide, it mattered little that the victims were Armenian: what concerned audiences and readers is that Christians were being persecuted.[57] This also explains the whitewashed images of Mardiganian on the advertising posters. The narrative for Gates had to be compelling enough to "invoke both compassion and outrage in American audiences,"[58] but clearly the film needed excitement. Thus, in one poster advertising the film, her experiences of genocidal brutality are labeled "adventures."[59]

The sequences of suggested rape and of Christian iconography resulted in attempts to ban the film. The Armenian National Union sought to stop the film because of the exploitation of Mardiganian; the suggestions of rape and the images of crucifixion proved too unsavory for the public.[60] The crucifixions of naked females that survive in the film reels today were a substitute for what Mardiganian witnessed: vaginal impalements. As Liz Ohanesian writes, "the crucifixions are based on something closer to impalement. This image, though, of women on the cross is actually less brutal and heightens the way the genocide was framed in Western media as a crime committed specifically against Christians."[61] The perception of Mardiganian as a Christian martyr suited both the ACASR and Hollywood, and thus, Mardiganian's experience of the genocide was patronized. Stardom dehumanized her and her experiences as a female genocide victim from the outset.

MARDIGANIAN AS VICTIM OF GENOCIDE AND HOLLYWOOD

The apparent goodwill and benevolence behind the making of the film proved traumatic for Mardiganian. She was not prepared in any way for acting out her genocidal narrative, nor was she equipped to cope with the publicity. When she stepped out of her dressing room and was confronted with men wearing fezzes and swords she thought, "they fooled me. I thought they were going to give me to these Turks to finish my life."[62] During the production, she fell off a high set and broke her ankle, but was still required by the director of the film to act in the film and walk on her foot in spite of the pain. Slide pointedly remarks that audiences would believe that the bandages around her ankle "covered wounds inflicted by the Turks rather than the barbarians of Hollywood."[63] Mardiganian had to endure this after she witnessed the horror that many other Armenian genocide survivors experienced: the murder of her parents and siblings.[64] Because of the film, Mardiganian was forced to participate in a frantic publicity tour that included "a 21-city campaign ... [where she] toured with the film, speaking at screenings, dinners and other fundraisers."[65] She refused, had an emotional breakdown, then was sent to a convent to recuperate and was replaced with seven Mardiganian lookalikes,[66] or more aptly, "impersonators."[67] Slide speculates that some members of the audience may have wondered whether Aurora Mardiganian "was perhaps not a real person, but rather an amalgam of all the tortured, suffering, and murdered young women of Armenia."[68] As filmmaker Atom Egoyan has written, not only was Mardiganian a victim of one of the earliest genocides in the twentieth century, "she was also one of the first victims of contemporary celebrity culture," culminating in "Hollywood's uneasy marriage of glamour and atrocity,"[69] a concoction that usually befalls women as victims.

EMPOWERING THE VOICE OF AURORA MARDIGANIAN

Between the early 1930s and 1994, when the reels of *Ravished Armenia* were found in Yerevan, the film and Mardiganian were largely forgotten. The crumbling of the Soviet Union and the restoration of the Republic of Armenia coincided with the 1994 discovery of the reels and of Mardiganian's death, and thus with nation-building, pride, and the rehabilitation of the collective psyche of Armenians. In the last twenty years, efforts to resurrect her from exploitation have been increasing, both in Armenia and the diaspora. On the longtime neglect of Mardiganian and the film, Hayk Demoyan, Director of the Armenian Genocide Museum-Institute (AGMI) in Yerevan, explains that, "Many in the Armenian community turned their backs on her possibly because of the 'shameful' part of the story, namely rape and trafficking, pain that they wanted forgotten and unmentioned. Another possible explanation was that the hero was in fact a heroine, a young girl."[70]

The sexual assaults perpetrated against Mardiganian, and that came to symbolize her, did not conform to the "'cleansing' and 'cleanliness' [that] formed the basic characteristics of the idealized woman who for her nation was called to give life."[71] However, with the increasing body of scholarly work on the Armenian genocide in recent years, and genocide studies testimony in general, scholars are beginning to understand the worth and significance of Mardiganian's unique story as a victim of genocide, and of Hollywood.

In 1988, Slide discovered that Mardiganian was living in Los Angeles and interviewed her in a video testimony.[72] Knowing that the genocide was denied, and thus forgotten for many years, he now discovered that Mardiganian's extraordinary stories of genocide and reenactment in a Hollywood film were also absent in scholarly genocide studies history. Mardiganian said she was "thrilled to have someone speak with her because she said that no one had ever spoken to her about the film."[73] Despite her broken English, Mardiganian's video testimony depicts the suffering she endured during the genocide, even in a transcript that omits body language, facial and voice expression, pauses, tone, and silences. It reads as follows:

> AM: Made the second exile with them and killed them, before reaching to the desert and burned them. All.
>
> AS: Could you tell about your family that perished?
>
> AM: Parish [sic] that's where I...
>
> AS: No, No, your family.
>
> AM: My mother, [nods in understanding] my mother, was perished and then they killed my and then they killed right before, [shakes head as in "no"] I didn't see the body, I see, found the body, I didn't see right before my eyes. But my aunt, my two aunts [smacks her chest] was killed right before my eyes. They tie up my hair, and I said and then they killed and I said "please save them" "no, no, sooner or later all you going to die. There will be not one single Armenian to live. We're going to get all your dogs, all your girls" and all these kind of words they were calling and yelling and all. And whipping me [touches hair] and using those horse whip. It was so painful and all. And that's the way they want to finish us. So they will have all our own lands. Our country. And then the rape of the Christianity. Er, both ways. I was so small I wouldn't be able know many other things. You know. [silence, nods head].[74]

As with Holocaust victims who have told their genocide narrative for the first time in a video testimony, Mardiganian's narrative appears unrehearsed, unmethodical, and lacks a chronological storyline, unlike the classically structured Hollywood narrative that she was forced to abide by.

Another video testimony of Mardiganian from the 1980s reveals more on the genocide. In 1915, Turkish authorities arrested Mardiganian's father and brother and along with many other Armenian men they were sent to prison. Living close to the prison, Mardiganian and her siblings were able to hear the cries from the prisoners who were being tortured. During her deportation, Mardiganian met with two men who escaped the prison. They told her that her father killed her brother with a stone, knowing their captors were about to enflame the prison, and thus "saving" his son from the torture of being burnt alive. As Mardiganian explains in the video testimony, holding her head: "I can never forget the screams from the prison."[75] While such "mercy killings" were known to have occurred, the effects on the survivor family are ineradicable.[76]

The exploration of Mardiganian's personal narrative in both video testimonies accentuates that many women and children during the Armenian genocide were often witnesses to the torture and the death of their family members, highlighting the mental harm imposed on female genocide victims. To be fair, *Ravished Armenia* was perceived as testimony in its day and thus comparisons to the rawness of her words in the video testimonies from the 1980s are unfair. However, both testimonies are valuable lessons regarding the importance of victims' voices for history and memory.

The recent growing interest in Mardiganian and the film has produced artistic renditions of the Mardiganian narrative, including Egoyan's visual installation *Auroras/Testimony*. It explores the tropes that manifested themselves through the representation of the biological absorption and resulted in the double exploitation of women in the Armenian genocide. Egoyan's *Auroras* installation are videos of seven Mardiganian look-alikes reading sections of the book *Ravished Armenia*. *Auroras* raises issues of mediated narratives and voices, and points to the silencing and absorption of Mardiganian's voice, evidencing that the young woman who had experienced genocidal acts specifically aimed at female biological destruction was commercialized and fetishized through the dominant male Gates. As Shushan Avagyan astutely notes, Egoyan's mediation of the tropes of Mardiganian signal the "discourse of voices"[77] surrounding the spokespeople for Mardiganian and her genocidal narrative.

In the wake of the reevaluations of Mardiganian and her narrative, the Armenian Genocide Museum-Institute (AGMI) has incorporated her story of the genocide, stardom, and exploitation into its main exhibition. Recently, the director of the AGMI discovered Mardiganian's large leather touring trunk, lined with floral wallpaper, with drawers and compartments, marked in large letters on the outside: "Aurora Mardiganian Auction of Souls Co."[78] Its poignancy lies in the reminder that Mardiganian was treated with Hollywood lavishness by Gates, who acted as her narrative agent for the brutal crimes committed against her by Ottoman men.

CONCLUSION

What does this story mean to Armenians, whose genocide has been denied and unacknowledged by the perpetrator country and whose recently created matriarchal symbol of the genocide was abused first by Ottoman Turks and then Hollywood? The answers partly lie in the reels of the lost film that highlight Mardiganian's exploitation. Her miraculous escape from death and her abusive treatment by her supposed American caretakers illuminate the importance and imperative of understanding gendered experiences of atrocity.

The film and the book, at the time, despite their claim to documentary truth, "actually did the opposite, casting doubt on the urgency, modernity, and reality of Mardiganian's experience, and diminishing the threat of genocide to humanity."[79] The prevention of genocide, of course, was not on anyone's mind in 1919, nor was there a deep understanding of what had occurred. However, the rediscovered reels of the film point to the dislocated memory of the genocide, a memory that is muted by denial and lack of political will to acknowledgement it. This chapter has highlighted how the newly found recognition of Mardiganian's plight as a female genocide victim has created an understanding of gendered notions of absorption. Her exploitation by Hollywood mirrors present-day Turkey's unconscionable denial of the genocide; the denial of *her* voice through Gates's narrative and the Hollywood film illuminates Turkey's attempt to silence recognition of the Armenian genocide. The rise of Atatürk may have coincided with the beginning of the vicious denial campaign of the genocide, which is why *Ravished Armenia*, released four years before Atatürk's presidency, is an important source of both evidence and tropes of the genocide.

The indefatigable work by Demoyan and others in resurrecting Arshaluys Mardigian from her exploited Hollywood phantom underscores the injustices committed on women in the genocide due to their biology and ethnicity. The increasing awareness of the Armenian genocide (once dubbed "the forgotten genocide") and Mardiganian's narrative encourages new knowledge about genocidal destruction, and, in particular, how gender-specific destruction is as crucial in understanding genocide as in understanding mass murders. For many genocide scholars, as the details of Mardigian/Mardiganian's life are further revealed, much can be gained that will aid in understanding biological absorption policies as acts of genocide.

DONNA-LEE FRIEZE is a Research Fellow at Deakin University in Melbourne. She is editor of Raphael Lemkin's autobiography *Totally Unofficial* and coauthor with Steven Cooke of *"The Interior of Our Memories": A History of Melbourne's Jewish Holocaust Centre.*

NOTES

Many thanks to the editors of this volume, Elissa Bemporad and Joyce W Warren, for their patience and helpful feedback, and to the anonymous reviewers of this chapter. Gratitude to Eduardo Kozanlian and Hayk Demoyan and the staff at the Armenian Genocide Museum-Institute.

1. Alin K. Gregorian, "Scholar Captures Tragedy, Miracle of Aurora Mardiganian's Life Story," *Armenian Mirror-Spectator*, March 24, 2014, http://www.mirrorspectator.com /2014/03/24/scholar-captures-tragedy-miracle-of-aurora-mardiganians-life-story/.

2. Vartan Matiossian, "The Quest for Aurora: On 'Ravished Armenia' and its Surviving Fragment," *Armenian Weekly*, April 15, 2014, http://armenianweekly.com/2014/04/15 /aurora/. See this article for an exploration of the missing film. Matiossian also argues that of the "10,919 silent films produced between 1912 and 1929 in the United States, only 3,313 still exist."

3. Vahakn N. Dadrian and Taner Akçam, *Judgment at Istanbul: The Armenian Genocide Trials* (New York: Berghahn Books, 2011), 13.

4. Dadrian and Akçam, *Judgment at Istanbul*, 14.

5. Jay Winter, "Under Cover of War: The Armenian Genocide in the Context of Total War," in *America and the Armenian Genocide of 1915*, ed. Jay Winter (New York: Cambridge University Press, 2003), 40.

6. Peter Balakian, *The Burning Tigress: The Armenian Genocide and America's Response* (New York: Harper Collins, 2003), 211.

7. For further discussion about pregenocidal actions see Donna-Lee Frieze, "The Destruction of Sarajevo's *Vijećnica*: A Case of Genocidal Cultural Destruction?" in *New Directions in Genocide Research*, ed. Adam Jones (London: Routledge, 2012), 57–74.

8. Balakian, *Burning Tigress*, 176, 178.

9. Katherine Derderian, "Common Fate, Different Experience: Gender-Specific Aspects of the Armenian Genocide, 1915–1917," *Holocaust and Genocide Studies* 19, no. 1 (2005): 5, 6.

10. Balakian, *Burning Tigress*, 179–80.

11. Vahé Tachjian, "Gender, Nationalism, Exclusion: The Reintegration Process of Female Survivors of the Armenian genocide," *Nations and Nationalism* 15, no. 1 (2009): 65.

12. Raphael Lemkin, *Totally Unofficial: The Autobiography of Raphael Lemkin*, ed. Donna-Lee Frieze (New Haven, CT: Yale University Press, 2013).

13. Henry Morgenthau, *Ambassador Morgenthau's Story* (New York: Doubleday, 1918), 306–8.

14. Fatma Ulgen, "Reading Mustafa Kemal Atatürk on the Armenian Genocide of 1915," *Patterns of Prejudice* 44, no. 4 (2010): 369.

15. Taner Akçam, *A Shameful Act: The Armenian Genocide and the Question of Turkish Responsibility* (New York: Metropolitan Books, 2006).

16. Ulgen, "Reading Mustafa Kemal Atatürk," 371.

17. Derderian, "Common Fate, Different Experience," 3.

18. For a more complete account of how biological absorption is an act of genocide see Donna-Lee Frieze, "'Simply Bred Out': Genocide and the Ethical in the Stolen Generations," in *Hidden Genocides: Power, Knowledge, Memory*, eds. Alexander Laban Hinton, Thomas La Pointe, and Douglas Irvin-Erickson (New Jersey: Rutgers University Press, 2013), 126–46.

19. Katherine Derderian problematically uses the term "biological assimilation." See Derderian, "Common Fate, Different Experience," 1–25.

20. Lerna Ekmekcioglu, "A Climate for Abduction, a Climate for Redemption: The Politics of Inclusion during and after the Armenian Genocide," *Comparative Studies in Society and History* 55, no. 3 (2013): 530.

21. See Derderian, "Common Fate, Different Experience," 4.

22. Ekmekcioglu, "Climate for Abduction," 530.

23. Derderian, "Common Fate, Different Experience," 1.

24. Ibid., 9.

25. Armenian Genocide Museum-Institute, "Becoming Someone Else: Genocide and Kidnapped Armenian Women," accessed March 3, 2016, http://www.genocide-museum .am/eng/online_exhibition_2.php#sthash.VNaEE2Eq.dpuf. See also *Grandma's Tattoos*, directed by Suzanne Khardalian (New York: Cinema Guild), DVD.

26. Derderian, "Common Fate, Different Experience," 10.

27. Tachjian, "Gender, Nationalism, Exclusion," 70, 74. See also Ara Sarafian, "The Absorption of Armenian Women and Children into Muslim Households as a Structural Component of the Armenian Genocide," in *In God's Name: Genocide and Religion in the Twentieth Century*, eds. Omer Bartov and Phyllis Mack (New York: Berghahn, 2001).

28. Ibid., 74–75.

29. Derderian, "Common Fate, Different Experience," 9.

30. Ekmekcioglu, "Climate for Abduction," 545–46.

31. Derderian, "Common Fate, Different Experience," 2.

32. Ani Baghdasarian, "'Ravished Armenia' Screened at San Francisco Library," *Asbarez*, 2009, accessed November 29, 2017: http://asbarez.com/61773 /ravished-armenia-screened-at-san-francisco-library/.

33. Armenian Genocide Museum-Institute, "'Auction of Souls,' or 'Memorial of Truth," 2014, accessed April 11, 2016: http://www.genocide-museum.am/eng/online _exhibition_6.php.

34. Anthony Slide, *Ravished Armenia and the Story of Aurora Mardiganian*, (Lanham, MD: Scarecrow Press, 1997).

35. Ibid., 6–7.

36. Shushan Avagyan, "Becoming Aurora: Translating the Story of Arshaluys Mardiganian," *Dissidences: Hispanic Journal of Theory and Criticism* 4, no. 8 (2012), http:// digitalcommons.bowdoin.edu/dissidences/vol4/iss8/13.

37. Slide, *Ravished Armenia*, 7.

38. Gregorian, "Scholar Captures Tragedy."

39. Hayk Demoyan, personal conversation with author, July 2015, Yerevan.

40. Avagyan, "Becoming Aurora."

41. Slide, *Ravished Armenia*, 3.

42. Meg McLagan, "Introduction: Making Human Rights Claims Public," *American Anthropologist* 108, no. 1 (2006): 191.

43. Leshu Torchin, "*Ravished Armenia*: Visual Media, Humanitarian Advocacy, and the Formation of Witnessing Publics," *American Anthropologist* 108, no. 1 (2006): 214.

44. McLagan, "Introduction," 193.

45. Ibid., 194.

46. Matiossian, "Quest for Aurora."

47. Avagyan, "Becoming Aurora."

48. Donald M. Miller and Lorna Touryan Miller, *Survivors: An Oral History of the Armenian Genocide* (Berkeley, CA: University of California Press, 1993), 102–3.

49. Baghdasarian, "Ravished Armenia."

50. Oscar Apfel, quoted in Slide, *Ravished Armenia*, 10.

51. Avagyan, "Becoming Aurora."

52. Ibid.

53. Vahan Malezian in Tachjian, "Gender, Nationalism, Exclusion," 69.

54. Anthony Slide in Liz Ohanesian, "I Am Armenian: The Intriguing Life of Aurora Mardiganian," *KCET*, accessed January 13, 2016: https://www.kcet.org/shows/artbound/i-am-armenian-the-intriguing-life-of-aurora-mardiganian.

55. Tachjian, "Gender, Nationalism, Exclusion," 76.

56. See Janice Okoomian, "Becoming White: Contested History, Armenian American Women, and Radicalized Bodies," *Melus* 27, no. 1 (2002): 213–37.

57. Anthony Slide in Ohanesian, "I Am Armenian."

58. Avagyan, "Becoming Aurora."

59. Armenian Genocide Research Institute, The First National Exhibitors' Circuit Inc, Poster advertising *Auction of Souls*, n.d.

60. Matiossian, "Quest for Aurora."

61. Ohanesian, "I Am Armenian."

62. Slide, *Ravished Armenia*, 9.

63. Ibid., 9.

64. Balakian, *Burning Tigress*, 314.

65. Torchin, *Ravished Armenia*, 216.

66. Liam Lacey, "Painful Stories, Powerful Work from Egoyan and Ataman," *Globe and Mail*, June 5, 2007, R4.

67. Torchin, *Ravished Armenia*, 216.

68. Slide, *Ravished Armenia*, 5.

69. Atom Egoyan, "Forward," in *Ravished Armenia and the Story of Aurora Mardiganian*, ed. Anthony Slide (Jackson, MS: University Press of Mississippi, 2014), Kindle edition.

70. Gregorian, "Scholar Captures Tragedy."

71. Tachjian, "Gender, Nationalism, Exclusion," 69.

72. Matiossian, "Quest for Aurora."

73. Ohanesian, "I Am Armenian."

74. Aurora Mardiganian interviewed by Anthony Slide, "Armenian Survivor Aurora Mardiganian on Genocide," April 22, 2015, USC Shoah Foundation, https://www .youtube.com/watch?v=oTlqnStssEA.

75. Aurora Mardiganian video testimony. Armenian Genocide Museum-Institute, 1985.

76. Miller and Miller, *Survivors*, 228.

77. Avagyan, "Becoming Aurora." See this article for an interesting discussion on a simulacrum of Egoyan's installation.

78. *Auction of Souls* was an alternative title for the film *Ravished Armenia*.

79. Avagyan, "Becoming Aurora."

"Hyphenated" Identities during the Holodomor

Women and Cannibalism

Olga Bertelsen

The 1932–33 famine in Soviet Ukraine, known as the Holodomor, was a politically engineered calamity that claimed the lives of at least four million people.[1] Among the cluster of Soviet famines, two famines in particular—the 1932–33 Ukrainian-Kuban Holodomor and the 1931–33 Kazakh famine—should be identified as genocides, deliberate attempts by Stalin and his lieutenants to subdue and neutralize populations that were associated with nationalism and resistance to Soviet collectivization.[2] The collectivization campaign was launched by Stalin in 1928, and was designed to control agricultural production and distribution by eliminating individual peasant farms and replacing them with collective farms. To suppress resistance to the project, the Bolsheviks implemented political and cultural terror against the peasantry, the intelligentsia, and the clergy in Ukraine through a series of conscious decisions in November 1932 to June 1933. They charged the Ukrainians with nationalism and separatism, and eliminated a significant portion of Ukrainian society. The most recent studies and overwhelming archival evidence confirm the Soviet government's intent to solve the national question by using famine as a weapon, which places the Holodomor in the category of genocide as defined by the United Nations.[3]

However, like the history of other genocides,[4] the history and the implications of the Holodomor have not been fully examined. In particular, some crucial aspects rooted in the realms of anthropology, psychology, biology, and medicine have not received enough scholarly attention, and still constitute gray areas of study. Similarly, very little has been written about the gender aspects of the Holodomor. Some studies have discussed the central role of women in communal resistance to collectivization. Women's riots (bab'i bunty) against collectivization were a widespread phenomenon by 1930,[5] but there were some women who supported the state's efforts at collectivization and elevated themselves to the status of authority figures in the countryside. They were broadly hated, ostracized, and even murdered for their cooperation with the Soviet secret police by the women who resisted.[6] This study focuses on women without power or state privileges, those who suffered the most in 1932–33 because of extreme starvation and psychological trauma. A discussion about the Holodomor in gender terms seems to be necessary in order to recover women's voices, which will help personalize the history of the Holodomor. Women's voices will deepen our understanding of people's survival strategies during genocide, adding specific knowledge to the already rich studies about human suffering under authoritarian rule.

More often than not, women have been victims and specific targets of ethnic cleansing and genocide. Norman Naimark has posited that "ethnic cleansing is inherently misogynistic."[7] Conveniently for the abusers, women usually do not abandon their homes, and are punished and mistreated because they are the "cultural and biological repository of the nation."[8] Men are not around to protect them. As a result, women are raped, exiled, or shot; they are displaced and often join underground resistance detachments; in environments of chronic starvation, in order to survive and save their families from death, they forage for food, and quite dramatically change their behavior, committing crimes and resorting to necrophagia (trupoyidstvo) and cannibalism (liudoyidstvo), as often happened in Ukraine in the early thirties.[9]

The problem of women's victimization, dehumanization, and their pathological and criminal behavior are given priority here because there is virtually no scholarship on this aspect of the Holodomor. Generally, very little has been written about drastic transformations in human beings experiencing famine across time and space. Thus, mapping these places and times of genocide that dehumanized people in the process of their extermination is crucial.[10] Knowledge about one place where people experienced violence adds to the wealth of human knowledge about many other places where similar tragedies occurred. Such an accumulation of information encourages historical and sociological generalizations and increases individual and societal self-awareness of individual, collective, and state violence.

The Ukrainian famine and state violence transformed many women into psychiatrically disturbed and mentally confused individuals with the capacity to kill to survive.[11] The biochemical and hormonal stress caused by extreme starvation induced severe changes in people's behavior and self-identification, and cannibalism was integrated into the system of their delusions.[12] This condition inevitably entailed changes in their understanding of moral values and norms.[13] Women's new values, emotional ambivalence, and deranged state of mind, incited by state violence, led to aggression directed outward (toward their victims and the state), and to confusion directed inward (toward themselves). Consequently, a new "hyphenated" identity emerged during the Holodomor, an identity that provides an idiom for women's strategies of social survival and their confused self-identification.[14] Having adopted this new identity, they simultaneously resented and resisted it.

To decode the meaning of this paradox, this study will explicate women's behavioral changes under prolonged starvation, explore the highly personalized voices of women who resorted to cannibalism, offer more nuanced understandings of women's behavior during the Holodomor, and provide an overview of the state's response to the criminal behavior of its victims.

STARVATION AND BEHAVIORAL CHANGES

Almost a century ago, analyzing unresolvable sequences of human experiences, the English anthropologist Gregory Bateson coined the term "double bind." Among various components that constitute a double bind situation, Bateson stressed the significance of repeated victimization, the impossibility of escaping from a double bind situation, and punishments that threatened survival. Through a number of injunctions that are often contradictory, and punishments that are always unavoidable, the victims finally learn to identify the reality in double bind patterns, which leads to chronic psychological trauma.[15] The victims are caught in a situation in which they are sent two messages, and one of these denies the other. Bateson has argued that in impossible situations, individuals often "shift and become somebody else." In this case, the double bind no longer has an effect on the victims because they are not themselves. The victims conjure a solution. This may well be the case with people who became cannibals during the Holodomor.

People were categorized as "hoarders" and "saboteurs" during collectivization. They were punished if they were found to be storing food. Deprived of any foodstuffs, they stopped working, which, in the eyes of the state, redefined their status as saboteurs and led to further punishment. Faced with starvation and unavoidable punishment, they discovered a solution—killing humans and eating their flesh—for which they were also punished. Incessantly guilty, they were caught in a double bind situation, and their only escape from it was through dramatic changes in their personality and self-identity.

The Soviet state learned how to manipulate the population into submission by hunger at a very early stage. In Lenin's top-secret March 19, 1922 letter addressed to the members of the Politburo, he wrote:

> Now, and only now, when they have started to eat human flesh in the regions where there is famine, and when hundreds if not thousands of bodies lie on the roads, is the moment in which we can (which means we must) confiscate the goods of the Church with the most savage and merciless energy, not hesitating to crush any resistance ... so that we can lay our hands on a fund of a few hundred millions of gold roubles.[16]

The Soviet government became infamous for using hunger as a weapon against the regime's various enemies: the famines of 1921–22, 1927–29, 1931–34, and 1946–47 terminated the lives of millions of people.[17] The famine geography was colossal, extending through the Russian Soviet Federative Socialist Republic (RSFSR, including the Kuban and Volga regions, Siberia), the Ukrainian Soviet Socialist Republic (UkrSSR), and Kazakhstan.

According to numerous accounts and memoirs, the majority of women understood the Holodomor as a deliberate destruction of people, a state-organized and politically motivated mass killing. Moreover, many explained the famine in spatial terms—by reason of their geographical belonging and membership in the Ukrainian peasantry, and their association with disobedience, resistance, and nationalism—imposed by the state.[18] They claimed that their world was turned upside down: their villages became desolate places and their culture and traditions were completely eradicated. Making handicrafts, embroidering, weaving, singing, and dancing were no longer part of their lives. Instead, women existed in a space of death and impossible choices, where they played a new role and engaged in new, incomprehensible, and dangerous activities of survival.

Sex determines the forms of abuse, torture, and killing during genocide. When state activists searched peasants' huts for grain in Ukraine during collectivization, women were tortured, beaten, and raped. They were stripped naked and brought outside in subzero temperatures.[19] Certain stereotypes, prejudices, and attitudes toward women existed among the party leadership. Predominantly male Bolshevik heads of collective farms (*kolhospy*) and the village councils (*silrady*) believed in their superior status over women, perceptions that were rooted in the historically patriarchal traditions of Tsarist Russia. This factor, amplified by the males' chronic alcoholism, unleashed their basest instincts, and many took advantage of women, who were weak and vulnerable from starvation.[20] With a complete breakdown of social and legal order and in the absence of husbands who had been exiled, shot, or had gone on illegal trips outside the zones of starvation to get provisions, these women were defenseless. The state prevented people's escape from the villages by surrounding them with armed troops of secret police. In their search for food, women visited silrady where they were often raped by the heads of kolhospy and party bosses of the primary party cells, or had sex with them in exchange for bread. Prolonged torture by starvation, however, became the most dreadful experience for them, which reduced, and in many cases eclipsed, their psychological and physical suffering after being raped or sexually assaulted. While the individual tragedy of rape united women who survived it, the collective experience of starvation dehumanized and divided them.

Indeed, hunger reduced sociability. "Nobody is concerned about any-one else, and only the communists have a life, or those who have a revolver," a witness of the 1932 famine wrote.[21] As a result, the social and communal fabric of Ukrainian society suffered and was eventually destroyed in the early thirties.[22] The Ukrainian case has also demonstrated that at the peak of the famine, opportunities for women's traditional social activities (maintaining proper hygiene, intellectual development, and participating in social rituals such as marriage) declined dramatically. Moreover, pro-longed starvation produced major hormonal, epigenetic, and behavioral changes. Hunger led to the formation of obsessions, in which satisfying hunger became the fundamental priority.[23] Desperate girls and women agreed to have sex with men who offered them some food. Sex crimes and prostitution were a product of uneven relations between those who were starving and those who were not.[24] In addition, the suicide rate among children and adults increased enormously during the famine.

Yet because of the uniqueness of individual biology, physiology, and psychology, human reactions to starvation vary. During famines, one may observe the disintegration of people's body, spirit, and mentality or just the opposite effect: the consolidation of their physical and mental integrity. Pitirim Sorokin has noted that under stress and in the face of physical and mental challenges, sometimes "one becomes like well-tempered steel,—a moral hero,—whereas another turns into a coward, a nervous wreck, or a criminal."[25] Truly, the Holodomor produced wide-ranging effects on people's mentality and behavior, which strongly correlated with their expo-sure to hunger and suffering, and the degree of physical and psychological damages caused by starvation.

In her study of women's roles and participation in the nationalist under-ground in Western Ukraine in the 1940s–50s, Oksana Kiss has demon-strated that traditional femininity was curtailed and diluted through women's mobilization efforts and their participation in the resistance and liberation movement against the Soviets and the Nazis.[26] Women's wartime experiences facilitated their social mobility and increased their visibility in social life, enhancing their political competence and activity.[27] In contrast, women's experiences during the Holodomor truncated their abilities to advance themselves physically, morally, and intellectually, forc-ing them into isolation and delusions. The biological need for food and survival transformed them in a much more dramatic way than ideological commitment ever could.

Prolonged food deprivation, which for many in Ukraine lasted from 1928 to 1934, determined and reinforced people's behavior and social patterns. Some women, especially the elderly, were sluggish and broken: the protracted torture by hunger made them beg for death.[28] Others behaved aggressively, especially toward the Soviet authorities. By late November 1932, many women refused to work in kolhospy because they were being attacked and murdered in the fields *en masse* by starving individuals looking for a piece of bread, or a potato, or anything else of value they might possess.[29] Between 1932 and 1933, at the peak of the famine, people's behavior severely departed from conventional norms to the point of psychotic reactions and cannibalism. The majority were disoriented and confused, and developed hallucinations, delusions, and memory loss accompanied by profound cognitive and emotional upheaval.[30] Contemporary scholars and psychiatrists are unanimous in claiming that those who engage in necrophagia and cannibalism are the most psychiatrically disturbed and deviant individuals, no matter what triggered these inclinations.[31] Tremendous physical suffering gradually redefined people's identities, and the distance between the moral and the immoral withered away.[32] In Ukrainian villages, fathers murdered and ate their children, wives killed their husbands and vice versa, and children murdered their siblings and consumed their raw flesh. Women gave birth and buried their children in the garden, or drowned them in the estuary.[33]

Armed with this background understanding of the implications of prolonged starvation, it seems prudent to explore what was central, peripheral, transient, and permanent in this space of violence and impossible choices, and what role women played in the communal havoc and mass madness provoked by the Holodomor.

NECROPHAGIA AND CANNIBALISM

Catalin Avramescu has posited that the history of cannibalism illuminates not only the origins of the modern state but also clarifies the boundaries of modern civilization.[34] Importantly, this history is rich in places where the

state manifested itself as the supreme and new "agent of absolute cruelty."[35]
The history of cannibalism in Ukraine in 1932–33 places Soviet Ukraine on
the map of moral geography and discourse about the depth of individual
and collective moral degradation. To conceal the famine, the state sealed
Ukraine's borders. People's unsanctioned movements in or out of villages
were also forbidden. This ghettoization exacerbated the famine. Ultimately,
the entire republic was transformed into a "border-to-border concentration
camp,"[36] where people's movements in or out were restricted.[37]

Any demarcation zone where the resources necessary for human survival are scarce eventually becomes a zone of death where cannibalism
reigns. As Nicolas Werth has described, the island of Nazino in Siberia,
where thousands of people were deported by Stalin's regime in the early
1930s, became such a place: bodies were lying everywhere cut up for
"human flesh [which was] cooked and eaten."[38] The Soviet government
created a situation in which a person's right to physical survival and self-
preservation was incompatible with the same right for another person,
often a relative. Some relatives willingly sacrificed their bodies, and ultimately their lives, for the survival of their dearest. As letters sent from
Ukraine to the United States reveal, in August 1930 people felt the threat
of cannibalism approaching: "When this autumn comes, then shall be our
decline ... We will eat each other."[39] By early 1932, starving people, clinging to life, lived in fear: groups of cannibals ambushed their neighbors
and strangers, and broke into people's huts in the middle of the night,
robbing and killing their victims.[40] Necrophagia and cannibalism became
embedded in people's everyday life, dissociated from moral concerns or
pangs of conscience.[41]

Frank Dikötter has suggested that survivors are rarely heroes, and
their moral choices and compromises can be grim and appalling.[42]
Necrophagia, cannibalism, and body dismemberment constitute only
part of the Holodomor's tragic history. One might argue that this is the
most important part, because it reveals the brutal nature of Soviet rule,
which desensitized and demoralized people. Cultures in which humans
are forced to consider other humans as a potential source of nourishment
are self-destructive, as history has shown.

In the ascending order of horror and immorality, necrophagia became
a widespread practice by early 1932. People began to eat the corpses of

animals and deceased people. For many, human corpses became the only available source of nourishment, and a trade commodity. For instance, in the Kyshenkivskyi district of the Kharkiv region (*oblast*), a group of people collected corpses and stored them in the cellar of a hut. Meat sliced from corpses was sold on the black market. The speculators were discovered and tried in court.[43] During the search of the hut, the investigators discovered seventeen corpses in the cellar, dissected and prepared for sale.[44] The state left no choice for people but to devour each other. It created a community grounded in a savage economy in which new trade commodities and new rules were established. They were subordinated to one goal—to alleviate extreme hunger.

Official statistics on necrophagia are scattered. Some oblast prosecutors, however, claimed that the ratio of cannibalism to necrophagia was approximately ten to one. For instance, over the four months from February to May 1933, fifty-four cases of cannibalism and six cases of necrophagia were registered in twenty districts of the Dnipropetrovsk oblast.[45] Yet, there were oblasts, such as the Kyiv oblast, where the ratio was nearly one to one. From January to early March of 1933, fifty-four cases of necrophagia and sixty-nine cases of cannibalism were registered by the secret police.[46] This phenomenon was also brought to light through oral histories, memoirs, and diaries.

In urban centers, necrophagia was common. The morgues worked at full capacity, but unburied human corpses could be found on the streets of Kharkiv and Kyiv, at the railway stations, in ditches alongside roads and in almost all village huts.[47] In the countryside, only a few had the strength to bury their dead:[48] their corpses lay exposed for eight to ten days, often becoming a food source for the starving. Parents put their deceased children in the cellars instead of burying them, and consumed their flesh piece by piece, or sold it in the market.[49] In some cases, the dead were dragged from burial pits at the outskirts of villages to appease hunger. In others, collectors of corpses extracted the livers from those who died from hunger or typhus, and used them as a filling for meat pies for sale.[50]

The famine also drove people to the next level of dehumanization—cannibalism. By the early autumn of 1932, cannibalism also became commonplace, reaching its peak in late February to early March of 1933.[51] Fellow living beings were considered as a potential meal. Archival documents frequently depict graphic stories of Ukrainian cannibals who ate their own children. Official statistics on cannibalism, however, are unreliable and incomplete, reflecting only cases with solid evidence of murder committed by cannibals. Sometimes cannibals operated within a group or a family: men did the killing; women prepared human flesh for consumption. On April 27, 1932, Petro Moroz from the village Stepkivtsi killed his two-year-old child and dissected the body. His wife cooked the flesh and they fed themselves and their four-year-old child for two days.[52]

What was the profile of a typical Ukrainian cannibal? According to the official statistics, the Holodomor cannibals were predominantly under-educated women.[53] Their behavior was ruthless and cold-blooded, and could usually be observed in households where there were no adult males. To feed their children, they killed people, often assisted by their eldest daughters. Some scholars have suggested that women are fundamentally emotional, and their aggressiveness and irrationality might be driven by their biological nature.[54] Whatever the case, in traditional families with husband, wife, and children, husbands—not wives—were usually the executors of premeditated murders.

The most "innocent" portrait of a female cannibal is drawn from crimi-nal cases, in which several adults linked by family ties formed a group that conceived and committed the crimes. Quite frequently, the victims were the conspirators' weak and small children, or passersby. Any stranger was welcomed into their huts, which is where the homicide typically occurred. Sometimes, it took an effort to lure the victim inside. The offer to share some bread worked well: the victim, unable to resist the prospect of food, would step inside the inner porch (*siny*), where he or she would be brutally murdered with an ax, scythe, or shovel.

Children's naiveté and hunger facilitated the cannibals' task, often becoming their prey.[55] On May 28, 1932, Onysym Hutsulenko's three-year-old son from the village Molodetske of the Bukskyi district disappeared. His neighbor Sivachenko became an immediate suspect because of his frequent invitations for the little boy to visit his apartment. The search of Sivachenko's apartment by the village council commission revealed traces of blood on Sivachenko's ax and scythe, human bones, and pieces of human skin. But the most graphic scene observed by the commission occurred outside the cannibal's apartment: they exhumed the boy's head that was buried nearby. The face was preserved, which allowed the commission to establish the boy's identity, although the skull had been opened and the brain had been extracted. According to Sivachenko's deposition, he was part of a group that consisted of five people who during the last several months had murdered and consumed seven people. Among the members of the group was a woman, Natalia Kuzmyk, whose responsibility was to cook the meat, to make preserves, or to pickle the meat in a large wooden barrel (*kadushka*). She also cleaned the blood from the floor and the tools.[56]

Sivachenko claimed that the procedure was well organized and everyone followed a pre-arranged plan. The flesh of the dead victim was divided equally among the participants. In addition, the conspirators had a common meal to celebrate the event. Natalia cooked the internal organs. Usually, the feast was accompanied by the massive consumption of alcohol. Natalia drank and ate together with the men.[57]

These sorts of depositions were included in detailed secret police reports written by top officials, and were forwarded to the secret police's central headquarters in Moscow and the Central Party Committees in Kyiv and Moscow. Some women repented and were devastated by what they had done.[58] Many were almost lethargic when they were killing their victims: "We were very hungry, my head was spinning, I did not remember myself when I cut them into pieces," a woman claimed.[59] Most women were imperturbably violent and indifferent to the victim's cries.[60] At the peak of a delirium provoked by hunger, women killed their own children in order to feed the rest of the family.[61] They did not seem to express any remorse or regret, estranging themselves from the experience of killing, as well as from the victim. Apparently, by distancing themselves from this reality, it was easier for them to explain their behavior in simplistic terms of practical necessity, and to efficiently implement the task.[62] They presented themselves as victims of particular circumstances and state violence. For instance, Ksenia Bolotnikova from the village Sofievka (Berdiansk district) described her cannibalistic temptation as a necessity to feed her little son. She killed her eighteen-month-old daughter by slashing her throat, placed her on a bench, covered her with a rug, and went to bed. The next morning, she boiled her daughter's head and parts of the girls' left calf, and gave her son the boiled brain, telling him that it was veal.[63]

Women did not dare to kill strong men—they were too weak for this challenge, unless mothers persuaded their teenage daughters to work as a group. Typically, they killed young boys, girls who were barely alive, and women for food.[64] The victims' size mattered to cannibals: soberly calculating the profit, they searched for larger women. On May 2, 1932, a woman from Odesa murdered another woman. Her flesh was consumed by the cannibal family over three days. The murderer also melted the body fat, poured it in three bottles, and sold them in the market as goose oil.[65] Women's ovens and gardens became the burial places for the "unusable" parts of people's bodies—the heads and the bones.[66]

Eric D. Weitz has posited that "like rape, like torture, cannibalism symbolizes the utter, complete degradation of the individual."[67] Indeed, the scarcity of food dictated new rules of survival, and quite a few succumbed to them, discovering a new way of life, dangerous and immoral. Novice cannibals carried out their crimes secretly, and their operations were usually a nocturnal affair. But as the brutality and intensity of the famine progressed, they became less cautious. Cannibals and the village administration were the only individuals who were still mobile in the countryside. And it was precisely the cannibals' mobility that would eventually bring them to the secret police's attention.

THE STATE'S RESPONSE TO CANNIBALISM

Despite the fact that by 1933 cannibalism had become a mass phenomenon in the Ukrainian countryside, cannibals were considered by their community, whatever was left of it, as outcasts. Their healthy appearance betrayed them. They were denounced, and often ambushed, attacked, and killed by their neighbors.[68] In contrast, the state was completely silent about the famine in general, and cannibalism in particular. In the collective illusion of a socialist country of abundance, cannibalism and food shortages were unthinkable, and reports of them were considered "harmful rumors": those who raised questions about the famine or about anthropophagy were labeled anti-Soviet propagandists and counterrevolutionaries.[69] Thus, no definition of these transgressions or public acknowledgement of the famine can be found in the press at the time. Official circulars provided some statistics and reported on cases of cannibalism in the context of the raging famine in Ukraine, but these were secret and accessible only to a narrow circle of party or secret police bureaucracy.

Historically, cannibalism as a crime has rarely been included in world penal codes by legislators. Perhaps the unthinkable moral monstrosity of the aberration prevents them from translating it into legal terms and identifying it as a state offense.[70] In Ukraine, the state isolated the cannibals because they were socially dangerous individuals and murderers, but more importantly because they were the living confirmation of a widespread famine that was nevertheless a state secret. Cannibals were usually caught by the local militia, which was informed about missing people by the community. As a rule, the authorities recovered solid evidence of crimes—parts of dead bodies (buried, pickled, or cooked), walls covered with blood, and a distinct stench in the hut. The suspects were arrested and accused of criminal activity pursuant to Articles 139 and 174 of the Criminal Code of the UkrSSR, which were employed in 1933 by the prosecutors dealing with cannibals. Neither article contained a definition of cannibalism but rather referred to violent robberies that resulted in serious damage to a human body or death. Women's verdicts were as harsh as men's—the death sentence or ten years in prison. Occasionally, they received only five years in prison. In these cases, the prosecutors took into consideration the fact that they did not consume the flesh of their victims; they fed their own children.[71] Many ended up in the northern labor camps.[72]

Stalin continuously ignored secret messages from officials about the disaster in Ukraine, exacerbating the double bind situation, from which there was no way out for the peasants. He also remained deaf to thousands of women's petitions addressed directly to him. Among them were texts like this one:

> I am speaking on behalf of five thousand semialive people, not animals, who tore ourselves from the strong claws of artificial famine.... We know that our letter will not receive a response and will be simply ripped apart.... You will pretend that this is counterrevolutionary language.... We broke our noses, our fingers are cut off by the closing doors of the trains.... We are still alive because we ate garbage thrown at pigs ... People are ready to

eat the flesh of those who eat good bread, rather than the corpses of dead horses dragged from the earth.... We are returning to a primitive savage period.[73]

Indeed, the Kremlin remained silent. The authorities continued to starve people and to punish cannibals. To an extent, cannibalism became a means through which the Kremlin reinforced and expanded its authority. Thousands of people were executed and exiled to the gulag for this transgression, although the official statistics are quite modest and have not been systematized yet. According to some sources, the Soviets convicted at least 2,505 Ukrainians for cannibalism.[74] Women were separated from men, put like livestock in cattle cars, and sent to labor camps. Olha Mane, a Jewish woman who was repressed in the 1930s and exiled to the Solovetski Islands, claimed that three hundred Ukrainian women served their terms there for cannibalism.[75]

EPILOGUE

The Ukrainian peasants' lives and the system in which they lived no longer made sense to them. They were punished twice: by hunger for resistance and separatist tendencies, and by imprisonment for eating human flesh because of forced starvation. Such double-victimization made women further suffer, changing everything in their world, including their identity. State-sponsored violence and near-death experiences dramatically affected their traditional roles in the family—tilling the land and taking care of their children and households. Moreover, because of their appearance, it became problematic to identify their sex without close examination (unless they were dressed in traditional women's clothing).[76] Women were robbed of their reproductive capacities by the famine: most could not get pregnant; those who could gave birth to stillborn children. Being women, they felt that they were no longer women—in a cultural, social, and biological sense.[77] They understood the meaning and the implications of their criminal activities, but at the same time they resented their criminalization as cannibals by the state. They estranged themselves from their crimes and rationalized them. Their ghettoization made them criminals through force and coercion: they were victims of a double bind. They developed ambivalent attitudes toward their new "hyphenated" identities as women-criminals.

Hunger has been employed as a weapon to subjugate nations and individuals throughout human history. Zygmund Bauman has reminded us that the goal of genocide is achieved when the will and resilience of the victims are broken. They are subsumed by the new order demanded of them. In the absence of food, necessary for resistance, the continuation of the struggle becomes impossible.[78] People's morbid fixation on food produces social spaces in which moral principles are completely annihilated: what ultimately counts is "to outlive the others."[79] In the Ukrainian case, the state used violence to act as a morality-silencing force and accelerate people's return to a presocial state—"a primitive savage period," as the aforementioned petitioner stated.

There were, however, many men and women whose boundaries of morality, although skewed and polluted, had the strength and the internal fortitude to restore them daily to yesterday's norms. To remain human, they had to make a choice, and often they chose to die with dignity. Isaiah Berlin was convinced that humans "are doomed to choose, and every choice may entail an irreparable loss."[80] Genocide excludes and destroys people because of their ethnicity, nationality, religious affiliation, and the like, but involves all—perpetrators, victims, innocent, and guilty—in its deadly bacchanalia because of their everyday choices that drive the pendulum of morality. These choices help identify people's survival patterns. The gender survival patterns in Ukraine in 1932–33 are generally consistent with those registered for many other genocides: adult females were more likely to survive than males, the elderly, and children.[81] Yet, the questions of whether cannibalism was a gender-specific phenomenon, and whether women's performance[82] and their propensity to act violently were limited to a particular place, such as starving Ukraine in 1932–33, remains open.

The history of the Holodomor and cannibalistic practices serves as a lens through which the incompatibility of the Soviet system and a moral philosophy becomes more evident and transparent. Importantly, cannibals' transformations and their projections into the future should be central to this history because, ultimately, women who turned to necrophagia and cannibalism had a better chance of surviving the famine, subsequently becoming a part of Ukraine's post-famine realities, associated with raising children and contributing to Ukraine's cultural development. Not surprisingly, the tremendous cultural disruption, the erosion of people's moral values, and the de-civilization, which occurred at all levels in Ukraine in the early thirties, remain a serious concern for contemporary Ukrainians, and these phenomena beg a series of questions about how quickly such a society is able to recover, at what cost, and whether it can recover at all.

OLGA BERTELSEN is a visiting scholar at the New York University Jordan Center for the Advanced Study of Russia. She is author of *The House of Writers in Ukraine, the 1930s: Conceived, Lived, Perceived,* and editor of *Revolution and War in Contemporary Ukraine: The Challenge of Change.*

NOTES

1. I am grateful to the editors of this volume, anonymous reviewers, Andrea Graziosi and Dale A. Bertelsen for their comments and suggestions on earlier drafts of this text. "Holodomor" is a Ukrainian term for the famine that consists of two words, "holod" and "mor" which, when combined, literally means "killing by hunger."

2. Andrea Graziosi, Lubomyr A. Hajda, and Halyna Hryn, "Introduction," in *After the Holodomor: The Enduring Impact of the Great Famine on Ukraine,* eds. Andrea Graziosi, Lubomyr A. Hajda, and Halyna Hryn (Cambridge, MA: Ukrainian Research Institute, 2013), xv.

3. Andrea Graziosi, "The Impact of the Holodomor Studies on the Understanding of the USSR," *East/West: Journal of Ukrainian Studies* 2, no. 1 (2015): 73; Andrea Graziosi, "Why and in What Sense Was the Holodomor a Genocide?" in *Holodomor: Reflections on the Great Famine of 1932–1933 in Soviet Ukraine,* ed. Lubomyr Y. Luciuk (Kingston, ON: The Kashtan Press, 2008), 139–57; James Mace, "Is the Ukrainian Genocide a Myth?" in Luciuk, *Holodomor: Reflections,* 49–60.

4. Timothy Snyder, *Black Earth: The Holocaust as History and Warning* (New York: Tim Duggan Books, 2015), xii.

5. *Bab'i bunty* were women's riots during collectivization. For a discussion about *bab'i bunty,* see Lynne Viola, *Peasant Rebels Under Stalin: Collectivization and the Culture of Peasant Resistance* (New York: Oxford University Press, 1996), 181–204; Lynne Viola, "*Bab'i bunty* and Peasant Women's Protest during Collectivization," *Russian Review* 45, no. 1 (1986): 189–205. See also TSDAHOU (*Tsentral'nyi derzhavnyi arkhiv hromads'kykh ob'iednan' Ukrainy*), 1/20/5401/22-26. Approximately 60–70 percent of the protesters in various places in Ukraine were women (May, 1932).

6. Lynne Viola, "Introduction," in *Contending with Stalinism: Soviet Power and Popular Resistance in the 1930s,* ed. Lynne Viola (Ithaca, NY: Cornell University Press, 2002), 6.

7. Norman M. Naimark, *Fires of Hatred: Ethnic Cleansing in Twentieth-Century Europe* (Cambridge, MA: Harvard University Press, 2001), 83, 195.

8. Ibid.

9. Necrophagia is the consumption of cadavers' flesh or the flesh of those who just passed away. Cannibalism involves the killing of a human being for subsequent consumption.

10. On the dehumanization of the victims of genocide, see Leo Kuper, *Genocide: Its Political Use in the Twentieth Century* (New Haven, CT: Yale University Press, 1981), 104; Naimark, *Fires of Hatred*, 23; Eric D. Weitz, *A Century of Genocide: Utopias of Race and Nation* (Princeton, NJ: Princeton University Press, 2003), 222.

11. V. I. Marochko, "Kanibalizm v roky holodomoru," in *Holod 1932-1933 v Ukraini: prychyny ta naslidky*, ed. V. M. Litvin (Kyiv: Naukova dumka, 2003), 568. In psychiatry, cases of cannibalism are usually associated with severe mental illness and changes in self-identity. See, for instance, Ortiz O. Medina, Galvis D. Contreras, N. Sánchez-Mora, and López C. Arango, "Cannibalism in Paranoid Schizophrenia: A Case Report," *Actas Esp Psiquiatr* 34, no. 2 (2006): 136–39; Jean-Luc Senninger and Adele Senninger, "Cannibalism, Schizophrenia and Cannabis Use," *European Psychiatry* 29, S. 1 (2014): 1 (an abstract of this study presented at the 22nd European Congress of Psychiatry).

12. Michele Ernandes, Rita Cedrini, and Marco Giammanco, "Aztec Cannibalism and Maize Consumption: The Serotonin Deficiency Link," *Mankind Quarterly* 43, no. 1 (2002): 3–40. According to several studies, during starvation serotonin deficiency is responsible for aggressive behavior and cannibalism.

13. This phenomenon should not be conflated with ritual cannibalism.

14. The term is borrowed from the 1915 essay "Democracy Versus the Melting Pot: A Study of American Nationality, Part Two" (*The Nation* 100, no. 2590 [18–25 February 1915]: 217) by Horace M. Kallen, Jewish-American philosopher, who emphatically espoused the notion of hyphenated identity, asserting that American identity is "a chorus of many voices each singing a rather different tune" (ibid.).

15. Gregory Bateson, *Steps to an Ecology of Mind* (New York: Ballantine Books, 1972), 206–10.

16. Quoted in Catalin Avramescu, *An Intellectual History of Cannibalism*, trans. Alistair Ian Blyth (Princeton, NJ: Princeton University Press, 2009), 232.

17. See O. M. Movchan, "Holod v 1921–1923 rr. v pivdennykh huberniiakh USRR," in *Istoriia ukrainskoho selianstva*, eds. V. M. Lytvyn et al. (Kyiv: Naukova Dumka, 2006), 20–26; O. M. Veselova, "Holod 1946–1947 rr.: prychyny i naslidky," in Lytvyn et al.; Liudmyla Hrynevych, *Khronika kolektyvizatsii ta Holodomoru v Ukraini: 1927–1933*, vol. 1, kn. 1–3 (Kyiv: Krytyka, 2008; 2012); Vladyslav Verstiuk, Volodymyr Tylishchak, and Ihor Iukhnovskyi, *Holodomor: Henotsyd ukrainskoho narodu, 1932–1933* (Kyiv: Vyd-vo imeni Oleny Telihy, 2008); Stanislav Kulchytskyi, *Holodomor 1932–1933 rr. iak henotsyd: trudnoshchi usvidomlennia* (Kyiv: "Nash Chas," 2008); Vasyl Marochko and Olha Movchan, *Holodomor v Ukraini 1932–1933 rokiv: Khronika* (Kyiv: KMA, 2008); Bohdan Klid and Alexander J. Motyl, eds. *The Holodomor Reader: A Sourcebook on the Famine of 1932–1933 in Ukraine* (Edmonton; Toronto: CIUS Press, 2012); Andrij Makuch and Frank E. Sysyn, eds., *Contextualizing the Holodomor: The Impact of Thirty Years of Ukrainian Famine Studies* (Edmonton; Toronto: CIUS Press, 2015).

18. DAKhO (*Derzhavnyi arkhiv Kharkivs'koi oblasti*), R856/3/22/130.

19. TSDAHOU, 1/20/5488/17; 1/20/6395/99.

20. Food was scarce, but there was plenty of cheap vodka in Ukraine. Alcohol, despite the fact that it is a central nervous system depressant, also serves as a social lubricant, capable of removing sexual inhibitions. See Jim Penman, *Biohistory: Decline and Fall of the West* (Newcastle upon Tyne, UK: Cambridge Scholars Publishing, 2015), 20–23.

21. From a private letter to relatives in North Dakota, May 20, 1932, cited in Ronald J. Vossler, ed., *We'll Meet Again in Heaven: Germans in the Soviet Union Write Their Dakota Relatives, 1925–1937* (Fargo: North Dakota State University Libraries, 2003), 160.

22. For a discussion of similar trends in Rwanda, see Jennie E. Burnet, *Genocide Lives in Us: Women, Memory, and Silence in Rwanda* (Madison: The University of Wisconsin Press, 2012), 65.

23. Abraham H. Maslow, *Motivation and Personality*, 2nd ed. (New York: Harper & Row, 1970), 20, 37; Ernest Dichter, *Motivating Human Behavior* (New York: McGraw-Hill Book Company, 1971), 2; Penman, 14, 23.

24. Pitirim A. Sorokin, *Man and Society in Calamity: The Effects of War, Revolution, Famine, Pestilence upon Human Mind, Behavior, Social Organization and Cultural Life* (New York: E.P. Dutton, 1946), 59–63.

25. Ibid., 14, 159.

26. Oksana Kiss, "National Femininity Used and Contested: Women's Participation in the Nationalist Underground in Western Ukraine in the 1940s–50s," *East/West: Journal of Ukrainian Studies* 2, no. 2 (2015): 53–82.

27. Ibid., 76.

28. TSDAHOU, 1/20/5255/5.

29. TSDAHOU, 1/20/5252/119-22.

30. DAKhO, R856/3/22/149.

31. David Lester, John White, and Brandi Giordano, "Cannibalism," *OMEGA-Journal of Death and Dying* 70, no. 4 (2015): 428–35. According to several studies, exposure to starvation provokes the development of schizophrenia and psychosis. See David St. Clair et al., "Rates of Adult Schizophrenia Following Prenatal Exposure to the Chinese Famine of 1959–1961," *Journal of the American Medical Association* 294, no. 5 (2005): 557–62; Ezra Susser and Katherine M. Keyes, "Prenatal Nutritional Deficiency and Psychosis: Where Do We Go From Here? *JAMA Psychiatry* 74, no. 4 (2017): 349–50; Ezra Susser, David St. Clair, and He Lin, "Latent Effects of Prenatal Malnutrition on Adult Health," *Annals of the New York Academy of Sciences* 1136 (2008):185–92; Ezra S. Susser and Shang P. Lin, "Schizophrenia after Prenatal Exposure to the Dutch Hunger Winter of 1944–1945," *Archives of General Psychiatry* 49, no. 12 (1992): 983–88.

32. On behavioral patterns and mechanisms triggered by deprivation and satiation, see Jack Michael and Lee Meyerson, "A Behavioral Approach to Human Control," in *Control of Human Behavior: Expanding the Behavioral Laboratory*, eds. Roger Ulrich, Thomas Stachnik, and John Mabry (Glenview, IL: Scott, Foresman, 1966), 29.

33. Vossler, *We'll Meet Again in Heaven*, 136.

34. Avramescu, *An Intellectual History*, 3.

35. Ibid., 262. During the Chinese 1959–62 famine, at least forty-five million people died within four years because of starvation and its complications, and thousands if not millions of people engaged in necrophagia and cannibalism. See Frank Dikötter, "The Great Leap Backward," *History Today* 60, no. 11 (November 2010): 4 (3/4); Xun Zhou, *Forgotten Voices of Mao's Great Famine, 1958–1962: An Oral History* (New Haven, CT: Yale University

Press, 2013); Ralph Thaxton, *Catastrophe and Contention in Rural China: Mao's Great Leap Forward Famine and the Origins of Righteous Resistance in Da Fo Village* (Cambridge, New York: Cambridge University Press, 2008).

36. R. J. Rummel, *Death by Government* (New Brunswick, NJ: Transaction Publishers, 2007), 26.

37. TSDAHOU, 1/16/19/19.

38. Nicolas Werth, *Cannibal Island: Death in a Siberian Gulag* (Princeton, NJ: Princeton University Press, 2007), 138-41.

39. Vossler, *We'll Meet Again in Heaven*, 107.

40. TSDAHOU, 1/20/5255/40.

41. TSDAHOU, 1/20/5255/36,40,50; Steven Bela Vardy and Agnes Huszar Vardy, "Cannibalism in Stalin's Russia and Mao's China," *East European Quarterly* 41, no. 2 (2007): 230. Some witnesses spoke of "mass cannibalism" which occurred in Ukraine in the early thirties.

42. Frank Dikötter, *Mao's Great Famine: The History of Mao's Most Devastating Catastrophe* (New York: Walker & Co., 2010), xv.

43. TSDAHOU, 1/20/6275/129.

44. In the regions of starvation, people were selling human flesh on the black market, claiming it was pork or beef. Sausages made out of children's flesh were sold at 7 karbovantsi, and children's flesh at 28 karbovantsi per kilogram. See Marochko, "Kanibalizm," 574.

45. DADO (*Derzhavnyi arkhiv Dnipropetrovs'koi oblasti*), R-1520/3/1/500.

46. Marochko, "Kanibalizm," 572.

47. TSDAHOU, 1/20/5255/18.

48. Vossler, *We'll Meet Again in Heaven*, xxxv.

49. Tamara Polishchuk, *Stolytsia vidchaiu* (Kharkiv: "Berezil," 2006), 46, 53, 109.

50. Andrea Graziosi, "Lettres de Kharkov: La famine en Ukraine et dans le Caucase du Nord a travers les rapports des diplomates italiens, 1932–1934," *Cahiers du monde russe et sovietique* 30, no. 1 (1989): 79.

51. TSDAHOU, 1/20/6274/151; 1/20/6276/42,47. According to the official statistics, which are far from accurate, by June 1, 1933, 221 incidents of cannibalism were registered in the Kharkiv oblast alone; from June 1 to June 10, 245 such incidents in 41 districts of the Kharkiv oblast were registered by the secret police.

52. TSDAHOU, 1/20/5255/50.

53. Marochko, "Kanibalizm," 571.

54. See, for instance, Daniel A. Georges-Abeyie, "Women as Terrorists," in *Perspectives on Terrorism*, ed. Lawrence Zelic Freedman and Yonah Alexander (Wilmington, DE: Scholarly Resources, 1983), 71–84; for an analysis of emotionality and feminist approaches, see Catherine Lutz, "Feminist Emotions," in *Power and the Self*, ed. Jeannette Marie Mageo (New York: Cambridge University Press, 2001), 194–215.

55. TSDAHOU, 1/20/5488/46.

56. TSDAHOU, 1/20/5255/62-64.

57. TSDAHOU, 1/20/5255/64.

58. Marochko, "Kanibalizm," 571.

59. TSDAHOU, 1/20/6274/171.

60. TSDAHOU, 1/20/5255/71.

61. Ibid.

62. For a similar rationale and psychology, see Zygmund Bauman, *Modernity and the Holocaust* (Ithaca, NY: Cornell University Press, 2000), 155.

63. TSDAHOU, 1/20/5255/74-75.

64. TSDAHOU, 1/20/6274/77; DAChO (*Derzhavnyi arkhiv Cherkas'koi oblasti*) R-5625/1/949/1.

65. TSDAHOU, 1/20/5256/36.

66. TSDAHOU, 1/20/5488/46, 49.

67. Weitz, *A Century of Genocide*, 179.

68. Vossler, *We'll Meet Again in Heaven*, xxxiv.

69. TsDAHOU, 1/16/19/85; Werth, *Cannibal Island*, 138, 144. By 1932, the famine was no longer a secret. The information about mass starvation and cannibalism leaked through foreign intelligence and diplomats. See Graziosi, "Lettres de Kharkov;" Robert Kuśnierz, "The Impact of the Great Famine on Ukrainian Cities: Evidence from the Polish Archives," in Graziosi, Hajda, and Hryn, *After the Holodomor*, 17.

70. Interestingly enough, the Soviet legal system identified cannibalism as a specific crime that deserved a death sentence only during the Leningrad siege. See Richard Overy, *Russia's War* (London: TV Books, 1998), 107.

71. Marochko, "Kanibalizm," 571.

72. DAVO, R-2700/9/396/47-48; DADO (*Derzhavnyi arkhiv Donets'koi oblasti*), P-326/1/130/6.

73. TSDAHOU, 1/20/5255/26-29.

74. Timothy Snyder, *Bloodlands: Europe Between Hitler and Stalin* (New York: Basic Books, 2010), 51; Paul G. Pierpaoli Jr., "Cannibalism in the Holodomor," in *Modern Genocide: The Definitive Resource and Document Collection*, vol. 4, ed. Paul R. Bartrop and Steven Leonard Jacobs (Santa Barbara, CA: ABC-CLIO, 2015): 1875.

75. UCRDC (Ukrainian Canadian Research and Documentation Centre), A Collection of Unpublished Memoirs, file no. 41.

76. Roman Serbyn, "Photographic Evidence of the Ukrainian Famines of 1921–1923 and 1932–1933," *Holodomor Studies* 2, no. 1 (2010): 63–94.

77. Vossler, *We'll Meet Again in Heaven*, 220.

78. Bauman, *Modernity*, 119.

79. Ibid., 169, 234.

80. Isaiah Berlin, "The Pursuit of the Ideal," in *The Proper Study of Mankind: An Anthology of Essays* (New York: Farrar, Straus and Giroux, 1998), 11.

81. See, for instance, the Chinese case in Dikötter, *Mao's Great Famine*, 262.

82. For a discussion about "performance" and the idea of an original and natural gender, see Judith Butler, *Bodies that Matter. On the Discursive Limits of "Sex"* (New York: Routledge, 1993). Similar questions have been raised in the context of terrorism and gender issues. See Dominique Grisard, "History of Knowledge, Terrorism and Gender," *Historical Social Research* 39, no. 3 (2014): 82–99.

Gender

A Crucial Tool in Holocaust Research

Marion Kaplan

Feminist scholarship, which uses gender analysis much as class or ethnic analyses are used by traditional historians, has been crucial to my work on German-Jewish daily life under the Nazis. Gender—the culturally and hierarchically constructed differences between the sexes—made a difference in the way the oppressors treated Jews. Gender also made a difference in the ways Jews perceived and reacted to daily events. A gender analysis reveals dimensions in private life that are otherwise untouchable—the decision-making process between husbands and wives regarding emigration, for example, or the way fathers and mothers reacted to the persecution of their children at school.

It is clear to scholars who study the Holocaust that Jews were persecuted *as Jews* and murdered *as Jews*. But feminist scholars look beyond this general truth to ask more complicated questions. As Carol Rittner and John Roth have pointed out, "much that happened to men and women during the Holocaust was devastatingly alike. But, much that happened was devastatingly different, too."[1] There were differences between men and women, in how they were treated as well as how they reacted. Mary Felstiner insists that, "along the stations toward extinction ... each gender lived its own journey."[2]

GENDERED SUFFERING AND SURVIVAL STRATEGIES

To be more specific, although the calamity that hit German Jews affected them as Jews first, they also suffered based on gender. First, racism and sexism were intertwined in the minds of the torturers. The Nazis attacked Jewish men first, demolishing their careers and businesses. The Nazis were not original thinkers. Historically European–majority cultures led by men focused on the "dangerous" minority male. Men in power saw male "others" as potential rivals, threats to be kept down, whether in German antisemitism or in the American South, for example. Women might have been seen as manipulative or demanding, but men in power understood women's impotence, and successfully reinforced their exclusion from authority and influence until the late nineteenth century.[3] Thus, like other racists and sexists, Nazi propaganda put the emphasis on Jewish men—the "Jew" or "der Jude"—usually strangely distorted males with huge noses and stomachs. Hence, Nazi propaganda usually conflated Jewish men and Jews. For example, at a dinner party in late 1933, the vice mayor of Berlin assured the Jewish journalist Bella Fromm that, "I am only against Jews, not against Jewish women. Especially not against charming Jewesses."[4] Jewish men were also far more vulnerable to physical assault and arrest. (Even in mixed marriages, the Nazis privileged the marriage of Aryan men to Jewish women over Jewish men to Aryan women.) When men faced arrest, women often remained to carry the burden of maintaining their homes and families, of keeping their households and communities together. Even if ultimately Jewish women, the procreators, were also enemies doomed to perish in the Nazis' race war, at the beginning of the Nazi era Jewish women saw their men's status slip precipitously and tried to alleviate the distress, saw their men endangered and tried to rescue them.[5]

Not only was early Nazi racism and persecution gendered, so too were the victims' survival strategies in both practical and psychological terms. The victims reacted not always and not only as Jews, but as Jewish women and men. A focus on gender led me to recognize, for example, that most women took the early warning signals of Nazism far more seriously than did most men. Women eagerly trained for jobs and crafts useful abroad, whereas men continued to hope that they would be able to maintain their careers or professions. And women made do on smaller budgets, shopped in hostile stores, and tried to create cheer in cramped spaces, while, at home, husbands were asked only to limit their expectations.

Gender made an enormous difference in deciding between fight and flight. In the early years, Jewish women were more sensitive to discrimination, more eager to leave Germany, more willing to face uncertainty abroad rather than discrimination and ostracism at home. Jewish men thought they had a great deal more to lose by leaving Germany. Over 80 percent of Germany's approximately 525,000 Jews lived middle-class lives. These men had to tear themselves away from their lifework, whether a business or professional practice. Usually more educated than women, Jewish men felt a deep attachment to German culture. Additionally, many had fought in World War I and believed that their service and patriotism would count for something. Most important, as long as they made a living, many breadwinners were unwilling to face poverty abroad. And men were the primary breadwinners. In 1933, most Jewish men worked, with about 62 percent in business and commerce, whereas about 27 percent of Jewish women worked outside the home, half in retail or offices and family enterprises. In light of men's primary identity being associated with their occupation, they often felt trapped into staying. Women, whose identity was more family oriented, struggled to preserve what was central to them by fleeing with it.[6]

Those men whose businesses declined as a result of the Nazi boycott of April 1, 1933, (and sporadic, increasing boycotts thereafter), and who lost their jobs due to the anti-Semitic "April Laws" of 1933 (which restricted Jews in the civil service, medical, and legal professions), had little choice but to leave. Ironically, this proved to be lifesaving for them and their families. The April laws affected primarily males, since women had been accepted to German universities only since 1908, and hence had just entered the professions. The two exceptions to these laws—those who had held the job at the start of World War I, around August 1, 1914, or those who had served at the front during that war did not usually apply to women. Immediately after these laws were implemented, about half of Jewish judges and prosecutors and almost a third of Jewish lawyers lost their jobs. A fourth of Jewish doctors lost their German National Health Insurance affiliation. In September 1933, the Nazis excluded Jews, again, mostly males, from the worlds of art, film, music, literature, and journalism. Restrictions, official and unofficial harassment, and economic boycotts increased in their frequency and fervor. By April 1938, 60 percent of all Jewish-owned businesses no longer existed. Still, until November 1938, some of those who had not lost their jobs and businesses hung on, either hoping the regime would collapse or trying to get the papers necessary to flee.

In addition to different experiences in the world of work, men and women also led relatively distinct lives and often interpreted daily events differently. Women were more integrated into their communities: there were the daily interactions with neighbors, regular exchanges with the grocer, and, often, participation in local women's organizations. Raised to be sensitive to social situations, women's social antennae were finely attuned to and directed toward more unconventional—what men might have considered more trivial—sources of information, what the baker said, whether the neighbor gave her usual greeting, and so on.

Women seem to have been more acutely aware of their children's unhappiness, another reason to flee. When children suffered from taunts and abuse at school, mothers and fathers often disagreed as to the solution. Toni Lessler, the founder and director of a Montessori school in Berlin that became a Jewish school, remembered: "The ... city schools became evermore difficult for the Jewish children.... If the parents had only guessed what the children had to go through there.... And it must probably have been a false pride that caused the fathers in particular to keep their children in city schools." Lessler pointed not only to fathers' aspirations to give their children a quality education but also to their "stand-tough" approach.[7] Memoirs furthermore attest to fathers' unrealistic hopes that their children would not suffer and to their insistence that they develop thicker skin. When a sixteen-year-old, the only Jewish girl in her class, balked at participating in a class trip during which the class would eat at a hotel that displayed a "Jews Undesired" placard, her mother supported her. The mother dreaded the anxiety her daughter might experience—"she'll worry about what might happen during the entire trip." Her father, however, insisted that she participate.[8] Sometimes even the Aryan wives of Jewish men took the lead. Verena Hellwig, for example, feared for her two mixed (*Mischling*) children, even as her husband, also of "mixed blood", insisted on remaining in Germany until his approaching retirement. When her teenage son could not find an apprenticeship, she spoke to a Nazi official. He told her that people of "mixed blood" were "our greatest danger. They should either return to Judaism ... and suffer the fate of the Jews or they should be prevented from procreating." She had reached her turning point, saying Germany was dead for her. She soon immigrated to England with her children. This meant a temporary separation from "her husband, [her] best friend," but she had to find a future for her children.[9]

A widespread assumption that women lacked political acumen—stemming from their primary role in the domestic sphere—gave women's warnings less credibility. And, the prejudice that women were "hysterical" in the face of danger worked to everyone's disadvantage. Many men insisted that men were more attuned to political realities. One man pulled rank on his wife, saying, "You're a child.... You mustn't take everything so seriously. Hitler used the Jews ... as propaganda to gain power—now ... you'll hear nothing more about the Jews."[10] Men claimed to see the broader picture, to maintain an objective stance. When Else Gerstel urged her husband, a judge who had lost his job, to emigrate, he responded: "the German people, the German judges, would not stand for much more of this madness."[11] Men mediated their experiences through newspapers and broadcasts. Politics may have remained more abstract to them, whereas women's narrower picture—the minutiae (and significance) of direct everyday contacts—brought politics home.

Recalling debates within Berlin families, Peter Wyden summed it up, saying: "It was not a bit unusual in these go-or-no-go family dilemmas for the women to display more energy and enterprise than the men.... Almost no women had a business, a law office, or a medical practice to lose. They were less status-conscious, less money-oriented than the men. They seemed to be less rigid, less cautious, more confident of their ability to flourish on new turf."[12]

GENDER ROLE REVERSALS

Gender differences in perceiving danger do not mean that gender roles remained static. On the contrary, in what Holocaust historian Raul Hilberg has described as communities of "men without power and women without support,"[13] we find, for the most part, active women who, early on, greatly expanded their traditional roles. Anxious but highly energetic women took note of the political and social environment and strategized ways of responding to it. Many experimented with new behaviors rarely before attempted by any middle-class German women: interceding for their men with the authorities, seeking paid employment, sending off children on *Kindertransporte*, selling their homes, and deciding on countries of refuge. The November Pogrom of 1938 known as "Crystal Night" or *Kristallnacht*, highlights women's activities under dire circumstances. Organized by the government and supported by local mobs, the attacks ranged from homes and businesses destroyed by assailants wielding hatchets and axes to synagogues destroyed by means of incendiary bombs and dynamite. Mobs plundered Jewish property. The Nazis also invaded Jewish hospitals, old age homes, and orphanages. Finally, the Nazis systematically rounded up thirty thousand Jewish men and imprisoned them in concentration camps,[14] where brutality, humiliation, and outright murder reigned.

The November Pogrom claimed the lives of at least one hundred Jews, not including the deaths or suicides that occurred as indirect results of the pogrom. Moreover, the men who were lucky enough to return from internment "with shaved heads, unrecognizably dirty and with frozen limbs" were often physically and psychologically ravaged.[15]

The marauders primarily beat and arrested men. There were exceptions: some women were publically humiliated, bloodied, beaten, and murdered.[16] Nonetheless, most women were forced to stand by and watch their homes torn apart and their men abused. Later, they were to anguish as the men disappeared into camps. Rescuing their men was the most crucial task confronting Jewish women in the days following the pogrom. Wives, mothers, and daughters of prisoners were told that their men would be released only if they could present emigration papers. Women summoned the courage to overcome gender stereotypes of passivity in order to find any means to have their men freed from camps. One woman whose husband was in hiding teamed up with a friend whose husband had been taken to the Dachau concentration camp, near Munich: "We ran from early morning to late evening ... nothing mattered anymore, except to save your family and yourself."[17] Charlotte Stein-Pick wrote of the November Pogrom: "From this hour on, I tried untiringly, day in and day out, to find a connection that could lead to my husband's release. I ran to Christian acquaintances, friends, or colleagues, but everywhere people shrugged their shoulders, shook their heads and said 'no.' And everyone was glad when I left. I was treated like a leper, even by people who were positively inclined towards us."[18] Undaunted, Stein-Pick entered Nazi headquarters in Munich, the notorious Brown House, to request her husband's release based on his status as a war veteran. There she was shown her husband, twenty pounds thinner. The Nazis required that she explain the finances of her husband's student fraternity, of which he was still treasurer. She could do this and—on his release—she was required to return to the Brown House monthly to do the fraternity's bookkeeping until they left Germany.[19]

Ruth Abraham impressed not only her family but also the Nazis with her determination and bravery. During the November Pogrom, it was she who pulled her fiancé out of his store and led him through the teeming crowds to safety. She then traveled to Dachau to ask for the release of her future father-in-law. Arriving in a bus filled with Hitler's elite troupe, the SS, she entered the camp, where she was ignored. She assumed that because of her Aryan looks—blond hair and blue eyes—those in charge took her for a member of the League of German Girls (BDM). Finally, she requested an interview with the commandant and begged for the release of her elderly father-in-law. She succeeded, again attributing her success to her looks, since the men who helped her refused to believe that she was a "full Jew" and seemed to take pity on her. Abraham's highly unconventional behavior found a more conventional reward: the couple married immediately. The rabbi who performed the ceremony did so with bandaged hands, an indication of the treatment he had received in a concentration camp.[20]

Some women not only arranged the release of loved ones, but also sold property and made all emigration decisions. Accompanying her husband home after his ordeal in a camp, one wife announced that she had just sold their house and bought tickets for the whole family to Shanghai. Her husband reflected: "Anything was okay with me, only not to stay in a land in which everyone had declared open season on us."[21] Edith Bick recalled in an interview in 1972 that "when my husband was in a concentration camp, whatever there was, I had to take over, which I never did before. Never. He didn't like it. [But] he not only accepted it. He was thankful."[22] One prominent lawyer, rescued by his wife, wrote about the November Pogrom: "Our wives ... worked tirelessly to obtain our release.... Women ... thought nothing of going to authorities we normally did not approach without a good deal of trepidation."[23] Similar expressions of thankfulness, tinged perhaps, with a bit of surprise at women's heroism, can be found in many men's memoirs. They continued to be indebted to women even after their ordeals, when many men were too beaten in body and spirit to be of much use in the scramble to emigrate.[24]

Once the Nazis began releasing some men, women organized emergency assistance near the concentration camps. At the Weimar train station, a group of Jewish women waited for men freed from Buchenwald. They gave them coffee, fresh socks, and handkerchiefs and tried to clean their clothing a bit before sending them on trains to their various destinations.[25] But not all Jewish men were that lucky: "On a daily basis one heard that the ashes of a dead person had been delivered to this or that family. These urns were sent COD (for which the post office took the sum of 3.75 marks)."[26]

It is striking that in the testimony of both men and women, women's calm, dry-eyed self-control in the midst of turmoil is emphasized. Even in desperate circumstances, women's dignity was not merely a proclamation of female strength to counter the stereotype of female frailty. Emphasis on composure also resulted from the decorum stressed in Jewish bourgeois upbringing. Moreover, it asserted Jewish pride in the face of Aryan savagery, human dignity in the face of general dishonor.[27] But women's perseverance is also more than the sum of its parts, suggesting a new role for women. Traditionally, men had publicly guarded the honor of the family and community; now, suddenly, women found themselves in the difficult position of defending Jewish honor. Often, in taking on traditionally male roles both within and outside the family, women transformed their own female identities—at least for the duration of the crisis—while seeking to save their families.

Even though women transcended certain gender roles, gender as such continued to have serious consequences during the emigration of Jews from Germany. Gender made a difference in matters of life and death. For example, more women than men remained trapped in Nazi Germany. While there are many explanations for this—including a high number of male deaths in World War I, a higher number of widows, the intention of men to emigrate first and bring their families over when they had settled, and so on,[28]—it is also clear that more men got out before the doors were tightly shut, through connections, capitalist visas, or because they were in physical danger earlier than women and the women sent them out first. The disproportionate number of elderly women that the Nazis murdered suggests that gender and age were a lethal combination.

MEMORY AND MEMOIRS

Just as gender made a sharp difference in the destiny of German Jews, it also played a role in how the Nazi era is remembered. There is a relationship between gender and memory in the memoirs, diaries, letters, and interviews I have reviewed. Women and men concentrate on different memories and offer different perspectives, even when describing the same events. It should not be surprising that women and men remember differently. Their original experiences, gendered as they were, provide for the different perspectives they offer. Women's memories tend to focus on family and friends, on the ways in which a variety of Jews coped within the privacy of their homes or in public, while men's tend to focus on their work, business, or political environments. In fact, women typically depict themselves in relationships, drawing sketches of partners, children, and friends and describing events that befell others as well. Men, on the other hand, more frequently see themselves as independent actors, so that women are often rather shadowy figures.[29] A good case in point is the diary of Victor Klemperer, a Jewish professor married to an Aryan woman in Dresden. Between 1933 and 1945, Klemperer wrote in elaborate detail about his academic projects, his political and personal fears, his acquaintances, and his daily routine. He also noted in passing how his wife scurried for food from morning until night and gave piano lessons in exchange for food. He described his terror when she was taken ill, since his very existence depended on his marriage to her. Still, she remained a shadowy figure. He related her physical ailments, her migraines, and moments of desperation, far more than her thoughts or feelings.[30]

Women's memoirs also highlight entirely new dimensions of history. For example, men write of the public spectacle of the November Pogrom, describing the broken shop windows and burning synagogues, the lasting images of broken glass from which the Nazis cynically extracted the name "Crystal Night." A powerful, if more mundane, image, mentioned often in Jewish women's memoirs, is that of flying feathers—feathers covering the internal space of the home, hallway and front yard or courtyard. Similar to pogroms in Russia at the turn of the century, the marauders tore up goose feather blankets and pillows, shaking them into the rooms, out the windows, down the stairways.[31] Bereft of their bedding, German Jews lost the kind of physical and psychological security and comfort that this represented and that they had once known. In addition, not only were these items expensive, but they could no longer be readily replaced, in part because of their cost, and because, in the looming war economy, linens were severely limited.[32] Broken glass in public and strewn feather beds in private spelled the end of Jewish security in Germany.

CONCLUSION

Feminist scholarship has two interrelated goals: to give women a voice long denied them *and* to offer a perspective long denied us. Today an emerging literature, starting very late in the 1990s, offers gendered perspectives on the Holocaust. These volumes include but are not limited to the following: *Different Voices: Women and the Holocaust* (Rittner and Roth, 1998); *Between Dignity and Despair: Jewish Life in Nazi Germany* (Kaplan, 1998); *Women in the Holocaust* (Ofer and Weitzman, 1998); *Double Jeopardy: Gender and the Holocaust* (Baumel, 1998); *Experience and Expression: Women, the Nazis, and the Holocaust* (Baer and Goldenberg, 2003); *Resilience and Courage: Women, Men and the Holocaust* (Tec, 2004). In addition, there are books about Jewish women in the resistance, in concentration camps, and even some studies of Nazi women. Further, scores of women have written memoirs of life during the Holocaust.[33] And the list keeps growing, offering a vast diversity of perspectives.

Examining women's experiences during the years of persecution and genocide raises questions. Why until recently, for example, have we looked primarily at men in studying the Holocaust? And, why do some historians of the Holocaust accept a gender analysis only with the greatest reluctance, while others shun it entirely?[34] In part, this has to do with the broader perspective of Jewish history in general. Gender analyses have not been seen as vital by the majority of Jewish historians, although a productive minority has stepped forward to challenge the mainstream at every turn.[35] Traditional historians have focused on men's public and communal activities or their philosophical, religious, or political contributions, neglecting women's powerful and sustained influence on European Jewry in the families and the culture of Jewish and national communities. This reluctance to address gender continues with Holocaust studies, although here old as well as new roadblocks can be seen: the old ones—"what of importance can we really learn by studying women?"—are reinforced by new ones— "are women's historians (read feminists) trying retrospectively to divide Jews during the most tragic moment in modern Jewish history?"[36] My own answer is as follows: It seems clear that "the *end*—namely, annihilation or death—does not describe or explain the *process.*"[37] To raise the issue of gender does not place it above racism in some hierarchy of horrors. We know, to quote philosopher Hannah Arendt, that the Nazis did not want "to share the earth with the Jewish people."[38] Neither does raising the issue of gender place blame on survivors for the disproportionate deaths of Jewish women. Blame rests with the murderers. Rather, gender helps us to tell a fuller and more nuanced story, to emphasize the multiplicity of voices and experiences in the war against the Jews. Studying the ways in which women and men were treated differently and the frequently distinctive manner in which they reacted demonstrates how gender influenced decisions and destinies. Gender mattered, especially in extreme situations.

MARION KAPLAN is the Skirball Professor of Modern Jewish History at New York University. She is author of *The Making of the Jewish Middle Class: Women, Family, and Identity in Imperial Germany*; *Between Dignity and Despair: Jewish Life in Nazi Germany*; and editor, with Deborah Dash Moore, of *Gender and Jewish History*.

NOTES

From my *Lessons and Legacies IV: Reflections of Religion, Justice, Sexuality, and Genocide*, ed. by Larry V. Thompson. Copyright © 2003. With permission of Northwestern University Press. All rights reserved. With additional material © 2015 by Marion Kaplan.

1. Carol Rittner and John Roth, eds., *Different Voices: Women and the Holocaust* (New York: Paragon House, 1993), 3. Although my work focuses on Germany and German Jews, the issue of gender in the Holocaust more generally throughout Europe was raised early on by Joan Ringelheim whose research shows that "being male or female mattered during the Holocaust. Antisemitism, racism and sexism were not separated in the theory of the Nazis or in their practice—nor was sexism absent from the responses of the Jewish community. Sexism, the division of social roles according to biological function, placed women at an extreme disadvantage during the Holocaust. It deprived them of skills that might have enabled more of them to survive. At the same time, the group that was supposed to protect them—men—was not able to do so." From her essay "Women and the Holocaust: A Reconsideration of Research," in Rittner and Roth, *Different Voices*, 400.

2. Mary Lowenthal Felstiner, *To Paint Her Life: Charlotte Salomon in the Nazi Era* (New York: HarperCollins, 1994), 204–7.

3. Gerda Lerner, *The Creation of Patriarchy (Women and History Vol. I)* (New York: Oxford, 1987) and also Lerner's *The Creation of Feminist Consciousness (Women and History Vol. II)* (New York: Oxford, 1994).

4. Bella Fromm, *Blood and Banquets: A Berlin Social Diary* (New York: Harper and Bros., 1942), 119–20.

5. For a fuller, more detailed history of this period, see my *Between Dignity and Despair: Jewish Life in Nazi Germany* (New York: Oxford, 1998).

6. For examples, see Else Gerstel, memoirs, Leo Baeck Institute, NY (hereafter LBI), 71, and John Foster, ed., *Community of Fate: Memoirs of German Jews in Melbourne* (Sydney: Allen & Unwin, 1986), 28–30.

7. Toni Lessler, memoirs; LBI, 22.

8. Mally Dienemann, 23a, from Harvard University, Houghton Library, BMS GER 91, written for contest "Mein Leben in Deutschland vor und nach dem 30. Januar 1933." Publication of all citations is by permission of the Houghton Library.

9. Verena Hellwig, Harvard, 25–26.

10. Gordon W. Allport, Jerome S. Bruner, and E. M. Jandorf, "Personality under Social Catastrophe: Ninety Life-Histories of the Nazi Revolution," in *Character and Personality: An International Psychological Quarterly* 10, no. 1 (September 1941): 3.

11. Gerstel, LBI, 71.

12. Peter Wyden, *Stella* (New York: Simon and Schuster, 1992), 47.

13. Raul Hilberg, *Perpetrators, Victims, and Bystanders* (New York: Aaron Asher, 1992), 127.

14. Three camps absorbed all of the Jewish men: Dachau (11,000), Buchenwald (9,845), and Sachsenhausen (9,000). Rita Thalmann and Emmanuel Feinermann, *Crystal Night* (New York: Coward, McCann & Geoghegan, 1972), 117.

15. Wolf Gruner, "Die Reichshauptstadt," in *Jüdische Geschichte in Berlin*, ed. Reinhard Rürup (Berlin: Hentrich, 1995), 239.

16. These exceptions seem to have occurred mostly in small towns (although for examples from Nuremberg and Düsseldorf, see Rita Thalmann and Emmanuel Feinermann, *Crystal Night* (New York: Holocaust Libr., 1974), 70, 8l. If one collected all these tales, one would notice that women were not exempt from violence even as early as 1938. Erna Albersheim reported, "My daughter's fiancé came from a small town in East Prussia. His mother and his ten- and fourteen-year-old sisters were arrested. The girls were released almost immediately, but his mother, as well as the other Jewish

women, were imprisoned for about two weeks. It was the only case I heard of where women were arrested." (Harvard University, Houghton Library, BMS GER 91), 63. Alice Baerwald (p. 58) described the same town: "Among the fourteen Jewish women in this small community were a niece of mine and her mother-in-law. They were brought to jail, organized in pairs, and made to walk through town saying 'we have betrayed Germany.' The mob ran alongside and shouted 'kill them, why are you still feeding them!'" She believed that they attained freedom in two days—at least her relatives did. (Harvard University, Houghton Library, BMS GER 91). For examples of women who were beaten, see "Lest We Forget!," Anonymous, memoirs, LBI. Visiting a hospital, the woman recalled, "in the waiting room an old woman was sleeping, terribly beaten up, as she had tried to cover her husband from attack. In the sitting room many women were lying, all of them had escaped from small towns," 5.

Also, see Francis Henry, *Victims and Neighbors: A Small Town in Nazi Germany Remembered* (South Hadley, MA: Bergin and Garvey, 1984), 116–7, which describes a Jewish woman, blood dripping down her face as she ran down the street in "Sonderburg" and another elderly couple forced to run through the town's streets followed by SA throwing stones at them. Reports from the cities of Nürnberg and Fürth describe Jews being driven from their homes with leather straps and Jewish women with evidence of strap marks on their faces. Klaus Behnken, ed., *Deutschland-Berichte der Sozialdemokratischen Partei Deutschlands, 1934–1940* (Frankfurt: Petra Nettelbeck/Zweitausendeins, 1980), 920. [Cited as *Deutschland-Berichte*]. In addition, some women were also taken hostage for husbands who had hidden. In Frankfurt, for example, they were taken hostage, but a few were released after a day in jail in order to care for their children at home. Andreas Lixl-Purcell, *Women of Exile* (Westport, Conn.: Greenwood Press, 1988), 71. In Dresden, women were taken hostage until their husbands turned themselves in. *Deutschland-Berichte*, 1939, 922. Finally, the elderly, female and male, were not spared physical brutality either. On the edges of Berlin, rioters set the tiny shack (Laube) of an elderly couple aflame. When the couple tried to escape in their nightshirts, the band tried to force them back into the house. The man died of a heart attack and the woman needed to be institutionalized as a result of their treatment. *Deutschland-Berichte*, 1938, 1340.

17. "ARALK" in Margarete Limberg and Hubert Rübsaat, eds., *Sie durften nicht mehr Deutsch sein: Jüdischer Alltag in Selbstzeugnissen 1933–1938* (Frankfurt, Germany: Campus, 1990), 344.

18. Charlotte Stein-Pick, memoirs, LBI, 41.

19. Ibid., 43–5.

20. Ruth Abraham, memoirs, LBI, 3–5.

21. Siegfried Neumann, in *Sie durften nicht mehr Deutsch*, 325.

22. Edith Bick, b. 1900, Hamburg, emigrated Nov. 1938 to USA (interviewed in Jan. 1972), 18. Research Foundation for Jewish Immigration, NY.

23. Max Moses Polke, a Breslau lawyer from *Before the Holocaust: Three German–Jewish Lives, 1870–1939*, ed. and trans. Thomas Dunlap (Bloomington, Indiana: Xlibris, 2010).

24. Charlotte Stein-Pick, memoirs, LBI, 45. See also Gerdy Stoppleman, memoirs, LBI. Her husband left Sachsenhausen in March 1939. "More than his body, my husband's mind was deeply affected. Almost every night he experienced Sachsenhausen Concentration camp anew in nightmares so alarming that I feared for his sanity" (5).

25. *Deutschland-Berichte*, 1939, 924.

26. Margot Littauer, Harvard University, Houghton Library, BMS GER 91, 33.

27. Erna Albersheim, memoirs, 33, found at Harvard University, Houghton Library, BMS GER 91.

28. See Kaplan, *Between Dignity and Despair*, chap. 5.

29. The diaries of Victor Klemperer, published to much acclaim in Germany and translated into English, exemplify this. His wife's existence—her Aryan status as well as her bravery in working for and finding food—saved his life, but we learn little of her thoughts and see only snippets of her actions as he reports on the books he has read, the conversations he has had with others, his forced labor, or the books he is writing. *Ich will Zeugnis ablegen bis zum letzten: Tagebücher.* Vols. 1 and 2 (Berlin: Aufbau Verlag, 1995) and *I Will Bear Witness: A Diary of the Nazi Years 1933–1941*, trans. Martin Chalmers (New York: Random House, 1998); Vol. 2, *I Will Bear Witness, 1941–1945: A Diary of the Nazi Years* (New York: Random House, 2000).

30. Klemperer, *Ich will Zeugnis*, Vols. 1 and 2.

31. For feathers during the November Pogrom, see Henry, *Victims and Neighbors*, 116–18. See also from Harvard University, Houghton Library, BMS GER 91: Erna Albersheim, 28; Elsie Axelrath, 43; Alice Baerwald, 72.

32. See from Harvard University, Houghton Library, BMS GER 91: Erna Albersheim, 28; Elsie Axelrath, 43; Alice Baerwald, 72.

33. A basic bibliography on women and the Holocaust is available at the US Holocaust Memorial Museum website http://www.ushmm.org/research/research-in-collections /search-the-collections/bibliography/women, accessed July 1, 2015.

34. Ringelheim, "Women and the Holocaust," 400. At a "Women and the Holocaust" conference at the Hebrew University, Jerusalem, in June 1995, several participants thought a gender analysis was "obscene" in the face of the destruction of the Jewish people.

35. There is a growing literature in this field. See for examples Paula Hyman, *Gender and Assimilation in Modern Jewish History: The Roles and Representation of Women* (Seattle: University of Washington Press, 1995); Judith R. Baskin, ed., *Jewish Women in Historical Perspective* (Detroit: Wayne State University Press, 1991); Marion Kaplan and Deborah Dash Moore, eds., *Gender and Jewish History* (Bloomington: Indiana University Press, 2011). For a bibliography on American Jewish women's history, see http://jwa .org/discover/resources/books/bibliography, accessed June 30, 2015.

36. Although there is no broad-based critique on issues of gender and the Holocaust, Gabriel Schoenfeld's article in *Commentary* of June 1998, titled "Auschwitz and the Professors," (44–46), singled out such scholarship as part of its attack on Holocaust studies. *Lilith* magazine responded to Schoenfeld a few months later (vol. 23, no. 3 [fall 1998])

37. Felstiner, *To Paint Her Life*, 204–7.

38. Hannah Arendt, *Eichmann in Jerusalem: A Report on the Banality of Evil* (New York: Viking, 1965), 279.

6

German Women and the Holocaust in the Nazi East[1]

Wendy Lower

In 1945 Margaret Bourke-White, a pioneer female war correspondent and *Life* magazine photographer, trudged through the wasteland of the Third Reich, conducting interviews and snapping photos. Among her photographs is the image of Buchenwald concentration camp survivors with gaunt, ghostly faces and striped garb, standing behind the barbed wire looking more puzzled than jubilant about their liberation. Actually, most of Bourke-White's photos of Nazi Germany were not of victims, but portraits of ordinary and famous Nazis. The daughter of an orthodox Jew, Bourke-White did not whitewash with her lens, especially when she photographed and interviewed Nazi women such as Hildegarde Roselius. Roselius was a socialite who proudly admitted her Nazi convictions as she cooked in her bombed-out apartment kitchen in Bremen, which lacked two walls and provided a view of the ruins below. She still gushed about Hitler's "strong manly handshake," and fumed about the regime's victims. "Those people from concentration camps really are behaving very badly," Roselius remarked. They crowded the marketplace. They were demanding. They were suspicious.[2] Bourke-White introduced and ended her book, *Dear Fatherland, Rest Quietly*, with Frau Roselius.

The message in Bourke-White's images and text was this: The Germans of the Third Reich, men *and* women, were hardened ideologues. Those who did not commit suicide for the Führer soldiered on with uncompromising bitterness and arrogance. In her opinion, a Nazi was a Nazi, male or female. Her harsh condemnation and moral outrage were understandable. Assigned to the United States Third Army under General Patton, Bourke-White was among the camp liberators; she witnessed, smelled, and touched the horrors of the war and the Holocaust. Reading her book, which is part memoir and part photojournalistic investigation, one realizes that in the many years since she snapped those raw images and interviewed Frau Roselius, perceptions of women in Nazi Germany have changed dramatically.[3]

Today when one speaks of crimes of the Third Reich, one is mostly referring to the "ordinary men" who committed them. To be sure, the vast majority of the crimes of the Holocaust were planned, organized, and implemented by men. However, the men were assisted by women, and women also bloodied their hands directly in the mass murder. This essay focuses on German women who were not trained guards, rather on those who participated in the crimes of the Holocaust *outside* of the formal camp system.

Although women may have comprised a minority of the perpetrators, their actions were nonetheless extremely important for several reasons. Women were central to the regime's politics of national cohesion. They were integral members of the society of perpetrators and the new elite in the occupied territories. A defining feature of Nazism was a terror and violence that in the twelve-year history of the Third Reich became socially embedded. Crossing public and private spheres, transgressing gender norms, the genocidal campaigns of the Reich became a perverse form of mass mobilization.[4] Particularly during the war and in the occupied territories of the East, one demonstrated loyalty to the regime through the abuse of racial inferiors and rituals of violence. Women as well as men were expected to perform, condone, or at least accept these acts as "necessary" to secure Germany's future. The Nazi utopia of a peaceful Aryan Lebensraum ("living space") was a sinister mirage, even a ploy, because peace was antithetical to a regime that defined itself as a perpetual revolution forged through a war at home and abroad, in Europe and beyond. Civil courage was not about resisting such immoral, criminal acts, but was distorted into an acceptance of them as a necessary self-vindication, even as historian Saul Friedländer discerned, as a form of redemptive antisemitism.[5]

To understand how a political movement develops into a genocidal society, we must look at all members of that society. We must scrutinize more critically the role of gender as a force of radicalization, and specifically the views and behavior of German women who committed crimes in the Reich and Nazi-occupied territories of Europe. Can we better understand the perpetration of the Holocaust through the lens of gender? Did ordinary German women engage directly in the violence with or without men? Was there a dynamic between men and women that aggravated or ameliorated the violence? Were female acts of violence or contributions to the genocide distinctively feminine or aligned with what was considered female propriety at the time? What could women do? What was within their means, realm of action? How much access to power did they have, and how was it wielded? This essay cannot answer all of these questions, but will focus on key examples of German female perpetration of the Holocaust in Eastern Europe and trends in the literature that have obfuscated this history.

In many ways, the German women who came of age professionally, socially, and ideologically during the interwar and Nazi eras occupied a time and space that seems foreign to us now. However, as the first generation of women empowered with the vote and entering the workforce of the emerging modern state in unprecedented numbers and in professional fields, these women had similar ideals and motivations. Though of varied socioeconomic background and education, they shared a common sense of adventure and were ambitious and patriotic. The young German women in the Eastern occupied territories were especially so. They were not powerless, neither the playthings of their husbands and lovers, nor the puppets of their bosses. They shattered perceptions of femininity, and for that were not ostracized or marginalized. On the contrary, they embodied the Nazi revolution and empowering notions of individual will and collective sacrifice. German women found themselves charting a complicated, dynamic system that on the one hand opened up new doors, including possible career advancement and travel in the East, while closing others at home with quota systems that barred women from university degrees and professions. The paths that they pursued as wives, mothers, and working women were determined by several factors: individual choices and preferences, social relations and expectations, economic needs, ideological and religious orientation, ethnic and ancestral background, class and social standing, and age. Such factors were part of the extraordinary circumstances of Nazi fascism—the pairing of a nondemocratic, patriarchal police state with a racially defined social experiment. Once accepted into the Volksgemeinschaft (people's community) most German women enjoyed a sense of belonging and were expected to do their part.[6] Those who did not were severely punished. Indeed hundreds of thousands branded as political resisters, asocials (e.g. prostitutes, alcoholics, work shirkers), and racial degenerates were incarcerated, tortured, and sterilized. The wives of communists, such as Lina Haag, endured years of imprisonment.[7] The wives of SS men were not safe from persecution. On the contrary, if they stood in the way of their husbands' careers or expressed any disagreement with SS policies, they were also threatened and persecuted. But these were rare cases of outright resistance to the regime and to the pressures of patriotism that swayed women as much as men.[8] When Melitta Maschmann, an early Nazi activist in the League of German Girls, was posted to occupied Poland to do "a sort of colonization work," she recalled in her 1963 memoir that the assignment reinvigorated "the sense of national honour that had been so wounded in [her] childhood and early youth." While stationed in the Warthegau, Maschmann and her colleagues were called to assist the German police in "evacuation" actions against Polish inhabitants; it was, as she stated, "men's work" that she disliked, but had to do nonetheless.[9]

Hitler propagated that a woman's place was in the home as well as in the movement. At the Nuremberg Party Rally of 1934, he employed the typical martial rhetoric declaring: "What man offers in heroism on the field of battle, woman equals with unending perseverance and sacrifice, with unending pain and suffering. Every child she brings into the world is a battle, a battle she wages for the existence of her people ... for the National Socialist Volksgemeinschaft was established on a firm basis precisely because millions of women became our most loyal, fanatical fellow-combatants."[10] In Hitler's 1935 and 1936 speeches to the National Socialist Woman's Organization (which later boasted 2.3 million members, representing nearly 6 percent of the German female population), he proclaimed that a mother of five, six, seven children who are all healthy and well brought up accomplishes more than a female jurist. He rejected equal rights for women as a Marxist demand, "since it draws the woman into an area in which she will necessarily be inferior. It places the woman in situations that cannot strengthen her position—vis-a-vis both man and society—but only weaken it."[11] Or as Alfred Rosenberg, the Nazi Party ideologue summed it up: "all possibilities for the developments of a woman's energies should remain open to her. But there must be clarity on one point: only man must be and remain a judge, soldier and ruler of the state."[12] Women in Nazi Germany were barred from certain professions, such as the judiciary, and they could not rule in formal government positions. But they swelled the ranks of Party organizations. Out of a population of about forty million women, some twelve to thirteen million became members of a Nazi Party organization. As the war dragged on they were given more responsibility. They were drafted like soldiers into military formations (female air defense units) and endured physical and ideological training.[13]

Recently published letters of a German Red Cross nurse who was on the eastern front illuminate the enthusiasm of women in the East. After volunteering for the Patriotic Women's Association, training as a nurse and taking an oath to the Führer as a member of the German Red Cross, Brigitte Penkert left her unhappy marriage and small daughter at home, and headed east. In letters she sent from the front while stationed in Belarus and Ukraine (Gomel, Kiev, and Kowel) she expressed her loyalty to the Nazi campaign as a "manly" honor. She enthused over the chance to stand guard just like the men with a weapon in her hand. Penkert's official role as a nurse was clearly women's work, but when she experienced the unusual assignment of handling a weapon and standing guard she enjoyed a moment of equality, or, in the Nazi ideology of racial unity, a comradeship of Aryan men and women. The East was her liberation from an unhappy marriage and the burdens of motherhood. As a single mother, she continued to neglect her daughter's needs after the war; she entered a Carmelite cloister and spent the rest of her years in obscure poverty.[14]

Hundreds of thousands of young single women who had to fulfill their labor duty chose to do so in the occupied territories, working as nurses, secretaries, and auxiliaries in the armed forces and Himmler's SS and police agencies. Most of these women had not ventured beyond their hometowns, and in the early years of the war when victory seemed to be on the horizon, they were excited to don a new uniform and to receive a paycheck. Nazi propaganda posters exhorted young women, "The East Needs You," and enticed them with higher salaries and career opportunities.[15] Rumors of the East as the land of "milk and honey" and source of foodstuffs (the breadbasket of Ukraine) were also appealing. An estimated five hundred thousand German women went east, including thirty thousand clerks in SS police offices and fifteen thousand in the regional occupation administrations, plus thousands of teachers and welfare workers. These figures do not account for the large number of spouses and other female family members who visited and resided in the Nazi empire in special German–only housing and settlements.

Prior work on the Holocaust and Nazi Germany paid scant attention to this phenomenon. The collapse of the Soviet Union, which opened up access to the regional archives and killing fields of the eastern territories, made it possible to place German women on the map of mass murder, or, in historian Timothy Snyder's words, the "Bloodlands." Postwar trial proceedings and a few scholars, such as Claudia Koonz and Gudrun Schwarz, established that women were accomplices and perpetrators. However, the scope and scale of their participation across Nazi-dominated Europe had not been fully appreciated. Instead the focus of trials and scholarship was on the vast network of Nazi concentration camps and killing centers and other killing institutions (such as euthanasia centers) where German women fell into a variety of roles as guards, block elders, senior administrators, commandants' wives, and nurses.[16]

SS female camp supervisors and guards accumulated their own records of Nazi crimes, including beating prisoners and carrying out selections of prisoners who were sent to their death. Besides association with the SS through the camp system and marrying SS men, women could also join the SS as auxiliaries. In early 1942, Reich leader of the SS and police Heinrich Himmler ordered the establishment of a female reporting and clerical corps of the SS (SS-Frauenkorps). With the expansion of the Nazi empire, Himmler realized that there would be a shortage of elite colonial administrators. Women are valuable workers, Himmler argued, who should be placed into wartime service in the annexed and occupied territories. An SS school for training women was later established in Alsace. The school was designed to train women for specific functions, such as radio operators, technicians, medical orderlies, drivers, and guards. But racial screening, physical fitness, and ideological indoctrination were all part of this program that intended to develop a female SS elite. Recruits were young, single women who had a strong track record in the Association for German Girls (BDM), especially those who had volunteered for service in the East and had demonstrated some leadership ability. Graduates of the SS program were assigned to SS-police outposts, concentration camps, and field headquarters of mobile units. By the end of the war, there were about ten thousand women in this SS-corps occupying auxiliary and command positions. But they could never issue an order to an SS man.

Not enough attention has been paid to informal roles of women outside the camp system, and in other administrative agencies. For example, secretaries were assigned to the mobile killing units, the Einsatzgruppen, and stationed in Heinrich Himmler's field headquarters. There were twenty-two female typists assigned to the Einsatzgruppe A, which covered the Baltics. Gestapo chief Heinrich Mueller entrusted his special assistant and girlfriend, Barbara Hellmuth, to certify and transmit orders.[17] Women prepared thousands of pages of reports and orders on mass shootings, sent the death tallies back to Berlin, and assisted with their distribution there. They were an integral component of the SS-led machinery of destruction.

Research on German female perpetrators has also established the significant role of nurses in the Nazi euthanasia campaign. In the Reich, approximately two hundred thousand Germans and people of other nationalities (such as Polish, Russian, and Ukrainian slave laborers) were killed in asylums, hospitals, and other medical facilities. German nurses assisted in the racial screening and selection, and in the mass sterilization, starvation, gassing, and lethal injections of those deemed "unworthy of life."[18] Besides administering lethal injections and overdoses of Luminal by mouth, clerical staff (almost entirely women ages 18–22 years) typed up the death notices and processed the shipment of common ashes randomly placed in individual urns. Support and technical staff who had taken an oath of secrecy to the Führer's "mercy killing" program were sent for "Osteinsatz with the Organisation Todt" in early 1942.[19] Organization Todt was the engineering and construction agency that supported civilian and military projects for the state. In this instance, it may have been used as a cover agency that would allow a delegation of civilian personnel to access military sites, including hospitals and prisoner of war camps. Historians have surmised that the reasons for this deployment were the development of mass gassing operations in Belarus and Poland (later applied to the "Final Solution"), and a system to carry out "mercy killings" against critically wounded, and mentally and physically disabled German soldiers returning to field hospitals from the front. One of the first testimonies to mention this deployment was that of nurse Pauline Kneissler, an ethnic German originally from Ukraine who became a career killer in the Nazi euthanasia program,[20] killing patients almost every day for five years.

The Latin term perpetrator means to carry through or accomplish by the "pater," or father. Male agency is embedded in the term as it has come to also mean the execution of a crime. When we think of violent criminals, we do not think of women, and statistically across cultures and over time, women commit a small percentage of homicides—today, less than 10 percent in the US. When women do kill, their victims are usually family members and people they know. However, in genocidal societies and terrorist movements, where violence is a defining feature of the system of rule and ideology, women have become mass murderers.

In Holocaust studies the foundational study of perpetration was written by scholar Raul Hilberg. Yet in his exhaustive three volume reconstruction of the Nazi machinery of destruction, Hilberg does not place women in the killing apparatus, certainly not as an integral feature. To correct this omission, one might simply edit Hilberg's description as follows.

> [The machinery was] diffused in a widespread bureaucracy, and each man [and woman] could feel that his [and her] contribution was a small part of an immense undertaking. For these reasons, an administrator, clerk, or uniformed guard never referred to himself [or herself] as a perpetrator. He [or she] realized, however, that the process of destruction was deliberate, and that once he [or she] had stepped into this maelstrom, his [or her] deed would be indelible. In this sense, he [or she] would always be what he [or she] had been, even if he [or she] remained reticent or silent about what he [or she] had done.[21]

Of course writing women into this history is not as easy as automatically inserting them into the narrative, but the extensive research on Nazi perpetrators should be applied to the history of German women.

Over the years, a few portraits have emerged in the literature. One is the desk murderer who excelled as an administrator but allegedly was ignorant of the outcome of his actions, or just thoughtless. This type was fashioned most notably by the self-serving testimony of Adolf Eichmann and others who were high-ranking administrators and technocrats.[22] Another image is the lower ranking killer such as the Order Police battalion member who was pressured by his comrades (presented by historian Christopher Browning), or the random soldier who was drafted on the spot to participate in a massacre (depicted controversially in the 1995 German exhibit, *Vernichtungskrieg. Verbrechen der Wehrmacht 1941 bis 1944*).[23] These types of people were not bloodthirsty sadists and fanatical anti-Semites, another portrait discussed in Daniel Goldhagen's work, *Hitler's Willing Executioners*. Finally, we have the elite professional, the expert such as the medical doctor, the *gebildeter* and cultured German who listened to Wagner and Beethoven or sipped cognac while planning the deaths of millions, seen in the various studies of Nazi doctors, scientists, academics, population planners, and civil servants, some depicted at the Wannsee Conference.[24] Hilberg's middle-ranking bureaucrat comprised the multitude of part-timers and functionaries who ensured the system ran smoothly, including the Reich railway timetable-keeper who kept the trains running and the shipments of Zyklon B and bullets delivered. Women can be identified among these portraits; their mug shots appear in this rogues' gallery, although not among the decision-makers, not as evenly distributed across professions, and not in such large numbers as the men in military and SS-police units.

But there are the notable exceptions, which must be taken seriously because the documentation on women is lacking and because it points to important developments in the history of modern genocide, in which women do play a significant part. Holocaust historians have scrutinized German documents from summer and fall 1941 to reconstruct the origins of the "Final Solution." Many clues to the decision making that precipitated the Holocaust are found in regional initiatives. For example, on August 31, 1941, Gertrude Slottke, a secretary stationed in the German secret police in the Netherlands, prepared such a document, titled "Combating Jewry in its totality," which proposed "the final solution of the Jewish question by way of the removal of all Jews."[25] Slottke had her own support staff of typists and clerks, and she actively participated in meetings with her boss, the commander of the security police and service, Wilhelm Harster. She drafted lists of names of Jews deported to Mauthausen, Auschwitz, and Sobibor. She decided who should be deported, and observed at least one roundup of "hysterical" Jewesses, as she described them in her report of May 27, 1943. One name on her list of deportees was the Frank family.

Situating women in this history is not about giving women their rightful place, because female perpetrators were in many ways in the wrong place at the wrong time. Rather, the history of the Holocaust, and genocide more broadly, must be understood as a social phenomenon. Genocide is by definition the collective, systematic act of one group killing another, of one social entity bent on destroying another. The totality and thoroughness that defines genocide would not be possible without the broad participation of a society of perpetrators and accomplices. The division of labor that included women is largely unclear. German women such as Maria Cramer, the wife of the district commissar who lorded over the Kovno ghetto, was known for her exploitation and plundering of Jews in the ghetto. She was named in the investigation of crimes in Kovno, but did not stand trial, and died in 1992.[26] While the topic of non-German local collaboration has been a central topic in recent decades, the other piece in this larger social history of the Holocaust, the role of women across Europe, has barely been touched. Why is this so?

Of course there are established explanations for the absence of women in the writing of history. There is a lack of documentation on the private realm of women's activity and women remained silent about their complicity. Bedside confessions about one's Nazi past were suppressed by surviving family members, and in any case were not the realm of historical research.[27] Most scholars were oblivious to the topic or were focused on the male perpetrators who predominated. Ideological and methodological shifts that fostered the growth of social history (of gender, class, and race) emerged in the 1970s. Holocaust studies as a research field did not take off until the late 1980s and 1990s. While women's history of Jewish Holocaust victims made important strides, the history of female Holocaust perpetrators and bystanders lagged behind. In the 1980s and early 1990s, the concept of "gender" was disputed, and postmodern approaches may have inhibited, more than encouraged, research in Holocaust studies.[28] The mere mention of "gender" has the power to excite interest from audiences as well as cause some to roll their eyes. Rather than question the concept's utility or theoretical definitions, I apply it fundamentally as the *perceived* differences between the sexes. We know that the sexes are biologically different organisms of the same species. We know that in most cultures men and women perceive themselves as different and that such perceptions, usually delineating weakness versus strength, have shaped and defined power relations and resulted in various forms of discrimination against women (and against men who are perceived as feminine).

Genocide studies presents yet another analytical challenge. How do we account for the extremely violent and even sadistic behavior of women such as Erna Petri, who shot Jewish children in a ditch near her home, or Johanna Altvater, who threw Jewish children from the balcony of a ghetto infirmary in Volodymyr-Volynskyi, Ukraine? Were women expressing a femininity or maternity through violence, or mimicking men? Were they acting on a human impulse that was not specifically female or male? At what point does individual behavior turn violent, challenging accepted legal, moral, ethical, and gendered rules and expectations? Besides a lack of documentation to this point, research on female Holocaust perpetrators has been hampered by a reluctance to look squarely at the puzzling, horrific fact that German women brutalized and killed innocent men, women, and children. A psychiatrist might not diagnose these women as sociopaths or criminally insane (which does not mean that they were not). They were something else, but what exactly?

In fact, many, like Erna Petri (1920–2000) and Johanna Altvater (1919–2003), were nurturing mothers, wives, and daughters. After the war, they did not continue to kill. The wartime witnesses who observed female perpetrators and the postwar prosecutors who questioned them were dumbfounded by their cruelty. As one Holocaust survivor from Volodymyr-Volynskyi remarked about Johanna Altvater's murder of children in the ghetto on September 16, 1942: "Such sadism from a woman I have never seen, I will never forget this scene." These women stood out in their actions and appearance—they were described as she-men and sexual deviants. In survivors' memories, they are not blurred into the mass of crew-cut, uniformed German soldiers and police. It was expected that men could and did kill, but women? How could women act this way?

Prosecutors, judges, and scholars have often minimized female violence, attributing it to social pressures, the bad influences of male bosses, husbands, and colleagues, or to emotional—not ideological—drives. Nazi Germany was a participatory dictatorship in which women fully contributed, and our standard for measuring this contribution should not be defined exclusively by power as we know it in a "man's world" of political office and social standing. Rather, studying the roles and behavior of women who were agents of a criminal regime should begin by identifying who they were, what they did, and why they supported a violent system. Explaining the causes of female genocidal behavior is as difficult an undertaking as trying to pin down the motivations of their male counterparts, and given the gendered bias then and now, arguably more complicated.

What orders was Erna Petri following when she shot naked Jewish children on her farm and beat Ukrainian maids in her household? Unlike the men in the Reich's formal administrative chain of command, women who committed crimes in their domestic settings could not rationalize their actions during or after the war with the claim that it was necessary to follow orders—"Befehlsnotstand." How did they explain their actions, if they admitted to them, after the war? Were they able to find refuge within the masses of victimized German women, aggrieved widows and mothers who suffered the aerial bombings on the home front, the mass rapes by Red Army soldiers in a country reduced to rubble with the end of the war?[29]

Another framework for analyzing female perpetrators is within the literature about women and war. In *Women and War in the Twentieth Century*, editor Nicole Dombrowski delineates three female roles during wartime: the "warrior, maid-in-waiting, and helpless victim." She finds that "wives, girlfriends, and soldiers' loved ones have played a more passive, but perhaps equally important, role in sustaining and supporting military culture." As passive subjects at home, women embodied the home front, the icons of wartime propagandists who exhorted soldiers to fight to protect families. This "rhetoric of chivalry" sent many innocent men to their deaths on the battlefield. But, Dombrowki asks, "If women do bolster soldiers' morale, then what is their political or historical responsibility for atrocities or war crimes committed, in part, in their name?"[30] Moreover, how do we incorporate the history of women who joined their men on the front and crossed the line from home front to battleground as direct perpetrators of war crimes?

Trial records have fostered scholarly work on the role of gender in the courtroom,[31] particularly the cases against Ravensbrück guards and individuals such as Hermine Ryan-Braunsteiner, who was a deputy warden at Majdanek, and Ilse Koch at Buchenwald. At the trial against secretary Gertrude Slottke and her male bosses stationed in the Netherlands, Anne Frank's father, Otto, questioned the defendants and showed them the photograph of Anne on the cover of her published diary. The defendants insisted they were innocent. Slottke received a five-year jail sentence for her role as an accomplice in the murder of nearly fifty-five thousand deported Jews.[32] A few days after her sentencing, an unrepentant Slottke complained about the verdict.

The relatively few women who were tried after the war were featured in sensationalistic press coverage, portrayed as beasts, sadists, and seductresses. Much of this coverage perpetuated pornographic images of Nazi women that distorted their violent behavior as a form of sexual deviance. The multitude of roles and professions and postwar depictions of German female perpetrators defy generalizations. In short, we have moved beyond the stark portraits in Bourke-White's book, and cannot speak in terms of the "nature" of German women in the Third Reich, let alone categorize them as innocent or guilty.[33]

But much more work needs to be done. Though rich in documentation and more nuanced than earlier studies, nearly all of the recent work on German women and Nazism has not moved beyond the borders of Germany. It has not tapped the rich regional archives of the former Soviet Union. It has not geographically taken the broader view of the Nazi system, nor has it delved into microanalyses of the implementation of Nazi policies including the Final Solution as it occurred in the territories of Ukraine, Belarus, and the Baltics.[34]

What has been overlooked and under-researched is the actual presence of women outside of the camp system. In the killing fields, war zones, and imperial setting of the eastern territories, the boundaries of private and public were blurred. If the population of ethnic Germans in a particular region was significant, then additional women were sent from the Reich to serve as social workers and educators (teachers, childcare providers).

They were the ideological conduits of Nazism, trained to transform local ethnic Germans into Hitler loyalists. They were sent on "official business" as representatives of National Socialist People's Welfare (NSV).

This was the case in Chudniv, Ukraine. Dr. Paul Blümel set up his Chudniv office with his personal secretary, Frau Gretl Tazl, arriving from Vienna in November 1941.[35] Soon after, a platoon of German gendarmerie and agricultural specialists joined Bluemel and his secretaries.[36] This closed racial community of German occupation administrators shared the same canteen. In fact the chief agricultural inspector, Kurt Heinemann brought his wife with him to Chudniv to help run the kitchen. She also donned the gold-brown uniform of the civil administration while doing volunteer work in the kitchen, making sure that all the local Germans enjoyed home-style cooking.

Located in historic Volhynia, Chudniv was home to several thousand ethnic Germans, Volksdeutschen who had migrated to the area in the eighteenth and nineteenth centuries and had settled into about fifteen villages. Though many (including entire families) had been deported by Stalin in 1937–38, a significant number remained, mostly women, since usually Stalin's deportation policy targeted the heads of households. In the 1930s, Sovietization encouraged the intermarriage of nationalities, so many ethnic Germans had Ukrainian and Jewish spouses, which complicated the Nazi attempt to order the East along strict racial lines. The local German school had been shut down, but many Volksdeutschen whom the Nazis encountered in 1941 were proficient enough in German to serve as interpreters (few Germans from the Reich spoke Russian or Ukrainian).[37]

The concentration of ethnic German settlements in this district meant that more German women from the Reich were deployed to build up the colony into a stronghold of Nazi-style Germania. A twenty-two-year-old, Elisabeth Held, a district advisor for the childcare center, arrived from Nuremburg. Fraulein Elisabeth Frank was assigned to Romanow to manage the Hitler Youth program. A German language school was established in 1942, and two more teachers arrived from Berlin and Hamburg. Otille Jehn arrived from Kassel to work in the agricultural office in August 1942. Ethnic German women from Ukraine were also consolidated in the area to assist with these programs and assigned to the local administration. Florentina Bedner, a collective farm worker and the wife of the local forester, was recruited as a teacher. Elsa Marx, who was in Kiev serving as a translator for the Germans as of August 1941, moved to Chudniv and cooked for the agricultural chief inspector Heinemann. Frau Paulina Wenzler also joined the local German staff. An ethnic German from Chudniv, she evidently befriended several of the Reich German men and had an affair with a gendarme who committed suicide. At the time it was rumored that Ms. Wenzler was married to a Jew, and that her lover, the German gendarme was ordered to kill him. This is a complicated story that cannot be substantiated fully, but representative of the overlapping private and public realms that women tried to navigate, whereby race, antisemitism, and ethnicity become blurred in the machinations of wartime love affairs and life and death struggles for survival in this criminal system. In fact the Wenzler story extended beyond the war. Ms. Wenzler may have been motivated by revenge when she initiated the war crimes investigation in West Germany of her ex-boss Heinemann, who had sexually harassed her during the war, and allegedly started the rumor about her Jewish husband. Because most of the ethnic Germans in the wartime administration had been evacuated and settled in West Germany, these tangled relationships, vendettas, and even blackmail continued into the postwar, and reappeared in the "he said, she said" accusations and denunciations found in criminal investigations and courtrooms.[38]

During the Nazi occupation of the Chudniv district, some five thousand Jews were murdered there. The massacres began at the end of August 1941 with the shooting of 890 Jews carried out by units of Order Police Battalion 303 and Sonderkommando 4a (attached to Einsatzgruppe C). In October or November 1941, a unit of EK5 arrived in Romaniv from Zhytomyr, under the command of August Meyer. The remaining Jews were gathered in a school building. The skilled laborers, that is, handworkers, doctors, and their families, were selected and allowed to go home. (According to postwar German testimony and investigations, there was no ghetto in Romaniv.) Hundreds of Jews (as many as 1200) were placed on trucks under the guard of local ethnic German and Ukrainian militia and brought to the edge of town, forced to dig mass graves, and shot near a local park. A few weeks later in December 1941, the workers' families were targeted, and at least eighty women, children, and elderly were shot at the same site. At this massacre the Ukrainian Hilfspolizei and the German

SD men (EK5) took turns doing the shooting. The remaining workers were killed in June or July 1942 by the same combination of SD men (this time sent from Berdichev) and the local Ukrainian police led by a German gendarme post leader in Romaniv, a Swabian named Karl Malich.[39]

What did the local German women witness in regard to the Holocaust? Did they contribute to the implementation of the "Final Solution"? Bluemel's secretary Gretel Tazl typed up reports about the deaths of Jews and non-Jews and sent them to superiors in the regional capital of Zhytomyr. Florentina Bedner recalled in her postwar testimony that many Jews lived in the forests near Romaniv, and her husband was aware of that in his position as the forester. Bedner does not state that her husband did anything to help the Jews, and given the context of her testimony (a criminal investigation on the Holocaust), if she could associate herself with any rescue or aid activity, she might have mentioned this. This omission suggests that her husband did nothing to aid the Jews, and perhaps assisted in revealing their whereabouts. Bedner admits that the Jews were shot, and that she herself saw the two large pits in Romaniv where their bodies were buried. She described the grave, saying, "It was as big as our house, about 10 meters wide.... I passed by it every now and then."[40] Bedner insisted in her interrogation that she did not actually witness the mass shootings being carried out. On the other hand she does not deny any involvement in the preparatory measures, such as the gathering of the Jews at the local school where Bedner worked as a teacher. Ethnic German Elsa Marx, the interpreter and cook for the district agricultural leader Konrad Heinemann, accompanied him as he moved around the region inspecting the collective farms. Did she join him as well when he participated in the mass shootings? According to several eyewitnesses, he was actively involved in the planning and implementation of the mass murder. On one occasion Heinemann asked a local technical inspector, named Barth, if he wanted to join him for a little target practice. Barth realized that the targets would be living persons, so he declined the offer.[41] After the war, Elsa Marx portrayed Heinemann as a decent man.

During the war, Elsa Marx prepared food for about forty-five Reich men and women who worked in the commissariat and gendarme office and interacted with them on a daily basis. She admitted that she had heard stories at the canteen, over meals. She heard about the large booty depot near her boss Heineman's office, where one could get just about everything. She obtained a nice winter coat. It had been taken from the gravesite where the Jews had been shot (near the Oelberg). A Ukrainian took it from the grave, and then traded it to Elsa.

In the division of labor that made the Holocaust possible and overlapped with the everyday functioning of the Nazi administration, we can place Marx and Bedner in an auxiliary position of someone who was a direct witness and partial contributor. Marx was admittedly a beneficiary, having referenced her "Jewish" coat taken from the massacre site. Field kitchens and translation work were necessary for the implementation of the large massacres as well as gathering places, such as the school. We cannot assume that Marx's interpreting and cooking skills were lent to the genocidal actions, or that Bedner was involved in discussions about the use of the school for gathering Jews. In fact, according to Father Desbois's recent research on Ukrainian eyewitnesses, it seems that Ukrainian girls and peasant women, not German women, were routinely requisitioned by German officials to do the most gruesome work at the mass murder scenes.[42] But it seems more than possible, and indeed likely, that German female auxiliaries were involved more than they admitted. The prosecutors did not press them about such activities. Marx and Bedner were certainly not going to provide more information than was necessary, especially anything incriminating.

Most Germans who faced prosecutors after the war, even those who were working in places such as Ukraine where the killing was an open secret, where thousands of fresh mass graves marked the landscape, claimed that they saw and knew nothing. But in the Chudniv investigation we learn that Reich German women were told just as they entered the region that massacres were occurring and that they should not be alarmed. Elisabeth Held arrived in Chudniv-Romaniv in April 1942 with a commission to establish a German kindergarten. She was sent from Berlin with several teachers. Held recalled that on their way to Ukraine they were stopped at the border, and were introduced to a man wearing a goldish-brown uniform. He assembled them for a short speech, explaining that they should not be afraid when they heard gunfire; it was "just that a few Jews were being shot."[43] When pressed about such crimes after the war, Held tried to dismiss the entire investigation as "all part of that Jewish thing from the Second World War."

Elisabeth Hoeven from Kassel worked in Heinemann's office. She arrived in early 1942 (at the age of nineteen), trained as a law clerk. She volunteered for service in the East and was the main typist in the economics office. Hoeven's reckless enthusiasm is also demonstrated by the fact that she agreed to be transferred to Retchiza in 1943, one of the more dangerous spots for German civil servants in Ukraine, where partisan warfare was a real threat, and German economic and labor officials had been assassinated as they went about their "requisition" work. Hoeven admits to seeing a reprisal action, a public hanging of three Ukrainians at the local train station. They were killed for trying to steal food. She went with her female colleague in the office to see the bodies hanging, since it had become a local spectacle in town. But other than this incident, which her interrogators had documented and substantiated with other eyewitness accounts, Hoeven did not divulge any additional information about the crimes she might have witnessed. Instead, in her testimony she shows herself to be well versed in the art of defense language, invoking the standard lines: "mir ist nichts daruber bekannt" ("I know nothing about that"), "ich kann nicht sagen" ("I cannot say"), "ich weiss nicht mehr" ("I don't know anymore"), "ich habe nichts davon gehoert" ("I heard nothing about that").[44]

In Tarnopol (a town in present day Ukraine, which was in wartime Nazi–occupied Poland), a twenty-two-year-old ethnic German Helene Dowland, originally from Odessa, was one of several female typists working in the Gestapo office. She noticed the special meetings in her office during August 1942, when all the SS-men were gathered. After such meetings, her boss informed her that the office would be empty the following day and that the women would have to "hold down the fort." That evening, or the next day, staff returned and told stories about the mass shootings, often in gruesome detail. One time, SS man Horst Guenther extended his hand to Dowland after a shooting and asked Dowland to shake it. She refused because she told him it was dirty. "Yes," he replied laughing, making a gesture as if shooting, and then pointing to his uniform and boots, "look, here is a drop of blood, and here still another, and another." Dowland also recalled that the gold teeth and metal prostheses from the victims were stored in their office. She served as an interpreter, but did not state in her postwar interrogation whether she was present at one of the many massacres carried out by the Tarnopol SD.[45]

Historians Goetz Aly and Susanne Heim's pathbreaking study on the intellectuals and technocrats who drafted and implemented the Nazis' grand, sinister, imperial projects devote a few pages to female activists and scientists, though more were involved than has been sufficiently studied. The Nazis' German Institute for the East was a wartime platform for intellectuals who served as racial science screeners and researchers in Poland. Frau Doctor Kalich and Frau Doctor Elfriede Fliethmann, esteemed Viennese anthropologists, led a team of examiners who measured the facial features of one hundred Jewish families in the Tarnow on the eve of their "extinction," their deportation to the nearby killing center at Belzec, in July 1942. Some were also given psychological tests and their facial features were photographed. Those selected were "the most typical of the original Galician Jewry." When some of the men on the team were drafted to the front, Fliethmann enthused about how productive the team was without them: "See what women can do!"[46] At home in the Reich, educated women, writers, journalists, editors, and filmmakers did their part. The writer Thea Haupt (whose book on the war against the Soviet Union had been praised by Reich labor leader Robert Ley and chief of the Nazi Party Chancellery Martin Bormann) wrote to the chief of the German Institute for the East in Cracow in June 1944. As a commissioned author for the educational ministry, Haupt offered her services. She produced a special calendar for mothers and children with the theme, "thoughts on the Eastern Settlement of children." Through literary images and romantic stories about Indians and soldier-farmers, the calendar educated children (five to ten years old) about the importance of Germany's Eastern settlements.[47]

While German women may not have obtained formal positions of power at the highest levels of the Third Reich, they contributed in various ways to the creation and furthering of Nazi racial policies including the terror system within Germany and in the occupied territories. In a 2004 article "Does Atrocity Have a Gender?" scholar Susannah Heschel criticized feminist historiography on Holocaust perpetrators for assuming that violence was an expression of masculinity whereas nurturing and caring for other victims as well as for the perpetrators (by SS wives) was an exclusively female role and form of behavior. Various accounts of women's history in the Third Reich diverge in their evaluations of the power and influence that German "Aryan" women possessed. Leaving aside the fact that Nazi racism was inherently misogynist, "Aryan" women lorded it over so-called non-Aryan inferiors. As Heschel aptly points out, their indirect role is underappreciated and their direct role under-researched.[48] The number of female perpetrators is estimated at less than 1 percent of the German female population at the time.[49] However this amounted to thousands—and perhaps tens of thousands—of women who held positions in the proliferating German agencies in Nazi-dominated Europe.[50] Yet one might ask, why bother to delve into this minority? As Hilberg observed, the history of the Holocaust reveals that low-ranking officials "had relatively small roles in operations of massive proportions."[51]

To summarize, the prevailing trends in the literature and some of the blind spots that have persisted amount to the following:

1) The notion that "women were victims" has obscured the reality that German women were accomplices and perpetrators, and integral to the smooth functioning of the Nazi machinery of destruction.[52]

2) If not victims, then as perpetrators, women appear as marginal, even freakish, sexual deviants (collaborators with the enemy), sex slaves, sadomasochists, psychopaths, Nazi sycophants, or groupies (wives of Nazi leaders).

3) Preconceived notions of female behavior assume that women are incapable of committing atrocities and genocidal violence, and therefore innocent.

4) Traditional women's work is understood as outside the realm of genocidal activity. Yet the totality of genocide requires that otherwise harmless activities can become criminal and lethal. The perversion of professions that are supposed to be life preserving (such as nursing), or the politicization and mobilization of activities that in a "normal" society are mundane (such as secretarial work), or valued as charitable or social work (such as welfare and education), contributed to the Holocaust.

5) The history of material deprivation in genocidal perpetration has not shown that women were central to this history of theft and consumption. German men who plundered in the East sought to appease wives on the home front. Women in the East plundered as consumers and caregivers for their own families and Volksdeutschen refugees.

6) A skewed picture of power relations has overstated the political and understated the social. Because German women were not placed in leading government positions, their role as functionaries appears as mere window dressing.

One of the ways that we can begin to answer the questions of how and why the Holocaust happened is to look at the ordinary individuals who wielded extraordinary power and committed the crimes, specifically the men and women who shared in the business of genocide.

WENDY LOWER is John K. Roth Professor of History and George R. Roberts Fellow and Director of Mgrublian Center for Human Rights. She is author of *Nazi Empire-Building and the Holocaust in Ukraine; Hitler's Furies: German Women in the Nazi Killing Fields;* and coeditor of *The Shoah in Ukraine: History, Testimony, Memorialization* (IUP, 2008).

NOTES

1. Parts of this chapter previously appeared in the book, *Hitler's Furies: German Women in the Nazi Killing Fields* (Boston: Houghton Mifflin Harcourt, 2013).

2. Margaret Bourke-White, *"Dear Fatherland, Rest Quietly," A Report on the Collapse of Hitler's Thousand Years* (New York: Simon and Schuster, 1946), 4–5, 136.

3. Ruth Kempner and Robert M. W. Kempner, *Women in Nazi Germany,* vol. 1 (Washington, DC: Government Printing Office, 1944), 28–9.

4. Michael Geyer and Sheila Fitzpatrick, eds., *Beyond Totalitarianism* (New York: Cambridge University Press, 2009), 30–31, 34.

5. Saul Friedländer, *Nazi Germany and the Jews, The Years of Persecution, 1933–1939* (New York: Harper Collins, 1997).

6. On the importance of the racial community for men and women, see Peter Fritzsche's *Life and Death in the Third Reich* (Cambridge: Harvard University Press, 2008); Gisela Bock, "Ordinary Women in Nazi Germany: Perpetrators, Victims, Followers, and Bystanders," in *Women in the Holocaust,* eds. Dalia Ofer and Lenore J. Weitzman and Ofer (New Haven, CT: Yale University Press, 1999): Atina Grossmann, "Feminist Debates about Women and National Socialism," *Gender and History* 3, no. 3 (1991): 350–58.

7. See Lina Haag's 1947 memoir, *Eine Hand voll Staub—Widerstand einer Frau 1933 bis 1945* (Fischer Verlag, 1995). Among those in the earliest camps at Gotteszell and then Lichtenburg was the communist Lina Haag. Haag briefly recalled the conditions during my interview with her and Dr. Boris Neusius, February 9, 2012, Munich Germany. Interview is available in the US Holocaust Memorial Museum Archives. Gisela Bock, *Zwangssterilisation im Nationalsozialismus: Studien zur Rassenpolitik und Frauenpolitik* (Opladen, Germany: Westdeutscher Verlag, 1986).

8. See the case of Maria Dietrich (b. 1904), SpruchkammerAkten, v. 285. Staatsarchiv Muenchen.

9. The excitement was expressed years later in Melitta Maschmann's memoir, *Fazit: Mein Weg in der Hitler Jugend* (Munich, 1979). Maschmann joined the Nazi League of German Girls (BDM) in 1933 and rose quickly to the position of Officer, Press and Propaganda. She was also leader of a Reich Labor Service Camp in the Warthegau.

According to Ute Frevert, as BDM Press Officer she could issue directives to male subordinates. Ute Frevert, *Women in German History: From Bourgeois Emancipation to Sexual Liberation*, trans. Stuart McKinon-Evans (New York: Berg, 1989), 241. Elisabeth Harvey, *Women and the Nazi East: Agents and Witnesses of Germanization* (New Haven, CT: Yale University Press, 2003), 13, 153. Geoff Eley, "Missionaries of the Volksgemeinschaft: Ordinary Women, Nazification, and the Social," in *Nazism as Fascism: Violence, Ideology, and the Ground of Consent in Germany 1930–1945* (New York: Routledge, 2013), 91–130. Also see, Margarete Dörr, "*Wer die Zeit nicht miterlebt hat …*": *Frauenerfahrungen im Zweiten Weltkrieg und in den Jahren danach: Kriegsalltag*, Vol 2 (Frankfurt, Germany: Campus, 1998).

10. Speech excerpted in *Inside Hitler's Germany: A Documentary History of Life in the Third Reich*, eds. Benjamin Sax and Dieter Kunz (Lexington: D. C. Heath, 1992), 262–63.

11. Adolf Hitler, 1935 Speech to National Socialist Women's Congress, excerpted in George Mosse, ed. *Nazi Culture: Intellectual, Cultural and Social Life in the Third Reich* (New York: Grosset and Dunlap, 1966), 39.

12. George Mosse, ed., *Nazi Culture: Intellectual, Cultural, and Social Life in the Third Reich* (New York: Grosset and Dunlap, 1966), 39–43.

13. Franka Maubach, *Die Stellung halten: Kriegserfahrungen und Lebensgeschichten von Wehrmachthelferinnen* (Goettingen, Germany: Vandenhoeck & Ruprecht, 2009). Nicole Kramer, *Volksgenossinnen an der Heimatfront: Mobilizierung, Verhalten, Erinnerung* (Goettingen, Germany:Vandenhoeck & Ruprecht, 2011).

14. Marita Krauss, ed., *Sie waren dabei: Mitläuferinnen, Nutznießerinnen, Täterinnen im Nationalsozialismus*, (Göttingen, Germany: Wallstein, 2008), 13. Brigitte Penkert, *Briefe einer Rotkreuzschwester von der Ostfront*, eds. Jens Ebert und Sibylle Penkert (Göttingen, Germany: Wallstein, 2006).

15. Thanks to Elizabeth Harvey for bringing this recruitment poster to my attention.

16. Elissa Mailänder Koslov, *Gewalt im Dienstalltag: Die SS—Aufseherinnen des Konzentrations—und Vernichtungslagers Mayjdanek 1942–1944* (Hamburg: Hamburg Institute for Social Research, 2009). Daniel Patrick Brown, *The Camp Women. The Female Auxiliaries Who Assisted the SS in Running the Nazi Concentration Camp System* (Atglen, PA: Schiffer Publishing, 2002). Jürgen Matthäus, ed., *Approaching an Auschwitz Survivor: Holocaust Testimony and its Transformations* (New York: Oxford University Press, 2009). Christina Thürmer-Rohr, "Frauen als Täterinnen und Mittäterinnen im NS-Deutschland," in *Frauen als Täterinnen und Mittäterinnen im Nationalsozialismus: Gestaltungsspielräume und Handlungsmöglichkeiten*, ed. Viola Schubert-Lehnhardt and Sylvia Korch (Halle, Germany: Martin-Luther-Universität Halle-Wittenberg, 2006).

17. For years after the war, Hellmuth was questioned and under surveillance by West German and American authorities who hunted for Mueller. She appears in the recently declassified CIA name files: http://www.archives.gov/iwg/declassified-records/rg-263 -cia-records/rg-263-mueller.html. Mueller's mistress, Anna Schmid, was also questioned. See Richard Breitman, Norman Goda, Tim Naftali, and Robert Wolfe, *US Intelligence and the Nazis* (New York: Cambridge University Press, 2005), 150.

18. See the case of nurses at Eglfing Haar, e.g., Maria Spindler, who earned a monthly bonus of twenty-five RM for killing children, in SpKA K1558, Staatsarchiv Muenchen.

19. See the interrogation summaries of nurses and office personnel at Hadamar in trials against Wahlmann, Gorgass, et al., CLG Frankfurt am Main, SS 10.48, 188/48. B162/28348 fol. 1. Urteil, 68–98; Susan Benedict, "Caring While Killing: Nursing in the 'Euthanasia'

Centers," in *Experience and Expression: Women, the Nazis, and the Holocaust*, eds. Elizabeth R. Baer and Myrna Goldenberg (Detroit: Wayne State University Press, 2003); Ulrike Gaida, *Zwischen Pflegen und Töten: Krankenschwestern im Nationalsozialismus* (Frankfurt am Main: Mabuse Verlag, 2006).

20. Michael Burleigh, *Death and Deliverance: "Euthanasia" in Germany, 1900–1945* (New York: Cambridge University Press, 1994). Henry Friedlander, *The Origins of Nazi Genocide: From Euthanasia to the Final Solution* (Chapel Hill: University of North Carolina Press, 1997).

21. Raul Hilberg, *Perpetrators, Victims, Bystanders: The Jewish Catastrophe, 1933–1945* (New York: HarperCollins, 1992), 9.

22. This portrait was developed by Hannah Arendt, Zygmunt Baumann, and others. See Hannah Arendt's *Eichmann in Jerusalem: A Report on the Banality of Evil* (New York: Penguin, 1963), Zygmunt Baumann's *Modernity and the Holocaust* (Ithaca, NY: Cornell University Press, 1989) and the recent critique by Donald Bloxham, "Organized Mass Murder: Structure, Participation and Motivation in Comparative Perspective," *Holocaust and Genocide Studies* 22, no. 2 (October 2008): 203–45.

23. Hamburger Institut für Sozialforschung, ed., *Verbrechen der Wehrmacht: Dimensionen des Vernichtungskrieges, 1941–1944* (Hamburg, Germany: Hamburger Edition HIS, 2002) and Hannes Heer and Klaus Naumann, eds., *War of Extermination: The German Military in World War II, 1941–1944* (New York: Berghahn, 2000).

24. Robert J. Lifton, *The Nazi Doctors: Medical Killing and the Psychology of Genocide* (New York: Basic Books, 1986). Götz Aly and Susanne Heim, *Vordenker der Vernichtung: Auschwitz und die deutsche Pläne für eine neue europäische Ordnung* (Frankfurt am Main: Fischer, 1993). Mark Roseman, *The Wannsee Conference and the Final Solution: A Reconsideration* (New York: Picador, 2002).

25. Yaacov Lozowick, *Hitler's Bureaucrats: The Nazi Security Police and the Banality of Evil* (New York: Continuum Books, 2000).

26. Maria Cramer (b. 1903), wife of SS Brigadefuehrer SA, Gebietskommissar Kaunas, Hans Cramer, lived in Kovno, 1941–44. Staatsanwalt Traunstein, NG Akten, carton 20264, case KLS 37/49, Staatsarchiv Muenchen. On the greed of German women and their involvement in the Aryanization of Jewish property, also see the case of Sophie Ueberreiter, carton 20299/1–5, Staatsanwalt Traunstein, Staatsarchiv Muenchen.

27. Eric A. Johnson and Karl-Heins Reuband, *What We Knew: Terror, Mass Murder, and Everyday Life in Nazi Germany, an Oral History* (Boston: Basic Books, 2005). Also see, Johnson's response to my book *Hitler's Furies: German Women in the Nazi Killing Fields* (New York: Houghton Mifflin Harcourt, 2013): Eric A. Johnson, "Hitler's Female Executioners?," *East Central Europe* 44, no. 1 (Summer 2017): 164–69.

28. Judith Butler, *Gender Trouble: Feminism and the Subversion of Identity* (New York: Routledge, 1990); Joan W. Scott, *Gender and the Politics of History* (New York: Columbia University Press, 1999).

29. On the mass rapes of German women, and discourses of German victimization, see Atina Grossmann's "A Question of Silence: The Rape of German Women by Soviet Occupation Soldiers," in *Women and War in the Twentieth Century: Enlisted with or without Consent*, ed. Nicole A. Dombrowski (New York: Routledge, 1998), 162–83; "Die deutschen Truemmerfrauen," Documentary Film, Hans Dieter Grabe (1968); Elizabeth Heineman, "The Hour of the Woman: Memories of Germany's 'Crisis Years' and West German National Identity," *American Historical Review* 101, no. 2 (April 1996): 354-95; and

Anonymous, *A Woman in Berlin: Eight Weeks in the Conquered City, A Diary* (New York: Metropolitan Books, 2005).

30. Nicole Ann Dombrowski, "Soldiers, Saints, or Sacrificial Lambs? Women's Relationship to Combat and the Fortification of the Home Front in the Twentieth Century," in *Women and War in the Twentieth Century: Enlisted with or without Consent*, ed. Nicole A. Dombrowski (New York: Routledge, 2004), 2–3.

31. Sybil Milton "Women and the Holocaust: The Case of German and German-Jewish Women," in *When Biology Became Destiny*, eds. Renate Bridenthal, Atina Grossman, and Marion Kaplan (New York: *Monthly Review Press*, 1984), 297–333. See also Gudrun Schwarz, *Eine Frau an Seiner Seite: Ehefrauen in der 'SS-Sippengemeinschaft'* (Berlin: Aufbau Taschenbuch, 2000) and recent work by Sarah Cushman ("The Women of Birkenau, [PhD diss., Clark University, 2010]). For East German cases against women in particular, see Insa Eschenbach, "'Negative Elemente': Ermittlungsberichte des MfS über ehemalige SS-Aufseherinnen," in *Helden, Täter und Verräter: Studien zum DDR-Antifaschismus*, eds., Annette Leo and Peter Reif-Spireck (Berlin: Metropol, 1999), 197–210.

32. The 1967 trial against this female desk murderer Slottke and the convictions were unusual. It seems that the international attention, media coverage, and involvement in the case of witness Otto Frank, as well as prominent Nazi hunter Simon Wiesenthal and former Nuremberg attorney Robert Kempner, strengthened the prosecution. For Gertrude Slottke's testimony and other trial material, BAL, 107 AR 518/59, Band II. After the war, Slottke settled in Stuttgart, and was working as a sales clerk before her arrest. Coverage of the trial was in *Newsweek*, January 30, 1967. Slottke's speciality was deciding on the "immunity cases" of about forty thousand Jews (e.g., German war veterans) who had been protected from deportation; she analyzed each case, and ultimately sent all to Poland between 1942 and 1944. Besides reviewing paper files, Slottke examined individual Jewish prisoners. Lozowick, *Hitler's Bureaucrats*, 165–66, 171, 269. Kohlhaas, "Weibliche Angestellte der Gestapo," *Sie waren dabei: Mitläuferinnen, Nutznießerinnen, Täterinnen im Nationalsozialismus*, ed. Marita Krauss (Göttingen, Germany: Wallstein, 2008), 154–61.

33. Gisela Bock, *Zwangssterilisation im Nationalsozialismus: Studien zur Rassenpolitik und Frauenpolitik* (Berlin: Schriften des Zentralinstituts für Sozialwissenschaftliche Forschung der Freien Universitat Berlin, 1986). Claudia Koonz, *Mothers in the Fatherland: Women, the Family and Nazi Politics* (New York: St. Martin's Press, 1987). Gudrun Schwarz, *Eine Frau an seiner Seite: Ehefrauen in der "SS-Sippengemeinschaft,"* (Berlin: Aufbau Taschenbuch, 2000). Alison Owens, *Frauen: German Woman Recall the Third Reich* (New Brunswick, NJ: Rutgers University Press, 1993). See Elisabeth Harvey on educators, welfare workers, and "resettlement advisors" in *Women in the Nazi East* (New Haven, CT: Yale University Press, 2004). Only in passing are women analyzed in *Die Täter der Shoah: Fanatische Nationalsozialisten oder ganz normale Deutsche?*, ed., Gerhard Paul (Göttingen, Germany: Wallstein, 2002).

34. The few exceptions are Elizabeth Harvey's book, discussed here, and a recent PhD dissertation by Mara Lazda, Indiana University, on "Gender in Collaboration and Resistance: Nazi Occupation in Latvia, 1941–1945," published in part as a book chapter, "Family, Gender, and Ideology in World War II Latvia," in *Gender and War in Twentieth Century Eastern Europe*, eds. Nancy Meriwether Wingfield and Maria Bucur (Bloomington: Indiana University Press, 2006). Waitman Wade Beorn's study

of Belarus contains some excellent material and analysis of German women in Slonim and elsewhere, see Beorn's *Marching into Darkness: The Wehrmacht and the Holocaust in Belarus* (Cambridge, MA: Harvard University Press, 2014), 160–70.

35. After the war, Bluemel was denounced by female staff. After the case against him was dropped, he fled to Ocala, Florida, to be with his daughter. He was identified there and questioned by the US Department of Justice's Office of Special Investigations and escorted home to West Germany in April 1984. Telegram from German Embassy Washington to Ministry of Justice, Bonn, April 5, 1985, regarding OSI/DOJ questioning of Bluemel. Bundesarchiv Ludwigsburg, B 162/3263. Newspaper articles on the departure of Bluemel were printed in the *New York Times* (AP "2 War Crime Suspects Leave United States," April 30, 1985, http://www.nytimes.com/1985/04/30/us/2-war-crime-suspects -leave-united-states.html), *San Francisco Chronicle*, *Palm Beach Post*. Thanks to David Sandler for sharing these articles with me.

36. Elisabeth Harvey, *Women and the Nazi East*. West German investigation and trials against Gebietskommissar Paul Bluemel and Agricultural Leader Konrad Heinemann, Bundesarchiv Ludwigsburg, Sta Munich, 35-320 Js 16 839/75 and Kassel, 3 Ks 5/57; BAL 162/7354. Chudniv lay on the train lines that ran between Lviv, Miropol, Berdichev, and Fastow. Its administrative borders encompassed Liubar and Dzerzhyns'k (Romanow). The total area was 1900 square kilometers with a population of about 156,000 persons. The judgment against Heinemann, who was acquitted, is reprinted in *Justiz und NS-Verbrechen: Sammlung deutscher Strafurteile wegen nationalsozialistischer Tötungsverbrechen 1945–1966*, eds. C.F. Rueter and D.W. de Mildt (Amsterdam: University Press Amsterdam), volume 14, 137–46.

37. "Der Generalbezirk Shytomyr," RmfdbO, Hauptabteilung 1 Raumplanung, 15 Maerz 1942. Zhytomyr State Archives, Zhytomyr Ukraine, P1151-1-51.

38. West German investigation and trials against *Gebietskommissar* Paul Bluemel, and Agricultural Leader Konrad Heinemann, Sta Munich, 35-320 Js 16 839/75 and Kassel, 3 Ks 5/57; Bundesarchiv Ludwigsburg, 162/7354.

39. Vorermittlungsverfahren der Zentralen Stelle der Landesjustizverwaltungen wegen NS-Verbrechen im Bereich des ehemaligen Generlbezirks Shitomir/Ukraine, II 204a AR-Z 131/67, Abschlussbericht, Das Gebietskommisariat Tschudnow.

40. Testimony of Florentina Bedner, November 29, 1976. Bundesarchiv Ludwigsburg, Bayer. Landeskriminalamt 76-K 41676. Koeln.

41. Heinrich Barth testimony of March 2, 1977, Bundesarchiv Ludwigsburg, 76-K 41676-Koeln.

42. See Father Patrick Desbois, *The Holocaust by Bullets* (New York: Macmillan, 2008).

43. Elisabeth Held, born Frank, Neustadt. August 11, 1977, Bundesarchiv Ludwigsburg, 76-K 41676-Koeln.

44. Elisabeth Hoeven, born Bork 1922, Kassel. Bundesarchiv Ludwigsburg, Testimony October 10, 1978, 634-K41676-Koeln.

45. Helene Dowland, Euskirchen, April 21, 1966, Bundesarchiv Ludwigsburg, B 162/2110. Fol.1. Dowland explained that the men were often drunk when they returned in the evenings, and in a festive mood. She learned at the time that the shootings were done with the use of a large plank, "like a diving board" placed over the mass grave. Jews were made to walk on the plank, and fell into the grave when shot by sharpshooters from a distance. Jews from Tarnopol, Skalat, and Brzezany were killed by staff of this office,

according to Dowland. I am grateful to Marie Moutier for this testimony. A similar testimony was given by the ethnic German cook from Lida. She was in charge of feeding the local policeman. One day the German gendarme captain told her to quickly prepare meals for one hundred persons who would be arriving in town the next day for a special action. In the early morning hours she fed them, they left into the darkness, and a few hours later the gunfire started. The executioners (whom she described as German SS officers and green-gray uniformed Lithuanian auxiliaries) came back to eat periodically during the day as they worked in shifts. This went on past midnight, and into the next day. Local auxiliaries told her the horrific details of the execution site, the throwing of babies in the air, burying those who were still alive, and other atrocities. She recalled SS executioners and their auxiliaries beating a Jewish woman on the street outside the gendarme office and hunting down other Jews who had worked in their office. See testimony of Maria Koschinska Sprenger, April 20. 1966, BAL 162/3446. The massacre on May 8, 1942, was carried out by former members of *Einsatzkommando* 9 (based in the SD office in Baranovichi) and native auxiliaries. *The Yad Vashem Encyclopedia of the Ghettos during the Holocaust* (Jerusalem: Yad Vashem, 2009), volume 1, "Lida," 396–97. The local auxiliaries might have been Belarussian, Latvian, Lithuanian, or Polish; the testimony on their nationalities is inconsistent. See Wolfgang Curilla, *Die Deutsche Ordnungspolizei und der Holocaust im Baltikum und in Weissrussland* (Paderborn: Schöningh, 2006), 885–86.

46. Aly and Heim, *Vordenker der Vernichtung*, 200–202.

47. Thea Haupt letter to Institut für Deutsche Ostarbeit, June 27, 1944. National Anthropological Archives, Smithsonian Institute. I am grateful to Götz Aly for sharing this file with me.

48. Susannah Heschel "Does Atrocity Have a Gender? Feminist Interpretations of Women in the SS," in *Lessons and Legacies: New Currents in Holocaust Research Volume VI*, ed. Jeffrey Diefendorf (Evanston, IL: Northwestern University Press, 2004), 300–321. Dana Britton, *The Gender of Crime* (Lanham, MD: Rowman & Littlefield, 2011).

49. In 1939, there were about twenty-eight million middle-aged German women in the Reich. If one defines perpetrator broadly to include accomplices, operators in the administration of the genocide (such as desk clerks and interpreters at crime scenes), then the percentage of female accomplices within the state, private industry, and Nazi party workforce is significant. Those who were violent and directly caused deaths and cruelties in the camps, killing fields, and euthanasia sites amounted to more than four to five thousand German and ethnic German women. As women managed labor on the home front during the war years, the occurrences of physical abuse of forced laborers by German women in homes, farms, and factories were probably frequent, but scarcely documented.

50. This rough estimate of the Gestapo offices is from Elisabeth Kohlhaas's "Weibliche Angestellte der Gestapo, 1933–1945," 148.

51. Hilberg, *Perpetrators, Victims, Bystanders*, 53.

52. And they played a major role in shaping the modern system of administration. Leaving them out of this history in Nazi Germany implies that women are outside of modern history altogether. See Ann Taylor Allen, "The Holocaust and the Modernization of Gender: A Historiographical Essay." *Central European History* 30, no. 3 (1997): 349–64.

No Shelter to Cry In

Romani Girls and Responsibility during the Holocaust

Michelle Kelso

Anuța Brânzan (née Radu) remembers vividly the morning that her family of six was deported from Romania in September 1942.[1] Living in a provincial town a few hours southwest of the capital Bucharest, Anuța, then eight years old, loved playing outside and was looking forward to starting second grade. Her older sister Marieta also attended school, while her younger sisters, Margareta and Verginia, stayed home with their mother, Constantina, a housewife. Their father Pavel was a cobbler and part-time musician who Anuța recalled spoiled the children, much to their delight. Unbeknownst to the Radus, who were part of the country's ethnic Roma minority, Romania's pro-fascist dictator Ion Antonescu (1940–44) had ordered the deportation of Romani families like theirs as part of a policy of genocide enacted against Jews and Roma in a bio-racial purification plan similar to that of his Nazi allies.[2]

Anuța was playing in the yard when police arrived. Authorities had decided that Roma would be resettled in the newly acquired eastern territory of Transnistria (1941–-1944), stretching from the Dniester River to the Bug River, ostensibly to bolster the new Romanian administration there. Antonescu, whose troops were fighting alongside the German army on the Soviet front after Romania entered WWII, received Transnistria from Hitler to administrate during occupation for their shared victories in the 1941 invasion of the Soviet Union.[3] The territory would become Romania's killing fields, as Jews and Roma were interned, suffered, and died in Transnistrian ghettos and camps. Anuța recalled: "The police lied to us. They told mother not to gather our things, not to take anything, because they were not taking us to a place of suffering but someplace where we'd have everything. They were deporting us, but they would give us things we needed there. Just to take strict necessities."[4]

To assuage Romani fears, police invented scenarios that made the removal of Roma both easier and more profitable for the state, which seized Romani assets before liquidation could occur.[5] The lightning speed with which the authorities accomplished the deportation of twenty-five thousand Roma provided little opportunity for resistance, although some Roma tried to escape the deportations.[6]

Under orders to pack lightly and quickly, Constantina gathered a few amenities like a drinking cup and linens, clothing for her family, and several days' worth of food. While Constantina did her best to hastily prepare for departure, her young daughters, then ages one through ten, accompanied their aunt Zozica to a local photography studio. Zozica worried she might not see her beloved nieces for a while and wanted a keepsake portrait. She begged Anuța's father Pavel to leave at least the two youngest girls with her. Pavel, misled by the fiction that police told him that a good life awaited them in the resettlement, refused, telling her that he wanted all his children with him.

Within a few days that September, authorities rounded up 13,176 Roma they categorized as "undesirable."[7] Roma who could not prove stable employment, such as those working in seasonal agriculture and manual labor, or those who had criminal records, even for minor transgressions like chicken thieving, were deported. Entire families were crammed into cargo trains heading east because of their presumed moral turpitude.[8] Over the next months, authorities deported several hundred more Roma. Already the previous spring and summer, police had forced 11,441 nomadic Roma using their own caravans across the country to Transnistria in what for many was an arduous, weeks-long trek.[9] The removal of Roma followed on the heels of the persecution of Jews, which began nearly a year before.[10]

In this chapter I delve into gendered experiences of Romani girls who, like Anuța, shed their childhoods in Transnistria. Children and youth, especially girls, were undoubtedly in the most vulnerable positions in camps for several reasons that included the perpetrating regime's policies, such as the work-for-food plans that benefited adults that contributed to the suffering and deaths of children, as well as an internal Romani cultural hierarchy that, for example, privileged sons over daughters. As historian Stefan Ionescu noted, Romani children suffered high mortality rates in Transnistria.[11] How then did Romani girls experience and survive the Holocaust in Romanian territories? What factors did gender and culture play, if any, in their survival? These questions center this work, which aims to understand how individual agency, grossly constrained by the most horrific genocidal conditions, affected the decisions and actions of Romani girls and their families.

I focus on the intersection of youth and gender in the case of the Roma during the Holocaust because they are little studied in literature and can shed further light on perpetration and survival during genocides. While Holocaust research virtually ignores the plight of Roma, historian Sybil Milton recognized that works on Romani women's experiences were even more scarce, calling them "scattered and isolated," and, at best, "fragmentary."[12] Ethnicity, gender, and age affected persecuted Roma, just as they did Jewish victims.[13] The intersectionality of these identities played a prominent role in the survival of Romani women and girls.[14] The majority of Romani deportees were children.[15]

In addition to age, gender was a critically important factor in Romani experiences in Transnistria. Several scholars have highlighted the importance of studying gender and the Holocaust to acknowledge the differing aspects of perpetration embedded in gender,[16] to decentralize the master narrative of the Holocaust away from a male-dominated paradigm,[17] and to deepen understanding of the Holocaust as an event.[18] Myrna Goldenberg and Amy Shapiro suggest that gender also enriches the study of the Holocaust because it allows for the exploration of "relationships between humans, specifically in terms of issues of power and control,"[19] which is what I will focus on in this writing.

I begin with a brief section on methods and theoretical framing, followed by a historical overview of the Holocaust in Romania. I then turn to survivor accounts and my analysis of them.

METHODOLOGY

To understand how Romani girls were subjugated by the Antonescu regime and the means they used at times to thwart the power and control authorities and others exerted over them, I turn to survivors' testimonies. Because most archival sources reveal little of the specific experiences of children, teenagers, or women, I therefore rely on survivors' narratives as my primary data source. I chose the narratives of three Romani women who were girls at the time of their deportations to Transnistrian camps. These narratives illustrate the constraints, fears, and role inversions forced on them, as well as their mechanisms for survival. By providing fuller accounts from three individuals, I intend to provide a more holistic view of girls' experiences, thus addressing concerns of feminist scholars like Janet Jacobs, who raise the question that those writing about gender may stereotype women as merely helpless victims.[20]

These interviews were recorded fifty or more years after the traumatic events occurred.[21] Over a thirteen-year period, from 1995 to 2008, I did intermittent fieldwork in Romani communities, interviewing over two hundred Romani survivors.[22] Working in partnership with Romani women and men, many of whom were prominent elders in their communities and survivors themselves, we crisscrossed bumpy backroads of Romania gathering life stories of those deported *ando Bugo* (to the Bug River). The Bug marked the periphery of the Romanian regime's control over their lives, and Roma conflated all the horrors they lived onto the river along whose banks they suffered and died. The three interviewees were all unmarried Romani girls aged thirteen and under at the time of their deportations, who did not yet have the experiences of their own households or children, and remained with their parents during deportation and internment.

In taking testimony, I followed in the footsteps of many others collecting survivors' voices and advocating their use as a means through which to understand the Holocaust.[23] In Geoffrey Hartman's words, testimony allows survivors to speak and "look toward an establishment of a legacy."[24] This is especially so for Romani communities where diaries, journals, and other victim-perspective sources are scarce. Placed contextually alongside archival records, survivors' accounts personalize the Holocaust and allow for a shift of perspective from perpetrator to victim, elevating the voices upon whom genocide was carried out.

Testimonies can additionally offer a gendered perspective on genocide. The ability to gather data on how gender roles affected Romani families deported to Transnistria is limited. Although perpetrator records provide much comprehensive information about deportations and camp life, they do not focus on gendered experiences. Testimonies thus provide perhaps the most essential source for understanding how Roma not only made sense of the state's persecution of them, but also shed light on the differing experiences of women, men, girls, and boys.

In Transnistrian camps, girls, subjected to stringent cultural gender norms governing their behavior, had more caretaking responsibility than did boys. Before internment like children elsewhere, Romani children relied on their parents and elders for their daily sustenance and emotional needs. Transnistria, however, shook the foundation of familial bonds. The camps brought brutality, starvation, disease, and a systematic breakdown of the social structures. Age worked as both an asset and a liability, depending on circumstances. Some children were orphaned and struggled alone to survive, while others remained and struggled within their family units. Youths acquired new roles as providers and caretakers, eking out an existence for themselves and family. For example, children and teens, either on their own initiative or by request of adults in their lives, turned to begging and stealing to obtain food. Some were beaten, raped, and killed for their efforts.[25] Agility and size often allowed youths to procure food or supplies when adults could not; guards appeared less inclined to physically punish or kill children disobeying camp rules. In food distribution, however, age worked against youths. Authorities allocated half rations for children under fourteen, who were at greater risk for starvation because they had few opportunities to work or gain access to local resources.[26] Romani testimonies reveal the myriad ways in which children and youths subverted and survived, as well as sometimes succumbed, to genocide.

ROMA AND THE HOLOCAUST IN ROMANIAN-CONTROLLED LANDS

Romania entered WWII after allying with Nazi Germany, attacking the Soviet Union alongside its Axis allies in June 1941. The Antonescu regime used the fog of war to unleash massacres and deportations of Jews.[27] The Romanian military and police, working mainly alone and occasionally in conjunction with special German mobile killing units, murdered many Jews from Northeastern provinces before deporting the survivors and Ukrainian Jews into ghettos and camps created in Transnistria. Authorities, experienced in the removal, terrorization, and killing of the Jews, then turned to eradicating the so-called Roma problem. As historian Roland Clark stated, Romania would become the largest perpetuating state after Nazi Germany, authoring its own genocidal policies against Jews and Roma.[28]

The Holocaust, a watershed in the destruction of Roma life across Europe, was not the first systemic persecution that Roma had faced in Romania. Less than a century before the Holocaust, some Roma were enslaved in Romanian territories just as African Americans were enslaved in the United States. Romani slavery spanned five centuries and ended only in 1855–56.[29] Following emancipation, the majority of former slaves and their families had few economic, social, or political opportunities.[30] Slavery's legacy of social isolation and its accompanying poverty dogged Romani communities well into the first half of the twentieth century, which only began to systematically change when postwar communist governments ushered in assimilation policies in the mid-1950s. Few Roma escaped the grinding poverty and its associated social problems that came to characterize their neighborhoods, which were often segregated and stigmatized.[31]

Despite their destitution, Roma were in various states of integration, ranging from the least integrated, like the nomads, who spoke and kept Romani language and traditions, to the most integrated who had completely assimilated into Romanian society, with the majority falling somewhere in between. Nomadic Roma were undoubtedly the most marginalized and distinguishable to outsiders, which later made them easier to target for genocide. They traveled the country in their colorfully painted caravans, and their specific dress and hairstyles were cultural markers that made them easily identifiable as Roma. Men often had extended moustaches and beards, and both men and women wore their hair long. Women wore ankle-length, brightly colored skirts and headscarves. Women also frequently wore part if not all of their families' wealth—gold and silver coins—either woven into their braids, or as jewelry.

Roma lived a patriarchal family lifestyle much like their neighbors. Like women elsewhere, Romani women were responsible for raising children and keeping the household, while men worked as agricultural day laborers, or in trades, such as coppersmithing and shoemaking. While gender norms were cohesive among Roma subgroups, traditional Roma placed more restrictions on women, who had almost no control over the major decisions in their lives. Hierarchies in households were based on sex and age, with men and older individuals having more status and retaining decision-making roles. For example, girls and young women had little or no say in the choice of their marriage partners, the age at which they married, or the number of children they bore. As in other patriarchal societies, there was a birth preference for boys by parents and grandparents. Sons grew into men who would then care for elderly parents, while daughters left their families upon marriage to live with and care for their spouses' families.

Roma were one of several ethnic minorities living in Romania, which also included Bulgarians, Germans, Hungarians, Jews, Serbians, Turks, and Ukrainians, among others. The number of minority groups increased after WWI, when Romania nearly doubled in size after it gained territories like Transylvania, which were awarded in peace settlements. Rapid expansion meant that ethnic Romanians, although remaining the majority (even increasing in number), decreased in overall population proportions, falling from 92.2 percent in 1899, to 71.9 percent in the 1930 census. A larger and more ethnically diverse Romania brought not only administrative challenges, but also produced some discontent that sparked the rise of extremist movements in the 1920s. Anti-Semitic and xenophobic, they agitated for an ethnic state composed of Orthodox Christian Romanians. Politicians and administrators were largely preoccupied with the Germans, Hungarians, and Jews, who comprised respectively 4.1, 7.9, and 4 percent of the population, according to 1930 census data, making them the largest ethnic minorities in the country. While extremists viewed Hungarians and Jews as the most threatening to an ethnic Romanian state, few other than a handful of staunch eugenicists perceived Roma as threats.[32]

In 1941 when the Antonescu regime began killing and deporting Jews, their persecution was framed in terms of security, claiming that "communist Jews" were a national security threat. Months later, a similar argument was extended to justify the measures taken against "criminal Roma" whom Antonescu accused of threatening national stability.[33] In actuality, Antonescu was enacting his own bio-racial policies, dubbed "Romanization," that shared characteristics with Nazi Germany's "Aryanization" plans.[34] Notably Antonescu chose not to deport Romanian Jews or Roma to German–controlled camps as requested by his Nazi allies; rather, he devised his own plans to "Romanianize" the country. In 1942, Antonescu announced to his cabinet additional motives for the war, which included purging Romania of Jews, and as historian Jean Ancel noted, of Roma.[35] Transnistria became one of the means through which Antonescu and his advisors could achieve those goals by massive deportations of Jews and Roma to the region. Much like Poland for the Nazis, Transnistria became a space in which to rid the nation of so-called ethnically polluting elements.

In late summer and fall 1941, hundreds of thousands of Jews were rounded up and dumped into ghettos and camps.[36] By the end of September 1942, the Antonescu regime had deported to Transnistria all nomadic Roma and some settled groups, or around 12 percent of the Romani population.[37] Ancel wrote that "Roma and Jews were deported to Transnistria to perish."[38] He noted that both Jews and Roma were robbed, humiliated, suffered, and died from diseases and killings. The family life that Roma knew prior to deportation nearly ceased to exist. Nomads had their caravans confiscated, rendering them homeless and without means of surviving. Settled Roma had been forced to part with their properties and goods before boarding trains to Transnistria. Arguably more integrated than their nomadic countrymen, many settled Roma lost more than their homes: their social networks—grounded in neighbors, extended families, and churches—were torn apart.

Once in Transnistria, authorities placed most deportees on large state-owned or state-run agricultural farms, where some lived in pig-pens or animal barns. Others were temporarily housed in overcrowded institutional buildings such as schools. Some Roma entered camps that had previously held Jews before their executions, such as Bogdanovka or Dumanovka.[39] Several hundred Roma were placed in camps also interning Jewish deportees who had survived earlier massacres. However, most Roma were concentrated in rural areas along the River Bug, placing them at the farthermost point of Romania's control.

Romanian authorities maintained a starvation policy with infrequent or no delivery of food. Survivors reported eating whatever they could find: grass, the soles of shoes, and even spoke of cannibalism in camps. In the Oceacov district, gendarmes reported that *țiganii*, or Gypsies, were reduced to "mere shadows" and were "almost wild" due to the regime's policies.[40] Diseases like typhus, brutality by guards, lack of food distribution, and forced exposure to cold through inadequate housing contributed to the deaths of Roma. One report documented that Roma were saying, "Better to shoot us than to keep us in this situation we are in."[41] By November 1942, camp commanders and local officials reported large numbers of Roma dying daily. Unable and unwilling to stem the typhus outbreak or to distribute adequate food rations, administrators ordered shallowly dug mass graves for the dead. Able-bodied Roma and locals were charged with removals and burials. One woman recalled witnessing her parents and then her brother die from typhus. She said, "There was no cemetery, of course, no priest, no candle, no nothing. We were dying like dogs; we were just left there. Killed by hunger and typhus. Naked and miserable bodies."[42] Young women and girls were particularly vulnerable due to the hardships of forced treks, starvation, diseases, and internment.

In Transnistrian camps, men, from the male Romanian administers and guards to the Romani fathers, husbands, and brothers whom the regime directed to oversee work and ration deliveries, controlled the daily life of women. This placed women and children in dependency positions vis-à-vis both the regime and their own families. Women and girls, as traditional keepers of home and hearth, were expected to continue their preexisting roles as wives, mothers, and daughters. One woman remembered, saying, "It was harder for women than for men" because they were strained trying to meet their families' needs while laboring for the regime as well.[43] Romani women and girls were also at great risk of sexual violence, and associated health and trauma complications. Ancel found that both Jewish and Romani women in Transnistria were victims of perpetrator sexual violence.[44] His findings dovetail with research that indicates that sexual violence can be systematic for "the explicit purpose of destabilizing populations and destroying bonds within communities and families. In these instances, rape is often a public act, aimed to maximize humiliation and shame."[45]

The internment in Transnistrian camps had decimated the Romani deportees. The situation changed in early 1944 when the Soviet army recaptured its occupied territories, and Axis troops retreated across Transnistria. Liberation of camps effectively occurred through abandonment by their

Romanian administrators, leaving Jews and Roma to the perils of an oncoming front line. Thousands flooded the roads alongside locals and military personnel fleeing the Red Army. Relations between Romani families, already strained, rarely improved. Women who were pushed by extreme conditions sometimes abandoned their assigned cultural roles as caregivers and nurturers. One Romani woman confessed to abandoning her grandmother on the roadside after liberation because the older woman had a stroke and could no longer walk.[46] Unable to care for her and frightened about the advancing front line, she hoped for the best for her grandmother and continued. A Romani teen told of setting her baby daughter out to die because she could not care for the girl in the chaos of liberation from the camps.[47] Another woman recalled, "Your daughter died, your father died. You didn't even bother to look anymore, you just looked at your feet and continued on."[48] At the war's end, a little over half of those Roma deported had survived.[49]

ANUȚA'S JOURNEY

In Transnistria Anuța's family eked out their existence in improvised camps like Vladimirovka, situated near the Bug River. With little to no food provided by Romanian authorities, the Radus would have starved to death if Constantina had not been a thrifty packer. At first Pavel traded their clothes and linens with locals in exchange for small portions of food. He was then forced to trade the girls' gold earrings and any remaining valuables for cornmeal, potatoes, salt, and grains. To keep the family fed as the weeks dragged on, Pavel even sold the clothes the children wore, leaving Anuța and her sisters dressed in rags with a brutal winter approaching.

The deterioration of the Roma in the camps was noted by Jewish prisoners and authorities alike. One Jewish survivor witnessed the devastation unleashed on the Roma: "Closed in by barbed wire, without food, they had to sell their clothing to survive."[50] The state of the Roma's undress was also discussed in field reports filed to headquarters in Bucharest that noted that due to the terrible conditions, many women and children were naked. One report predicted unequivocally: "with the first snow or freeze, the women and children will perish."[51] In the overcrowded living conditions, with virtually no medical assistance or food, typhus quickly ravaged deportees weakened by stress and hunger.[52] The Romanian prefect of one Transnistrian district estimated that during the 1942–43 winter alone, three to four thousand Roma deportees in areas under his control died from typhus.[53]

Crammed in a single-family house with too many other Romani families, Anuţa recalled the toll that overcrowding, starvation, and disease took on her family.[54] Her mother Constantina was one of the first to perish from typhus. Anuţa explained that Constantina's fast decline came from seeing her children in such a terrible state. A neighbor, deported with the family, later told Anuţa that Constantina would go outside to the cow barn and beat her head against the wall, crying because the girls did not even have water to drink. "My mom lasted only for four months. When she saw the state we were in, she immediately got sick."[55] Anuţa learned that Constantina's body, taken away by locals, was thrown into an unmarked mass grave. At the time of our first interview, Anuţa still dreamed of going back to Transnistria to locate the pit her mother was buried in, hoping that some sort of marker or cross honored the dead there.

Pavel kept the girls alive, even attempting an escape. As Anuţa reckoned, her father thought there was nothing else to lose. By 1943, hundreds of Roma fled the ghettos and camps, desperately trying to reenter Romania.[56] Authorities were slow to crack down on escapes, but soon stepped up their efforts to catch Roma, fearing a spread of typhus into the country. A Romanian patrol captured the bedraggled Radus and the other escapees with them, taking them to a nearby camp. Anuţa said other Roma tried to persuade Pavel to abandon his children and run away on his own, but her father refused. He never wavered in his dedication, saying he preferred to die with his children.

The Radus stayed together until early in 1944, when German and Romanian troops retreated. The family fled alongside thousands of war refugees and interned prisoners like themselves. One day when sheltering in a barn during a bombing raid, German soldiers entered and took away several Romani men, including Pavel. Anuţa never saw her father again. Within days, her elder sister Marieta died, overcome by exhaustion and illness. Anuţa, then ten years old, took on the role of sole caretaker for her two youngest sisters in an ever-moving warzone, emulating her father's behavior. Food and shelter were her priorities, along with learning some basic Russian to survive. "I learned bit of Russian so that I could ask for bread, to say my name and that was it, to ask for water," said Anuța. The Radu girls traversed Transnistria, finding "shot up villages, lots of bullets, howling cats. There was nobody left, everyone had fled." Occasionally they ran into Soviet soldiers, who Anuța recalled were kind to the girls. "If they had a piece of bread or some canned food they gave it to us, crying that after so many years on the front when they didn't go home, they didn't know if their children were still alive." The sisters arrived in Odessa, where they heard a train would take them to Romania. They stayed in a nearby field where a paint and glass factory had been bombed:

> We gathered some aluminum, some bricks, and we made like a little dog house, so that we could shelter from the rain and hail. We would go to the market and beg. I went to the market, where Russian ladies were around the train station because there were apartment blocks, and they took pity on us. There were old Russian ladies that told us their daughters were on the frontlines, and they made us little shirts. They gave us something to eat. We went to the market to beg so that we could live.[57]

Anuța said that Russian women would ask after her sisters, wanting to keep them. "They were little girls, so cute, but I told them: 'No, I am going home, to my mother's house, and I'm taking them.'" She continued: "I cannot even tell you, we were full of lice, lice on us that you would pull off by the fistful. Misery and lice all over us. I don't know how we survived." When they learned that it was impossible to get a train to Romania, Anuța and her sisters continued walking toward the border. The girls' legs swelled so badly that every step was painful. To motivate Margareta and Verginia, Anuța told them about their aunt Zozica, who loved them very much and was waiting for them in Romania. Anuța kept up the encouragement daily, saying repeatedly that it was just a little farther until their aunt's house. It took the girls six months to reach home. She relates, "Can you imagine, we had no bed, no straw, nothing on the ground [to sleep on] and to walk an entire summer, from spring until fall... there was rain, cold, and we slept on the ground. I lay on the ground like animals do, like dogs over their puppies, to keep them warm with my body. First on the one, and then on the other. I lay over them to warm them up again.... Hungry, beaten down by the wind and rain, all the miseries possible."[58]

Anuța had used her wits to dodge marauding soldiers, to outsmart border guards so that she and her sisters could cross back into Romania, and to continue finding them places to sleep and scraps to eat. Even after arriving at their aunt Zozica's house, Anuta's role as surrogate mother did not end. The state had confiscated the Radu's house and land in 1942, leaving no resources with which to care for and educate the girls. The rest of the extended family were by then so impoverished they could not keep the girls, and the sisters rotated living with relatives. Anuța abandoned school, working instead to provide for her younger sisters.

LUCIA'S CHOICE

When Lucia "Flower" Mihai was born, her family gave her two first names, as was often the custom among nomadic Roma coppersmiths. Lucia was her official name used for the Romanian state (in records like her birth certificate), and *Luluji*, or Flower, was her Romani one used by her family and friends.[59] However, both names were entirely insignificant for the Antonescu regime. In 1942 when authorities drew up deportation lists of nomads, they wrote only the names of Romani men heading households. Women and children were included on the lists but only as numerical figures written in alongside their men. Thus authorities erased the identities of Romani women and children even before sending them to perish in Transnistria.

Lucia, one of three children, recalled being around eight years old when police rounded up their caravans, forcing the clan from village to village until they reached the banks of the Bug. Left in a large field guarded by Romanian police, the family shared a cramped *bordei*, or earthen dugout, with four other families after their caravans were confiscated. The scarcity of food and water contributed to the daily death tolls. Nearby, a large pit was dug for the dead, serving as a reminder to those yet living of their intended fate. Lucia's parents, Urda and Luba, constantly took risks to ensure the family's survival. They stole corn from nearby fields and wood from the forest for cooking, making a thin porridge to sustain the family. But as Lucia noted, stealing corn was a dangerous undertaking, as guards sometimes shot Roma who got caught. With no place in or near the camp to buy food, her mother Luba bribed guards with gold coins to allow her to go out to neighboring villages. Sometimes she went thirty kilometers to sell their clothes to villagers in exchange for flour, cheese, and meat. The main water source was the Bug River, but it was too far to access easily. Lucia's father and some other men dug makeshift wells, finding sandy water that they scooped out and gave the children to relieve their thirst.

Luba was pregnant when police forced them from Romania; in Transnistria, she gave birth to a son, Valerica. Weeks after his birth, Lucia's parents began fighting because they no longer saw how they could keep the baby and their other children alive. One day Luba sent Lucia to throw the baby in the mass grave. Lucia vividly recalled her actions:

> I took him in my arms and I brought him there and I stayed there with him in my arms. And I told him, "I won't throw you away, little brother, don't be scared." He was small, two or three weeks old.... And I was crying like that with him in my arms.
>
> Out of nowhere my sister Tinca appeared, and seeing us there next to the pit, she said, "Throw him now. What are you waiting for? Mama said to throw him away. And you are still holding him in your arms?"
>
> "Go away! [I said.] Aren't you afraid? How can I throw him in this ugly pit, where the dead are piled one on top of the other, in that darkness? How can we get him out of there? Don't you have any mercy?"[60]

Lucia refused to let go of her brother. Tinca ran to tell their mother that the two were still at the pit. Crying, her mother came to bring them both back, saying that she would keep all four of her children and their fate was in God's hands. Her father was surprisingly pleased by Lucia's defiance. When relatives heard what had happened, her mother told them: "If my husband was fighting with me, what could I do? I felt bad for [the baby] and sent my daughter to throw him away and she stayed with him in her arms next to the pit and didn't throw him to kill him."[61]

Lucia's story was recorded by both her daughter, Luminiţa Cioabă, a Romani activist, and by the University of Southern California's Shoah Foundation Visual History Archive. Although we briefly met once in 1995, I did not have the chance to speak with Lucia directly about her experiences. However, I did interview her brother Valerica in 2007.[62] His incredible birth story centers his identity, and his parents, Urda and Luba, spoke openly of the horrible choices that they faced to circumvent genocide. Growing up, Valerica heard from almost everyone in his immediate and extended family of the horrors inflicted on nomadic and sedentary Roma *ando Bugo*. In telling me of his parents' attempted infanticide, Valerica understood the pain suffered in the camps and acknowledged his good fortune in life. He had two mothers: his mother Luba, who birthed and raised him with love, and sister Lucia who, in loving him, gave him life by saving him from death.

ENUȚA'S COURAGE

Enuța Spiridon (née Gotu) was deported with her parents and three sisters when she was thirteen.[63] According to Enuța, approximately ten families from her village in Galati County were packed into cargo trains and transported to Transnistria, where they were left in a field near the Bug River. For three days they scrounged the fields for potatoes, eating whatever they could, before authorities evacuated locals and crammed several Romani families into a single-family home. Enuța recalled receiving less than half a pound of oatmeal as their food ration. "We stayed there that winter dying of starvation," she said, adding, "We put boots on the fire ... could a scrap of shoe leather keep hunger away?" Romani survivors recounted scrounging for roots and grasses, eating carrion, and even turning to cannibalism to survive.[64] A camp officer reported the haunting sights of *tiganii* who "die worse than animals" and "are buried without a priest."[65] Constantin, then a young boy in Transnistria, recalled the ground was frozen when his mother died. They had to leave her body exposed outside, where dogs devoured her during the night.[66]

Roma had only two means through which to leave Transnistria: illegal escapes or legal reentry permits. Roma who managed somehow to hold back money or hide jewelry occasionally bribed guards and border patrols to help them clandestinely return to Romania. Families of Romani soldiers fighting on the frontlines or those who could prove they were erroneously deported could receive reentry permits to Romania.[67] Enuța's mother and sister managed to coordinate their escape through such a reentry permit. An older Romani man who was granted a permit claimed them as part of his family. Enuța, her father Mihai, and her younger sister remained in Transnistria. After her mother left, Enuța was responsible for the near-impossible tasks of finding and cooking food, as well as caring for her ailing father. Within months of their arrival, Roma deportees exhausted every scrap of wood for cooking and heating that they could scavenge. Enuța remembers struggling to make a little porridge, which was often undercooked because she had no firewood.

The immense stress stretched Enuța nearly beyond her endurance. Both her father and sister died in the camps. Enuța felt guilty for their deaths, and for being alive, which is often discussed in Holocaust literature as survivors' guilt. She felt she should have been able to do more to save them, even though there was nothing she could have done. On the night of Mihai's death, Enuța anxiously sat watch over her father's body, fearing that other Roma would cannibalize his corpse. She states that, "When he died, I stayed to guard the body until they buried him, otherwise [some Roma] would have cut him to eat him. From hunger, from hunger [Roma] were eating each other. I was afraid until they came to bury him. They were just waiting for someone to die, to cut them to eat them. They waited for a woman to give birth to a child, to cut it and eat it, the [babies] who died."[68]

After Mihai's burial, Enuța took over caring for her sister. Orphaned and without any resources, they were at the mercy of the regime. The girls were transferred, along with ten or so other Roma, to a horse barn. Enuța strategized how to stay alive. When local women came looking for field laborers, she went with them. In exchange for her work, she received a piece of bread or some food. One day some Romanian soldiers entered the barn to stable their horses, and Enuța begged them for help: "Take us with you. Maybe God will give us luck and we can escape back into Romania." The soldiers agreed, but the girls' luck did not hold. A patrol spotted them and brought the sisters back to a camp. There guards beat the girls. Enuța told me: "They took us like this," she said, gesturing as my camera filmed her making two fists and knocking them together. "They took me like this and grabbed my head by the hair doing the same to her, and they knocked our heads together." Tears and emotion choked Enuța's voice, which cracked as she told me: "After that my sister died." Bereft, there was not even a shelter for her to cry in. Released from the beating, Enuța ran to hide in a pile a straw, and did not see what happened to her sister's body. In our 1999 interview, Enuţa still grieved for her sister, wondering if she was buried or worse, cannibalized.

Completely alone and desperate, Enuţa managed a harrowing escape back into Romania. Playing on her status as a child, she persuaded guards and patrols that she was mistakenly in Transnistria and her family awaited her back home. She told me that it was fortunate that she "was a bit whiter" and could pass as a Romanian. She met some strangers, an elderly Romani woman and her grandson, who were also trying to escape, and they stuck it out together. Enuţa invented a story for their perpetrators. When patrols asked about their wanderings, she related: "I told the old woman to let me do the talking because she didn't speak Romanian well, all broken like." The woman agreed, and Enuţa fabricated a story. She told various patrols, soldiers and police they encountered: "We are Romanians and we were brought to the Bug River. My father died on the front in Odessa and my mother died here, and I am left with my grandmother and the boy. It has been hard. We were beaten and badly treated, and we want to go home to our country, Romania."[69]

Enuţa's portrait of themselves as a fallen soldier's family displayed a keen understanding of her perpetrators. She assessed correctly that Romanian military and police would relate to and sympathize with an orphaned Romanian girl and her remaining family. She recounted that one soldier gave her some porridge and others helped the threesome to stow away on trains that brought them closer to the border. Eventually, they crossed back into Romania. Enuţa attributes their escape to her ability to perform a non-Romani identity.

CONCLUSION

During genocides and conflicts,[70] the stability of daily life and the social networks that offer protection against stress factors often collapse. The dislocation of families and communities disrupts their social and protective services, such as judicial systems, health facilities, and religious institutions. Bonds between families can break, and "behavioral norms can deteriorate as people focus on their own survival."[71] As Elisa von Joeden-Forgey noted, one of the underlying effects of genocide is the destruction of families.[72] In Transnistria, Romani family relationships sometimes began to deteriorate, collapsing under the extreme duress. For example, some Romani parents took drastic measures pursuing survival strategies. One man, who at the time was a boy, told me of his parents choosing to withhold food from his younger sisters who were ill.[73] His parents rationalized that typhus would kill the girls no matter what they did; thus it was better to feed their healthier children with their meager rations. The girls were cognizant of their parents' actions, asking continually before they died why they could not have anything to eat like their siblings. Mothers, placed in desperate situations, at times turned to infanticide because they saw no options for keeping their children alive.[74] Abandonment was often the fate of the young and the old as living conditions worsened.[75] As death spread, children and youths were orphaned and alone, suddenly finding themselves forced into new or extended social roles.

The testimonies of Anuța, Lucia, and Enuța reveal how some Romani girls experienced the Holocaust and how the key aspects of age and gender were at times extremely salient in navigating perpetrator spaces in Transnistria. Foremost, to survive, all three girls drew on their socially assigned, gendered caretaking roles, typically fulfilled by older women. In the absence of parental support due to death or abandonment, these girls displayed resiliency in taking on caretaking roles in the most horrific circumstances. Anuța and Enuța recounted painful moments after becoming orphans when they had to take charge, making decisions that affected the survival of themselves and others as well. Anuța found transportation, shelter, and food for her younger sisters, acting as a mother figure who protected them with her body. Enuța cared for her father and sister, securing and making food for them until their deaths. She protected her father's body with her own by sitting beside him until his burial, deterring others from cannibalizing him. Enuța's vigil in a Transnistrian camp was an extreme extension of the role she would have carried out back home in their Orthodox Christian tradition of sitting with the body of a relative until it was buried. She was unable to do this for her sister whose violent death yet haunted her. Enuța then bonded with new acquaintances, forming a makeshift family that she managed to bring back to Romania. Similarly, Lucia, despite nearly starving and freezing to death, inverted the parent-child relationship to save her brother Valerica, even though she knew it meant they all might starve. While on the one hand she defied her cultural role as a dutiful daughter, on the other, she upheld her sibling bond with her brother, following her own moral compass as a caretaker. Each girl through her actions ensured another person close to her was able to live.

In sum, a gendered analysis reveals these Romani girls' struggle to survive and to make sense of their experiences, which, because of their age, gender, and position as part of a marginalized ethnic group, might have otherwise been missed or obscured in scholarship. In turning a gender lens on the deportation of Romanian Roma to Transnistria, these accounts reveal instances in which the relationships forged by the youth withstood the mechanisms used by perpetrators to break Roma. Romani girls were thus at times essential in thwarting the Romanian regime's attempt to destroy them, using their individual agency in carrying out their socially assigned roles as young women and girls, saving themselves and others. All three girls understood the constraints of the regime and managed to circumvent genocide by leveraging their agency. As articulated in Sandra Harding's standpoint perspective theory,[76] women's experiences differ from men's, and incorporating them allows for a fuller understanding of phenomena.

MICHELLE KELSO is Assistant Professor of Human Services, Sociology, and International Affairs at The George Washington University. She directed a 2005 documentary film *Hidden Sorrows: The Persecution of Romanian Gypsies During WWII*. Special thanks to Linda Miller for providing instructive comments on this chapter.

NOTES

1. Michelle Kelso, trans., "Anuţa Brânzan," in *Tragedia romilor deportaţi in Transnistria 1942–1945*, eds., Radu Ioanid, Michelle Kelso, and Luminiţa Cioabă (Iaşi, Romania: Polirom, 2009), 111–142.

2. Vladimir Solonari, "An Important New Document on the Romanian Policy of Ethnic Cleansing during World War II," *Holocaust and Genocide Studies* 21, no. 2 (2007): 268–97.

3. Romanian National Archives (RNA), Presidency of the Council of Ministers (PCM), 292/1941, 3.

4. Ioanid, Kelso, and Cioabă, "Anuţa Brânzan," in *Tragedia romilor*, 111–162.

5. RNA, General Inspector of the Constabulary (IGJ), 126/1942, 10.

6. For more on Jewish and Romani resistance, see Stefan Ionescu, *Jewish Resistance to 'Romanization', 1940–44* (New York: Palgrave MacMillan, 2015).

7. RNA, IGJ, 126/1942, 209.

8. Ioanid, Kelso, and Cioabă, *Tragedia romilor*, 37.

9. Michelle Kelso, "Gypsy Deportations from Romania to Transnistria 1942–1944," in *In the Shadow of the Swastika: The Gypsies during the Second World War*, ed., Donald Kenrick (Hatfield, England: University of Hertfordshire Press, 1999), 109.

10. For more on the persecution of Romania's Jews, see: International Commission on the Holocaust in Romania, Elie Wiesel, Tuvia Friling, Radu Ioanid, Mihail E. Ionescu, and L. Benjamin, *Final report* (Iaşi, Romania: Polirom, 2005); Radu Ioanid, *Evreii sub regimul Antonescu* (Bucureşti, Romania: Editura Hasefer, 1997), 316–21.

11. Ionescu, *Jewish Resistance*, 134.

12. Sybil Milton, "Gypsies and the Holocaust," *The History Teacher*, 24, 4 (1991): 375–87; Slawomir Kapraliski, "Identity Building and the Holocaust: Roma Political Nationalism," *Nationalities Papers*, 25, 2 (1997): 269–83; Michael Stewart, "Remembering Without Commemoration: The Mnemonics and Politics of Holocaust Memories among European Roma," *Journal of the Royal Anthropological Institute*, 10, 3 (2004): 561–82; Sybil Milton, "Hidden Lives: Sinti and Roma Women" in *Experience and Expression: Women, the Nazis, and the Holocaust*, eds., Elizabeth R. Baer and Myrna Goldenberg (Detroit: Wayne State UniversityPress, 2003), 69.

13. Myrna Goldenberg, "Sex-Based Violence and the Politics and Ethics of Survival," in *Different Horrors, Same Hell: Gender and the Holocaust*, eds., Myrna Goldenberg and Amy H. Shapiro (Seattle: University of Washington Press, 2013).

14. For more on children and genocides, see Samuel Totten, ed., *The Plight and Fate of Children During and Following Genocide.* (New Brunswick, NJ: Transaction Publishers, 2014).

15. Michelle Kelso, "Romani Women and the Holocaust: Testimonies of Sexual Violence in Romanian–controlled Transnistria," in *Women and Genocide: Gendered Experiences of Violence, Survival, and Resistance*, eds., JoAnn DiGeorgio-Lutz and Donna Gosbee (Toronto, ON: Canadian Scholars' Press, 2016), 37–72.

16. Marion A. Kaplan, *Between Dignity and Despair: Jewish Life in Nazi Germany* (Oxford University Press, 1999); Elizabeth R. Baer and Myrna Goldenberg, eds., *Experience and Expression: Women, the Nazis, and the Holocaust* (Detroit: Wayne State University Press, 2003); Anna Reading, *The Social Inheritance of the Holocaust: Gender, Culture, and Memory* (New York: Palgrave Macmillan, 2002).

17. Joan Ringelheim, "The Split Between Gender and the Holocaust," in *Women and the Holocaust*, ed., Dalia Ofer and Lenore Weitzman (New Haven, CT: Yale University Press, 1998), 340–50; Joan, Ringelheim, "Women and the Holocaust: A Reconsideration of Research," *Signs* 10, 4 (1985): 741–61.

18. Carol Rittner and John K. Roth, eds., *Different Voices: Women and the Holocaust* (New York: Paragon House, 1993); Dalia Ofer and Lenore Weitzman, eds., *Women in the Holocaust* (New Haven, CT: Yale University Press, 1998); Goldenberg and Shapiro, *Different Horrors, Same Hell*, 2013).

19. Goldenberg and Shapiro, *Different Horrors*, 4.

20. While Jacobs is also speaking about sexual violence, her platform can be viewed more broadly. See Janet L. Jacobs, *Memorializing the Holocaust: Gender, Genocide and Collective Memory* (London: I.B. Tauris, 2010), 44–5.

21. All testimonies are available in Ioanid, Kelso, and Cioabă, *Tragedia romilor*, 2009. The English translations from Romanian are mine.

22. From 1994–96, and again in 2004, I was a Fulbright Grantee in Romania working on this research.

23. See Laurence Langer, *Holocaust Testimonies: The Ruins of Memory* (New Haven, CT: Yale University Press, 1991); Henry Greenspan, *On Listening to Holocaust Survivors: Recounting and Life History* (Westport, CT: Praeger Publishers, 1998); Dori Laub, "On Holocaust Testimony and Its 'Reception' within Its Own Frame, as a Process in Its Own Right: A Response to "Between History and Psychoanalysis" Review, *History and Memory* 21, 1 (2009 Spring/Summer):127–50; Annette Wieviorka, *The Era of the Witness* (Ithaca, NY: Cornell University Press, 2006); Dan Stone, *The Liberation of the Camps: The End of the Holocaust and Its Aftermath* (Cambridge, MA: Yale University Press, 2015).

24. Geoffrey Hartman, *The Longest Shadow: In the Aftermath of the Holocaust* (New York: Palgrave Macmillan, 2002), 136.

25. Kelso, "Gypsy Deportations," 113.

26. RNA, IGJ, 43/1943, 260–2.

27. Vladimir Solonari, *Purifying the Nation: Population Exchange and Ethnic Cleansing in Nazi-Allied Romania* (Washington, DC: Woodrow Wilson Center Press, 2010).

28. Roland Clark, "New Models, New Questions: Historiographical Approaches to the Romanian Holocaust," *European Review of History: Revue europeenne d'histoire* 19, 2 (2012): 303–20.

29. For more on Romani slavery, see Petre Petcuț, "Prețurile sclavilor rromi în țara românească 1593-1653," *Anularul Centrului de Studii Rome* 1 (2008.): 11–22.

30. Viorel Achim, *The Roma in Romanian History* (Budapest: Central European University Press, 2004).

31. Ibid.

32. Ben M. Thorne, "Assimilation, Invisibility, and the Eugenic Turn in the 'Gypsy Question' in Romanian Society, 1938–1942," *Romani Studies* 21, 2 (2011): 177–205.

33. Radu Ioanid, *The Holocaust in Romania: The Destruction of Jews and Gypsies under the Antonescu Regime, 1940-1944* (Chicago: Ivan Dee, 2000); Kelso, "Gypsy Deportations," 1999.

34. For more on Nazi racial policy, see Michael Burleigh and Wolfang Wippermann, *The Racial State: Germany, 1933–1945* (Cambridge, MA: Cambridge University Press, 1991). For more on Romanian eugenics, see Maria Bucur, *Eugenics and Modernization in Interwar Romania* (Pittsburg: University of Pittsburg Press, 2002); Thorne, "Assimilation, Invisibility," 2011.

35. Ioanid, Kelso, and Cioabă, *Tragedia romilor*, 4.

36. Ioanid, *Holocaust in Romania*, 2000.

37. Kelso, "Gypsy Deportations," 109.

38. Jean Ancel, "Tragedia romilor și tragedia evreilor din România: asemănări și deosebiri," in *Lacrimi rome*, ed., Luminița Mihai Cioabă (București, Romania: Ro Media, 2006), 32.

39. Ioanid, Kelso, and Cioabă, *Tragedia romilor*, 93.

40. RNA, IGJ, 130/1942, 127–31.

41. Ioanid, Kelso, and Cioabă, *Tragedia romilor*, 376.

42. Michelle Kelso, director. *Hidden Sorrows: The Persecution of Romanian Gypsies during WWII*. In the Shadow Productions, 2005. DVD.

43. Kelso, "Gypsy Deportations," 116.

44. Ancel, "Tragedia romilor şi tragedia evreilor," 17.

45. Jeanne Ward and Mendy Marsh, "Sexual Violence Against Women and Girls in War and Its Aftermath: Realities, Responses and Required Resources," in *Symposium on Sexual Violence in Conflict and Beyond*, 21 (2006), 4. Kelso, "Romani Women," 2016.

46. Ibid.

47. Ioanid, Kelso, and Cioabă, *Tragedia romilor*, 180.

48. Kelso, *Hidden Sorrows*, 2005.

49. Achim, *Roma in Romanian History*, 2004.

50. Radu Ioanid, "Studiu Introductiv," in *Tragedia romilor deportați in Transnistria, 1942–1945*, ed. Radu Ioanid, Michelle Kelso, and Luminița Cioabă. (Iaşi, Romania: Polirom. 2009), 46.

51. Ionescu, *Jewish Resistance*, 451.

52. Ioanid, Kelso and Cioabă, "Anuța Brânzan," in *Tragedia romilor*, 362.

53. Ioanid, "Studiu Introductiv," in *Tragedia romilor*, 44.

54. Locals had been resettled in other areas and their houses confiscated for the use of the Romanian regime for Roma deportees. Ioanid, Kelso, and Cioabă, *Tragedia romilor*, 344–5.

55. Ioanid, Kelso, and Cioabă, "Anuța Brânzan," in *Tragedia romilor*, 121.

56. RNA, IGJ, 130/1942, 516.

57. Ioanid, Kelso and Cioabă, "Anuța Brânzan," in *Tragedia romilor*, 130–1.

58. Ibid., 135–6.

59. Ioanid, Kelso, and Cioabă, "Lucia Mihai," in *Tragedia romilor*, 104–10.

60. Ibid., 106–7.

61. Ibid., 107.

62. Valerica Stanescu (Romani survivor) in discussion with author. October 2007.

63. Ioanid, Kelso, and Cioabă, "Enuța Spiridon," in *Tragedia romilor*, 153–64.

64. Kelso, *Hidden Sorrows*, 2005.

65. RNA, IGJ, 43/1943, 260–2.

66. Kelso, *Hidden Sorrows*, 2005.

67. Kelso, "Gypsy Deportations," in *In the Shadow*, 121.

68. Ioanid, Kelso, and Cioabă, "Enuța Spiridon," in *Tragedia romilor*, 156.

69. Ibid., 158–9.

70. For the effects of armed conflicts on gender-based violence, in particular sexual violence, see Mendy Marsh, Susan Purdin, and Sonia Navani, "Addressing Sexual Violence in Humanitarian Emergencies," *Global Public Health* 1, 2 (2006): 133–46.

71. Ibid., 137.

72. Elisa von Joeden-Forgey, "The Devil in the Details: 'Life Force Atrocities' and the Assault on the Family in Times of Conflict," *Genocide Studies and Prevention* 5, 1 (2010):1–19.

73. Dumitru Tranca (Romani survivor and retired construction worker) in discussion with the author, July 1999.

74. Kelso, "Gypsy Deportations," in *In the Shadow*, 117.

75. Kelso, *Hidden Sorrows*, 2005.

76. Sandra G. Harding, ed., *The Feminist Standpoint Theory Reader: Intellectual and Political Controversies* (New York: Routledge, 2004).

Birangona

Rape Survivors Bearing Witness in War and Peace in Bangladesh[1]

Bina D'Costa

On a mild September morning in 2011, three members from the International Crimes Tribunal (ICT) investigation team came to my house. The traffic in Dhaka city was horrendous. The investigators decided to make use of the precious time by interviewing me on our way to the ICT. They were interested to hear about my work with Birangona and the war babies. While I have much respect for everything that the investigators were doing to include the experiences of Birangona and war babies in their investigations into the violence during the 1971 war with Pakistan, I was quite taken aback by the abruptness of their questions: "How many did you find? Where? Give us their contact details please." My insistence that not many would be keen to share their stories publicly, especially with police investigators, was ignored; yet I did not give in easily. Women's testimonies, in this case, those of the Birangona, self-consciously serve within a liberation lineage where the most oppressed and invisible subject is the powerful, speaking woman. The narrating of history by Birangona and by other witnesses of sexual and reproductive crimes before the ICT importantly gives voice to the sexual and psychological torture used as a strategy by the Pakistani war machine during the war in 1971.

Waiting to testify for long periods before providing evidence and then having to face the accused and the defense team are not easy tasks. Yet, Birangona women testified in front of the ICT, in an attempt to share their experiences in a public tribunal in 1994. They also testified in other women-friendly platforms, such as the Liberation War Museum in Bangladesh, at the ECCC (Extraordinary Chambers in the Courts of Cambodia) in 2013, and at the Comfort Women's Public Tribunal in 2000, known as the Tokyo Tribunal.

Uncovering the truth from a shroud of erroneous national conscious-ness is a prerequisite for a nation's reconciliation with its own past. When the wall of silence that surrounds abuses of women's human rights breaks down with testimonies and evidence, how do we then translate emotions and passions into practical actions? I address this query by focusing on the vulnerability of women survivors of the 1971 war whose needs both the state and civil society have failed to address in a meaningful and responsive way.

This chapter focuses on two simultaneous processes that reveal the emerging paradox of recognition of rape as a crime of war. First, efforts by feminists and practitioners focusing on gender issues were directed toward making rape and sexual violence visible in formal war crime trial processes. These efforts contributed to a certain kind of *hypervisibility* making it difficult to distinguish between silence as a speech act that is useful for individual women's resilience, and silence that needs to be ana-lyzed to emphasize recognition for projects of justice.[2]

The second argument that this chapter follows, is that all representation—in language, narrative, image, or testimonies—is based on memory. Collective memory is not a fixed entity; instead, each genera-tion is influenced by social and political changes that cause the reshaping of a shared historical discourse.[3] Trials that bring forward processes of collective memorialization by questioning silence also homogenize the diversity of all women's reactions to rape. The feminization of vulnerabil-ity and shame in trial proceedings and texts can only be attributed to a system where women are subjected to everything except just laws. Based on primary research carried out in the International Crimes Tribunal of Rwanda (ICTR), International Crimes Tribunal, Bangladesh (ICT), and the International Criminal Court (ICC), this chapter articulates that these processes are manifested in the silencing of rape victims not only in society, but in the courts.

The chapter begins by examining women's experiences of sexual violence and torture in "Muktijudhyo" (the Bangladesh Liberation War of 1971). It then goes on to provide a brief account of the war and the responses to Birangona in the immediate aftermath of the war. Through a brief analysis of the Peoples' Tribunal of 1994, this chapter then argues for a gender-sensitive and safe space for women to share their memories of sex- and gender-based violence during this time. The final part of the chapter discusses the broader contexts of women's advocacy in the region and elsewhere, in redressing rape and sexual violence.

THE CONTEXT: RECOVERING THE PAST

The Cambodian Defenders Project, in partnership with the Victim Support Section of the ECCC convened the Asia-Pacific Regional Women's Hearing on Gender-based violence in 2012. Testimonies were presented by survivors and witnesses of sexual violence perpetrated during the conflicts in the region—Cambodia (1975–79), Bangladesh (1971), Nepal (1996–2006), and Timor-Leste (1974–99).[4] Saleha Begum, aged fifty-five, recounts her story. She was fourteen years old in 1971. Begum tells how the Pakistani army and their local collaborators, the "Razakars", abducted Begum, her sister, and one of her neighbors. She recalled, "The soldiers committed all kinds of sexual orgy on us,"[5] including sodomy. Begum was also a witness to the torture, rape, and murder of many girls during the conflict. For two months, she was repeatedly and brutally raped in front of her sisters and other girls, which caused severe vaginal bleeding and permanent scars. Then she was transferred to the Golmari Camp in Khulna, where she remained for another two months. Begum, her sister, and six other girls and women who became pregnant, were taken to a nearby bridge to be killed. Although she was shot in the leg, she survived; her sister and the other six rape victims, however, died that day. Begum gave birth four months after liberation, resulting in abandonment by her family and the community.[6]

Begum started working as a domestic helper, and got married following Bangladesh's independence. When Begum told her husband about her ordeals in 1971, he at first wanted to divorce her, but he was deterred because, at the time, she was again pregnant. She gave birth to a daughter. Begum's in-laws abandoned her, and rejected the daughter, who was unable to meet her paternal grandparents until she was fourteen years old. Begum's daughter is very proud of her mother for speaking out.[7]

Mosamma Rajia Khatun Kamla, aged fifty-five, in her testimony at the same hearing, said she was only thirteen years old when she suffered rape, sexual slavery, unlawful confinement, and torture.[8] To protect her from the Pakistani soldiers, Khatun's parents married her off and sent to stay with her in-laws. When the Pakistani army attacked the village, Khatun escaped to the forest along with her mother-in-law. The next day, she learned that her father had been killed, along with many other relatives. She was separated from her mother-in-law, and a Razakar tricked her into going to a military camp. There, she was stripped naked and tied to a pillar. She was raped by six soldiers, one after another, and was left tied to the pole for the entire night. Her vagina had been permanently injured due to the brutal sexual violence. She was detained in the camp for fifteen days and repeatedly raped during that time. When her rapists were no longer able to perform vaginal sex because she was very swollen, they performed anal and oral sex, spreading the semen over her face. She witnessed many other rapes, torture, and executions at the military camp. After fifteen days, she was ordered to work as a cleaner in the camp. She was given the task of washing the Pakistani army uniforms, although she could barely walk because of swelling and injuries to her anus and vagina. She managed to escape by hiding in a pond. When the soldiers could not find her, they randomly shot into the pond. Naked, she made her way to the other side of the pond with a bamboo stick. There she found the house of an old woman, and the two hid together. The old woman gave her some bananas and clothes, and advised her to go to India as a refugee. On the road to India, she, along with others, witnessed many atrocities perpetrated by the Pakistani military and their Bangladeshi collaborators, including rape and murder. Eventually she met "muktijodhyas" (freedom fighters) who took her to a safe haven and provided her with medical care. When one of the muktijodhyas took her to his own house, the woman there refused to allow her in. With no food, she slept in a cowshed, surviving by hiding and begging.[9] She recalls, "After liberation, I could not find work, because people could see from my scars that I was a rape victim, and no one gave me food or shelter."

The Hearing Report further documents how Khatun was deceived by a man into working in a brothel. He assured her that it was a place for rape victims to get help. The report continues to note that at first, the brothel owner, Shushuma, was much kinder than many others she had asked for help, giving her food and shelter, and allowing her to bathe. She was provided medical treatment for her vaginal injuries. She states, "Then I realized she was treating me so that she could use me as a prostitute."[10] When she refused to have sex with her first customer, she was beaten brutally. She was trapped and forced to stay there for three years, where she eventually met her husband as a customer. After buying her from the brothel owner, he brought her to his house, where she discovered he already had one wife and three children; she was rejected by his family. Still, she remained and gave birth to two sons. When her sons were still young (one, an infant, and the other five years old), her husband died. She and her children were thrown out by her in-laws. With nowhere else to turn and two sons to support, she returned to prostitution. She states, "I still remember those days, though forty years have passed, and still I have not received justice." Her sons, now fully grown, have faced stigma throughout their lives because their mother was raped during the Liberation War. She concludes, "I came here to share my story, but it is not about me only, but about the millions, all those who were killed, tortured and raped in 1971."[11]

These two testimonies vividly illustrate the strategic use of rape as a genocide tactic in Muktijudhyo.[12] Although no accurate statistics are available, in Bangladesh it is generally accepted that in 1971, an estimated two hundred thousand Bengali girls and women were raped by soldiers. This figure has been cited by feminist scholars elsewhere;[13] others cite that some twenty-five thousand were raped.[14] Based on my own research, especially interviews with medical practitioners, social workers, and government officials who worked at that time in Bangladesh, I believe that a very large number of women and girls, both Bengali and of other ethnic groups, such as the Biharis, were targeted during 1971.[15] Yet, women's narratives that directly speak to the war crimes of 1971 have been excluded from the official history. In this context, certain narratives were privileged and validated, while other narratives were silenced to create an "acceptable" national story.[16]

National interpretations of rape of women saw these experiences as being less about women themselves than about the challenge to Bengali nationalist and masculine identity. While the war ended Pakistani rule in Bangladesh, existing power relations, political hierarchies, and limited political and cultural ties with Pakistan persisted. The inevitable struggle for power in the years following the war, divisions between liberation leaders, and the heavy dependence of the governments on political and economic alliances, in particular with the Middle East, allowed conservative groups who sided or collaborated with Pakistan during the 1971 war to reestablish a power base and a limited legitimacy. It was in this context that the culture of impunity in Bangladesh developed. After the war ended on December 16, 1971, with Indian army intervention, the three states involved in the war, Bangladesh, India, and Pakistan began prolonged negotiations over the release of approximately ninety-three thousand Pakistani Prisoners of War (POWs), including fifteen thousand civilian men, women, and children captured in Bangladesh/East Pakistan, but detained under Indian authority.[17] The matter was complicated by the Bangladeshi Prime Minister Sheikh Mujibur Rahaman's insistence on trying 1,500 Pakistani POWs for war crimes, and the Pakistani President Zulfikar Ali Bhutto's reluctance to agree to it.[18] On August 28, 1973, India and Pakistan signed a treaty with Bangladesh's support, which provided repatriation of all POWs except 195 prisoners, whom Bangladesh wanted to prosecute for genocide and other war crimes.[19] Postwar tripartite diplomacy between Bangladesh, Pakistan, and India, such as the 1973 India-Pakistan Agreement and the Bangladesh-India repatriation proposals, stipulated that Pakistan would investigate and try those Pakistanis who were found guilty of war crimes. Pakistan also made similar promises in its submissions to the International Court of Justice on May 11, 1973. Unfortunately, these undertakings were not fulfilled afterward.

After 1975, when Sheikh Mujibur Rahman was murdered, Bangladesh was unwilling and unable to hold the perpetrators responsible for the war crimes, which led to a brittle peace in the postwar state. There was growing frustration and resentment among its citizens about the fabrication of history through textbooks and government-sponsored media to serve authoritarian regimes from the post-1975 period until Ershad's resignation in 1990. Additionally, there were various kinds of international, regional, and domestic pressures, including by families of persons stranded in Pakistan.[20]

Bangladesh's history has been written and revised during each change of political regime, a process further complicated by the influence of military and religious elites. Eventually the reinstatement of some of the infamous pro-Pakistani political leaders who were directly responsible for the genocide committed in 1971 led to the construction of separate and parallel histories: one that existed in the official discourse, and others that existed in micro-narratives, in memory, and in lived experience. While the gender aspects of this deliberate suppression of women's experiences of sexual violence during war have been investigated at length by feminist researchers, what remains is the question of how to bargain with a patriarchal state without compromising the agenda for justice, should suppressed stories come out.[21] Local initiatives by Bangladeshi feminist or civil society organizations made several attempts to organize platforms for silenced voices to be heard, but they remained marginalized and unstable. The People's Tribunal proceedings in 1993 discussed later in the chapter, and the Oral History Publication by Ain o Salish Kendra (ASK), which came out in 2001, are two examples in which pro-Liberation civil society[22] and feminist human rights organizations made efforts to bring women's voices to the foreground.[23] Before discussing these initiatives, it is important to first elaborate on the historical events of the 1971 war, and the initial responses to Birangona.

MUKTIJUDHYO: 1971

Anti-colonial nationalism reached its peak in South Asia after World War II. Finally, on June 3, 1947, the British Government announced the Mountbatten Plan, a policy that recognized the inevitability of the partition of India. The Plan was implemented with the birth of Pakistan on August 14, 1947, under the provisions of the British Indian Independence Act 1947. Pakistan was comprised of five provinces in two regions: Punjab, Sindh, the North-West Frontier Province (NWFP), Baluchistan in West Pakistan and East Pakistan, which later became Bangladesh.

During their twenty-four years of union, the two regions of Pakistan enjoyed an uneasy partnership marked by intermittent regional, economic, political, and cultural conflicts. Tension reached its peak after a national election in 1970 escalated into an armed conflict in March 1971. For over nine months the Pakistani Army tried to subdue the rebellious civilian Bengali population. A guerrilla insurgency began in March, and with armed Indian assistance, Bangladesh finally attained its independence in December 1971. Much has been written on this war, and in recent times various accounts have also documented women's diverse experiences of the war.[24]

The Liberation War of Bangladesh was very much a story of women. Although the exact number is unknown, many women participated as active combatants in the war. Women also assisted the freedom fighters in a range of ways, for example, by hiding them in their houses in times of crisis and providing them with food and medicine. When men in local communities fled the areas in fear of army persecution, or to fight in the guerrilla warfare, women took care of the families.[25] After the war, the many widows were responsible to take care of children and the elders alone. Finally, women were targeted for rape and forced impregnation by the Pakistani military.

"Birangona" was the term officially introduced by the first Prime Minister of Bangladesh, Sheikh Mujibur Rahman, popularly known as "Bangabandhu", to acknowledge the sacrifice of women for the freedom of Bangladesh in 1971.[26] The literal translation of the word is "war heroine." Originally its use was intended to honor all women—political activists, freedom fighters, rape survivors, and so on—who participated in the national struggle. The term Birangona was also intended to give rape survivors an honorary status and to provide them with equal access to privileges in the public sector, such as the education and employment rights granted to male freedom fighters.[27]

The term Birangona, however, became a distinct marker, or a boundary, that identified these women as victims of rape and often subjected them to humiliation and abuse. As Faustina Pereira points out, by its very nature, the term Birangona was a restrictive privilege. So strong was the stigma of rape in Bangladesh that most women did not take advantage of the title, "because to do so would be tantamount to focusing on the scar of rape on the victim, thus forcing her to risk a social death."[28] However, it was not only the naming that added to the stigma, but Bangladeshi society's rejection of the women and girls who were subjected to sexual torture in 1971. The presence of the Birangona is a stinging reminder to the state of how the norm of *purdah*, or female seclusion, collapsed during the war when men were unable to defend their women. Not only were women left unprotected and exposed to sexual violence during the war, but many were abandoned by their families afterward.

As a response to this complex situation, concerned Bengalis, especially the cultural elites of the country, recently coined a new term: "nari jodhya", or, "women combatants". Nonetheless, without an informed plan of action to change the patriarchal traditions and societal norms from which the stigma emanates, the introduction of new or innovative terms did not prove adequate to positively address the situation of the Birangona. Furthermore, jodhya in its conventional interpretation implies an active combat role. This interpretation does not take into account the experiences of many women whose lives were changed dramatically by war outside this paradigm. Indeed, their sacrifice has virtually gone undocumented, although not unseen. Despite some attempts to respond to their economic and security needs, as discussed below, the state was unable to counter the social rejection of Birangona. On the other hand, it also blurs the category between women combatants who were on the frontline, and women who were victims of rape and gender violence.

RESPONSES TO BIRANGONA

Men who fought in the Liberation war were referred to as Muktijodhya, "Mukti" meaning freedom and "jodhya" meaning combatant. The most common translation of this is, "freedom fighters." On April 4, 1971, the Bangladesh Armed Forces were formed with Bengali–manned battalions of the East Bengal Regiment (EBR) under the command of Col M. A. G. Osmani, a retired officer of the Pakistan Army. During the first Bangladesh Sector Commanders Conference for better management and coordination, July 11–17, 1971, the battle zones throughout Bangladesh/East Pakistan were divided into eleven sectors. Each sector had Bengali commanders in charge of the military operations; all of them had defected from the Pakistani armed force. Tajuddin Ahmed, the prime minister of Bangladesh's government-in-exile, stated in a speech on Free Bangla Radio on April 11, 1971, "Today, a mighty army is being formed around the nucleus of professional soldiers from the Bengal Regiment and EPR (East Pakistan Rifles) who have rallied to the cause of the liberation struggle."[29] The "Mukti Bahini" (Liberation Army) faced no manpower problem as Bengalis volunteered by the thousands to join them, numbering an estimated one hundred seventy-five thousand. This also included a large number of deserters from the East Pakistan Rifles, East Bengal Regiment, and the Bengali police force.[30]

While both men and women participated in the struggle for independence as Mukti Jodhya (freedom fighters), women were generally excluded from most honorific titles and awards; the highest bravery decorations of the Bangladeshi state were reserved for those who served in the armed forces. Internally, the overwhelming support for the Mukti Bahini created a sense of insecurity among the Awami League leadership, resulting in the setting up of yet another exclusive guerrilla force, the "Mujib Bahini" (named after Sheikh Mujibur Rahman), which consisted of die-hard supporters of both the AL and Mujib.[31] As Bangladeshi society transitioned from violence toward a more democratic or liberal political system, various forms of masculinity continued to influence the postwar society, forming yet another patriarchal social order. Countless Mukti Jodhya, those who surrendered arms and returned to their civilian lives, lived in dire poverty. There were also those who continued to carry weapons, and either became involved in criminal activities or were slowly absorbed by political parties. In addition, in the first five years of Bangladesh's sovereign life, the parallel politics between the Mujib Bahini and the Mukti Bahini created factionalism in Bangladesh politics, which influenced the consciousness of Bangladesh's armed forces.

Acknowledging the courage and sacrifice of the Mukti Jodhya, the government awarded them with public service quotas to enter into various government departments. Bangladeshis commemorated them through patriotic songs, poems, and literature. On the other hand, women were not beneficiaries of the actual or symbolic rewards. While there were no awards, even for women who were commended for their roles as active combatants, the government introduced a scheme for monthly pensions or grants, and job quotas. Although neither men nor women participated in the liberation war with some form of benefits in mind, the government's poorly planned and biased policies created frustration within the community.

Immediately after the independence, some Birangona were treated with respect. Mukti Jodhya, in formal and informal conversations with me, indicated that they helped the women rescued from the rape camps in any way they could, such as offering them food, water, and medicine, and taking them to health care units or back to their families.[32] One of the freedom fighters I spoke with stated, "We always treated the women with respect and we were genuinely concerned about their suffering."[33]

In contrast, the initial responses of the women's families were not positive. In middle-class families, the issue of rape was treated with secrecy, and many families never revealed their daughters were taken by the Pakistani Army. A shroud of silence covered their stories. Some families took pregnant women to clinics for abortions. When asked, respondent B said, "It still remains as a scar in my heart. The government allowed abortion on a mass scale. They did not want any Pakistani child. Either they were to be aborted or to get out of the country as soon as possible. We had incubators and we were prepared to take the premature babies."

Those families that could afford to exile their daughters to neighboring India or one of the Western countries preferred to do so in order to quietly get rid of their family shame. If the women were in an advanced stage of pregnancy, they were left in rehabilitation centers or clinics to give birth, after which the babies were given up for adoption.[34] When I asked Geoffrey Davis,[35] who worked as a physician in Bangladesh immediately after the war, if there were some women who were reluctant to have abortions or give up their babies for adoption he said, "Well ... a few of them did." When asked if he knew what happened to them he answered, "I have no idea. ISS (International Social Service) was there to get as many babies as they could. Because there were less and less babies available for adoption in America and Western Europe and they wanted to get as many babies as they could get."

As I stated earlier, twenty-five thousand cases of pregnancy were reported after the war. However, no statistics—official or otherwise—

exist to my knowledge indicating the number of women who had abortions or the number of babies sent to other countries.

Several political developments that have contributed to the silence surrounding rape in Bangladesh can be identified. First, because reintegration into society was given the highest priority, rape as a sexual and reproductive crime received no significant attention from the government and its elite segments despite its inclusion as a crime in the International Crimes Tribunal Act of 1973. Bangladesh signed the Rome Statute on the Establishment of an International Criminal Court on September 16, 1999, and now formally recognizes that rape, sexual aggression, and gender-specific violence constitute war crimes and crimes against humanity. The statute has still not been ratified by subsequent governments. Second, as mentioned earlier, the postwar diplomacy between Bangladesh, Pakistan, and India compromised the trial of war criminals and their collaborators and had serious consequences for those seeking justice in postwar Bangladesh. Pakistan never kept its promise to try those who were charged. Third, the gradual rehabilitation of Bengali collaborators of the Pakistani Army into Bangladesh politics at both local and state government levels silenced the micro-narratives through direct or indirect coercion. In particular, with the lifting of the ban on extremist religious political parties, the Birangona issue was buried further.[36]

Despite Mahila Parishad's and other senior women's strong support for rehabilitation, there was little space for protest and advocacy for women's justice during the fifteen years of military dictatorship. Instead of the advocacy for gender justice, senior women policymakers and practitioners were more focussed on getting the Birangona reintegrated in the wider Bangladeshi society. The demand for justice for sexual and reproductive crimes of 1971 was occurring in the larger context for demanding justice for all Bengali victims of war crimes, but not in the context of gender justice. Consequently, there was no coordinated and sustained feminist movement or consciousness to make available a "pro-gender justice" political language at that time.

While in the Pakistani context "purity" meant creating a "proper" Muslim identity that would fit the Muslim Pakistani imagination, in the context of Bangladesh, it meant purging the state of Pakistani blood.

Children were vivid reminders of the attack on a pure Bengali identity. Therefore, the Bangladeshi state responded to the issue of wartime pregnancy in a way it perceived as legitimate: it exercised its authority over women's bodies and their maternal role through abortion and forced-adoption programs. The needs of the women were insignificant in this nationalist construction of identity. Clinics, international adoption agencies, and religious organizations facilitated these programs, acting as surface mechanisms for the state, often against the wishes of some of the women, thereby victimizing them for a second time. As far as Bangladesh was concerned, the task of flushing out "impure" Pakistani blood was necessary for the honor of the new nation. The abstract notions of purity and honor are dangerous rationales for which women often pay heavily. The appropriation of birth, denying it, and, when possible, stopping it through state abortions, demonstrates the power of the state over women's bodies when women have little or no control.[37]

During this time women were symbolically distanced from birth by the nation state's narrative. The abortion and adoption programs carried out by the Bangladesh Government following the war indicate the forcible appropriation of women's bodies in the interests of the nation. In the context of the mass suicide of women during the 1947 Partition, Urvashi Butalia argued that these actions were approved because women were protecting the purity of the community whose borders they constituted.[38] Similarly, in 1971, the issue of choice became even more problematic in terms of the complex intersections of gender, religion, and national interests, in which women were trapped. Social workers, government officials, and medical staff working in the rehabilitation centers and clinics were, like the Mukti Jodhya, genuinely compassionate toward the survivors. Geoffrey Davis recalled many women's stories:

> Some of the stories they told us were appalling. Being raped again and again and again by large Pathan soldiers. You couldn't believe that anybody would do that! All the rich and pretty ones were kept for the officers and all the other ones were distributed among the other ranks. And the women had it really rough. They did not get enough to eat. When they got sick, they got no treatment. A lot of them died in those camps. There was an air of disbelief about the whole thing ... but the evidence clearly showed that it did happen.[39]

In my interviews, I was particularly interested in whether the Birangona women had a choice in the matter of pregnancy and the high rates of terminations that took place. When I asked Geoffrey if the social workers and the medical personnel involved respected women's choices to either have abortion or not to go through with it he replied, "Nobody wanted to talk about it. You could not ask questions and get an answer. Quite often it would be that they couldn't remember. And the men didn't want to talk about it at all! Because according to them the women had been *defiled*. And women's status in Bangladesh was pretty low anyway. If they had been defiled, they had no status at all. They might as well be dead."[40]

In interviews with the ASK oral history team, both Nilima Ibrahim and Maleka Khan, prominent social workers heavily involved in the rehabilitation program of Birangona, noted that given the nature of social relations and family attitudes, women effectively had no choice.

The attitudes and decisions taken by the social workers and medical staff in the rehabilitation centers similarly reflected patriarchal, traditional values about family, community norms, and state policies, and thus endorsed decisions to reintegrate women into society as soon as possible by keeping their trauma and ordeal a secret, contributing to the silencing in official documents and personal narratives. Respondent B, who worked in the rehabilitation projects, and was particularly involved in the adoption programs, commented, "There was a wound. We tried to rehabilitate them, tried to accept the situation they were in. And we would never write names, neither addresses. Stigma would remain if people knew."[41]

In the aftermath of the war in Bangladesh, Badrunnesa Ahmad, Bangladesh's first Minister of Education (1973–75), and Nurjehan Murshid, State Minister for Health and Social Welfare (1972–73) and Minister of Social Affairs and Planning (1973–75), in the Parliament demanded justice on behalf of the Birangona. Yet, there also existed a vast power discrepancy between the Birangona and the social workers, government officials, or others who were involved in the government's rehabilitation programs for the women. The shame and stigma attached to sexual violence were not challenged. Instead there was an implicit charity-focused approach that denied women the opportunity to voice their protests if they were unwilling to cooperate with the state's prescribed policies. Women were cast as victims, and only as victims did they deserve the state's assistance.

In these contexts, it was almost impossible for women to speak out as strong and outspoken survivors.

On January 7, 1972, in response to the development of women's movements, the Government set up the Central Organization for Women's Rehabilitation, to institutionalize women's rehabilitation programs and place them under the management of the national central women's rehabilitation board which coordinated the government's postwar policies with regard to women. The chairperson, Sufia Kamal, along with Taslima Abed, Shahera Ahmed, Hajera Khatun, and others, started the rehabilitation programs in two houses in Eskaton, Dhaka.[42] In 1974, the name of the board was changed by legislation to the Bangladesh Women's Rehabilitation and Welfare Foundation. Eventually, the government changed the profile of the Foundation and merged it under the Women's Division of the Women's and Children Affairs Ministry. Programs such as those "to free women from the *unchosen* [my emphasis] curse of motherhood" and to encourage men to marry Birangona reveal that patriarchal and traditional beliefs played out in decisions made in relation to Birangona rehabilitation programs.[43] The state-sponsored abortion and adoption programs clearly aspired to prioritize the national identity of Bengalis, identifying the children carrying Pakistani blood as liabilities to the purity of the nation-state. In an atmosphere filled with nationalistic passion and hatred toward Pakistanis, Birangona who were already vulnerable relied on the state's prescribed policies and were therefore unable to articulate resistance if they had any.[44] Since the pregnant body was a vivid reminder of the Pakistani father, Birangona's reproductive rights belonged to the nation.

As such, the primary goal of the state's rehabilitation programs in relation to Birangona was, not to emancipate, but to reintegrate the women into the traditional gender roles they had previously performed as housewives, mothers, or daughters, effectively silencing their experiences during the conflict. Women's own silence on the other hand guaranteed that the state's rehabilitation programs remained unchallenged. This silence also ensured that the elite narrative construction of the past gained official acknowledgement.[45] However, there were significant efforts made by notable individuals to reclaim the voices of women in the attempted prosecution of war criminals in the early 1990s. After the fall of Hussein Muhammad Ershad, women's groups, and a range of civil society actors, have been much more explicit in their demand for gender-sensitive justice for crimes committed in 1971 and for crimes against minority women, such as in the CHT.

QUESTIONING THE CULTURE OF IMPUNITY

The 1971 war in Bangladesh led to a complete breakdown of state and community. The question of justice assumed great urgency but there was no common understanding of how to achieve it. In the absence of legal norms or any nationally organized political forces, there were several individual and local efforts to respond to the demands for justice. The most successful of all these efforts were led by a single woman, Jahanara Imam. Rumi, her son, participated in the war as a mukti Jodhya (freedom fighter) and was brutally tortured and killed by the Pakistani army in 1971. Her book *Ekatturer Dinguli* (*Those Days of '71*) is an autobiographical record of the violence in 1971.[46]

Popularly known as *shahid jononi* ("martyr mother"), Jahanara Imam began a crusade in January 1992, directed against Golam Azam[47] and other collaborators who had supported Pakistan during the 1971 war and engaged in atrocities and sexual violence against Bangladeshi civilians.[48] On December 29, 1991, Golam Azam was appointed the Aameer (chairperson) of the Jama'at-i-Islami (hereinafter, Jama'at), an extremist Islamic, nationalist party of Bangladesh, that did not support the Liberation movement of Bangladesh, which had its roots in secularism and Bengali national identity.[49] The Jama'at members actively collaborated with the Pakistani army during the war, and as a consequence, was banned after 1971, along with other religious parties.[50] Following significant political changes in Bangladesh, in particular with the Amendment in the Constitution in 1977,[51] and the pro-Islamic tilt in the Zia and Ershad regimes policies, *Jama'at* got back into Bangladesh politics.

Under her leadership, the pro-liberation movement was coordinated and people from various corners, such as intellectuals, students, freedom fighters (both men and women) of the 1971 war, war widows, and families (especially children whose parents had been killed), organized under Projonmyo Ekattur (Generation '71), and supported a massive movement to hold a symbolic People's Tribunal to bring Golam Azam and other war criminals to trial. Imam was elected as the chairperson of the "Ghatok Dalal Nirmul Committee" (Committee for the Elimination of Killers and Collaborators), created on January 19, 1992, to demand the trials of the war criminals.[52] Under her leadership, the "National Coordinating Committee for Realization of Bangladesh Liberation War Ideals and Trial of Bangladesh War Criminals of 1971" was formed in February, 1992, integrating the opposing political parties and the cultural elites of Bangladesh to hold the People's Tribunal. In Jahanara Imam's words, "prompted by our commitment to the values of the Liberation War and love for our country and aggrieved by the failure of the government to try the war criminals," the Committee decided to unearth "evidence of complicity of all collaborators of war crimes, crimes against humanity, killings and other activities."[53]

After three months of intensive organizing and activism, the People's Tribunal was held in Dhaka on March 26, 1992, and nearly two hundred thousand people from all over the country participated as witnesses. This massive popular movement demonstrated that Bangladeshis were indeed interested in seeking justice for 1971. Unfortunately, however, the quality of the Commission reports was very poor, the language emotive rather than reasoned, and it lacked details that would lead to any possible criminal prosecutions. After Imam's death in 1994, political differences significantly weakened the movement.

Despite the intervening years, the silence surrounding the rape of women in 1971 was still prevalent and the sexual violence remained a well-guarded secret within the affected families. Some viewed the "digging into the past" as an unnecessary exercise that would cause them more pain and misery, especially because no organized effort to seek redress had occurred in the country. Moreover, various interest groups ignored the sensitive nature of the women's stories and the fact that disclosing their identities might contribute to the stigma they were forced to bear by their communities. For example, at the aforementioned Dhaka People's Tribunal in 1992, the court was not able to hold the hearings of the testimonies of victims and survivors of the 1971 war due to a government-sponsored assault by the police on the organizers.[54] The Government also filed cases of treason against the organizers, which stagnated the movements afterward.[55]

The three rape survivors who were brought in from the rural areas of Kushtia, a southern region in Bangladesh, to provide testimonies were also unable to narrate their experiences. None of them had clear ideas about the tribunal proceedings, what their testimonies actually signified, and what implications these public testimonies might have in their present lives.[56] The local activists who brought them to Dhaka did not ask them if they wanted to testify either, and they were left in the dark.[57] Yet, their photos and stories appeared in national newspapers the next day. Because of strong ideas around purity and honor, these women were subsequently persecuted and excluded from participating in the life of their communities.[58]

Their ordeals were printed in the media in 1996,[59] and fresh interest in their stories again brought them into the public arena. This experience had a significant impact on the women's increasing reluctance to speak with "outsiders." In addition, women's organizations became very skeptical about bringing Birangona women to speak openly and testify about their experiences at public platforms. Most women still do not feel comfortable in talking about the pain and trauma of 1971. Their discomfort is a combination of traumatic memories, traditional parameters of shame and purity, the stigma attached to the rape experience, and the need to reintegrate into their society and to address basic requirements for survival. In combination, all these have led the women to create their own negotiated survival techniques "just to get on with their lives."[60]

In 1994, Nilima Ibrahim published a two-volume book, *Ami Birangana Bolchi*, the only available collection of testimonies of women survivors in print until 2001 when Ain o Salish Kendra (ASK), a Bangladeshi human rights organization, published its oral history volume. In the preface of the 1998 edition she writes:

> I promised my readers to publish the third volume of *Ami Birangona Bolchi* ("I, the Birangona"). However, I no longer want to do so, for two reasons. First, my physical condition: Writing about the Birangona affected me both physically and emotionally. Second, the present society's conservative mentality. They [society] do not hesitate to call the Birangona sinners. Therefore, I don't want to insult those women all over again who were not allowed to live an easy and normal life even 25 years ago.... In addition,

many compassionate people requested me for their [*Birangona*] contacts. I believe, it wouldn't be right to rub salt on the wounds of those who we coldly banished from our community one day.[61]

In December 1996, the *Shommilito Nari Shomaj* (a broad network of feminist activists in Bangladesh, hereinafter SNS) organized four women's testimonies from Ibrahim's book to be read on Bangladesh Television (BTV). After the telecast, a few Birangona contacted Nilima Ibrahim and the feminist network SNS to share their stories.[62] There was a newspaper report on the communication between some Birangona and the SNS. It revealed that the SNS was approached by one of the women who bluntly said, "I was raped by Pakistani Army in 1971."[63] When SNS activists asked the women who contacted them why they were now coming forward after twenty-six years of silence, one woman replied, "… because now I am getting the courage to do so."[64] Several others gave similar explanations. One rape survivor stated, "I was raped and I would like to tell my son about it but do not know how to do so."[65] These women wanted the Pakistani government and its collaborators to be brought to trial internationally. It was the crucial factor in their decision to communicate with Ibrahim and other social workers whom they trusted. Despite the reactions of Birangona as a result of the TV show, with the memory of the previous trial in 1992 still fresh in their minds, women's groups remained sensitive in bringing the women into public.

Until her death in June 2002, Ibrahim refused to reveal any personal information about the women. In her conversation with me in 2000, she mentioned that she was very concerned about the renewed interest to publicize the stories of Birangona. I realized that she wanted to protect the women's privacy and did not want to cause any further harm to them.[66] This reaction was not surprising considering the way in which women's stories have been exploited or used without any legal, financial, or moral support offered in return.

Nonetheless, their testimonies are crucial for war crime trials to demonstrate the gendered nature of the 1971 war and state policies afterward. It is my contention that a gender-sensitive space can be provided for the Birangona to speak about their experiences in a way that keeps them and their stories safe from further persecution and violence. As I specify later in the chapter, informed strategies, in particular learning from women's groups and movements elsewhere in South Asia, can assist Bangladesh women's groups to pursue this sensitively, with the Birangona's interest first and foremost in mind.

> A small but significantly important number of Birangona have been prepared to come forward and document their narratives. Although women's groups did not pursue the issue, Birangona have also still maintained their demands for justice. Ferdousi Priyobhashini, another courageous Birangona woman who came forward with her story, wrote, I am one of the 250,000 raped women of '71. I am telling you these stories because, those who killed 3 million Bengalis in '71 and raped 250,000 women, still have not been brought to justice.[67]

When I visited Bangladesh in 2002 and spoke with Halima Parveen, she reiterated the demands of other women.[68] Halima's apa (sister) fought in the war and was raped in captivity. She indicated that she would testify and encourage other women to do so and stated, "I will fight with even the last bit of strength I have in my body to demand justice from Bangladesh government and from Pakistan."[69] It is evident that despite the hardship and possible consequences of disclosure, if an appropriate forum is provided, women will come forward to speak. Their desire to tell their stories and seek justice is evidence that if an action-oriented network is organized to seek justice for crimes committed during the 1971 war, some Birangona would be interested in participating. Sharing their war memories in a woman-friendly environment, sensitive to their traditional and cultural restrictions, can help facilitate the participation of many Birangona in this kind of network. Muktijudhyo Jadughar (Liberation War Museum, LWM) in Bangladesh recently has taken the initiative to record the experiences of Birangona. In documenting women's experiences of the war, LWM researchers have used gender sensitive approaches such as maintaining confidentiality and conducting closed-door interviews. In several conferences and public events, the LWM speakers, such as Mofidul Hoque, raised the importance of ensuring justice for Birangona.

Although making women visible is necessary, doing only that is not enough to enable feminists to provide a full analysis of women's exploitation within the nation-state system.[70] While it is possible to arrive at a macro-level understanding of nationalism's gender-blind approach, without looking at micro-level and regional politics a feminist scholarship of postconflict situations will be unable to address the "woman question" in diverse locations. Similar to other regions in South Asia, cultural and regional experiences of women vary immensely, and women respond quite differently—and sometimes from contradictory positions—according to their backgrounds, education, and politics. Birangona, especially those who live in rural areas, might lack the means to reflect on and articulate their own experiences except through the socially accepted norms with which they are already familiar. Focusing on the lived reality of women and offering them choices so that they can decide themselves whether or not they have been silenced in the national writing of history by the state may be more important. This might create the social awareness necessary to serve as the driving force behind a common platform of action.

FRAMING WOMEN'S ISSUES IN BANGLADESH

Despite holding diverse views, Bangladeshi women's organizations have successfully raised numerous feminist issues. The space of social activism is occupied by activists well versed in the social and political movements of South Asia. As political activists, Bengali women contributed to the anti-colonial nationalist struggle for the independence of the Indian sub-continent. During both the anti-colonial movement against the British and the Bangladesh national liberation movement, Muslim Bengali women appeared in public and participated in protests, demonstrations, and other forms of political campaigns for the freedom of their land. Their visibility became an important symbol in the Bengali national movement.

During the national movement of Independence for Bangladesh, women organized and participated in protests against the repressive measures taken by the military regime of Pakistan. The military regime detained numerous political activists and leaders without trial during 1966–70. A group of young women activists, most of whom were associated with leftist organizations, approached the Awami League (AL), the strongest political party in East Pakistan, and with the help of political leaders formed a joint women's action committee to organize the wives and mothers of political prisoners, who advocated for the men's release.[71] This eventually led to the formation of the Bangladesh Mahila Parishad

(Women's Caucus, BMP) in 1972, which is the oldest and largest women's organization in Bangladesh.

Movements for national liberation are rarely extended to the autonomy and liberation of women.[72] Both during the liberation struggle in 1971, and in the aftermath of the creation of Bangladesh, women activists enthusiastically expressed their solidarity in the construction of the new nation-state. However, as Rounaq Jahan observes, despite their significant role in the war, the new government soon marginalized women.[73] The policies for the rehabilitation programs in Bangladesh after 1971 were introduced irrespective of women's wishes and consent. While this was often done for pragmatic reasons, such as an alternative to their social rejection, these practices are evidence of the ways women's rights are subsumed and subordinated under national "rights." Generally, women's liberation has been regarded as being unfavorable to the identity and existence of the national group. During the 1971 nationalist struggle, Muslim Bengali women went out onto the streets in active resistance. This liberating gesture served several purposes: it demonstrated to the Pakistani rulers that Bengali culture was different from West Pakistani traditions, that Bengalis shared similar cultural values regardless of whether they were Hindu or Muslim, and that Bengali women were more liberated than West Pakistani women. Many Muslim Bengali women participated as activists in their country's national movement. Their unique cultural identity became their symbol, and the use of the phrase "Muslim Bengali woman" had a political rather than a religious connotation.

Although their political activism played a crucial role in achieving independence, after their country was born these women were encouraged to go back to their traditional roles as wives, mothers, and daughters, and as protected and vulnerable beings. Moreover, the national movement was not concerned with women's actual emancipation. As a result of their exclusion, the national Liberation War of Bangladesh failed to achieve freedom for all of its citizens. National liberation rhetoric had served to consolidate emotion in order to create an active struggle against the Pakistani Army, using the situation of women. In reality, women were still seen to belong in the private sphere, situated in a complex construction of traditional, religious, and cultural values.

Traditionally, the honor of the family is linked to the virtue of its women, and men are responsible for protecting this honor.[74] The image of Bengali women as cherished and protected mothers, wives, and daughters was, over the years, challenged by an awareness that women are subordinated in the hierarchical gender relations in Bangladesh, which deny them both social power and autonomy over their own lives. The experience of 1971 helped women to raise their concern about their subordination. The norm of female seclusion and the so-called safety of the private sphere was shattered by the 1971 war, when women could not be protected against aggression by their men, and were then abandoned, through no fault of their own.[75]

Since the Liberation War, a Bengali ruling class comprising an unstable class alliance of an underdeveloped bourgeoisie, the military, and the bureaucracy has been in power.[76] Though regimes have changed, rising impoverishment, social differentiation, and aid dependency have persisted. At the same time, increased violence against women in both the public and private spheres has helped to develop a greater awareness of the position of women in Bangladesh. This awareness has also been informed by communication with other states and increased participation in transnational feminist programs, including attendance at international conferences, workshops, and dialogues, and a significant interest worldwide in addressing gender inequality.

Interestingly, the nascent women's movement did not work actively to mobilize support for rape victims. In reflecting on the reasons for this, women leaders offer a variety of perspectives. Many groups and individuals were still hesitant to challenge the society's strong patriarchal traditions and feared that doing so would invite backlash that could hurt the victims more. The groups were very new, with limited scope and membership, and as such still quite vulnerable. Even some organizations, such as Mahila Parishad, that later vocally and successfully challenged the government's stand on gender violence, did not articulate a position on rape at this time.

Some organizations and individuals also wished to remain apolitical, implying that even after more than three decades of independence the stories of women can make some powerful groups uncomfortable and angry. Cautioned by the drastic curtailment of women's rights in Iran and Pakistan, which accompanied the rise of political power of Islamists, the Bangladesh women's movement sought to build public opinion in support of secular politics.[77] During the Decade of Women (1975–85) Bangladesh governments invited women's groups to advise them in preparing official reports for intergovernmental discussions and agreements that provided the opportunity to women's groups to articulate their positions in the government's agenda.[78] With gender equity and poverty alleviation programs at the forefront of development planning, Bangladeshi women researchers and NGO employees were invited to voice their opinions in international conferences and workshops, opening the possibilities of cross-border dialogues. To serve the interests of its development policies, governments encouraged dialogue and the sharing of views and information with women's groups in other countries. Despite the changing political situation in Bangladesh, this facilitated dialogues among women inside Bangladesh and enabled them to create partnerships with women's organizations overseas to address specific issues, especially development and women's empowerment.

While an increase in women's status is essential for gender equity, the issue of violence against women has also been addressed strategically by women's organizations. For example, Ain o Salish Kendra (ASK), BLAST, Shaishob, Shakti, and Nari Pakkhya publicized cases of dowry-related family violence and murder, acid throwing, and rape (including rape while in police custody, and rape of adolescents), creating a public outcry. Their history, activism, and the contemporary politics of Bangladeshi nationhood, within which a vibrant feminist movement thrived, saw these organizations adopt agendas that addressed violence against women, patriarchal dominance, common class problems, labor exploitation, and unequal economic arrangements within specific national contexts. The activism of non-state actors organized into local networks has had a positive impact on agenda-setting, framing and spreading norms, and changing state practices.

The similarities of women's movements in the Indian subcontinent derive from the fact that India, Pakistan, and Bangladesh have a shared colonial past that utilized the situation of women for the existence of the nation-state. Furthermore, regional workshops, conferences, and academic exchanges between activists and scholars regarding women's rights have contributed to the growth of a shared and coherent women's networking and intellectual activism in South Asia. Based on common cultural and traditional backgrounds, and on the shared history of nation-building in different states, these networks have exchanged ideas, formulated strategies, and developed new ways of addressing the historical abuse of women and seeking restitution in the present.

Feminist analyses have contributed to our understanding of sexual violence in armed conflicts, women's roles in peace building, masculinity and violence, gender and national identity politics, and testimonies and memory.[79] However, an assessment of jurisdiction, law, and evidence validate that these remain a challenge in prosecuting sex- and gender-based violence as an international crime. In a conference marking the tenth anniversary of the ICTR judgment on the Akayesu case, Navenethem Pillay, the UN High Commissioner for Human Rights, who also served as a member of the Trial Chamber, explained:

> Rape and sexual violence are sustained by the patterns of gender inequality which cut across geo-political, economical and social boundaries. Justice is needed on the individual and national level to redress rape and other expressions of sex inequality that women experience as a part of their everyday lives, as well as on the international level for sexual violence and other crimes perpetrated in times of conflict and war that are not effectively addressed at the national level.[80]

This case significantly expanded the international community's ability to prosecute gender-based war crimes; and the jurisprudence provided by this has been taken as a starting point to review rape laws elsewhere.[81] A collection of essays that came out of the conference provides critical appraisal of recent developments in rape laws across a range of diverse jurisdictions. Various national jurisprudences considered in this collection reveal that wide-ranging efforts have been carried out allowing a diversity of approaches and traditions.[82] The authors contributing in this volume explain national and international rape law concerns and developments. A particular insight offered by a number of authors, and relevant to this discussion, is that constant pressures from feminists have led to rape law reforms. For example, in postconflict Croatia, voices of feminism and women's activism have been crucial in placing concerns of sexual violence in the political agenda,[83] and in both Australia and the US, sustained feminist activism achieved changes in the formal laws and policies on rape.[84] It is also noted that England and Wales have one of the lowest rape conviction rates in Europe, and despite feminist pressures and reforms and convictions, the sentencing of individuals has been inadequate. Some of the prejudices of national law, such as the divide between private and public spheres, which usually left family relations and abuse in the domestic sphere outside of the protection of national law, is also present in foundational international law, which considers the treatment of citizens as a private matter for each state.[85]

It took decades for the international community to seriously consider and investigate sexual crimes. Four international criminal justice institutions, namely the ICTR, the ICTY (International Criminal Tribunal for the former Yugoslavia), the SCSL (The Special Court for Sierra Leone), and the ICC, played a key role in acknowledging that rape, forced marriage, sexual slavery, and forced prostitution are war crimes, crimes against humanity, and in some instances, acts of genocide.[86] The ground breaking Akayesu case before the ICTR was the first time that an international court recognized that rape constituted an act of genocide. The text of the Akayesu judgement made a discursive shift by naming both women and girls as victims of violence. The Tadić case before the ICTY was the first case where a defendant was specifically charged with rape and sexual violence as crimes against humanity and war crimes.[87] Also, the Kunarac (Foča) case, before the ICTY, resulted in the first international conviction for rape, torture, and enslavement of women and girls as crimes against humanity.[88] However, legal precedents are not enough to oppose sex- and gender-based violence. The capacity of women to be involved in designing their own empowering activities is crucial in any effective justice approach.

CONCLUDING REMARKS: INTERNATIONAL CRIMES TRIBUNAL AND BIRANGONA TESTIMONIES

Women's testimonies have been used in Bangladesh in the ICT in various cases. A prosecution witness in the trial of ATM Azharul Islam,[89] the commander of Rangpur district unit of Al-Badr, testified that the incumbent assistant secretary general of Jama'at-e-Islami along with three Pakistani army members tortured and raped a pregnant woman for about nineteen days at Rangpur Town Hall during 1971. As a result, she lost her six-month-old fetus in womb. Mujibor Rahman Master, in his seventies, testified at the International Crimes Tribunal-1 as the eighth witness, who heard the incident from the victim. Azharul Islam was found guilty on five counts of mass murder and rape, and was sentenced to death.

On May 8, 2014, Abu Asad, third prosecution witness in the case against Jama'at-e-Islami leader, Abdus Subhan, told the ICT how he was forced to work with Subhan, who carried out atrocities in Pabna during the war. Asad, a member of Mujaheed Bahini, a collaborating paramilitary unit, stated, "I also witnessed how the Pakistani army had raped wives and daughters before their husbands and fathers and shot the raped women." At this point he broke down and verified, "Subhan Saheb was present with the army at that time." Subhan has also been sentenced to death for his involvement in targeting Hindus during 1971.

Also, another witness, Momena Begum, gave her testimony in a camera trial that eventually led to the sentencing of Kader Mollah, another Jama'at leader. Mollah was executed in 2014. Momena Begum, similar to the women whose narratives are introduced earlier in the chapter, was only a young girl (twelve years old) during the war. As with other minors, she bears witness to the war. Momena's name was not disclosed when the original verdict of life sentence was announced. However, her testimony was publicized, and her name disclosed, when the Appellate Division converted his life sentence to a death sentence. Momena's testimony came under direct attack from critics of the tribunal who asked whether or not a young girl of that time could identify Mollah so easily. A senior justice campaigner in Bangladesh told me, "We have talked to many victims. Unfortunately, the ICT accidentally disclosed her name. This was quite traumatic for Momena in particular." As the chapter argues, to ensure justice, the women who were victims in 1971 and agreed to provide their testimonies, must first be protected.

The Parliament on January 29, 2015, passed a resolution to recognize the Birangona as freedom fighters by preparing a list of them. Monirul Islam, the Lawmaker from Jessore-2 constituency, placed the proposal before the national parliament. Liberation War Affairs Minister AKM Mozammel Huq said, "The Ministry of Education has been requested to include Birangona in the textbooks. Moreover, it has been discussed in making their allowance Tk. 10,000."[90] While this bill was passed unanimously, the House rejected another lawmaker's proposal to rename Birangona as "Bir Konya". AKM Mozammel Huq said "It will not be wise to rename Birangona as it was named by Bangabandhu Sheikh Mujibur Rahman."

BINA D'COSTA is Fellow and Director of Teaching at the Coral Bell School of Asia Pacific Affairs at the Australian National University. She is author of *Nationbuilding, Gender and War Crimes in South Asia,* and coeditor of *Gender and the Global Politics in the Asia-Pacific.*

NOTES

1. This is an updated and revised version of a previously published essay, Bina D'Costa, "Coming to Terms with the Past," 2005. My thanks to Hameeda Hossain, Amena Mohsin, and Justine Chambers for their comments on the drafts.

2. Sara Sharratt, *Gender, Shame, and Sexual Violence: The Voices of Witnesses and Court Members at War Crimes Tribunals* (UK: Ashgate Publishing, Ltd., 2011).

3. Bina D'Costa, *Nationbuilding, Gender and War Crimes in South Asia* (London: Routledge, 2011).

4. Cambodian Defenders Project, *Asia-Pacific Regional Women's Hearing on Gender-Based Violence in Conflict: Report on the Proceedings,* 2012, http://gbvkr.org/wp-content/uploads/2013/01/Asia-Pacific-Regional-Womens-Hearing-on-GBV-in-Conflict-2012-Report.pdf

5. Ibid., 17.

6. At this point, Begum became emotionally overwhelmed and ended her testimony. She left the Hearing accompanied by a psychosocial support person.

7. Cambodian Defenders Project, *Asia-Pacific,* 17–8, 39

8. Ibid., 38.

9. Ibid., 17–8.

10. Ibid., 18.

11. Ibid., 18–9.

12. D'Costa, *Nationbuilding.*

13. Rhonda Copelon, "Gendered War Crimes: Reconceptualizing Rape in Time of War," in *Women's Rights Human Rights: International Feminist Perspectives,* eds., Julie Peters and Andrea Wolper (New York: Routledge, 1995), 197; Rita Manchanda, "Where are the women in South Asian conflicts?" in *Women, War and Peace in South Asia: Beyond Victimhood to Agency,* ed. R. Manchanda (New Delhi: Sage Publications, 2001), 30.

14. Susan Brownmiller, *Against Our Will: Men, Women, and Rape* (New York: Bantam Books, 1975), 84;.

15. See Dina Siddiqui, "Left Behind By The Nation: 'Stranded Pakistanis' on Bangladesh,'" *Sites,* 10, 1 (2013): 1–33.

16. Y. Matsui, "History Cannot Be Erased, Women Can No Longer Be Silenced" in *Common Grounds: Violence Against Women in War and Armed Conflict Situations,* ed. I. L. Sajor (Philippines: Asian Center for Women's Human Rights [ASCENT], 1998), 26–32; K. Puja, "Global Civil Society Remakes History: 'The Women's International War Crimes Tribunal 2000,'" *Positions: East Asia Cultures Critique,* 9, 3 (2001): 611–20.

17. S. M. Burke, "The Postwar Diplomacy of the Indo-Pakistani War of 1971," *Asian Survey,* 13, 11 (1973): 1037.

18. Ibid., 1037–8.

19. *Statesman Weekly,* September 1, 1973.

20. For details see D'Costa, *Nationbuilding.*

21. On South Asia, see for example, R. Menon and K. Bhasin, *Borders and Boundaries: Women in India's Partition* (New Delhi: Kali for Women, 1998); U. Butalia, *The Other Side of Silence: Voices from the Partition of India* (New Delhi: Penguin Books India, 1998).

22. In Bangladesh, the terminology pro-liberation (*shadhinotar pokhye*) and anti-liberation forces (*shadhinotar bipokhyo shokti*) have been invoked by the media, activists, and academics to differentiate between interest groups such as civil society actors, political leaders, and others who supported the justice campaigns and who advocated against revisiting the atrocities of 1971. Many in the pro-liberation lobby either participated in the war or are sympathetic to it. Individuals in the anti-liberation lobby have often been accused of collaborating with the Pakistani army or showing some bias towards the religious right. After the International Crimes Tribunal proceedings began, these terms have acquired new meanings in the war of rhetoric and propaganda campaigns.

23. Ain o Salish Kendra (ASK) initiated the Oral History Project. Some of the important interviews were published in S. Akhter, *et al.* eds., *Narir Ekattur o Judhyo Porobortee Kothyokahini* (Dhaka: Ain-o-Shalish Kendro, 2001), 14–20.

24. On women's experiences see Akhter *et al., Narir Ekattur*; D'Costa, *Nationbuilding*; Nayanika Mookherjee, "Gendered Embodiments: Mapping the body-politic of the raped woman and the nation in Bangladesh," *Feminist Review, Special Issue on War* Vol. 88, No. 1 (2008): 36–53; Yasmin Saikia, *Women, War, and the Making of Bangladesh: Remembering 1971* (Durham, NC: Duke University Press, 2011).

25. This is particularly evident from Respondent A's (wishes to remain anonymous) interview. I spoke with her in Kolkata, India in January, 2000. She played a major role in the rehabilitation of the women. She mentioned that they focused on households headed by females after the war, as the numbers of these increased. She mentioned, "We also did some rehabilitation work for women on the other side of the Buriganga (a river next to Dhaka city). All were Hindu women. No men, no grownup boys. The army killed all the men. They dug up a big hole where they buried all the men. And also the grown-up boys. Women were left alone. We started a program for helping the women. I gave each woman rupees to do some small business. They made a little extra. Afterwards they continued to work with that small savings. Then we gave them geese, ducklings, chicks and goats. For the next three years we helped them to stand on their feet. That is how Jagoroni (a handicrafts shop in Dhaka city run by catholic nuns) came into being. It was the Widows' Program."

26. Nayanika Mookherjee revealed in her work that Minister Kamruzaman used this nomenclature in December soon after his arrival in Dhaka.

27. F. Pereira, *The Fractured Scales: The Search for a Uniform Personal Code* (Calcutta: Stree, 2002).

28. Perira, *Fractured Scales,* 62.

29. *Bangladesh Documents,* 2000, 282–6.

30. Hasan-Askari Rizvi, *The Military and Politics in Pakistan* (Lahore, Pakistan: Progressive Publishers, 1987).

31. *The Times,* May 20, and June 15, 1971, and *the Far Eastern Economic Review,* September 4, 1971.

32. Nilima Ibrahim, interview by D'Costa, Dhaka, Bangladesh, January 14, 2000; Respondent A, interview by D'Costa, Dhaka, Bangladesh, Muktijodhya, January 16, 2000; Respondent B, interview by D'Costa, Kolkata, West Bengal, India, February 7, 2000; Geoffrey Davis, interview by D'Costa, Sydney, Australia, June 1, 2002; Halima Parveen, interview by D'Costa, Dhaka, Bangladesh, December 25, 2002.

33. D'Costa, cited interview 1, 2000.

34. Davis, interviewed by D'Costa; Parveen, interviewed by D'Costa.

35. I gratefully acknowledge Roger Kilham's assistance in tracking down Geoffrey Davis.

36. Rounaq Jahan, *The Elusive Agenda: Mainstreaming Women in Development* (London: Zed Books, 1995), 97.

37. Veena Das, *Critical Events: An Anthropological Perspective on Contemporary India* (Oxford: Oxford University Press, 1995), 55–83.

38. The Partition of India in 1947, sparked violent communal riots between Hindus, Muslims and Sikhs. During March 1947, four months before the actual Partition, some Sikh villages in the Rawalpindi area of Punjab had been attacked in retaliation for Hindu attacks on Muslims in Bihar. The story of ninety women who drowned themselves by jumping into a well at Thoa Khalsa, a small village in Rawalpindi, when their men were no longer able to defend their honor, is still discussed today in tones of admiration and respect. For details, see U. Butalia, *Other Side of Silence*, 146–84.

39. Davis, interview by D'Costa. Davis worked with the International Planned Parenthood in Bangladesh 1971–72.

40. Ibid. Emphasis mine.

41. Respondent B, interview by D'Costa. Respondent B was a social worker.

42. Marianne Scholte, "Liberating the women of 1971," *The Daily Star*, December 8, 2014. Available at http://www.thedailystar.net/liberating-the-women-of-1971-54154.

43. For details on sexual and reproductive programs see, "Proceedings of the Seminar of Family Planning," November 21–5, 1972 (Dacca: Bangladesh); M. A. Gafur, *Shomaj Kolyan Porikroma* (Dhaka: Pubali Prokashoni, 1979), 429, 555. I thank Rahnuma Ahmed for alerting me to the former important publication.

44. It is not my contention that many Birangona did not want to go through abortions or the adoption programs. However, without recovering the voices of the women themselves we would not be able to decipher the meaning of choice that could be either voluntary or coercive, especially when motherhood that belonged previously in the private domain was now controlled by the state.

45. The Bangladesh Government gradually eradicated the programs principally designed for the Birangona, and were said to have allegedly destroyed their records.

46. The book was translated into English under the title *Of Blood and Fire: The Untold Story of Bangladesh's War of Independence* (Dhaka, Bangladesh: Academic Publishers, 1991).

47. Golam Azam fled East Pakistan just before it became Bangladesh. In 1978, he returned to Bangladesh and has lived there since as a Pakistani national. The ICT found Azam guilty of five charges and sentenced him to ninety years in prison. He died in late 2014.

48. Partha S. Ghosh, "Bangladesh at the crossroads: religion and politics," *Asian Survey*, 33, 7 (1993): 703–4. In March 21, 1981, there was a demand from freedom fighters under the banner of Bangladesh *Muktijodhya Shongshod* (A freedom fighters' association) to

try Golam Azam and other collaborators for war crimes in a People's Tribunal (Kabir, 1993: 15–9). This movement faltered due to government intervention. Shahriar Kabir, *Gonoadaloter Potobhumi* (Dhaka: Dibyo Prokash, 1993).

49. Ibid., 11.

50. Rounaq Jahan, *Bangladeshi Politics: Problems and Issues* (Dhaka: University Press Ltd, 1980), 58; Jahan, *The Elusive Agenda*, 93.

51. In May 1977, Article 38 of the Constitution, banning the use of religion for political purpose was revoked; that cleared the way for religious-based parties to get back into Bangladeshi politics. The Constitution of the People's Republic of Bangladesh (Dhaka: Government of Bangladesh, 1972), 13; M. Anisuzzaman, "The Identity Question and Politics" in *Bangladesh: Promise and Performance*, ed. R. Jahan (Dhaka: University Press Ltd., 2000): 59.

52. Shahriar Kabir, *Gonoadaloter Potobhumi* (Dhaka, Bangladesh: Dibyo Prokash, 1993).

53. Cited in Ahmed Ziauddin, "What is to be Done About the Pakistani War Criminals and Collaborators," *The Daily Star*, December 3, 1999.

54. The BNP–led (Bangladesh Nationalist Party) government was against this symbolic tribunal. BNP won the election in February 27, 1990, with 140 seats, and formed the government with the support of *Jama'at*. Shahriar Kabir, *Ekatturer Gonohotya, Nirjaton ebong Judhyaporadhider Bichar* (Dhaka, Bangladesh: Shomoy, 2000), 29.

55. Shahriar Kabir, "Introduction" in *Ekatturer Dushoho Smriti*, Kabir, ed. Shahriar (Dhaka, Bangladesh: Ekatturer Ghatok Dalal Nirmul Committee, 1999): 20.

56. Suraya Begum, "Masuda, elijan, duljan, momena: kushtiar charjon grihobodhu," in *Narir Ekattur o Judhyo Porobortee Kothyokahini*, eds., S. Akhter *et al.*, (Dhaka, Bangladesh: Ain-o-Shalish Kendro, 2001), 82, 86.

57. Ibid., 102.

58. The three women come from rural and traditional areas where *purdah* and *izzat* (honor) have very strong social meanings. The Tribunal organizers were not sensitive to this.

59. *Daily Shongbad*, November 11, 1996.

60. D'Costa, interview with Birangona, 1999.

61. Nilima Ibrahim, *Ami Birangana Bolchi* (Dhaka, Bangladesh: Jagriti Prokashoni, 1998).

62. Ibrahim, interviewed by D'Costa.

63. Khan, *The Daily Star*, December 12, 1997.

64. Ibid.

65. Ibid.

66. Ibid.

67. Ferdousi Priyobhashini, "Onek Mrityo Dekhechi, Nari Nirjatoner Kotha Shunechi Kintoo Kokhonou Bhabini Ami Tar Shikar Hobo" in *Ekatturer Dushoho Smriti*, ed. Kabir (Dhaka, Bangladesh: Ekatturer Ghatok Dalal Nirmul Committee, 1999), 67.

68. My sincere thanks to Shaheen Akhter for introducing me to Halima Parveen.

69. Halima Parveen, interview by D'Costa, Dhaka, Bangladesh, December 25, 2002.

70. G. Waylen, "Analysing women in the politics of the Third World" in *Women and Politics in the Third World*, ed. H. Afshar, (London: Routledge, 1996), 7–24; S. M. Rai, *Gender and the Political Economy of Development: From Nationalism to Globalization* (Cambridge: Polity, 2002).

71. Jahan, *The Elusive Agenda*, 93.

72. V. Moghadam, "Introduction: Women and Identity Politics in Theoretical and Comparative Perspective," in *Identity Politics and Women: Cultural Reassertions and Feminisms in International Perspective*, ed. V. Moghadam, (1994), 2.

73. Jahan, *The Elusive Agenda*.

74. Naila Kabeer, "Subordination and Struggle: Women in Bangladesh," *New Left Review*, No. 168 (March/April 1988), 100.

75. Jahan, *The Elusive Agenda*, 102.

76. Naila Kabeer, "Subordination and Struggle: Women in Bangladesh," *New Left Review*, No. 168 (March/April 1988), 99.

77. Jahan, *The Elusive Agenda*, 98.

78. Ibid.

79. Kelly Askin, War Crimes against Women: Prosecution in International War Crimes Tribunals, Hague: Kluwer Law International, 1997; Christine Chinkin, and Hilary Charlesworth, "Building Women into Peace: the international legal framework" *Third World Quarterly* 2, 5 (2006): 937–57.

80. Navanethem Pillay, Foreword, *Rethinking Rape Law: International and Comparative Perspectives*, eds., Clare McGlynn and Vanessa E. Munro (New York: Routledge), xiv.

81. Ibid, xv.

82. See generally, Clare McGlynn and Vanessa E. Munro, eds., *Rethinking Rape Law*, 137–251.

83. Ivana Radačić and Ksenija Turković, "Rethinking Croatian Rape Laws: Force, Consent and the Contribution of the Victim," in *Rethinking Rape Law*, 168–82.

84. Clare McGlynn and Vanessa E. Munro, eds., *Rethinking Rape Law*, 10–1.

85. Alison Cole, 2006, "International Criminal Law and Sexual Violence: An Overview," in *Rethinking Rape Law*, 46–50.

86. For an overview of the jurisprudence addressing sexual violence in international courts and hybrid tribunals, see Bina D'Costa and Sara Hossain, "Redress for Sexual Violence Before the International Crimes Tribunal in Bangladesh: Lessons from History and Hopes for the Future," *Criminal Law Forum*, 21 (2010): 331–59.

87. *Prosecutor v Tadić*, ICTY, Case No. IT-94-1-A, July 15, 1999.

88. Dragoljub Kunarac is one of the eight individuals named in the first indictment dealing with sexual offences, issued in June 1996. This significant indictment covers the brutal regime of gang rape, torture, and enslavement which Muslim women and girls of *Foča* and elsewhere were subjected to, between April 1992 and February 1993, by Bosnian Serb soldiers, policemen, and members of paramilitary groups, including some from Serbia and Montenegro. *Prosecutor v Kunarac* (Trial Judgement), ICTY, Case Nos. IT-96-23-T and IT-96-23/1-T, February 22, 2001.

89. He is now sixty-one years old, which means he was seventeen years old during the war.

90. *The Daily Star*, January 30, 2015.

Very Superstitious

Gendered Punishment in Democratic Kampuchea, 1975–1979

Trude Jacobsen

On April 17, 1975, Phnom Penh, the capital of Cambodia, fell to self-proclaimed communist forces, named the "Khmer Rouge"—"Red Khmer"—by former king and prime minister, Norodom Sihanouk. Cambodian communism had had to retreat underground after the Samlaut uprising of 1967, when leftist politics began to come under scrutiny by the ostensibly inclusive umbrella of the Sihanouk–headed Sangkum Reastr Niyum. As the 1960s gave way to the 1970s, these were joined by an increasing number of young Cambodians disillusioned with modern society, which seemed to maintain only a status quo of elite greed, and hardship for everyone else. After the March 18, 1970, ousting of Prince Norodom Sihanouk as head of state, disenfranshised youth had a symbol under which to rally: The Front uni national du Kampuchea (FUNK), or Kampuchean United National Front. Before long, Sihanouk and the FUNK had joined with the communist resistance.[1]

This ensured that the rural population—who still regarded Sihanouk as a divine king, despite his 1955 abdication—rallied to the maquis, the dense scrubland area of northern and eastern Cambodia. It was only a matter of time before the short-lived Republic of Kampuchea, headed by Lon Nol and Sirik Matak, collapsed.[2] The influx of refugees escaping the conflict in Vietnam along the Cambodian border did little to stem the inevitable collapse of urban infrastructure and the loyalty of the armed forces. Within days of the fall of Phnom Penh on April 17, 1975, cities and towns emptied, their inhabitants forced into agrarian-based livelihoods, where their former existences were eradicated by force, and the basic building blocks of society—family and Buddhism—were deliberately dismantled.[3] Deviation from prescribed behavior resulted in punishment and, increasingly, "reeducation," or execution.[4] Orders emanated from Angkar Loeu or Angkar Padevat,[5] meaning high or revolutionary organization, and were enforced by dedicated and deadly Khmer Rouge cadres—many of whom were women attracted by the opportunity afforded them to act on par with their male counterparts. Yet, despite adopting an ostensibly gender-neutral approach, the Khmer Rouge period displayed cultural perspectives toward gender roles and female sexuality ingrained from previous eras. Furthermore, many Khmer Rouge used their positions to sexually exploit and abuse women in their power. However, until recently, this side of Democratic Kampuchea has not received much attention—on the contrary, the Khmer Rouge regime was perceived as being morally opposed to sexual interaction of any sort between men and women.

This began to change on July 26, 2010, when the Extraordinary Chambers in the Courts of Cambodia (ECCC) found Kaing Geuk Euv, known during the Khmer Rouge regime as "Duch," criminally responsible for—although not personally guilty of—one rape perpetrated during the time he was in charge of the notorious reeducation center in Tuol Sleng, Santebal 21 (known as S-21). Other rapes had been alleged, but only one, according to the official judgment, could be proved to have occurred.[6] Although this was devastating to the many people who had risked social ostracism by coming forward to tell their stories of sexual abuse, degradation, and humiliation during the three years, eight months, and twenty days that Democratic Kampuchea lasted, it was a victory for those who had suffered in silence for so long. As many as 3.53 million people are estimated to have died during the regime; what demographers cannot tell is how many were victims of sexual and gender-based violence. We also have no clear idea of how many women were participants in enforcing work units, obedience to Angkar, and subjecting their fellow citizens to starvation, torture, and death.

Rape remains a taboo topic in Cambodian culture even in the twenty-first century. Now, as in the 1960s, women rarely press charges against rapists not only due to lack of trust in the judicial system, but because of a persistent stigma that had the woman not been in the wrong place at the wrong time, or had she been dressed more modestly, she would not have been assaulted. Loss of virtue has economic and social implications, even for married women; husbands may leave them due to their having "engaged" in extramarital sex, and families may cover up the rape of an unmarried daughter lest her lack of virginity keep potential suitors away.[7] Thus, for women to have come forward to constitute a victim group in the ECCC was a profound step. Telling their stories meant that their families and communities may have heard for the first time what befell them during Democratic Kampuchea, and their social status may have been affected. Yet their desire for justice overcame these concerns. The fact that Duch was found guilty of rape—albeit only in one instance—was a victory against a backdrop of ingrained suspicion of female sexuality, and men's helplessness in the face of it.

"KHMER ROUGE DIDN'T RAPE OR ROB"

Sexual activity of any sort was strictly regulated during the Khmer Rouge regime, and policed by its agents. When Phnom Penh was falling to the Khmer Rouge in mid-April 1975, Doctor Haing Ngor knew his nurses would be safe on their way to their home villages as the soldiers of the communist forces were known not to "rape or rob."[8] To ensure that temptation did not occur, men and women were kept apart in separate work units, categorized according to whether members had ever been married, were widowed, or had living spouses. These groups ate together, received rations at the same times, and were sent out on work details together. They were expected to attend compulsory village gatherings for political education, new directives, and self-criticism in their same groupings.[9] In some places, married couples were also expected to sleep apart, in huts with their work units;[10] the rationale behind this was that personal happiness would have to wait until the country had been reconstructed for the good of all its people.[11] New people—those who had been evacuated from the towns and forced into rural villages—were seen as particularly liable to transgress sexually; the members of one such group were made to attend a meeting in their new village and were told that, "Everybody should concentrate exclusively on work. Therefore, we have separated by sexes. Sexual relations among unmarried couples are strictly forbidden.... We do not have any sexual problems. A Red Khmer boy can spend the night under the same mosquito net as a Red Khmer girl, and no sexual relations will take place."[12]

The same announcement carried a warning that any young men and women caught holding hands would be killed.

Extramarital sexual activity of any sort—even if only suspected—could result in harsh punishment, even death.[13] Married people who had affairs with others, married or unmarried, were executed.[14] Single women who transgressed in this way were regarded as having unnatural sexual appetites and therefore must be sex workers—a trope from before the Khmer Rouge came to power, and one that remains embedded in the culutral collective consciousness.[15] Huot Bophana is the best-known example of women who were executed under these auspices. She had had a relationship with Ly Deth, who had joined the Khmer Rouge in 1965, well before the fall of Phnom Penh. Often separated as he was promoted, they exchanged letters whenever possible. These were eventually intercepted and she was sent for reeducation at the most dreaded of the prison camps—Santebal 21, in Phnom Penh. She was tortured and made to write countless "confessions" as to the ways she had transgressed against the regime. In one of her final such confessions, she stated that she had never loved Ly Deth and that she had tricked him into a relationship on the orders of the CIA, who had a plan in place to corrupt high-level Khmer Rouge officers. She was executed and presumably buried in a mass grave at the Chhoeng Ek site, known as the "killing fields," on March 18, 1977.[16] He, on the other hand, was not punished.

Both Huot Bophana and Men Pich, another woman executed at S-21 on suspicion of having illicit relationships during the regime, were described as prostitutes—Huot Bophana by the wife of her krom (commune leader), and Men Pich in her forced confession.[17] The existence of women who were sexually active outside of a recognized marriage seems particularly to have bothered the Khmer Rouge; an official told Haing Ngor that life was "much better now. There is no more corruption. No more gambling or prostitution."[18] Many women suspected of being sex workers were killed during the evacuation of the cities; a truck driver saw the bodies of twenty women piled outside a temple in Banteay Meanchey province in the first days of the regime, killed by a blow to the back of the head.[19] Prostitution, sexual permissiveness, and conspicuous consumption of Western products, music, and fashion were the hallmarks of the decadence of the previous regimes, and had to be eliminated so that Cambodia could move forward.

Yet the supposedly strict morality of the regime hid a sinister truth: Sexual abuse was rampant, and those Khmer Rouge rank-and-file who did commit sexual assaults usually killed their victims so as to leave no witnesses. Documented cases of rape were rare in Democratic Kampuchea, but they undoubtedly occurred.[20] The punishment for Khmer Rouge officials found guilty of sexual misconduct, even toward suspected enemies of the regime, was stricter than those for ordinary people. In Phum Andong, the village headman allowed two of his henchmen to rape a woman, then colluded with them in covering up the crime. He was purged as a result.[21] Similarly, although interrogators at S-21 were ordered to always question women with a witness present, several were arrested for sexual interference.[22] Not all Khmer Rouge were held to this standard, however; Someth May remembered teenaged cadres flirting with each other with no repercussions, and Hu Nim, Minister of Information, "liked to be known as a Don Juan,"[23] which at least implies liaisons with women other than his wife. Some Khmer Rouge officials took advantage of their positions and took lesser wives, thus continuing a traditional mechanism by which men in Cambodia had demonstrated their political and economic superiority; this despite the specific prohibition of polygamy in the Constitution of Democratic Kampuchea in an effort to distance the regime from its predecessors.[24]

"YOU DO NOT UNDERSTAND THE PROBLEM OF WOMEN"

The issue of marriages, forced on individuals and couples as part of Khmer Rouge policy, has spawned several studies, notably Peg LeVine's

Love and Dread in Cambodia: Weddings, Births, and Ritual Harm Under the Khmer Rouge (2010).[25] Writing in 1982, Michael Vickery doubted that such marriages ever occurred, due to the stringency of the moral code promulgated by Democratic Kampuchea.[26] Yet the evidence gathered since the early post-DK years indicates that free choice of marriage partners was as rare under the Khmer Rouge as it had been prior to the revolution, and that the state subsumed the formerly parental role of sanctioning marriage partners.[27] Indeed, if anyone dared attempt to follow the traditional pathway to marriage, namely the prospective husband's family visiting the prospective bride's family with gifts, it would be seen as a flaunting of agency in the face of the Khmer Rouge leadership. As one survivor of the regime recounted, if anyone fell in love and did not "inform Angka [sic], the penalty is death. If you talk to your fiancée's parents ahead of Angka, you're killed."[28]

The view that marriage is more about cementing political and economic bonds, than about the inclinations of the parties involved in the union, continued under the Khmer Rouge. Ta Mok, a senior figure in Democratic Kampuchea renowned for his brutality, married his daughters off to men in the Khmer Rouge hierarchy in order to ensure their loyalty to him. In return, he assisted them in ascending the ladder of the Khmer Rouge politburo.[29] Men who had fought in the civil war were rewarded with women from among the new people evacuated from the cities, who seemed exotic to rural folk. In one village, the chief distributed girls from the cities to men who had been injured during the war, or who had fought particularly valiantly in the cause. "Just think, these guys have not had a woman in five years! ... They paid for victory with their blood, and the weddings will be their reward."[30]

Women may have preferred marriage to the brutal workload of the agricultural projects of Democratic Kampuchea. Some areas allowed for a higher degree of personal choice than others, although at times the choice lay between marrying or working in the harshest conditions in an unmarried labor brigade.[31] Vickery tells us of a "beautiful, spoiled girl" who refused to participate in the agricultural work of the village, despite having received warnings as to the penalties for disobeying Angkar. After discovering that married women did not have to participate in the exhausting work in the fields, she opted for marriage. This practice varied from commune to commune; other married women were expected to work as before. Similarly, the daughter of a village official, taken with a handsome new arrival from the cities, tried to convince the latter to impregnate her so that her father would force them to marry.[32]

Marriages were permitted to occur according to personal inclination in most places for the first year of Democratic Kampuchea. A couple was required to inform the local authority, most often the Khmer Rouge official in charge of the village; once they had received permission to marry, they would nonetheless have to wait until a number of other couples had come forward, at which time a marriage ceremony was performed by the local official en masse.[33] The current Prime Minister of Cambodia, Hun Sen, and his wife Bun Rany were married in a group with twelve other couples.[34] This deviated sharply from life before Democratic Kampuchea, when couples and their union would be feted by their families, blessed by monks, and celebrated by the community. Marriage itself was also different. Romance was forbidden. Romantic songs from before the DK period were outlawed.[35] Couples were prohibited from calling each other endearing names or expressions; instead, the acceptable terms were "mit p'dai" (comrade husband) and "mit prapuoan" (comrade wife).[36]

Once the marriage had taken place, there was no guarantee that the newlywedswould be permitted to remain together, as described earlier. Husbands and wives were usually sent to separate work units, and were only permitted to see each other sporadically. This startled the Vietnamese delegation to Democratic Kampuchea in February 1977, given that the politburo had set a population target of twenty million by 1990. How were women to become pregnant given the segregation policy for husbands and wives? When the Vietnamese delegate posed this question to Khieu Thirith, she answered sharply, "You do not understand the problem of women at all."[37]

Once malnutrition, purges, and refugees fleeing across the borders began to decimate the number of able-bodied Cambodians left in the country, Angkar decided that something must be done to increase the number of Cambodians being born and surviving childbirth. To encourage women to have children, the 1976 Four-Year Plan made provision for two months of maternity leave and access to creches for their children upon their return to work.[38] What the policy failed to acknowledge was that because most Cambodians were either exhausted from their labors by the end of the day or were prevented from visiting their spouse, any steps toward procreation were unlikely to occur. In addition, many women suffered from dysmenorrhea and miscarriage as a result of the combination of poor nutrition and overwork.[39]

This spurred the regime into arranging marriages. Some people recounted being made to attend village gatherings where all unmarried men and women were lined up, single file; when they stepped forward, they were married to the person at the head of the other line. Often they had never met before. They were expected to leave the wedding and go straight to huts where marriages should be consummated immediately. At one of these mass weddings, a village chief "removed his cigarette, and his toothless lips broke into a leer. 'You women must be quiet if your husband gets angry,'"[40] he informed them. This is a reference to a line from the "Cbpab Srei," "Code of Conduct for Women," a piece of traditional Cambodian literature dating to the early nineteenth century which implied that women should submit to their husbands sexually as in all other ways.

"DON'T PINCH THEIR HAIR OR THEIR CHEEKS"

Given the strict morality of the Khmer Rouge, it is not surprising that officials were admonished for sexually assaulting women that they were reeducating—a euphemism for anything from interrogation to torture. One of the rules for officials at S-21, the notorious reeducation center in Phnom Penh, was "don't pinch their hair or their cheeks."[41] There were women on the staff at S-21, perhaps as a preventive measure; some of them interrogated men, but there is no evidence that women were responsible for torturing other women. Their presence was not always an effective deterrent, as has been detailed earlier; yet the same moral principle that condemned ordinary people for sexual transgressions was more severe for Khmer Rouge officials. Sometimes victims could use this higher standard against perpetrators. In one instance, for example, a woman was caught having sex with a Khmer Rouge cadre in her village. Realizing that she would certainly be executed, she claimed that she was also having illicit sexual relationships with two other men. One of the men she named was a notorious teller of tales to the Khmer Rouge whose (often false) testimony had resulted in many deaths, and the other was the secretary of the local branch of the politburo. She thus ensured that those left behind would also be free of future abuses at the hands of these three men. She was regarded as a heroine by the people of the village.[42]

Even when officials did not rape women, the methods used to punish and torture them were gendered, and revolved around traditional Khmer notions of female sexuality and the supernatural powers with which it was associated. In the first days of the regime, women suspected of being sexually active outside of marriage—that is, women who dressed in Western clothes and had Western hairstyles, or who were working or living in places associated with entertainment, such as restaurants, hotels, karaoke bars, beauty parlors, and casinos—were executed immediately. The female relatives of men known or suspected to have been members of the army or the government during the Lon Nol regime were also killed immediately. This did not happen to men as a matter of course. For example, two hundred women believed to be related to soldiers were killed outside of Sisophon around April 20, 1975. In keeping with the regime's policy toward segregation of the sexes, they were executed by "mit neary"—"female comrades."[43] Women learned early on not to talk about their past connections; the wife of a former Lon Nol general never spoke again about her family after her husband "disappeared."[44]

As Leo Kuper acknowledged nearly four decades ago, the killing of women and children incites more repugnance than the killing of men.[45] Yet in the Cambodian context, a preexisting cultural practice that associated supernatural powers and advanced pregnancies meant that pregnant women were targeted. Women who were sent for reeducation faced a humiliating and often fatal experience at the hands of Angkar. Witnesses attest to seeing women tied spread-eagled and covered with red ants, their breasts and vaginas burned with hot metal, their nipples cut off, and snakes and other poisonous beasts and insects placed on their bound bodies.[46] Pregnant women were particulary victimized in an effort to manufacture koan kroach, literally "smoked child." According to folk beliefs, the first child of a woman holds particularly potent supernatural powers; a man could elicit the words "it belongs to you" from the mother, after which he would remove the fetus from the womb—killing the mother—dry it, and wear the remains in a bag around his neck. The spirit of the dead mother would follow her child to protect it, and the wearer of the bag, from harm.[47] Another pregnant woman had her fetus impaled with a stick inserted through her vagina.[48]

As the regime began to fail, increasing numbers of Khmer Rouge themselves were purged, accompanied by an increased level of violence against women. The highest echelons of the Khmer Rouge leadership, unable to believe that their policies were not leading to the self-sufficient and productive country they had envisioned, placed the blame for the failure of the regime on spies who had infiltrated and were sabotaging the success of their plans. One woman in the Eastern Zone said that many of her friends and relatives fell victim to rape, torture, and execution at this time. In this same region, during the 1978 purge, women party members were forced to dig their own graves and raped before being killed. Elsewhere in the Eastern Zone men, women, and children, many of them members of the local party leadership and their families, were ordered out of Svay Chrum hospital naked and raped, tortured, and killed.[49]

"DAUGHTERS OF POL POT"

Article 13 of the Constitution of Democratic Kampuchea stated:

There must be complete equality among all Kampuchean people in an equal, just, democratic, harmonious, and happy society within the great national solidarity for defending and building the country together. Men and women are fully equal in every respect.[50]

As in many revolutions, the policies of the central authority either were not implemented at the local level, or failed entirely. It is true that many women—particularly young ones—were enthusiastic in their support of the revolution and the opportunities for acting outside the traditional realm it appeared to offer.[51] A 1973 propaganda piece described the heroism of four Khmer Rouge girls who outwitted armed Lon Nol soldiers. When girls renowned for being hard workers were hospitalized, they were lauded as being "Daughters of Pol Pot, because of the exemplary work they accomplished up on the mountain." The hospital staff was told to give them the best care—even if it meant letting "old women die." "Mit neary" received the same training in military combat as their male counterparts; some even rose to the rank of Battalion Commander. Yet the same young women who went with their brothers and classmates on patrol were expected to cook upon return to camp, thus adhering to the bourgeois ideals of society prior to the revolution. *Democratic Kampuchea is Moving Forward*, a propaganda piece distributed to Western governments sympathetic to Marxist ideals, published photographs of women with guns juxtaposed with those of women in the rice fields. At the same time, however, the mit neary who were seen barking orders, stripping soldiers of their uniforms, and marching people out of towns in the early days of the regime, were the same ones who had to carry out tasks traditionally associated with women in prerevolutionary Cambodia, such as keeping accounts and records, weaving, nursing, teaching, and caring for children.[52]

Even the women within the upper echelons of the regime were there because of their relationships to men, and their responsibilities were associated with traditionally female concerns. Upward mobility for women and attaining positions of power usually depended on their husbands or brothers. Sisters Khieu Ponnary and Khieu Thirith married Pol Pot and Ieng Sary, respectively. Thirith and Ieng Sary married first, in 1951; five years later, and with their Marxist-Leninist ideological leanings confirmed, Ponnary and Pol Pot got married. This union was unusual for two reasons. First, Cambodian women are almost universally younger than their husbands; however, Ponnary was eight years older than Pol Pot. Second, Cambodian women marry in their late teens and early twenties. Ponnary was in her mid-thirties, an age at which most Cambodian women would have been confirmed spinsters and undesirable for marriage. This marriage was clearly an alliance made to cement the men together through marriage to the sisters, although their commitment to the cause is well documented.[53]

Prince Sihanouk, who had agreed to join the Khmer Rouge on the understanding that he would be made head of state, and his fifth wife Princess Monique visited the liberated zones in 1973 along with Pol Pot, Khieu Samphan, Ieng Sary, and other high-ranking Khmer Rouge leaders and their wives. Photos show the women relegated to a subservient position relative to the men, or shown separately. The responsibilties given to these women also bespoke an association between femaleness and domestic concerns. Khieu Thirith was appointed Minister for Social Action and Vice-Minister for Education, Culture and Propaganda in 1976.[54] Yun Yat, married to Son Sen, himself heavily involved with security and defense, also served in the same capacity. Although Khieu Ponnary was president of the Women's Association of Democratic Kampuchea, and called "me padevat", "mother of the revolution," she seems to have held these in name only.[55] Significantly, all of these positions were ones that accorded with traditional ideas of what was appropriate for women.

CONCLUSION

Under the Khmer Rouge, women were promised equality and the opportunity for advancement and agency, yet women were never given portfolios such as defense, finance, or foreign policy. While many young women perpetators of violence during the Khmer Rouge regime believed that they were part of the liberation of their country from corruption and may have reveled in their comparative freedoms, it was only a matter of time before they too were relegated to roles deemed "more appropriate" for women.[56] Many Cambodians who survived the Khmer Rouge regime have spoken of their shock at seeing mit neary, female Khmer Rouge cadres, wielding weapons, dressing like their male counterparts, and enacting verbal and physical violence. This was not behavior displayed by any Cambodian women in their experience. On the contrary, women were expected to be quiet, gentle, and take care to display appropriate aspects of their femininity that men found attractive. Indeed, the existence of female perpetrators during the Khmer Rouge period continues to be used in Cambodia as a rationale for why women should not step beyond their traditional spheres of home, market, and children.

Although Democratic Kampuchea adopted a revolutionary, gender-neutral approach in its policies, its treatment of women displayed the continuation of ingrained cultural perspectives toward gender roles—and female sexuality. This is discernible in the rewarding of men with young women and localized practices of polygamy, marriages carried out for purposes of political and economic alliance, the expected submission of wives to their husbands, the control of female sexuality, the use of rape as a tool of oppression, and the use of torture and humiliation specifically applied to women. Yet, the recognition by the ECCC that Duch was responsible for even one rape is significant in the effort to recognize sexual crimes as war crimes. So many women—and men—are no longer alive to tell their stories, but perhaps this one instance will prove the tipping point for others whose testimony may matter in Case No. 2, currently in its concluding stages, in which the surviving members of Angkar—Khieu Samphan and Nuon Chea—are on trial for crimes against humanity. Their conviction will not only provide closure for a nation, but fulfill the Cambodian adage "twer la'or, ban la'or; twer akrok, ban akrok" ("do good, get good; do bad, get bad back").

TRUDE JACOBSEN is Professor in Southeast Asian History at Northern Illinois University. She is author of *Sex Trafficking in Southeast Asia: A History of Desire, Duty, and Debt* (London: Routledge, 2017).

NOTES

1. Craig Etcheson, *The Rise and Demise of Democratic Kampuchea* (Boulder, CO: Westview Press; London: Frances Pinter, 1984), 35–6.

2. David P. Chandler, *A History of Cambodia*, 3rd ed., (Boulder, CO: Westview Press, 2000), 207; Ben Kiernan, "Social Cohesion in Revolutionary Cambodia," *Australian Outlook* 30, 3 (December 1976), 373.

3. Ben Kiernan, "The Genocide in Cambodia, 1975–79," *Bulletin of Concerned Asian Scholars* 22, 2 (April–June 1990): 39; David Chandler, "Strategies for Survival in Kampuchea," *Current History* 82, 483 (April 1983): 150.

4. Michael Vickery, *Cambodia: 1975–1982* [1984] (Chiang Mai: Silkworm Books, 1999), 97.

5. Kiernan, "Social Cohesion," 371n2.

Versions of this paper were presented as "Gender and Power in Democratic Kampuchea, 1975–1979" at the *Sex in History Symposium*, Melbourne, November 19, 2004, and "Gender Roles and Gendered Punishment During the Khmer Rouge Regime" at the ECCC, Phnom Penh, July 24, 2008, and published in chapter seven of *Lost Goddesses: The Denial of Female Power in Cambodian History* (Copenhagen: NIAS Press, 2008).

6. Extraordinary Chambers of the Court of Cambodia, Judgment in Case 001, 192.

7. See for example LICHADO, *Rape and Indecent Assault* (Phnom Penh: LICHADO, 2004), 12–3; Rebecca Surtees, "Rape and Sexual Transgression in Cambodian Society," in

Violence Against Women in Asian Societies, eds., Linda Rae Bennett and Lenore Manderson (London: RoutledgeCurzon, 2003), 93–113; Jacobsen, *Lost Goddesses*, 264–5.

8. Haing S. Ngor, *A Cambodian Odyssey* (New York: Macmillan, 1987), 124.

9. David Chandler with Ben Kiernan and Muy Hong Lim, *The Early Phases of Liberation in Northwestern Cambodia: Conversations with Peang Sophi* (Clayton, Victoria: Monash University, Centre of Southeast Asian Studies, 1976), 10.

10. Someth May, *Cambodian Witness: The Autobiography of Someth May* (London: Faber and Faber, 1988), 233; Lawrence Picq, *Au-delà le ciel: Cinq ans chez les Khmers rouges* (Paris: Éditions Bernard Barrault, 1984), 22. This differed from region to region depending on the strictness of officials.

11. Picq, *Au-delà le ciel*, 54.

12. John Barron and Anthony Paul, *Peace with Horror: The Untold Story of Communist Genocide in Cambodia* (London: Hodder and Stoughton, 1977), 136.

13. Vickery, *Cambodia: 1975–1982*, 95.

14. François Ponchaud, "Social Change in the Vortex of Revolution," in *Cambodia 1975–1978: Rendezvous with Death*, ed. Karl D. Jackson (Princeton, New Jersey: Princeton University Press, 1989), 167.

15. See Jacobsen, *Lost Goddesses*, 286.

16. Tuol Sleng Prison Records [hereafter TSPR] Y06455.

17. Elizabeth Becker, *When the War Was Over* (New York: Simon & Schuster, 1986), 225; TSPR B16134.

18. Haing Ngor, *Cambodian Odyessey*, 199.

19. Barron and Paul, *Peace with Horror*, 77.

20. Judy Ledgerwood, "Changing Khmer Conceptions of Gender: Women, Stories, and the Social Order" (PhD thesis, Cornell University, 1990). I agree with Ledgerwood's assertion that the prevalence of rape is difficult to determine given the shame attached to rape in Cambodian society, in which the woman is always perceived as at fault.

21. Martin Stuart-Fox and Bunheang Ung, *The Murderous Revolution: Life and Death in Pol Pot's Kampuchea* (Bangkok: Orchid Press, 1999), 129.

22. David Chandler, *Voices from S-21: Terror and History in Pol Pot's Secret Prison* (St Leonards, New South Wales: Allen & Unwin, 2000), 131; Vickery, *Cambodia: 1975–1982*, 151.

23. Someth May, *Cambodian Witness*, 75; Barron and Paul, *Peace with Horror*, 44.

24. Article 13 of the DK Constitution, in Raoul M. Jennar, *The Cambodian Constitutions, 1953–1993* (Bangkok: White Lotus, 1995), 86.

25. Peg Levine, *Love and Dread in Cambodia: Weddings, Births, and Ritual Harm Under the Khmer Rouge* (Singapore: NUS Press, 2010). See also Patrick Heuveline and Bunnak Poch, "Do Marriages Forget Their Past? Marital Stability in Post-Khmer Rouge Cambodia," *Demography* 43, 1 (February 2006): 99–125.

26. Vickery, *Cambodia: 1975–1982*, 175.

27. Ponchaud, "Social change in the vortex of revolution", 166–7; Recollection of Thoun Cheng, in *Peasants and Politics in Kampuchea, 1942–1981*, eds., Ben Kiernan and Chanthou Boua (London: Zed Press; New York: M.E. Sharpe, 1982), 292.

28. Barron and Paul, *Peace with Horror*, 200.

29. Vickery, *Cambodia: 1975–1982*, 99.

30. Barron and Paul, *Peace with horror*, 96; Jean Morice, *Cambodge, du sourire à l'horreur* (Paris: Éditions France-Empire, 1977), 392.

31. Work units were divided according to gender, marital status, and age.

32. Chanrithy Him, *When Broken Glass Floats: Growing Up Under the Khmer Rouge—A Memoir* (New York: W.W. Norton & Company, 2000), 243; Stuart-Fox and Ung, *Murderous Revolution*, 104; Vickery, *Cambodia: 1975–1982*, 105; Ly Y, *Heaven Becomes Hell: A Survivor's Story of Life Under the Khmer Rouge* (New Haven, CT: Yale University Press, 2000), 151.

33. Stuart-Fox and Ung, *Murderous Revolution*, 102; Morrice, *Cambodge, du sourire à l'horreur*, 393.

34. Harish C. Mehta and Julie B. Mehta, *Hun Sen: Strongman of Cambodia* (Singapore: Graham Brash, 1999), 38.

35. John Marston, "Khmer Rouge songs", *Crossroads* 16, 1 (2002), 106.

36. Ngor, *Cambodian Odyssey,* 221; Barron and Paul, *Peace with Horror,* 136.

37. Ben Kiernan, *The Pol Pot Regime: Race, Power, and Genocide in Cambodia Under the Khmer Rouge, 1975–79,* (New Haven, CT: Yale University Press, 1996), 162.

38. "The Party's Four-Year Plan to Build Socialism in All Fields," in *Pol Pot Plans the Future: Confidential Leadership Documents from Democratic Kampuchea, 1976–1977,* trans. and ed., David P. Chandler, Ben Kiernan, and Chanthou Boua (New Haven, CT: Yale University Southeast Asia Studies, 1988), 112. What this meant, in practice, was that children who no longer depended upon breastfeeding exclusively were removed from their mothers and cared for by female Khmer Rouge cadres in collectives. See the recollections of Sat, in *Peasants and Politics in Kampuchea,* 335, and Someth May, *Cambodian Witness,* 132.

39. Peang Sophi, cited in Chandler, *Conversations with Peang Sophi,* 9–10; Maureen H. Fitzgerald, Vannak Ing, Tek Heang Ya, Sim Heang Hay, Thida Yang, Hong Ly Duoong, Bryanne Barnett, Stephen Matthey, Serrick Silove, Penny Mitchell, and Justine McNamara, *Hear Our Voices: Trauma, Birthing and Mental Health Among Cambodian Women* (Paramatta, New South Wales: Transcultural Mental Health Centre, 1998), 44.

40. Haing Ngor, *Cambodian Odyssey,* 293.

41. Chandler, *Voices from S-21,* 131.

42. TSPR B15847; Pin Yathay, *Stay Alive, My Son,* rev. ed. (Ithaca, NY: Cornell University Press, 2000), 172–3.

43. Barron and Paul, *Peace with Horror,* 85.

44. Ida Simon-Barouh, *Le Cambodge des Khmers Rouges: Chronique de la view quotidienne, recit de Yi Tan Kim Pho* (Paris: L'Harmattan, 1990), 49.

45. Leo Kuper, *Genocide: Its Political Use in the Twentieth Century* (London: Penguin, 1981), 204.

46. Haing Ngor, *Cambodian Odyssey,* 218; Becker, *When the War Was Over,* 235.

47. Haing Ngor, *Cambodian Odyssey,* 223, 245–6.

48. Ibid., 248.

49. Fitzgerald *et al.,* *Hear Our Voices,* 43; Stuart-Fox and Bunheang Ung, *Murderous Revolution,* 139, 142.

50. Article 13 of the DK Constitution, in Jennar, *The Cambodian Constitutions,* 86.

51. Molyda Szymusiak recalled that the seventeen-year-old me kong in charge of her work group was replaced by one aged fifteen. Molyda Szymusiak, *The Stones Cry Out* (New York: Hill and Wang, 1986), 174.

52. TSPR B16026 and B15377; Barron and Paul, *Peace with Horror,* 69, 126; Kiernan, *Pol Pot Regime,* 35; San Sarin, "For Victory," *New Cambodge* 5 (September 1970): 67; *New*

Cambodge 11 (June 1971), 38; *Democratic Kampuchea is Moving Forward*, [Cambodia?], [n.p.], August 1977, 11; Szymusiak, *Stones Cry Out*, 80; "Cambodian Women in the Revolutionary War for the People's National Liberation (1973)," *Cambodian Genocide Program Resources*, www.yale.edu/cgp/kwomen.html, accessed June 24, 2003; Vickery, *Cambodia: 1975–1982*, 109.

53. Communist Party of Kampuchea, "Decisions of the Central Committee on a variety of questions," March 30, 1976, trans. Ben Kiernan, in *Pol Pot Plans the Future*, 5; Barron and Paul, *Peace with Horror*, 44.

54. Becker, *When the War Was Over*, 247.

55. Etcheson, *Rise and Demise of Democratic Kampuchea*, 166-7; Vickery, *Cambodia: 1975–1982* [1984 version], 145; Kiernan, *Pol Pot Regime*, 160, 162.

56. As per Nira Yuval-Davis, *Gender and Nation* (London: Sage, 1997).

10

Sexual Violence as a Weapon during the Guatemalan Genocide

Victoria Sanford, Sofia Duyos Álvarez-Arenas, and Kathleen Dill

Judge Yasmín Barríos and her tribunal made world history on May 10, 2013, when they found former Guatemalan dictator José Efraín Ríos Montt guilty of crimes against humanity and genocide—the first time ever that a head of state has been convicted of these crimes in a national court. The eighty-year prison sentence was the just conclusion of a court process that was nearly derailed by threats to witnesses, presidential declarations denouncing the trial, and over one hundred appeals by the defense team. Perseverance, courage, and a commitment to the rule of law on the part of the survivors, prosecutors, and tribunal judges repeatedly pushed the case back on track. Although ten days later a corrupt Constitutional Court annulled the verdict on technical grounds,[1] the genocide sentence is an unforgettable moment in the historic struggle for justice in Guatemala. It was also the first time a Guatemalan court recognized the systematic rape and torture to which Maya women were subjected during Ríos Montt's reign of terror.

Beginning on March 19, 2013, the court heard 102 witnesses (94 for the prosecution and 8 presented by the defense) and 68 expert testimonies. The tribunal also reviewed hundreds of documents. The nine lawyers for the defense used every stalling tactic possible to avoid reaching the verdict—filing over one hundred separate appeals. As the trial wore on, Guatemalans read about it in newspapers, watched televised news coverage, and listened to it live on national radio and the Internet. This brought the testimonies of survivors into the homes of any Guatemalan willing to learn how criminal state violence destroyed hundreds of thousands of individual lives and families, and in hundreds of cases annihilated entire Maya communities.[2]

Like the genocide itself, the organized use of sexual violence by the state was a public secret. Though it was not the central focus of the court case, the information had long been available from human rights reports, survivor testimonies, and truth commission reports. Reports from both the Commission for Historical Clarification (CEH) and the Catholic Church's Nunca Más project documented the fact that the army systematically deployed sexual violence as a counterinsurgency weapon. Sexual violence was ordered by the high command and enshrouded with impunity by official denial. During the war, army soldiers and other security officers were responsible for 94.3 percent of all sexual violence against women.[3] Of the 1,465 cases of rape reported, fully one-third of the victims were minor girls.[4] Women who survived bore the physical and psychological consequences, including pregnancy and sexually transmitted diseases, as well as the social stigma attached to victims of rape.[5]

While female witnesses recounted in detail how they were gang-raped by army soldiers, indigenous women observing the trial covered their heads with their shawls in solidarity. Witness Elena de Paz Santiago told the court what Guatemalan soldiers did to her at the army base when she was a child: "I was twelve when I was taken to the army base with other women. The soldiers tied my feet and hands.... They put a rag in the mouth ... and started raping me.... I do not even know how many soldiers had a turn.... I lost consciousness and blood ran from my body. When I came to, I was unable to stand."[6] The fact that the prosecution called Ms. de Paz Santiago and other women as witnesses, and that their testimonies support claims that sexual violence was systematically used as a genocide strategy, signals a relatively new development in the practice of international law.

Sexual violence has long been explained as an unfortunate outcome of war in which men are placed in extraordinary circumstances that provoke aberrant behavior. This is no longer a tenable theory. The work of the

International Criminal Court, the United Nations Special Rapporteur on Violence Against Women, feminist scholars, and human rights advocates has done much to reframe the issue. This conceptual shift was clearly expressed by the United Nations Special Rapporteur on Violence Against Women, who reported in 2009 that studies of wartime rape "conclusively demonstrate that sexual violence is not an outcome of war, but that women's bodies are an important site of war, which makes sexual violence an integral part of wartime strategy."[7]

PLANNING A GENOCIDE

When oral arguments in the 2013 genocide trial came to a close, eighty-six-year-old Ríos Montt demanded to speak, breaking the silence he had held since the trial began. Far from displaying any remorse for the genocide committed during his regime, he stated: "I never authorized, I never proposed, I never ordered acts against any ethnic or religious group."[8] He also denied that he commanded army troops, despite leading the junta that came to power through military coup in March 1982. He then asserted that his role was purely administrative. Even if the latter claim were true, the Adolph Eichmann trial proved that pushing papers does not absolve one of responsibility.[9] But Ríos Montt was much more than an administrator; he had command responsibility of a vertical military organization.[10] As the de facto president of Guatemala, Ríos Montt initiated genocide, beginning with propaganda against the indigenous Maya and any other Guatemalan who dared to question repression, inequality, and poverty.

Following the US-sponsored overthrow of democratically elected President Jacobo Árbenz in 1954, successive military governments in Guatemala fought against "the enemy within" as defined by the United States' Cold War era anticommunist National Security Doctrine. The Guatemalan government applied the doctrine to justify eliminating any person who, by working to bring sociopolitical change to the nation, challenged the regime. Carrying a gun was not necessary to be considered a target. According to the Guatemalan truth commission, "the broad concept of enemy wielded by the State was re-launched with particular violence and intensity in the eighties, and included not only those actively seeking to change the established order, but all who might potentially decide to support the struggle at some point in the future."[11] Victims of the doctrine included men, women, and children from all strata: workers, professionals, religious leaders and lay workers, politicians, peasants, students and academics; in ethnic terms the vast majority of victims were Maya.[12] Once the security forces had destroyed the social bases of dissent in the city and assassinated rural community leaders, the war machine set its full attention on Maya communities.

Anticommunism, fused with patriarchal structures and centuries-old prejudices against the majority Maya population, produced a climate ripe for the dehumanization of a targeted population. The conflation of Maya identity with guerrilla insurgency was exaggerated by the dictatorship with the intent to deploy this alleged widespread Maya/guerrilla affinity to justify the elimination of present and future members of the Maya population. Genocide ideologues implicitly acknowledged the poverty and exploitation of Maya life as they argued that if the Maya were to join the guerrillas in their demands for social justice, the army would lose the war.[13]

When a *population* is classified as an enemy, as opposed to specific elements within a group, women become primary targets for sexual violence rather than collateral damage. Women are recognized as "reproducers" in both the biological and socioeconomic senses of the term.[14] Although women's work is undervalued by general populations, analysts understand that it is essential, especially during times of crisis.[15] Because sexual violence harms women's ability to perform their roles, military analysts know that when the goal is to destabilize or destroy a population, targeting women will help them reach that goal.[16]

There is another compelling reason why when a population is the target, sexual violence against women is considered militarily advantageous. Despite the fact that the crime is committed against the actual victims, men experience their inability to protect women as a demoralizing humiliation and perceive it as an attack on their own power and dignity. Sexual violence against women committed by an invading army is a potent symbol clearly intended to demonstrate victory over the opposition. As Radhika Coomaraswamy states: "It is a battle among men fought over the bodies of women."[17]

Thus, the Guatemalan state launched a campaign designed not only to crush communities suspected of resistance, but also to debase the reproductive bodies and degrade the sociocultural status of Maya women. Leaked (and authenticated) army documents refer to Ixil women as "cockroaches" and Ixil children as "chocolates."[18] Within this idiom, forced displacement, the organized rape of women and girls, the systematic slaughter of unarmed men, women, and children, and the burning of hundreds of villages were reduced to a simple order: "Kill the cockroaches and leave no chocolates."[19]

TRAINING SOLDIERS TO RAPE

Cynthia Enloe reminds us that historically, rape has provided cost-free recompense for soldiers and collaborators, converting captive young women into the "spoils of war."[20] However, when rape is used as a weapon of genocide, more is involved than the forfeiture of women to conquering forces. Under the direction of Ríos Montt, the military simultaneously identified the Maya population as the enemy *and* stipulated that soldiers have sexual contact with women. Psychological operations for the troops included "recreation zones designed to maintain the soldier's fighting spirit," which featured "contact with the female sex."[21] Military plans included sexual contact as part of the soldier's rest and recreation because the normalization of rape was utilized to maintain control over the troops.

According to testimonies gathered by the CEH, the women used by the army to accustom soldiers to the practice of rape were prostitutes: "The Army took prostitutes to the soldiers who went to the lieutenant before being passed on to the rest of the soldiers." The CEH documents that women identified as "prostitutes or whores were passed from the lieutenant to all the soldiers during one week." Then, the CEH reports that "some [soldiers] passed up to ten times." It is also noted that the army "changed" the women every three months.[22]

In its replication of this lexicon, the CEH is shockingly passive and vague in its reporting of sexual violence, utilizing the term "pass" instead of rape. It fails to identify the absolute impunity under which the military operated and, in so doing, the full magnitude of sexual violence against women. Under what conditions would a woman, even if she were a prostitute, willingly go to a military base to be "passed" among dozens of soldiers on a daily basis for three months? The CEH fails to specify the sexual violence to which these women were subjected, despite knowing that the army brought a new group every three months, which suggests the level of physical and psychological battery experienced by these women. Perhaps one of the legacies of genocide is that even those seeking to chronicle the truth of the unimaginable can fall victim to its doublespeak, a phenomenon Marguerite Feitlowitz refers to as "a lexicon of terror" in her magisterial work by the same title.[23] What is certain is that this training produced the expected outcome.

Maya women survivors interviewed by the authors in four different departments of Guatemala reported that they were selected by army officers to provide the service of delivering tortillas to the soldiers each day. It was understood that they would be gang-raped when they made their delivery to the army base, but the women went hoping to protect their daughters from the same fate. In Rabinal, women were forced into rotations at the local military base. Gilberta Iboy[24] described being part of a captive group: "There was so much fear, but by necessity we had to go to the plaza [in Rabinal] because they would not give the men permission to leave the village. In Rabinal, the soldiers captured us and took us to the outpost. We were assaulted .... They kept us there for a week and then they let us go."[25]

Tomasa Toj[26] was still unable to talk about what happened to her: "They kept us in the military outpost for twenty-five days. We were there with other young women from various villages. The soldiers raped the women and some ended up pregnant ... [The interview ended there because the woman could not continue]."[27] Given the fact that, along with other village women, Ms. Iboy was held for a week, and Ms. Toj for twenty-five days, their testimonies strongly suggest that the women previously identified by the CEH as "prostitutes" were also kidnapped and held on army bases as sex slaves.

A former G-2 (army intelligence) officer recounted rapes to Recuperación de la Memoria Histórica (REHMI) investigators, making clear the way in which superior officers organized massive sexual violence:

Some of the guys came and said, "Come on, don't you want to go grab some ass?" I thought to myself, "Wow, just like that?" One said to me, "There are some girls and we are grabbing them." I responded, "We'll see." There were only two girls. They were prisoners. The guys said they were guerrillas, right? And, they were massively raping them. When I got there, I remember there was a line of thirty-five or so soldiers waiting their turn. They were surrounding them and raping them. One got up and another *passed* on. Then he got off and another *passed* on. I calculate that those poor women were raped by three hundred soldiers or maybe even more. Sargent Soto García grabbed them. He was a bad man. He wanted whatever woman we found and he liked to rape them because he knew that we were going to kill them anyway.[28]

The G-2 officer went on to explain how gang rape was planned to reduce the spread of sexually transmitted diseases among the troops. On another occasion, some seventy men had raped a woman and some of them had raped her two or three times: "There were some soldiers who were sick with gonorrhea and syphilis, so the lieutenant ordered them to wait to *pass* last after the rest of us were done."[29]

Guatemalan soldiers were trained to think of gang rape as a bonding exercise among the troops as well as an effective weapon for the extermination of the civilian enemy. Because the troops were not being directed to engage an armed insurgency, but rather to annihilate villages and terrorize civilian communities, the army needed to dehumanize the soldiers as well as their intended victims. The *Counterinsurgency War Manual* (*Manual de Guerra Contrainsurgente*) states: "The soldier, normally has great aversion toward police-type operations and repressive measures against women, children, and sick civilians, unless he is extremely well indoctrinated in the necessity of these operations."[30] One survivor testified to the truth commission: "There were always rapes inside the army bases … sometimes by [soldier's] choice, other times by order [from superiors]. They would say: 'We have to break the asses of these whores' or even worse things."[31]

The army prepared its soldiers by subjecting them to brutality, torture, and psychological manipulation. Once their resistance was extinguished and a blood lust established, soldiers were taught that entire communities were breeding grounds for subversives. This process would ensure that the fully indoctrinated would carry out abhorrent attacks on women, children, elderly, and disabled persons, oftentimes in front of their families—while those who remained appalled by the violence were too afraid to disobey orders.

As the vessels from which new subversives would emerge, women's bodies were transformed into primary targets. Jean Franco recounts some of the most horrific CEH testimonies of rape in Guatemala: "Women were mutilated, their breast or bellies cut, and if they were pregnant, fetuses were torn from their bodies. In one case, a woman's breasts were cut off after the rape and her eyes were pulled out. Her body was left hanging on a pole with a stick in her vagina."[32] Franco rightly concludes: "Such ferocity can only be explained on the grounds that women represented a significant threat."[33]

MODERN-DAY CONQUISTADORS

The prosecutors of the Ríos Montt trial focused on the evidence of state violence against the Ixil Maya; however, the army's genocidal campaign was not limited to that region or that ethnolinguistic group. Rape survivors and witnesses have confirmed that it was common knowledge in Maya villages across the country that the army was committing massacres and that soldiers were raping women. That means that systemic rape was a "public secret" shared by the residents of a village and the army that occupied it. But within the context of military impunity, even if remaining silent might not save your life, speaking out would certainly end it. This further underscores the power and authority with which sexual assaults were deployed by the army.

Power in Guatemala is a racialized phenomenon and the symbolic superiority of white and *ladino* men over the Maya was a catalyst for genocidal violence. In the same way that racism fueled the fury with which Ríos Montt's military plans were carried out against hundreds of Maya communities throughout the country, patriarchal ideology fueled the misogynist spiral of violence against women. Within this rubric of racist patriarchy, Maya women were objectified as enemy property deserving cruel destruction. Thus, the Guatemalan army raped and tortured women with the same ferocity with which they torched fields of sacred maize, burned houses, and slaughtered animals, leaving these signs of destruction to further terrorize any survivors.[34]

The state achieved several goals by recreating and affirming the historic relations in which indigenous women were the property of, and thus subordinate to, masculine white European and *ladino* power. In 1999, the CEH concluded that "massacres, scorched earth operations, forced disappearances and executions of Maya authorities, leaders and spiritual guides, were meant not only to destroy the social base of the guerrillas, but above all were meant to disintegrate cultural values that ensured cohesion and collective action of communities."[35]

Michele Leiby uses data gathered by truth commission reports to compare the army's use of sexual violence in Guatemala and Peru.[36] She points out that in the case of Guatemala, there exists a direct relationship between the perceived threat to the state and the number of rapes committed by soldiers. Although the war continued through December 1996, only 11 percent of sexual violence occurred after 1984, when it was clear that the URNG (Unidad Revolucionaria Nacional Guatemalteca) had been defeated.[37] Leiby cites testimonies of Guatemalan soldiers that demonstrate that rape, and in particular gang rape, was as integral to the army's strategy as was the spectacularly violent killing of "subversives": "The commander has his group of killers, and he tells them how they have to kill. Today they are going to behead or hang them; today they are going to rape all the women. Many times, orders are given to the soldiers before they go out.... They were also ordered to do the 'percha' ... where twenty or thirty soldiers would rape a single woman."[38]

Other army sources asserted that if soldiers hesitated to rape, they were berated by their superiors, and those who refused to rape were punished.[39] Based on her analysis of the data, Leiby concludes that while the military in Peru targeted actual or suspected guerrillas or other opponents of the state, "sexual violence in Guatemala was an explicit tool of repression, employed indiscriminately against the indigenous peasantry. Victims were not punished for joining the insurgency. Victims were not interrogated for information. Instead, sexual violence was used to spread fear and terror through entire 'communities of interest.'"[40]

Thus, to be a Maya woman—the heart of a community of interest— was to be at the mercy of a merciless army. Juana Sis[41] described what happened when the army surrounded her settlement near the village of Chichupac, Rabinal: "The soldiers captured us and they tied us up. They marched us to Chichupac and they assaulted us. They threatened us and accused us of being guerrillas and they raped women. It was the same in the Xesiguan community. They raped women in the community and they ordered some to go to the outpost [in Rabinal] and they raped them there. The soldiers respect no one."[42]

At the same time, the army manipulated and indoctrinated Maya collaborators so they participated in this attack against their own communities. Dorotea Chen[43] of Buena Vista, Rabinal, was raped by Maya men from the neighboring village. The rapists were members of the local militia instituted by the military and referred to as the Civil Patrols (PACs). The state forcibly recruited Maya men into PACs in order to extend its reach into every indigenous municipality in the country. Like enlisted soldiers, PAC members were brutalized and threatened with death if they did not follow orders. Some indigenous men fled into the mountains to avoid having to serve in the PACs. Some stayed behind and were horrified by what they were forced to do, while still others were eager to take advantage of their newfound power and impunity: "The PAC from Xococ arrived here and dragged young women out of their houses and they took them to Xococ where they raped them. Afterwards, they would send them back home but they always returned [for more] every so often. A great many of the women here have been raped."[44]

Almost all cases of mass and organized rape perpetrated by the army and their proxies took place in rural Mayan communities, especially during the height of the violence between 1980 and 1983.[45] The Guatemalan Army's deployment of systematic sexual violence during the genocide devastated individual victims as well as the indigenous groups to which they belonged. Of the twenty-one ethnolinguistic Maya groups in Guatemala, the K'iche, K'anjob'al, Mam, Kekchi, Ixil, Kaqchikel, and Chuj communities were either most often the victims of massive rape, or were those whose victimization was most recorded by human rights observers. As researchers who have worked with K'anjob'al, K'iche, Kakchikel, Akateco, Achi, Mam, Ixil, and Tz'ujil communities, we have found that the rape of Maya women was intended to terrorize, subjugate, debilitate, and demoralize entire populations. We have not encountered a department in Guatemala where women were not raped.

THE POLITICAL ECONOMY OF RAPE

In addition to the demoralizing spectacle of power and impunity that the public secret of mass rapes provided, by aiding, abetting, and promoting rape as a military strategy, the Guatemalan state also achieved some economic goals. Drawing from research conducted in Rwanda and Mozambique, Meredeth Turshen argues: "In civil wars, armies use rape systematically to strip women of their economic and political assets. Women's assets reside in the first instance in their productive and reproductive labor power and in the second instance in their possessions and their access to valuable assets such as land and livestock."[46]

In Rabinal, families that lived in the Chixoy River basin were especially targeted for violence because the state wanted their land for a World Bank–funded hydroelectric dam.[47] It is not surprising, then, to learn that the first cases of mass rape in that municipality occurred in the villages located on the banks or on the approach to the river. Hermenegildo Cuxum,[48] a man from Canchún, Rabinal, recalls:

> In March 1980, soldiers assassinated three men from Canchún who were visiting in the nearby community of Río Negro. One man was shot in the hand, but was able to escape and return to the village. Later, more army troops came. Three hundred soldiers entered Canchún, demanded information about the guerrillas and threatened the community. This time, the soldiers raped five women and five young girls before they left. We knew that we had to escape into the mountains to save our lives, but two elderly women were unable to come with us. One woman's body trembled too much to travel and the other woman was blind [so we had to leave them behind]. When we returned to the village, we discovered that in a savage and incomprehensible act, the soldiers had killed them.[49]

Across the indigenous highlands of Guatemala, women were raped wherever the army displaced Maya communities: in villages during massacres as they razed their homes and fields, in public buildings and churches converted into army detention centers, in military bases, and in so-called model villages where the army forcibly concentrated massacre survivors.[50] For many Maya women, rape and the ensuing loss of their way of life defined how they experienced the war.

CONCLUDING REMARKS

Genocide is an all-consuming type of violence. As researchers, it is impossible to convey the measure of human suffering experienced by its victims. We are often reduced to making lists. All told, we know that the Guatemalan genocide took the lives of some two hundred thousand civilians, disappeared fifty thousand people, annihilated 626 villages, displaced 1.5 million people, and caused one hundred fifty thousand people to seek refuge in Mexico.[51] But we do not know how many women and girls were raped, how many were abducted by the military and forced into sexual slavery, how many gave birth to children who were the product of sexual assault, or how many suffered from the venereal diseases transmitted by rape. Despite real advances in international law, there has been little progress in prosecuting these crimes.

In this chapter, we have touched on a number of reasons why and ways in which the Guatemalan genocide operationalized rape: to terrorize the Maya population, destabilize the reproductive role of women, demoralize the enemy, provide soldiers with the spoils of war, and train them to commit hyperviolent acts, usurp land, and reaffirm historic relations of power between the Euro-American elite and the Maya. Jelke Boesten detangles the various types and intents of sexual violence during war by carefully analyzing what she calls "rape regimes."[52] Because her study focuses on Peru, which like Guatemala is a country with a large indigenous population, Boesten also recognizes that sexual violence can be used to reinforce racialized socioeconomic hierarchies present during peacetime. During the Ríos Montt regime, the systemized rape of Maya women was a weapon of genocide used to accomplish multiple ends, all of which supported the singular, operational goal—breaking emergent Maya communities.

On May 10, 2013, José Efraín Ríos Montt was sentenced to the maximum penalty of fifty years' imprisonment for genocide and thirty years for crimes against humanity. The tribunal found that racism played a key role in the execution of acts of barbarism and ordered the development of concrete measures to provide dignified reparation to the victims. One of the measures ordered was for then president of Guatemala, Otto Pérez Molina (who is also implicated in the Ixil genocide)[53], and several ministers to ask forgiveness from the Ixil people—and especially Ixil women—for the acts of genocide and sexual violence they suffered. The verdict offered a modicum of justice for the survivors and opened the possibility that Guatemalan society might reconcile itself with its own history of racist exclusion and genocide.

However, Guatemala's elite quickly seized back control. On May 20, 2013, the Constitutional Court overturned the verdict on the pretext of procedural irregularities. In February 2014, the same court ruled that Ms. Claudia Paz y Paz, the attorney general who indicted Ríos Montt, was to be removed from her post six months early. Then in April 2014, the College of Lawyers in Guatemala suspended Judge Yasmín Barrios. She was able to defend herself and has resumed practice, but these blatantly corrupt maneuvers lend a Kafkaesque quality to the state of governance in Guatemala and remind everyone that the rule of law has yet to be established. Nonetheless, justice continues to move forward under the leadership of Attorney General Thelma Aldana. In January of 2016, eighteen former high-ranking army officers were arrested for various war crimes. As this book goes to press, the historic Sepur Zarco sexual slavery case is being tried in Guatemala City marking the first time a domestic court has heard charges of sexual slavery during armed conflict as an international crime.[54]

KATHLEEN DILL is a sociocultural anthropologist. Her research deals with local forms of transitional justice and postwar social reconstruction in Guatemala, and the politics of natural disasters and humanitarian aid in Nicaragua.

SOFÍA DUYOS ÁLVAREZ-ARENAS is a lawyer specialized in human rights. Since 2000, she has been working in the Human Rights Office of the Archbishop of Guatemala, where she has conducted research on human rights violations, advocacy and awareness.

VICTORIA SANFORD is Professor and Chair of Anthropology, founding Director of the Center for Human Rights and Peace Studies at Lehman College. She is author of *Buried Secrets: Truth and Human Rights in Guatemala*, among others. She is coeditor of *Engaged Observer: Activism, Advocacy*, and *Anthropology Gender Violence in Peace and War: States of Complicity*.

NOTES

Victoria Sanford, Sofia Duyos Alvarez-Arenas, and Kathleen Dill. "Sexual Violence as a Weapon during the Guatemalan Genocide" in *Gender Violence in Peace and War: States of Complicity*, edited by Victoria Sanford, Katerina Stefatos, and Cecilia Salvi, 34–46. New Brunswick: Rutgers University Press. Copyright © 2016 by Rutgers, the State University. Reprinted by permission of Rutgers University Press.

1. Ten days later, the Guatemalan Constitutional Court vacated the guilty verdict and ordered that the trial restart from the point reached on April 19, 2013, the day a lower court called for the suspension of the trial due to unresolved appeals by the defense. See Kate Doyle, "Guatemala's Genocide on Trial," *The Nation* (May 22, 2013). On January 11, 2016, the defense team successfully delayed the start of the retrial. See Anna-Catherine Brigida, "Retrial of ex-dictator Rios Montt: Will a changed Guatemala shine through?" *The Christian Science Monitor* (January 11, 2016).

2. The Commission for Historical Clarification (CEH) documented 626 army massacres in Maya villages.

3. Commission for Historical Clarification (CEH), *Guatemala: Memoria de Silencio* (Guatemala: Informe de La Comisión para el Esclarecimiento Histórico, 1999), 2: 32.

4. CEH, *Memoria de Silencio*, 2:23. Based on our field experience and conversations with colleagues, we assume sexual violence against men and women was underreported. See Kimberly Theidon, "A Greater Measure of Justice: Gender, Violence and Reparations," in *Mapping Feminist Anthropology in the Twenty-First Century*, ed. Leni Silverstein et al. (New Brunswick, NJ: Rutgers University Press, 2016).

5. Recuperación de la Memoria Histórica (REMHI), *Guatemala: Nunca Más* (Guatemala: Informe de La Recuperación de La Memoria Histórica: Oficina de derechos humanos del Arzobispado de Guatemala, 1998), 2: 210.

6. Asociación para la Justicia y Reconciliación, Centro para la Acción Legal en Derechos Human (CALDH), *Sentencia por genocidio y delitos contra los deberes de humanidad contra el pueblo Maya Ixil*, 10 Mayo 2013 (Guatemala: Editorial Serviprensa, 2014), 514.

7. Yakin Ertürk, *15 Years of The United Nations Special Rapporteur on Violence Against Women, Its Causes and Consequences, (1994–2009)—A Critical Review* (New York: UN Human Rights Council, 2009), vol. 13456.

8. Jo-Marie Burt, "Historic Genocide Trial Nears End; Rios Montt Addresses the Court, Declares Innocence," *International Justice Monitor, Open Society Justice Initiative*. Accessed January 26, 2017, http://www.ijmonitor.org/2013/05/historic-genocide-trial-nears-end-rios-montt-addresses-the-court-declares-innocence/

9. Hanna Arendt, *Eichmann in Jerusalem: A Report on the Banality of Evil* (New York: Penguin, 2006).

10. Victoria Sanford, "Command Responsibility and the Guatemalan Genocide: Genocide as a Military Plan of the Guatemalan Army under the Dictatorships of Generals Lucas Garcia, Rios Montt, and Mejia Victores," *Genocide Studies International* 8, 1 (2014): 86–101.

11. CEH, *Memoria de Silencio*, Chapter 2, Vol. 2,381, epigraph 1947.

12. Ibid., Chapter 4, Vol. 5, 24-5, epigraph 15.

13. Ibid., Chapter 4, Vol. 5, 29, epigraph 31.

14. Mary K. Meyer, "Ulster's Red Hand: Gender, Identity, and Sectarian Conflict in Northern Ireland," in *Women, States and Nationalism: At Home in the Nation?* eds. Sita Ranchod-Nilsson and Mary Ann Tetreault. (New York: Routledge, 2003), 126.

15. Gita Sen and Caren Grown, *Development Crises and Alternative Visions: Third World Women's Perspectives* (New York: Monthly Review Press, 1987).

16. Conversely, when the goal is to eliminate individual targets without destabilizing and alienating the community, military leaders have an incentive to prevent their troops from perpetrating sexual violence.

17. Ertürk, *Fifteen Years of The United Nations*, 15.

18. Carlos Dada, "Guatemala Se Enjuicia," *El Faro*, April 18, 2013, Accessed January 26, 2017, https://elfaro.net/es/201304/noticias/11755/Guatemala-se-enjuicia.htm?st-=.

19. Dada, "Guatemala Se Enjuicia."

20. Cynthia H. Enloe, *Maneuvers: The International Politics of Militarizing Women's Lives*, (Berkeley: University of California Press, 2000); see also Moradi in this volume.

21. Ejército de Guatemala, *Plan Victoria 82* (Guatemala: 1982), appendix B, 39.

22. CEH, *Memoria de Silencio*, vol. 2, 27.

23. Marguerite Feitlowitz, *A Lexicon of Terror: Argentina and the Legacies of Torture* (New York: Oxford University Press, 1999)

24. Pseudonym.

25. Kathleen Dill, "Mediated Pasts, Negotiated Futures: Human Rights and Social Reconstruction in a Maya Community" (PhD Diss., University of California, Davis, 2004).

26. Pseudonym.

27. Dill, "Mediated Pasts."

28. REMHI, *Guatemala: Nunca Más*, vol. 3, 212–3. Emphasis mine.

29. REMHI, *Guatemala: Nunca Más*, vol. 2, 213–4. Emphasis mine.

30. Ejército de Guatemala: *Manual de Guerra Contrainsurgente (resumen)* (Guatemala:1965,), Anexo A, 10.

31. CEH, *Memoria de Silencio*, Testigo, T.C. 53.

32. Jean Franco, "Rape: A Weapon of War," *Social Text* 25, 2 (2007): 39.

33. Ibid., 27.

34. Victoria Sanford, *Buried Secrets: Truth and Human Rights in Guatemala* (New York: Palgrave Macmillan 2003).

35. CEH, *Memoria de Silencio*, Capítulo Cuarto, 29, epígrafe 32.

36. Michele L. Leiby, "Wartime Sexual Violence in Guatemala and Peru," *International Studies Quarterly* 53, 2 (2009): 445–68.

37. Ibid., 460.

38. Ibid., 459.

39. Ibid.

40. Ibid., 466.

41. Pseudonym.

42. Dill, "Mediated Pasts."

43. Pseudonym.

44. Dill, "Mediated Pasts."

45. CEH, *Memoria de Silencio*.

46. Meredeth Turshen, "The Political Economy of Rape: An Analysis of Systematic Rape and Sexual Abuse of Women During Armed Conflict in Africa," in *Victors,*

Perpetrators, or Actors: Gender Armed Conflict and Political Violence, eds. Caroline O. N. Moser and Fiona C. Clark. (London: Zed Books, 2001), 56.

47. Barbara Rose Johnston, "Chixoy Dam Legacies: The Struggle to Secure Reparation and the Right to Remedy in Guatemala," *Water Alternatives* 3:2 (2010): 341–61.

48. Pseudonym.

49. Dill, "Mediated Pasts."

50. CEH, *Memoria de Silencio*, Testigo CEH (T.C. 53).

51. CEH, *Memoria de Silencio*.

52. Jo-Marie Boesten, "Six Witnesses Recount Atrocities at Sepur Zarco on Day Two of Landmark Trial," *International Justice Monitor, Open Society Justice Initiative* (2014), Accessed January 26, 2017, 2014, https://www.ijmonitor.org/2016/02/six-witnesses -recount-atrocities-at-sepur-zarco-on-day-two-of-landmark-trial/.

53. Ex-president Otto Perez Molina was arrested on September 2, 2015, and charged with corruption. He is accused of directing a customs-fraud scheme, which eliminated government import taxes in exchange for payoffs. He is currently awaiting trial in a military prison. See Jan Martínez Ahrens (Translation by Martin Delfin), "Guatemala's jailed ex-leader: 'I didn't want any deaths just to save my skin," *El País*, December 15, 2015. In October 2015, Jimmy Morales, a television comedian backed by right wing military and elite business interests, won the presidential election with the slogan "Not corrupt, nor a Thief." See Elizabeth Malkin and NIC Wiritz, *NY Times, Americas* (October 25, 2015).

54. Burt, "Historic Genocide Trial Nears End."

Gender and the Military in Post-Genocide Rwanda

Georgina Holmes

INTRODUCTION[1]

As civil war took place in the north of the country and Hutu extremists prepared for genocide against Tutsi and moderate Hutu, Rwanda in the early 1990s saw a sharp rise in the persecution of men, women, girls, and boys. At the time, instances of rape and violence, forced marriage, disappearances, coercion, and torture were documented by the UN Mission in Rwanda (UNAMIR), opposition parties, local human rights groups, Human Rights Watch, and Amnesty International. State security forces promoted a climate of insecurity, often staging attacks on small communities and blaming their enemy, the Rwandan Patriotic Front/Rwandan Patriotic Army (RPF/RPA). The war between the government and the RPF displaced over one million Rwandans, forcing civilian men, women, and children to live in vulnerable conditions, and intensifying gender insecurities. In this climate, the architects of genocide instilled fear in the population, inciting Rwandan citizens to commit genocide against innocent people categorized as enemies of the state. More than twenty years after the genocide, the central role played by the Presidential Guard, the Forces Armèes Rwandaises (FAR), and the Gendarmerie Nationale in committing genocide in 1994, and of the Rwandan Patriotic Army in committing war crimes and contributing to the climate of insecurity in the early 1990s, continues to be a legacy issue for the former insurgent group, now ruling party the RPF. Consequently, the regime has been required to secure its legitimacy both domestically and internationally, and has embarked on an ambitious program designed to modernize state security organs and build trust among Rwandan citizens. Part of this program includes integrating more women into the Rwanda Defence Force (RDF) and developing a more gender representative and responsive security sector.

This chapter undertakes a process-oriented study of genocide to consider how the gendered nature of genocide continues to influence security policies in postconflict Rwanda, and informs Rwandan women's motives for joining state security organs. I argue that while the RDF's gender program supports once shared national policy goals to mainstream gender equality across politics, economy, and culture, the program has been designed to help improve the reputation of the national armed forces, and in doing so, sets out to strengthen the legitimacy of the authoritarian state. This is achieved in three ways: by supporting the implementation of internal security policy goals; by attempting to improve civil-military relations; and, by transforming societal perceptions of military women. The first part of the chapter discusses how societal perceptions of both military women and the national armed forces have evolved since precolonial times up until 1994. The second part outlines the RDF's gender program, before examining the challenges the RDF faces in recruiting military women. Here, the chapter draws on depth interviews with RDF female military personnel, RDF senior leaders, and government policymakers to consider how new societal perceptions about military women have emerged out of the complex dynamics of genocide and civil war. The final part of the chapter examines how integrating women into the national armed forces facilitates regime survival. In doing so, the chapter demonstrates how the Rwanda Defence Force's gender mainstreaming initiatives reflect the paradoxical nature of postconflict development in Rwanda. For the purposes of this research, gender mainstreaming is defined as the promotion of 'gender equality through [the] systematic integration of [gender in] all systems and structures, into all policies, processes and procedures, into the organisation and its culture' and into institutional 'ways of seeing and doing'.[2]

BACKGROUND

Between April and July 1994, some eight hundred thousand Tutsi and moderate Hutu were killed during a state-sponsored genocide. Planned by a group of extremist Hutu closely connected to the family of President Juvénal Habyarimana, the genocide was one of the swiftest of the twentieth century, with killings executed six times faster than in the Nazi Holocaust. Within an hour of the shooting down of Habyarimana's plane on April 6, 1994, government soldiers set up roadblocks in the capital, Kigali, and the Presidential Guard, an elite military unit, began seeking out and killing minority Tutsi and prodemocratic Hutus from opposition parties. Following the murder of the interim Prime Minister Agathe Uwilingiyimana, Hutu extremists took power in a military coup. As the genocide progressed, gangs of men, women, and children, many of whom were members of the Hutu extremist youth-wing, the Interahamwe, hunted down and killed "the enemy." The genocide took place four years into a civil war between the Rwandan Patriotic Front—an armed political movement comprised of predominantly Tutsi refugees from Uganda— and the Mouvement RépublICan National pour la Démocratie et le Développement (MRND) government, and within a year of the signing of the UN–negotiated Arusha Peace Accords by both parties to the conflict. The genocide ended when the Rwandan Patriotic Front took Kigali on July 4, 1994, and a state of emergency was declared. Although initially, the newly formed government was representative of Rwandan prodemocratic political parties, the RPF consolidated its powerbase in 2003 when, following the results of the first post-genocide elections, Rwanda became a single-party state.

The different ways in which men and women, boys and girls were targeted during the 1994 genocide in Rwanda has been well documented by academics and in the cases of the International Criminal Tribunal for Rwanda (ICTR). The UN estimates that between two hundred and fifty thousand and five hundred thousand women were raped during the genocide.[3] Rape was employed as a means to annihilate Tutsi, to kill, impregnate women, or infect them with HIV/AIDS. Rape and sexual violence, often inflicted in public by both men and women, was used as a means to subvert traditional Rwandan reproductive symbols, break familial bonds, and perpetrate violence on the wider community.[4] Hutu women—particularly those married to Tutsi men—were also raped and killed. Because many of the killings took place in small, close-knit communities, and often by perpetrators who were known to their victims, the population was left deeply divided and traumatized in the aftermath of the genocide. These societal divisions were further exacerbated by the legacy of the civil war.

Narratives about human rights abuses committed during civil war and genocide in Rwanda in the early 1990s continue to be employed in the mediatized conflicts of the Great Lakes region of Africa. Throughout the 2000s European based spokesmen of the non-state armed group the Forces Démocratiques de Libération du Rwanda (FDLR), comprised of former Hutu extremists and their supporters who sought to return to Rwanda as a political opposition party, attempted to garner 'ideological support for their political cause' by issuing reports and press releases detailing human rights abuses that they alleged the Rwandan Patriotic Front had committed in order to 'weaken the legitimacy of the Rwandan government—already called into question by critics of the administration'.[5] It is in the context of this political climate that the RPF regime has sought to stabilize its legitimacy, while implementing a controversial postconflict recovery and development program encompassing economic growth, modernization, community cohesion, and reconciliation.

STATE BUILDING AND CENSORSHIP IN RWANDA

In recent years, there has emerged a polarized debate within the academic literature on postconflict state-building in Rwanda, centered on the themes of freedom of speech and democracy, censorship, and surveillance. A major issue concerns the extent to which Rwandan citizens believe they have ownership of—and feel comfortable to openly and critically discuss—the postconflict recovery and development program led by the ruling party, the RPF, as well as decisions made to intervene in wars in the East of Congo. In this context, interviewing Rwandan military personnel inevitably presents challenges. First, the political environment in Rwanda and the tight control over official narratives about the modernization and development of postconflict Rwanda—and indeed, the 1994 genocide and civil war—may lead some research participants to ensure their responses conform to national narratives. This issue was of particular concern during the fieldwork because participants were currently employed in the Rwanda Defence Force. Almost all the interviews were conducted in official military spaces, which may have reminded participants of their duty to respond first as soldiers and loyal citizens. However, many women did express their views about gender issues within the RDF, even if some exercised caution in the way they responded to interview questions. There was also a higher probability that the participants interviewed for this project would present a more positive outlook on government state-building initiatives than many other Rwandan citizens. Rwandans who wish to join the RDF must enter into a highly competitive and rigorous selection process at the district-level. RDF senior leaders therefore aim to recruit only those Rwandans whose personal values closely align to both RDF institutional values and the vision of the RPF government, although officially soldiers do not need to be members of the RPF political party. Cadet training lasts one year, during which time new recruits are socialized into RDF military culture. The current government discourages the public use of Tutsi, Hutu, and Twa ethnicities, and research participants were not asked their ethnicity. However, many of the women volunteered information about their family's history and their relatives' attitudes toward military women in Rwanda.

In an attempt to mitigate these research challenges, interviews are complemented by additional documentary research and a discourse analysis of RDF gender policies. The chapter draws on the research findings collected from sixty-five semi-structured depth interviews with Rwandan female military service personnel and male senior staff within the Rwanda Defence Force conducted at the Rwanda Military Academy Gako Campus and the Ministry of Defence in Kigali, Rwanda, between February 2014 and December 2015. Interviews were conducted in either English, French, or Kinyarwanda before being translated and transcribed into English.

Research participants were informed in advance that all responses would be anonymized, and all participants consented to the interviews.

SOCIETAL PERCEPTIONS OF MILITARY
WOMEN IN RWANDA

Government officials and supporters of the ruling elite, the Rwandan Patriotic Front, often talk about the existence of two Rwandan cultures. The first, described as Rwanda's "traditional culture," is considered to have been deeply misogynistic and characterized by unjust social relations that oppressed and marginalized Rwandan women across social, economic, and political spheres. Regardless of their ethnicity, women had no land rights, little protection from gender-based discrimination and violence, limited access to education, and few opportunities for social and economic advancement.[6] The second culture is described as Rwanda's "new, modern culture," which embraces gender equality and the empowerment of women. This culture is considered to be the product of the Rwandan Patriotic Front's (RPF's) postconflict recovery and redevelopment program, the blueprint for reconstructing Rwanda in the aftermath of war and genocide. The RPF government's success in integrating women into Rwanda's political sphere has been much celebrated internationally. In 2003, gender equality was enshrined in Rwanda's Constitution, and all public institutions require by law that women hold 30 percent of positions. Currently, women constitute 64 percent of Rwanda's parliamentarians and 40 percent of ministers; they hold 50 percent of the seats in the Supreme Court, 32 percent of the seats in the Senate; and represent 35 percent of leaders within decentralized structures.[7] Rwanda's success has also been driven by women's activism within civil society, particularly in the years directly after the genocide, when civil society organizations were less restricted.[8]

Although depicting pre-1994 and post-1994 as distinct temporal periods lends itself well to the creation of an ideological divide between old and new Rwanda, the practice obfuscates continuities in behaviors and processes that have either led to change within Rwandan society, or have sustained the status quo. For example, the foundations for women's advancement were laid from the late 1980s onward, when a burgeoning women's movement campaigned alongside political parties in Rwanda in the bid to bring about democracy and end Habyarimana's twenty-seven-year dictatorship.[9] Conversely, entrenched societal attitudes and expectations of gender roles prevail in all regions of contemporary Rwanda, as well as among members of the political elite, and there are reports of a backlash by men against the government's positive discrimination initiatives that favor women. In this regard, the current RPF government's articulation of a modern Rwandan culture that embraces gender equality and women's empowerment is aspirational at best, and does not reflect the full reality of social change in Rwanda.

This leads us to consider how successive national militaries have either sustained or transformed gender roles in Rwanda. Feminists contend that the military institution typically functions as the primary agency for the construction of hegemonic masculinity and supports the gendered social order in a given society. Hegemonic masculinity is reproduced through "specific forms of socialization, disciplinary models, and authority patterns" to become "a core element of a soldier's self-definition," as well as the operative norm within the institution.[10] As Colleen Burke observes, these patterns of socialization, often encapsulated in military values, "contribute to the construction of narrow definitions of masculine and feminine characteristics."[11] Although age, life status, and class informed gender roles in traditional Rwandan society and varied from region to region,[12] gender stereotypes played on a narrow dialectic of male/female binaries. Historically, masculinities were defined by the societal perception of the soldier-warrior, and male adulthood was achieved through the socializing processes of army training, which taught men toughness.[13] Women were viewed positively when they were "reserved, submissive, modest, silent, and maternal, when they maintain a 'respectable' household, and when they raise 'wise' children." In contrast, men were expected to be "self-assured, dominant, logical, brave and physically strong."[14] Burnet writes that "The positive qualities associated with maleness are so strong that when a woman displays competence it can be a compliment to say 'Ni umumfabo' (she's a man), although this usage is rare. The more commonly used phrase, 'Ni igishegabo' (She's a big man-woman), is an insult to describe a woman who displays characteristics desirable in a man, such as outspokenness and aggression, but objectionable in a woman."[15]

In precolonial Rwanda, the national army was a patriarchal system of "social armies," much like battalions but structured along hereditary lines, and therefore closely integrated into society. According to Rwandan military historian and former RPF Brigadier General Frank Rusagara, "a man would usually remain in his military formation throughout his lifespan" and would "usually belong to the army subunit of his father."[16] These social armies would mobilize at the behest of the "Mwami" (king). Male dominance of the military was also preserved in Rwandan oral literature. One folktale describing the plight of Ndabaga, a young woman who disguises herself as a man in order to replace her frail father, warns women of the consequences of challenging traditional Rwandan gender roles. Ndabaga cuts off her breasts and dons men's clothing, and once in the military succeeds in becoming a champion archer. Her gender is discovered when other soldiers become suspicious of her search for privacy. When the "Mwami" hears of Ndabaga's duplicity, he is impressed, yet casts her out of the military.[17] Rangira Béa Gallimore notes that the exclusion of women from the military is linguistically reflected in Kinyarwanda, observing that ""the word for 'male' in Kinyarwanda is 'umugabo' where the radical 'gab(o)' denotes masculinity....The Kinyarwanda word for army is 'ingabo.' This same word signifies 'shield.' Here, the emphasis is on the protective role played by the male soldier in the society."[18]

Societal perceptions of the military under Belgian colonial rule, in the early years of independence and throughout the twenty-seven-year dictatorship of President Habyarimana, were far more pessimistic. The replacement of the traditional Rwandan army by the colonial military, the Force Publique, occurred in the late 1920s. Alongside the establishment of the colonial racial ideology, and the "Tutsification" of administration, (in which Hutu and Twa chiefs were replaced with Tutsi), chiefs were no longer required to train or mobilize military men. In this respect, the disbanding of the old social army, the Ingabo z'u Rwanda, saw the erosion of the protectorate role of the Rwandan male soldier, and reinforced the exclusion of women from the military. In the colonial era, soldiers were perceived to be more aggressive, and masculine dominance over the military was asserted through inflicting Sexual and Gender Based Violence

(SGBV) on civilian women. One Kinyarwanda word for rape, gufalinga, derives from the letters FAL, which referred to the Fusil Automatique Léger—a Belgian automatic gun used by the Force Publique.[19] According to Alison Des Forges, "hundreds of [poorly paid and badly treated African] troops" from the Force Publique battalion deployed in Rwanda sometimes "escaped the control of their [European] officers and robbed and raped" women at gunpoint and "at will."[20] Rusagara claims that prior to this colonial violence, no Kinyarwanda word for rape existed, since women were so well respected in Rwandan society.[21] Nevertheless, the linguistic association of rape with an external non-Rwandan military force serves to set apart military violence from other forms of gendered violence in society, thereby concealing the everyday realities of civilian women and girls subjected to domestic violence, including child abuse and rape in marriage. Successive national armies engaged in political violence have each perpetrated ethnically targeted gendered crimes against humanity. This includes the period during the Hutu Revolution in 1959, which saw the transition from Belgian administration and Tutsi control to Hutu-dominated Republica in 1961, and the failed genocides against Tutsi in 1962 and 1973.

THE EARLY 1990S

The interconnected nature of the precolonial "social army" with the identity and role of the Rwandan man provides an interesting perspective on how Hutu extremists in the early 1990s mobilized both Hutu men and women to commit genocide against Tutsi and moderate Hutu. However, to understand the gendered nature of the 1994 genocide in Rwanda and the Rwandan government's post-genocide state security policies, it is important to acknowledge that genocide is not a static event, but is born out of a series of complex social, political, and historical processes.[22] Genocide scholar Greg Stanton identifies ten stages of genocide: classification, symbolization, discrimination, dehumanization, organization, polarization, preparation, persecution, extermination, and denial. Yet genocide itself is not a single, linear process. As Rosenberg notes, both direct and indirect "methods of annihilation might occur at different points in the linear process and/or might reflect a jumping or collapsing of stages."[23] While the shooting down of President Habyarimana's plane by an unconfirmed assailant on April 6, 1994, is widely considered the trigger that led to the killing of some eight hundred thousand Tutsi and prodemocratic Hutu in one hundred days, the conditions that led a population to commit genocide can also be attributed to the disintegration of state security as well as the rapid militarization of citizens from 1990 on.[24] For the purposes of this discussion, I identify four factors contributing to the security breakdown:

1. The civil war between the MRND government and the Rwandan Patriotic Front, which began when the RPF invaded on October 1, 1990.
2. Internal power struggles between Rwandan elites of all ethnicities who called for genuine democracy and power sharing, and Hutu clientele of the president's family who had substantially profited during the twenty-seven-year dictatorship.
3. The collapse of the Rwandan economy in 1989, which also led to a rise in unemployment, particularly among Hutu youths.
4. The implementation of the Hutu extremist "Final Solution" to rid Rwanda of ethnic Tutsi and establish a pure Hutu state.

Hutu extremists infiltrated and created divisions within prodemocratic political parties as well as civil society groups, including burgeoning women's groups. This contributed to a political stalemate, with members of Prime Minister Agathe Uwilingiyimana's interim government failing to reach a consensus on key security issues including the problem of widespread famine and the high number of internally displaced people attributed to the civil war.[25] There was an increase in political assassinations, and large massacres of the Tutsi minority took place, including in Kilbilra (1990), Bogogwe (1991), and Bugesera (1992). These massacres were allegedly "instigated and organized by local authorities with the complicity of certain prominent persons from the President's circle."[26] As state security disintegrated, gender insecurities in all regions of Rwanda increased dramatically. Although previously there were high levels of domestic violence and child abuse, women's groups under the umbrella organization Pro-Femmes Twese Hamwe received increased reports of incidents of rape and SGBV, particularly in the north of the country.[27] Survivors of the genocide and war in northern regions claim that local government officials "advised women to wear both shorts (amagongo) and underwear beneath their skirts as an impediment to rape, rather than wearing nothing per custom."[28] Women in the capital Kigali felt threatened in spite of the nighttime curfew imposed.[29] Investigations conducted by Human Rights Watch and the International Commission on Human Rights Abuse in Rwanda in the early 1990s indicate that the RPF and their military arm, the Rwandan Patriotic Army, were "responsible for a number of serious human rights violations in the early years of the war in Rwanda," most notably in the northeastern province.[30] Hutu extremists were able to capitalize on the RPF's violence and the increased gender insecurities in all regions of Rwanda to perpetuate a climate of fear, thereby goading Hutu to partake in genocide as an act of revenge and retribution.[31] For example, in 1993, UNAMIR (UN Mission in Rwanda) reported that several massacres by soldiers from the then national armed forces, the Forces Armées Rwandaises (FAR), in which women and girls had been raped, were staged to look as though they had been committed by the RPF.[32]

In one of her final interviews with the international media on March 15, 1994, Prime Minister Uwilingiyimana lamented the declining security situation in Rwanda. Uwilingiyimana observed that few political assassinations and massacres were investigated by the government and those that were investigated "never reach[ed] a conclusion."[33] She was deeply concerned that the national army was not under her orders, and that the heightened levels of violence and insecurity across all regions of Rwanda were being dismissed as outside his remit by the then Minister of Defence Augustin Bizimana, an MRND party member and Hutu extremist. In one instance, Bizimana challenged her authority by signing a communiqué in which "there was a decision to arrest all the contacts of the RPF" without her permission. At the time, Uwilingiyimana feared Bizimana was undermining the power-sharing agreement set out in the Arusha Peace Accords, which called for the "integration of the two armies," the Forces Armées Rwandaises and the RPF. She continued, observing that, "He signed the communiqué and I did not know that he said it came from my office. I said to the President that he had to intervene, but the President said "No, leave him. If you say this communiqué is nothing to do with you—either I am proud of my government, or I am not." This shows you it is difficult to say that the army is under my orders. If the army was under my orders, I can assure you there would be security."[34]

In a similar vein to the concept of a call to arms of the precolonial "Ingabo z'u Rwanda," Hutu extremists militarized ethnic Hutu and encouraged a Hutu "social army" to rise up against the Tutsi enemy. In this respect, women were actively encouraged to engage in military activities, albeit under the guise of community service (umuganda). Hate propaganda developed by Hutu extremists militarized Tutsi women as enemies, spies, and complicit with the RPF. Hutu women who were members of moderate political parties, such as the Parti Libéral (PL), and rejected Hutu extremist ideology were not to be trusted, while those Hutu women who joined the extremist political parties the MRND, the Coalition pour la Défense de la République (CDR), and were members of the youth-wing the Interahamwe, were celebrated.[35]

During the 1994 genocide, the traditional female/male binaries were subverted, and it became socially acceptable for women to behave aggressively, to be physically strong, and to kill (though not all Hutu women did so). However, women were still excluded from the national army, the Forces Armées Rwandaises. Many conventional female roles were also valued during the genocide, such as singing and chanting—often to ululate men into action or to encourage male and female members of the Interahamwe to kill.[36] The militarization of Hutu women is perhaps epitomized by Rose Karushara, a counselor at sector level who "took an extremely active role in the genocide" and wore military fatigues throughout.[37] Indeed, one male witness used the insulting Ni igishegabo term when describing Karushara to African Rights in 1995: "She was a giant, very strong and often beat up the men who came to her house for beer [which she sold]. With the progressive advance of the RPF, Rose became more and more wild."[38]

By contrast, the socialist RPF was dependent on recruiting refugee women into the liberation movement, and into the Rwandan Patriotic Army. Women served on the frontline as soldiers and medics, although they represented just one percent of all RPA military personnel during the civil war.[39] Some, such as then Lieutenant Rose Kabuye and Aloiyse Inyumba (who would later serve in senior positions in Paul Kagame's government), were involved in financing, developing strategy, and gathering intelligence.[40] Minister for Gender and Family Promotion, Oda Gasinzigwa claims that "in the RPF liberation struggle, the inclusion [of women] was there. They were fighting for liberation of the country—so there was the mobilization of women. At all ages, young, old, the youth—all had something to do to liberate the country."[41]

Other women joined the RPF directly after the genocide, when the guerrilla army was establishing itself as a proto national army. One captain described her motives for joining the military, which she refers to as the Rwanda Defence Force:

> Actually, I didn't join during the struggle. I was already in the country. But just after the operation, I joined the liberation, I joined the RDF. Like any other person, when you see a liberation struggle, you wish you could be part of that movement—to have your input and your say in the liberation. Because, then, the RPF ideology was attracting us—young people. [They were saying]: "Your country has been under oppression for a long time". We wished that ideology could change—the ideology of oppression, of discrimination. So myself, I wanted the system to change. That's why I joined the RPF—to have a say in the liberation and the new ideology of the country. I joined in August 1994.

INTEGRATING WOMEN INTO THE RDF

The RDF's policy to recruit more women into the armed forces began a decade after the transitional government established the Rwanda Demobilization and Reintegration Commission in 1997, which set out to rebuild and modernize Rwanda's security forces after the RPF had consolidated its powerbase. In a move to rid the armed forces of ethnic sectarianism, the Rwanda Demobilization and Reintegration Programme focused on the following goals: the integration of ex-combatants from the ex-Forces Armées Rwandaises and the Rwandan Patriotic Army, as originally proposed in the 1993 Arusha Peace Accords, professionalization of military personnel, and social cohesion. Over the past two decades, the military's demographics have shifted from being predominantly Tutsi refugees (now returnees) from Uganda, Burundi, and the Democratic Republic of Congo (as they were in the Rwandan Patriotic Army in the early 1990s), to representing the breadth of ethnic and socioeconomic groups in Rwanda. Thus, the RDF is no longer a "Tutsi" military among the lower ranks, although senior leadership positions are dominated by former RPA personnel who fought in the civil war,[42] many of whom are either members of, or closely connected to the ruling elite. Since Paul Kagame became president of Rwanda in 2003 and the RPF consolidated its power base, there has been increasing concern that the current government is using the military as a means to extend the reach of the authoritarian state.[43]

The RDF is shaped by both "perceived and experienced origins, as well as the contextual environment" of the genocide and civil war.[44] Yet, the legacy of the origins of the Rwandan Patriotic Front remains entrenched. The RDF website states that "The Rwanda Defence Force (RDF) was previously a liberation force known as the Rwandan Patriotic Army (RPA). Law No. 19/2002 of 17/05/2002 renamed the RPA as the Rwanda Defence Force."[45] There is also a strong belief both among RDF troops and elements of the Rwandan population, that the new army is a continuation of the older Rwandan Patriotic Army. This is evident in some of the phrases used by military personnel, most notably those who joined the military prior to the security sector reform program. As one woman commented, "I joined the RDF in 1992 when it was still called the RPF. Then it changed to the RDF."[46] Similarly, in informal interactions and discussions with RDF soldiers, the author observed a sense of pride among male and female military personnel who had fought in the RPF liberation war, some of whom commanded significant respect and awe from newer, younger recruits who had never before engaged in fighting on the frontline. Cadet training and subsequent training sessions that military personnel receive ensure that they are socialized, and remain socialized into RDF military culture, which promotes old RPF "liberation" values, including discipline, patriotism, and support for building a new, modern Rwanda.

Rwanda has gained an international reputation for its success in integrating women into political institutions at all decision-making levels. Yet, as is often the case with national militaries, the Rwanda Defence Force is one of the last public institutions to integrate a gender perspective and is significantly further behind in the process than Rwanda National Police. There is increasing pressure from Parliament to mainstream gender equality in the armed forces. In 2014, parliamentary oversight of the RDF gender budget was agreed on in order to allow the Ministry of

Gender and Family Promotion, and the Gender Monitoring Office (GMO) greater opportunities to lobby for change.[47] Since 2004, the number of female military personnel has increased from 241 to 633 in 2014, with the greatest increase seen after the RDF Gender Desk was established.[48] However, there are still fewer women in the armed forces today than there were in the Rwandan Patriotic Army directly after the genocide. As the Director of the Gender Desk explains:

> The RDF is a mixture of former government forces and the people who were fighting who decided to join, and the RPA, and other [militia] groups which joined later. Four hundred females have already decided to voluntarily retire, for demobilization, because they had reached the age of retirement. Because of the conflicts and the effects of the genocide, these women have decided to retire from the former forces, the former RPA, so the number [of female military personnel] of course has continued to reduce.... We are concentrating on recruitment and retirement of those who can't go far. I think the force will be increasing with professional people—not only females but also men.[49]

More female military personnel are required to support the RDF in delivering on its national and international commitments to address the different ways in which conflict affects men and women—both within the state and while engaged in peace support operations. Here, the Government of Rwanda takes a holistic approach to combating domestic insecurity issues and is attempting to incorporate a gender perspective into its national security policies, which emphasize human security. According to an RDF presentation during a planning meeting for Rwanda's first UN Security Council Resolution 1325 Action Plan (2010)—which details how state apparatus will protect women and girls during and after conflict, and enable women's participation in conflict prevention and peacebuilding—security "in the current context" is "no longer defined in terms of defence and protection of national sovereignty or homeland security; the security concept also takes into account nonmilitary aspects such as the economy, society, environment, politics, and diplomacy."[50]

The RPF government's policy approach to addressing gendered insecurities is also informed by the legacy of the fragmentation of state security in the early 1990s and the effects civil war had on the population, although the 1325 National Action Plan only emphasizes how the government "has worked hard to rehabilitate the country" after it was "devastated by the genocide perpetrated against the Tutsi in 1994."[51]

Implementing the government's prevent-sexual and gender based violence (SGBV) strategy is the RDF's priority, as it is for the Rwanda National Police, and female soldiers play a role in engaging with women across all regions and districts. Here, the RDF's vision is to improve "human security" through a series of objectives, including "promot[ing] gender equality, equity and women's empowerment" in the community; preventing and responding to HIV/AIDS as a consequence of SGBV; encouraging women to "play a significant role in decision-making processes;" working with local community leaders to "establish adult literacy programs and skills development for women as a strategy for effectively combating Gender Based Violence;" and "empowering women to contribute meaningfully to national poverty reduction."[52] A final objective "to follow up on gender related issues in the community through research, monitoring and evaluation" is proposed, though the RDF Gender Desk lacks the resources to do so.[53] In this regard, the government's holistic approach to addressing gender insecurities is a positive development since it challenges the perceived separation of (externally perpetrated) military-led gender violence from other forms of gendered violence, including domestic violence, as previously promoted in Rwandan culture. Female military personnel also believe that the RDF's gender program does support Rwanda's broader gender equality policy priorities by opening up the military to women and encouraging and empowering women to pursue a career in what is becoming an increasingly professional and disciplined military. However, further research is required to understand the impact of RDF gender-sensitive civil-military operations, and to ascertain whether these initiatives are perceived to benefit the local population.

RECRUITING FEMALE MILITARY PERSONNEL

Ideological and practical reasons motivate Rwandan women to join the armed forces in the post-genocide era. Many of the women interviewed, regardless of ethnicity, spoke of supporting the state in rebuilding Rwanda, and joining the army enabled them to "do their bit" for the country.

Others believed being a soldier empowered them and were in favor of the RPF government's policy to promote gender equality. Yet a career in the RDF also provides job security, a competitive salary, access to paid maternity leave, and a chance to gain a military-funded, degree-level education. As in any society, there are women who have a strong desire to serve in the military and have held ambitions of becoming soldiers from a very early age. Indeed, several of the women interviewed had watched and admired soldiers at work, including female Rwandan Patriotic Army soldiers, in the months and years directly after the genocide. Representatives of the RDF Gender Desk maintain that Rwandan women are reluctant to join the military because traditional societal values and attitudes toward military women prevail. All of the female military personnel interviewed emphasized that traditional societal perceptions depicting military women as aggressive and uncomfortably masculine still circulate, and that, in contrast to Rwanda's political institutions, the military institution continues to be regarded by many Rwandan citizens as a domain of male privilege. One relatively senior ranking female soldier observed that "in Rwandan culture, and not only in Rwandan culture, very few women would like to join the military. They still think that the military is a man's job."[54]

When asked how her family reacted when she told them of her intention to join the RDF, a female Captain remarked: "Do you know our past culture? There were no women in the military. [They would say] It's a tough duty, then women cannot do that. It is a difficult duty, so the women are too weak. That was the perception.... Some of them [the Rwandan population] still have that perception."[55]

However, new attitudes toward military women have emerged in the wake of the genocide and civil war and there exist competing societal perceptions about military women in postconflict Rwanda. The negative perception of Rwanda's national armed forces stems in part from the legacy of the Forces Armées Rwandaises and the Presidential Guard's involvement in perpetrating genocide in the early 1990s. Societal perceptions are also informed by collective historical memories of the actions and behaviors of Rwandan Patriotic Army soldiers, who are accused of killings during combat, summary executions, and other human rights abuses, both during the genocide and after they won the civil war.[56] Some sections of the population are critical of the Rwandan Patriotic Front and the newer Rwanda Defence Force's

intervention in conflicts in the east of Congo from 1997 to 2007, and later in
2012, when the RPF government was accused of supporting the M23 rebellion
against the Congolese government. All of these factors generate distrust of the
newly formed Rwanda Defence Force. Military women who have retired from
the Rwandan Patriotic Army, and women who are currently employed by the
RDF are perceived negatively by some because of their association with the
current ruling elite. Publicly, many Rwandans speak positively of the Rwandan
Patriotic Front and the Rwandan Patriotic Army, in spite of the war crimes they
committed, because they helped to end the genocide, establish security in the
aftermath of genocide and war, and rebuilt the country. A corporal interviewed
suggested that her mother was supportive of her wish to join the military in 2003
because she believed her daughter owed allegiance to the post-genocide government and the Rwandan Patriotic Front. She stated, "I had finished high school
and then I heard that announcement and I asked them [her parents] if I can
join. Because I have one parent, I asked her if I could join. Then she said, go and
work for our country. You see how they [the Rwandan Patriotic Front] helped
us and when we were in a bad situation. So go and work together with them."[57]

Another legacy of the role of the military and militarized individuals during the 1994 genocide concerns the extent to which societal perceptions of
female military personnel in contemporary Rwanda reflect the view that the
national armed forces is an unprofessional, corrupt institution. One inter-
viewee revealed how female soldiers were often regarded as prostitutes and
mistresses of, what were perceived to be, undisciplined RDF men: "Before
I joined the army [in 2003], there were rumors saying that women in the
military were bitches of men in the army. But I found that it is not true. We
come and work as usual and then go back to our homes."[58]

A twenty-five-year-old private also observed, that "at that time [of my
joining the RDF], the parents could not accept it, but for now they agree.
At that time, their mindset was that a life of a soldier was very bad, and
they would think that I would be sleeping with all the soldiers because,
at that time, not many girls loved to join the army. So people would think
that the number of men was too big to the [number of] girls."[59] However,
none of the research participants spoke openly about whether women
experienced sexual harassment in the RDF.

The suggestion that the female soldier is a prostitute or sexually promis-
cuous reflects the negative images of militarized Tutsi women published

in Hutu extremist hate propaganda prior to April 1994, which portrayed them as mistresses and prostitutes of RPF soldiers and UN peacekeepers.[60] This contemporary societal perception also serves as a warning to Rwandan women that if they join the RDF, they risk losing their status and value within society—either as young, unmarried and virtuous girls, or as respected women and mothers whose position of power resides in the home. The emphasis on the military woman's immoral sexual relations with military men is particularly detrimental, since in traditional Rwandan culture, women who have premarital relations dishonor their family, while those who have children outside of marriage are considered an "abomination," regardless of whether the pregnancy is the result of rape or a consensual relationship. In the past, these women and girls were often banished to remote locations.[61] The image also stands in stark contrast to Ndabaga, from the precolonial folktale, who was admired by the *Mwami* for her military prowess, courage, and purity, even though he cast her out of the precolonial army.

The emergence of new and often competing societal perceptions about military women in postconflict Rwanda can also be observed in the treatment of female Rwandan Patriotic Army soldiers who were demobilized during stage one and two of the Rwanda Demobilization and Reintegration Program. According to research conducted in 2013 by a Rwandan at the National University of Rwanda, female ex-combatants who have been reintegrated into local communities are struggling more than their male colleagues. Former female Rwandan Patriotic Army soldiers feel ostracized and excluded, rather than respected for their role in ending the genocide—a respect the women believed they had earned. One former combatant remarked: "Those women who have never been involved in the military see us as rough people just because we were involved in the military and this is against cultural norms. Instead of considering us as heroes we are seen as abnormal."

Another woman preferred to conceal her past identity during interactions with people in her community and felt uncomfortable once her former role with the RPA/RDF was made known: "I have people asking me my role during the war whenever they know that I am an ex-combatant, which is not the case for male combatants. And when you analyze this statement thoroughly, you find that they disapprove of women's active contributions."[62]

Many female ex-combatants believed they were among the poorest in their communities, but felt excluded from community programs and locally organized financial initiatives because there was a perception, even among local officials, that former RPA/RDF women were wealthier than their civilian counterparts. These women strongly disputed the claims that they received adequate financial support from the Rwanda Demobilization and Reintegration Commission and the Ministry of Defence, or were favored and protected by RPF elite.[63]

In response to these negative societal perceptions, the RPF government and the RDF have developed official narratives that eulogize the integral role women play in securing the state and a traumatized society left divided by genocide and war. RPA women helped to win the "liberation war" in 1994, and the importance of local women's networks in establishing security immediately after the genocide is celebrated. Attempting to reduce the tensions between traditional and modern (policy-driven) narratives about military women, the RDF have also reappropriated the folktale of Ndabaga to suggest that military women are not exceptional or a social deviance, but revered in Rwandan culture. As one representative of the RDF Gender Desk reflected:

> There is what we call mindset—the background, the history. Our history never saw that women can be soldiers, like men. They never thought about that. In our history we have only one girl called Ndabaga—that lady, I think she was the first who proved that even women can fight for their motherland, can go on the frontline and can do well like men. So there is that mindset which is in both women and men, but when you look at today, now things are changing.[64]

These official narratives are promoted during annual recruitment campaigns, when RDF representatives visit schools and universities, in advertisements broadcast on television and radio to motivate women to join the RDF, and on a frequent basis in the national press.[65]

STRENGTHENING THE LEGITIMACY OF THE STATE

State-led gender programs in Rwanda have been criticized for supporting economic modernization, community cohesion, and reconciliation policy goals, rather than viewing the transformation of gender relations as an end goal in itself.[66] Mainstreaming gender equality in the RDF and establishing the Gender Desk's program of work do indeed support the government's broader policy goals. However, an intended outcome of the RDF's gender program is to improve the reputation of the national armed forces among Rwandan citizens. In doing so, the RPF seeks to establish [new] links with the local Rwandan population[67] strengthen the legitimacy of the authoritarian state. This is achieved in three ways: by implementing collective domestic security policy goals; attempting to improve civil-military relations; and transforming societal perceptions of military women.

In much the same way as the government's support for gender equality draws on both RPF liberation ideology and the political goals of Rwanda's pre-1994 women's movement, preventing the recurrence of violent ethnic extremism and a commitment to development were shared policy goals developed by Rwanda's political elite in the early 2000s. These included members of the former prodemocratic parties who were targeted by Hutu extremists in 1994.[68] Combating ethnic sectarianism thus forms one component of the political settlement in Rwanda that was established prior to 2003, when the RPF consolidated its powerbase, and is enshrined in the Constitution.[69] The RDF is particularly concerned that civil-military operations developed by its Gender Desk support the government in maintaining macro-level postconflict stability in order, as they understand it, to reduce the risk future genocides, by reducing conflict in the domestic sphere. The RDF training manual for the gender module for all military personnel observes that addressing gender insecurities reduces conflict and ethnic sectarianism. Sexual and gender based violence "creates the violated (Victims) and violators (Perpetrators)" and is "a cause of insecurity, mistrust and fear amongst the population, which is a key recipe for conflict and attendant insecurity in society."[70] The training manual informs military personnel that Hutu extremist genocide ideology still directly affects personal relations, including between some Hutu and Tutsi who are married: "ethnic difference ... is yet to be done away with at domestic and community level." Accordingly, "in marriages, spouses assault one another and exaggerate mistakes of their spouses as they blame the other's ethnic group on what happened or did not happen" during the genocide.[71] To prevent the rise of ethnic sectarianism and divisionism and to instill confidence in the population, the national armed forces are expected to support the government by establishing gender security, and through this demonstrate that the state is in legitimate control of the national security.

"[Child abuse and SGBV] is always a security issue because it has the power to destroy good human relationships ..., security [and] enhance Human Rights violations ... the sum total of which is increased security risk and attendant control from a security point of view.... This in turn affects the way the population views the government's sense of control and ability to protect her citizens from all sources of insecurity."[72]

Male and female military personnel are taught that once the perception that the government has lost control and is unable to protect citizens "becomes entrenched in the collective psyche of the masses, there is no security because security is not what is believed to have been given but how it is perceived by the beneficiary."[73] Later in the training manual it is observed that "negative forces in society can also take advantage of this perception to wreak havoc on the population for [their] own benefit, which then becomes a challenge."[74]

The presence of female military personnel in local communities and their interactions with Rwandan citizens assist the RDF in their efforts to improve civil-military relations and garner support for the modernized national armed forces. The RDF gender program enables military personnel, many of whom are no longer associated with the original Rwandan Patriotic Front or who were born after the genocide, to engage with citizens in more informal settings, for example, during the Inter-women's Football Club competition and sector-level prevent-gender based violence (GBV) clubs. By supporting the implementation of gender awareness-raising initiatives, often working in conjunction with local authorities and women's groups, female military personnel demonstrate the strength and effectiveness of the state in postconflict Rwanda. Efforts to transform the reputation of the Rwanda Patriotic Front and to consolidate the image of the new RDF as the "people's army"[75] are also reliant on female military personnel acting as ambassadors of Rwanda's national armed forces. Like their male colleagues, female soldiers are encouraged to talk to their friends and family about the positive experiences they encounter while working for the RDF, and thereby extend the reach of the military state. Female military personnel were keen to observe how within their own networks and spheres of influence, societal perceptions of both the military and military women were changing. When asked what her family thought about her joining the RDF, one twenty-eight-year-old private remarked: "It was hard for them to understand why I wanted to join the army as a girl. They thought it would be hard for me, but they finally accepted it because I did it well and they found it was better than they thought.[76]

CONCLUSION

This chapter has explored the dynamics of gender, genocide, and the military in postconflict Rwanda to examine how the RPF government benefits from integrating women into the national armed forces. Senior leaders within the Rwanda Defence Force contend that women in Rwanda are reluctant to join the national armed forces because negative attitudes toward military women in traditional Rwandan culture still circulate. The present research has shown that new, often conflicting societal perceptions about military women have emerged in the aftermath of the 1994 genocide and civil war, which the RPF government and RDF will need to address if they are to convince more women to enter into military service. These are informed by the negative perceptions of the Rwandan Patriotic Army and the Habyarimana regime's Force Armées Rwandese prior to their assimilation into the Rwanda Defence Force, as well as contemporary attitudes toward the RDF's interventions in conflict in the east of Congo in the post-genocide era. Reflecting on the paradoxical nature of postconflict development in Rwanda, the chapter has also demonstrated how the RDF, and thus the ruling party the Rwandan Patriotic Front, have been able to turn to their advantage the once shared policy goal of mainstreaming gender equality in Rwandan society. The female military personnel interviewed for this project maintain that the military's gender program, of which they themselves are beneficiaries, contributes to improving the social and economic position of women in Rwanda. However, through active engagement with Rwandans in local communities and within their own networks, female military personnel help to promote the image of the RDF as a modern, professional, and disciplined people's army, and support the strategic aim to reassure Rwandan citizens that the RPF government is in control of security. Engaging in civil-military operations within Rwanda, young RDF female military personnel, and ethnic Hutu women in particular, bear special symbolic significance by demonstrating that the RDF is a cohesive yet diverse force comprised of members of a society that is moving toward reconciliation. Thus, an intended outcome of the gender program is to support RDF policy goals and strengthen the legitimacy of the authoritarian state. In view of these findings, further research is required to gather local-level perceptions of civil-military relations in Rwanda and to ascertain the degree to which citizens regard RDF gender initiatives as a positive development.

GEORGINA HOLMES is a Leverhulme Early Career Research Fellow in the Department of Politics and International Relations at the University of Reading. Her current research concerns gender and security sector reform in African militaries and the integration of African female uniformed peacekeepers into peacekeeping operations. She is author of *Women and War in Rwanda: Genocide, Media and the Representation of Genocide* (I.B.Tauris, 2013).

NOTES

1. Acknowledgements: The author would like to thank the British Academy/ Leverhulme for funding field research to Rwanda in 2014 and 2015 (Small Research Grant: Ref SG131357); staff at the Rwandan Ministry of Defence for facilitating access to female military personnel; Ilaria Buscaglia, and the research participants who agreed to take part in the project.

2. Theresa Rees. "Reflections on the uneven development of gender mainstreaming in Europe", *International Journal of Feminist Politics*, 7:4 (2005): p. 560.

3. UN Fact Sheet. Violence against women: forms, consequences and costs. October 9, 2006. http://www.un.org/womenwatch/daw/vaw/launch/english/v.a.w-consequenceE-use .pdf, accessed November 1, 2015.

4. See Elisa von Joeden-Forgey, "The Devil in the Details: 'Life Force Atrocities' and the Assault on the Family in Times of Conflict", *Genocide Studies and Prevention*, 5:1 (Spring, 2010): 1–19.

5. Georgina Holmes, "Negotiating narratives of human rights abuses in conflicts in the east of Congo", *Images of Africa: Creation, negotiation and subversion*, edited by Julia Gallagher (Manchester: Manchester University Press, 2015).

6. See Villia Jefremovas, "Brickyards to Graveyards: From Production to Genocide in Rwanda," (Albany: SUNY Press, 2002).

7. Representative of Gender Monitoring Office, Interview with the author, Kigali, Rwanda, June 20, 2014.

8. Jennie E. Burnet, "Gender Balance and the Meanings of Women in Governance in Post-Genocide Rwanda," *African Affairs*, 107/428 (2008): 361–86.

9. See Georgina Holmes, 2013, *Women and War in Rwanda: Gender, Media and the Representation of Genocide* (London/New York: I.B. Tauris, 2014), chapter Three.

10. Helena Carreiras, *Gender and the Military: Women in the Armed Forces of Western Democracies* (London/New York: Routledge, 2006), 41.

11. Rangira Béa Gallimore, "Militarism, Ethnicity, and Sexual Violence in the Rwandan Genocide," *Feminist Africa*, 10 (August 2008): 9.

12. Peace Uwineza and Elizabeth Pearson, *Sustaining Women's Gains in Rwanda: The Influence of Indigenous Culture and Post-Genocide Politics*, (Cambridge, MA: The Institute for Inclusive Security, 2009), 9.

13. Gallimore, "Militarism, Ethnicity," 12

14. Jennie E. Burnet, *Genocide Lives in Us: Women, Memory, and Silence in Rwanda* (Wisconsin: Wisconsin University Press, 2012a), 44–5.

15. Ibid.

16. Frank Rusagara, *Resilience of a Nation: A History of the Military in Rwanda* (Kigali: Fountain Publishers Rwanda, 2009), 209.

17. Gallimore, "Militarism, Ethnicity," 111.

18. Ibid.

19. Rusagara, *Resilience of a Nation*, 121.

20. Des Forges in Rusagara, *Resilience of a Nation*, 121.

21. Rusagara, *Resilience of a Nation*, 121.

22. See Holmes, *Women and War in Rwanda*, 63–6; Sheri P. Rosenberg, "Genocide is a process, not an event," *Genocide Studies and Prevention: An International Journal*, 7:4 (2012): 18.

23. Rosenburg, "Genocide is a process," 20.

24. See Georgina Holmes, The Postcolonial Politics of Militarizing Rwandan Women: An Analysis of Extremist Magazine Kangura and the Gendering of a Genocidal Nation-State, *Minerva Journal of Women and War*, 2:2 (2008): 44-54.

25. Agathe Uwilingiyimana, Interview with François Ryckmans, March 15, 1994, Linda Melvern Archive.

26. International Criminal Tribunal for Rwanda, "The Prosecutor v. Pauline Nyiramasuhuko and Shalom Ntahobali," Case Number ICTR-97-21-I, 1.20 (2001):8. http://41.220.139.198/Portals/0/Case/English/Nyira/indictment/index.pdf, accessed November 2, 2015.

27. Zaina Nyiramatama, Interview with the author, Kigali, April 10, 2006.

28. Jennie E. Burnet, "Sexual Violence, Female Agencies, and Sexual Consent: Complexities of Sexual Violence in the 1994 Rwandan Genocide," *African Studies Review*, 55, (2):97–118 (2012b): 108.

29. African Rights, *Rwanda: Death, Despair and Defiance* (London: African Rights, Revised Edition, 1995a), 60.

30. Human Rights Watch, "Leave None to Tell the Story: Genocide in Rwanda" (New York: Human Rights Watch, 1999). https://www.hrw.org/reports/1999/rwanda /Geno15-8-03.htm, accessed January 6, 2016.

31. Holmes, *Women and War in Rwanda*, 113–5.

32. Ibid., 120.

33. Uwilingiyimana, 1994.

34. Ibid.

35. See Holmes, *Women and War in Rwanda*, chapter Five.

36. African Rights, *Rwanda: Not So Innocent: When Women Become Killers* (London: African Rights, 1995b), 72.

37. Ibid., 111.

38. Ibid., 112.

39. Rwanda Demobilization and Reintegration Commission, 2015, http://www .demobrwanda.org.rw/78.0.html, accessed January 6, 2016.

40. Holmes, *Women and War in Rwanda*, 23.

41. Oda Gasinzigwa, Minister for Gender and Family Promotion, Interview with author, Kigali, February 28, 2014.

42. Marco Jowell, "Cohesion through socialization: Liberation, Tradition and Modernity in the Forging of the Rwanda Defence Force (RDF)," *Journal of Eastern African Studies*, 8:2 (2014): 279.

43. Andrea Purdekova, "'Even If I Am Not Here, There Are So Many Eyes': Surveillance and State Reach in Rwanda," *Journal of Modern African Studies*, 49:3 (2011): 475–97.

44. Jowell, "Cohesion through socialization," 280.

45. Rwanda Defence Force, 2015, http://mod.gov.rw/about-the-rdf/rwanda-defence -force/#.VseH-fmLTIU, accessed January 6, 2016.

46. Director of RDF Gender Desk, interview with author, Kigali, June 9, 2015.

47. Representative of the Gender Monitoring Office, Interview with the author, Kigali, June 10, 2014.

48. Georgina Holmes, "Gendering the Rwanda Defence Force: A Critical Assessment," *Journal of Intervention and Statebuilding*, 8:4 (2014b): 329.

49. Director of RDF Gender Desk, Interview with the author, Kigali, June 9, 2015.

50. Government of Rwanda, "1325 National Action Plan 2009–2012" (2009), 10, http:// www.peacewomen.org/assets/file/NationalActionPlans/rwandan_national_action _plan_1325.pdf, accessed October 15, 2013.

51. Government, "1325 Plan," 4.

52. Rwanda Defence Force website, http://mod.gov.rw/other-activities/campains /against-gender-based-violence-in-rdf/#.VsjdkPmLTIU, accessed January 6, 2016.

53. RDF Gender Desk Representative, Interview with the author, Kigali, June 10, 2014.

54. Female military personnel 6, Interview with the author, Kigali, June 6, 2015.

55. Female military personnel 22, Interview with the author, Kigali, June 10, 2014.

56. Human Rights Watch, "Leave None"; See also Burnet, *Genocide Lives in Us*.

57. Female military personnel 9, Interview with the author, Kigali, June 9, 2015.

58. Female military personnel 8, Interview with the author, Kigali, June 9, 2015.

59. Female military personnel 15, Interview with the author, Kigali, June 12, 2015.

60. Holmes, *Women and War in Rwanda*, 115–7.

61. Uwineza and Pearson, *Sustaining Women's Gains in Rwanda*, 11.

62. Anonymous, "Female Ex-Combatants in Post-Genocide Rwanda" (National University of Rwanda, 2013), 46.

63. Anonymous, "Female Ex-Combatants," 48.

64. Female military personnel 7, Interviewed by the author, Kigali, June 9, 2015.

65. RDF Gender Desk Representative, Interview with the author, Kigali, June 10, 2014.

66. Petra Debusscher and An Ansoms, "Gender Equality Policies in Rwanda: Public Relations or Real Transformation," *Development and Change*, 44:5 (2013): 1112. See also Erin K. Baines, "Les femmes aux mille bras: Building Peace and Rwanda", in *Gender, Conflict, and Peacekeeping*, eds., Dyan Mazurana, Angeal Raven-Roberts, and Jane Partpart (Oxford: Rowman & Littlefield Publishers, 2005).

67. Will Jones, "Between Pyongyang and Singapore", 232.

68. Frederick Golooba-Mutebi and David Booth, "Bilateral Cooperation and Local Power Dynamics", 2013.

69. Frederick Golooba-Mutebi and David Booth, "Bilateral Cooperation and Local Power Dynamics: The Case of Rwanda" (London: ODI, 2013), 4, http://www.odi.org/sites/odi.org.uk/files/odi-assets/publications-opinion-files/8605.pdf, accessed March 23, 2014.

70. Rwanda Defence Force, "Gender Training Manual" (Rwandan Defence Force, 2008), 12.

71. Ibid., 4.

72. Ibid.

73. Ibid., 12.

74. Ibid., 5.

75. Senior RDF military personnel, Interview with the author, Kigali, June 6, 2014.

76. Female military personnel 20, Interview with the author, Kigali, June 15, 2015.

12

Narratives of Survivors of Srebrenica

How Do They Reconnect to the World?

Selma Leydesdorff

BACKGROUND

When war erupted in Bosnia in 1992, what used to be Yugoslavia—the multiethnic communist state held together for decades—had crumbled. New nations had begun to declare their independence; Bosnia did so in 1991. In eastern Bosnia, Muslims became the victims of a brutal and bloodthirsty purge by the various Serbian forces, involving murder, rape on a massive scale, plundering, and forced relocation.

The situation was so out of control in 1993 that the United Nations designated "safe areas" or "safe enclaves" in the region and sent troops to protect the Muslims. Srebrenica, a small town sequestered in a fertile valley in eastern Bosnia, was one of them. After it was declared a UN Safe Area, thousands of Muslims from surrounding villages fled to it in search of safety.

Despite the UN's guarantee of protection, Srebrenica was under constant shelling from the surrounding hills. The peacekeepers could not prevent a humanitarian disaster. There were no medical supplies, water and electricity had been shut off, food convoys were denied access, and the population was starving.

The troops sent by the UN had a limited mandate and were insufficiently armed to keep peace in an area where a violent war was raging. Srebrenica was first protected by the Canadian army, later by soldiers of the Dutch army under United Nations command. Despite promises of safekeeping, the town fell into Serb hands on July 11, 1995. Before the massacre of Srebrenica began, UN soldiers herded women, children, and older men into the UN compound at Potočari where they expected to find shelter. However, in the days after the fall of Srebrenica, 7,749 people were killed, mostly men. The large majority who entered the compound of Potočari perished in the massacre. Many younger men opted to flee through the woods to territory controlled by the Bosnian army rather than enter the compound, but only a few of them made it to safety. Since 2002, I have interviewed female survivors, many of them still living in temporary shelters.

When I wrote my book on the women survivors of Srebrenica I wanted their voices to be heard and I wanted to send a message to the world.[1] The army sent by my country, Holland, had stood by while all these men were slaughtered. Whether the outcome could have been different we shall never know, but, as I have already argued elsewhere, better command, better armament, and better instructions might have changed the course of events. It is only in the Netherlands that people still deny the complicity and the cowardliness of the Dutch army; elsewhere, there is agreement that the Dutch army failed. However, today even in the Netherlands the tide of thinking is changing.

Since my book was published (2011) I have gone back to Bosnia several times and I realize that hearing the women's voices is not enough. The collective trauma demands forms of healing that must be invented. At the moment there is a cure for individual women, but we know collective healing is only possible when there is support like that which has been provided in South Africa or Rwanda. But no one seems interested in the Bosnian women's healing, except for some understaffed NGOs lacking financial support.

The women I interviewed lived in villages, refugee camps, and small towns with no access to the centers of power, even if that power was local. Many of them are still uprooted; few have found a place they can call home. A growing number of them returned to their homes in Srebrenica because life as a refugee is harsh. But today, Srebrenica is still a desolate place offering few facilities and even less employment, and many of the surrounding villages are still in ruins. One occasionally meets women there who are living with their children in what were once inhabited farms before the villages were shelled. The returnees have had a hard time putting together the bits and pieces of their lives. Material conditions are appalling, and to make matters worse for the Muslims who return, Srebrenica is now "enemy" territory, belonging to the Republika Srpska, which is predominantly Christian.

STORIES OF DESPERATE WOMEN DO NOT FIT THE OFFICIAL NARRATIVES

The displaced obviously want economic conditions to improve, but more importantly they want to know why their husbands, fathers, and sons were killed. They also want to know what happened elsewhere during the war. They wonder what took place on the international stage and whether the fate of their town was negotiated in exchange for raising the siege of Sarajevo. In short, they want to preserve the memory of what so many seem to want to forget. And they wait for news.[2] Even those who know that their men are dead are waiting for their deaths to be confirmed and their bodies found.

The memories of these genocide survivors contrast sharply with the reports and analyses through which the political debate is conducted, documents which rarely mention the survivors and are for the most part commissioned by national governments.[3] It is vital to the survivors that their voices be heard in the public domain; they want their ordeal to be known and their suffering acknowledged. The history of the war should include their own stories of betrayal, survival, and isolation. It should reflect their recollections of the mass murder and their efforts to come to terms with it. Their memories of the war have led them to accuse the international community and the Dutch army of—as they say in their own words—"betraying them."

THE WAR CONTINUES IN THE MIND

War never ends with the type of peace agreement the Dayton Accords pretend to be. "War" and "peace" are not mutually exclusive phenomena in history, but are intimately related. As Michel Foucault argued in *Society Must Be Defended*, peace is the continuation of war by other means.[4] This becomes even more apparent when the war was recent and was orchestrated to perpetuate hate-filled sentiment, as Edina Bećirević describes the Bosnian War.[5] The genocide was twenty years ago, but hatred and pain are still present for the survivors of Srebrenica. While many are still displaced in refugee camps, and others return to a place that is drenched in blood, the war goes on in the minds, imaginations, and nightmares of the survivors.

The outcome of the war has been extensive, with monumental suffering, but except in the private sphere of the survivors, the pain has become nearly invisible. While the West intervened in the Balkan Wars of the 1990s—only after the deaths of countless Bosnians—not enough thought has gone into how to bring about peace in damaged communities and to assuage the unsettled feelings of the many traumatized people living either in Bosnia or in the Diaspora.[6] Sorrow, poverty, and isolation persist.

Although there are no reliable statistics, I am inclined to follow those authors who connect the widespread occurrence of domestic violence with war trauma.[7] In Bosnia most families have become single-parent, and the women are not able to provide adequate role models for the many young men who were children during the war. Hence crime and unemployment are rampant in the camps; an entire generation has grown up in mud and dirt with a hostile attitude toward a world that has forsaken them, failed to recognize their desire to be acknowledged, and which has not helped them to find their loved ones. In refugee camps, single women have taken on the tasks previously reserved for men. They are responsible for family finances and for maintaining their pensions, chopping wood, keeping a farm or a shop afloat, and rebuilding houses with inadequate tools. The war lives on in domestic violence, in the form of violence against women and children if there are men in the household, or if not, violence of mothers against their children. In general, families are unable to cope with new roles and social networks.

A THEORETICAL FRAMEWORK FOR UNDERSTANDING

To create a theoretical framework for understanding the destruction, I make use of the work of anthropologist Victor Turner, who developed the concept of "social drama" to analyze crisis and change over time in the social relationships within African village life.[8] His model is often chosen to study change in small societies resulting from change on a larger scale. Social drama addresses disruptions in communities, and constitutes a limited focus of deep transparency on the otherwise opaque, uneventful surface of social life. In Turner's work, social drama consists of four successive phases: breach, crisis, redressive action, and reintegration. He also explores another possible outcome of social drama: schism, rupture, and the destruction of social relations. This latter model is helpful in understanding the women of Srebrenica. While there is some work being done on women speaking up in the former Yugoslavia, few studies have done more than provide a glimpse into the world in which the war took place. The entire society was affected, and the suffering is more than personal trauma. In what follows I explain that we cannot understand what happened to these women if we do not place their war experience in the context of an entire life. Indeed, the outcome of the social drama of Srebrenica is the rupture and destruction of social relations.

When we hear Bosnian women speaking up in the public arena, it is in a court of law prosecuting perpetrators, which means their words are about the war and the genocide.[9] Lawsuits are not about current living conditions and how social networks have been destroyed and upward social mobility impaired. Perhaps more time is needed. As we have seen in the academic study of the Holocaust, it took decades for the effects and aftermath of trauma to be studied seriously. Initially, only psychiatric studies that focused on individual suffering were undertaken. Out of psychiatry came the impulse to look, not only at the individual, but also the community as a whole; in the case of the Holocaust, this meant looking at the destroyed Jewish community.

The failure to protect so-called safe areas and the desperate situation of the survivors demonstrate the need for the international community to acknowledge its failures in response to the Balkan wars of the 1990s and to take seriously the perspectives of the survivors. The victims' core desire was and is not the financial compensation they are demanding, but recognition. Compensation is the juridical translation of this wish. Political philosopher Nancy Fraser has described recognition as a reciprocal relation between subjects, in which each sees the other both as its equal and also as separate from it. This relation is necessary for subjectivity: one becomes an individual subject only by virtue of recognizing, and being recognized by, another subject. Recognition from others is thus essential to the development of a sense of self. To be denied recognition—or to be "misrecognized"—is to suffer both a distortion of one's relation to one's self, and an injury to one's identity because the ability of traumatized survivors to restore their identity depends on reconnecting to a society and a world that seem to have been lost.[10]

Apparently, the world is reluctant to hear the widows' voices; neither does it want to be confronted with their overwhelming grief. This seems to be a pattern after genocide in other times and places as well. In *The Order Has Been Carried Out*,[11] oral historian Alessandro Portelli noted the social unease brought on by the lament of the widows of 335 unarmed male civilians who were mass murdered in one day by the German occupiers in Rome during the Second World War. The women marched throughout the city and openly expressed their grief, but this was considered unacceptable. As Portelli writes, "the city was in sympathy with them, but only as long as they stayed in their place." It did not want "to have to face this excessive death in the everyday space of ordinary life."[12] Portelli describes how the Italian widows were always given priority in stores, and while women thought that this was out of respect for them, in reality, it was because the other shoppers wanted them to leave the shops as quickly as possible. The women's evident pain and their ongoing misfortune could not be accommodated, because they made it impossible for everyone to forget the past. The confrontation with grieving widows in search of answers was too intense for Rome's residents. Srebrenica women face similar resistance. Their irate shouting filled with tears during the trials in the International Court in The Hague was dismissed as a form of hysteria since Bosnian is a language not widely spoken. Years of denial of what they endured have made the women of Srebrenica angrier.

WOMEN'S WORDS

The way in which the women of Srebrenica have been isolated and denied recognition is an expression of the world's inability to recognize its own failure to keep a promise. It would have been more humane to recognize their agony, admit responsibility for complicity in the massacre, and set up programs that would enable the women to build new lives. However, since the end of the war, the victims have lived in miserable conditions—in a country that is unable to deal with staggering unemployment in the present economic crisis. There is no money now to help the women, and pensions are so low that hunger has become routine. While many of them come from families that were middle class by prewar Yugoslav standards, they are now unable to give their children a decent education. Years of poverty have inflicted a psychological and physical strain. But, the worst consequence is the isolation and loneliness.

Although the story of Aiša has been documented on several occasions, I present it here as a striking example of the suffering experienced by most of the women. Aiša is elderly and lives with her daughter-in-law. They once occupied two rooms in a deserted school, but recently they moved to a better house. In an interview in 2004, Aiša said:

> There is no man to come and help you, to cut a tree branch, no. There are no pensions, either. We are bound to pay a debt for this house, about KM 15,000. But, by God, we have no money, we have been reduced ... to nothing. I swear by God ... I have lost all my children, my husband, son-in-law, cousins, nieces. I have no one. I am so glad that you have come. Only you have come to see me. Nobody else has visited me, at least ... Bairams comes ... Bairams comes, New Year's. I close myself in the room and cry all day long. You have no one to come to your door, to come to you, to tell you at least, "Where are you granny, where are you mother?" Nobody.
>
> I come from a large family. My mother had six of us. And all my family died. Mother, brothers, father, everybody, everybody. Nobody stayed. Nobody.
>
> *During the war?* (interviewer)
>
> They all died. They were young. It is very hard to become old, I know.
>
> *How many children did you have?* (interviewer)
>
> I had six, and now, nobody. I have only Mejra [her daughter-in-law]. Nobody else. Two of them died, four did not return.

THE TABOO OF RAPE[13]

Many women, not only in Srebrenica but in the whole of Bosnia, have been raped, and the rape of women has become a metaphor for ethnic cleansing in Bosnia.[14] Rape was a weapon of a policy of aggression, ethnic cleansing, and war. Some studies have dealt with the large number of rapes, particularly in Foca. The violence in Foca has prompted the International Criminal Tribunal for the Former Yugoslavia (ICTY) to consider rape a war crime.[15] The Parliamentary Assembly of the Council of Europe estimated that twenty thousand women were subjected to rape and other forms of sexual violence. In the 2010 PBS documentary, *I Came to Testify: Women, War and Peace in Bosnia*, the women who were employed at the tribunal made public how hard they had to fight for this acknowledgment. But there was no woman who wanted to speak up about rape. During my research women did not want to be recorded when they talked about sexual violence. They felt ashamed. Today some women raped in Potočari have found the courage to speak up in a society where one does not talk about such events. Balkan Transitional Justice, an online news site, published the following account of one woman's experience of rape:

> "I wish he had killed me instead of doing that to me. The fear inside you cannot be described with words—when it is night, when he is armed, you do not know who he is, and he makes you take off your clothes," said a woman who wanted to be identified only by the initials "H. M." as she recalled what happened to her in July 1995 in Srebrenica. She was 45 years old.... She said that after Serb forces seized Srebrenica, soldiers took her and her injured husband, along with other sick and wounded people, to a nearby house where two men called Savo the shoemaker and Sulejman lived. On their second night in the house, the military police officer took her upstairs, pushed her into a room and onto the bed, and pointed his gun at her. "He forced me to take off my clothes. I cried and begged him not to. He seemed to me like he was 20 years old. I was telling him: "I am an old woman; I could be your mother." He said: "I have been in the field for a month, I have no woman, I want to ...." He forced her to have oral sex. She is still haunted by nightmares and said: "I dream that they are coming, I am running, I beg them not to touch me, I beg them not to kill my man, I scream. When I wake up, I cannot feel my legs, I need at least an hour to realize that I am in my own house." She knows other women who had the same fate but, as she said: "We were raised in a patriarchal way,

this [Srebrenica] is a small village. I believe they are ashamed to tell their brothers, their children.... They are afraid to say who did it; they are afraid someone will burn their house, because that has happened before."[16]

When I interviewed women, they would hint of rape when we were alone. In the aforementioned narrative, I recognize the woman who is speaking, and at that time I was certain she had been raped. One woman I interviewed, "H," was raped in front of her small children. She felt ashamed, but despite this, she wanted to tell me about it:

There were four soldiers coming up to me [pause; H is crying]. They shouted, pointing a finger at me: "You with a little baby, go there to get some food." Two Dutch and two Serb soldiers. One was the interpreter. The last one was laughing. He had a helmet, a flak jacket and a gun. A Dutch soldier. I did not expect anything, I could not imagine that anything would happen. I only thought how I would get food. I and my children did not have anything to eat for three days. I followed them, took my children and went with them behind the factory. I saw a white tent there. They told me to wait there. They closed the zipper from outside and told me to wait for food. I waited. It was very hot, I think it was forty degrees. It was stuffy and very hot. I and my kids were sweating. We did not have enough air. I could not open the tent from inside, there was no other opening. It could be opened only from outside. I saw through the tent that the sun had set down and that it was getting dark. Nothing could be seen any longer. I could see through the tent that somewhere there was a little light. I could see someone coming behind the factory. The tent opened and one hand showed itself. I saw one hand. The tent was opened from outside and they were coming in. I thought that they had brought me food, so I got up to take the food, I expected it.... They were the same persons from the factory. The one that laughed was blond, very fair, very blond. I remember that hair, those eyes, those hands.... I remember everything.... They were drunk. When the interpreter was speaking near me I could smell alcohol, his breath was smelling of alcohol. One of them came up to me and slapped my face. Very hard. I think he hit me on the left side. When he slapped me I felt something break here. Then my nose started bleeding. I saw blood from my nose, and then I do not remember anything. My children were near me. But I do not remember anything, not a single thing. I only remember something as in a dream, and in that dream I was struggling, I was pushing something in front of me, I do not know. I do not remember but in that dream I had pain in this part of my body.[17]

Her children are adults now, and it is hard for her to look them in the eye. Shame has never left her. Similarly Edina, who was an adolescent when she was raped, feels shame, but she spoke openly about her rape and testified at ICTY. She was a social outsider, a Bosnian Muslim girl, who had the support of her psychiatrist; together they decided Edina could be immensely useful for the court as she knew the names of the perpetrators, and her testifying would not put her at risk. In the end, I believe her testifying made her even stronger:

> We came to a house and they made us get out of the car. They (Serb soldiers) made us again go into the house, upstairs. It was done quickly—get out of the car, get into the house, go upstairs. There was a kind of a corridor, or an anteroom there and a bed. That soldier, my neighbor, pushed me onto the bed. They took the other two girls into rooms. All that happened in five minutes I think, until they brought us upstairs. He pushed me onto the bed and started undressing me. I started screaming. I did not know what was happening. That neighbor of mine attacked me again. He tore my clothes. I started screaming. And all the time he shouted at me asking why my father had not returned. I did not know where my father had been taken and whether he was alive.
>
> So, he raped me there. I was scared very much, I cried a lot. After he raped me, he pulled me by my hair and hit me with his leg into my back. He pushed me to the door of another room. I fell down in front of the door. The soldiers took one girl out of the room. They dragged me into that room onto a bed that was in that room. Another one of them raped me. I do not remember his family name. He raped me there. When he finished, another came and he raped me too. When the second one finished, a third came. As I screamed all the time, they tied my hands and put a piece of paper or cloth into my mouth. As I cried my nose got blocked. I could not breathe with the paper in my mouth. I lost consciousness, I did not remember anything. When I regained consciousness I saw that I was wet all over, that my hands were tied.
>
> The first one who raped me and who pushed me into that room, my neighbor, returned. He raped me again. It was already morning. He lay there for some time. I do not remember whether it was an hour or two. It was daylight already. He left the room. I stayed on the bed. He returned and told me to get out.[18]

The violence these women experienced is like a movie that starts at odd moments in their dreams. They feel they will never get rid of it. The images of war are no longer raw; new stories and new images have been attached to the violence. And no one seems to listen to their pain. Women lament the fact that they were largely excluded from postwar negotiations; their experiences of physical violence and rape and their contributions to the resistance to Serbian aggression were not taken into account.

There are many examples of how people are unable to return to the life they knew before the war. Of course there was loss, and loved ones did not come back despite wives and mothers waiting for them. Even if they knew their husband was dead they waited. As Suhreta said:

> They maltreated him and tortured him terribly. I asked the man to tell me where he had been buried. I would like to transfer him, so that I could be buried next to him one day. But the man told me that he had not been buried anywhere, he had been thrown into the river, into the Drina. I would like to go to Skelani, to the bridge, to get some flowers and a loaf of bread and to offer a prayer for my husband at the place where he had lost his life.[19]

NO TIES TO THE WORLD: THE NEED FOR LIFE STORIES

But there is more to these women's loss than mourning the dead. Their connection to the wider world has been severed; they are alienated from old friends and neighbors who were part of the strand that connected the women to their communities. In short, there is loss of social context. For decades they lived in a peaceful society held together by an authoritarian state. Their world changed into a war that had started years before. Even if they had felt the rise of hostility and heard talk about it, they were used to a world in which you visited with people, ate together, and were close friends. In my interviews, some women were able to talk about this past world, while others denied they had ever been friends with any of the "others." Even during the genocide, however, some appealed to these old ties and asked for assistance.

To deny the deep feelings around this loss is to deny a part of these women's lives. Losing ties to their communities created a black hole in the vision of their future place in the world, and there was an inability to deal with loves and friendships that had been betrayed.

In an article I wrote on one of the survivors called Hanifa, I have tried to demonstrate the way dissociation (as we might call it) represents the inability to define a place in the world.[20] Hanifa grew up in a small village, and she lost both her parents at a young age. She spoke with sadness about a childhood without parental love. She eloped, and she and her husband then started a family. When the war began they left their village and found shelter in the "safe area" of Srebrenica. Together they went to Potočari from whence they were deported. Her husband was killed, and she started a long trajectory of travel through refugee camps. Hanifa's world has changed dramatically: the reality of her small, remote village not reachable by car has been replaced by a crowded camp deserted by the world. She is again alone. But I would never understand her feelings of isolation without knowing she had become a lonely orphan during her childhood. I did not only interview her about the genocide but also about her happy marriage, the way she felt protected after she married, and her lonely life now.

As I argue, life stories in oral history, with the methodological approach I use, do not just describe the historical trajectory of oneself; they are also the expression of someone's being in the world. Narratives of the self show how our lives are interwoven with our families, communities, and traditions. They show how we interpret the past and our experiences; they tell about our background and our expectations of our future life; they tell what we want to be and become. But in order for this to happen, our story needs to be believed and recognized, while others need to convey the importance of our stories to us. It is a precondition for reestablishing a sense of connection with others. Establishing such a connection is especially problematic when bonds and connections have been broken, and the image of the self has been fragmented. Trauma breaks social bonds and human connections, and shatters a sense of self. The denial and distortion of the survivors' voices is partly the result of their stories not being recognized. During the interviews I noticed, however, that the telling of a story can bring healing and can help in the long process of reassembling fragments of memory in the process of reconstructing a life story.

Trauma and solitude permeate the whole personality. Nezira, who lives in a suburb of Sarajevo, no longer cares for life. She says, "I cannot help crying, I think that this is the end of my life. First my father's remains were found and then my son's. My husband died ... forty days had passed after his death when I buried my son. I went with my only child. There was no one to lay him in the grave. Neighbors and people—somebody—put him in the grave; I don't really know what happened."[21]

Zumra told one of my co-interviewers in an interview in Sarajevo:

> Not one day passes that I haven't said something about it. That means it is on my mind all the time. I can't understand. Sometimes I visit a happy family, where all the members are there together, and they have problems buying a fridge, or they need to change the curtains or something else in their house. I'm not interested in that. I don't—I don't have the power inside me to listen to that. I don't worry anymore about which dress I have on, what kind of shoes, which bag. All I worry about now is that I'm neat, that I'm not filthy, and I pray to dear Allah to keep me sane, to keep me aware and reasonable, so that I can communicate normally with people.[22]

Zumra feels she should have done more:

> I couldn't say anything more. I had the feeling that I was paralyzed and I cried rivers of tears. I didn't shriek or scream. I didn't say that they must not take him. I didn't ask, "Why him?" Nothing, nothing. I'm not saying now that, if I had said something, it might have saved him. But I couldn't help…. They just told us to go along. I couldn't do anything, not a thing. And he was so gentle, worrying all the time. It was very hot that day, to faint. I felt a bit sick; he held my hand all the time, kept telling me everything is going to be all right. His arm on my shoulder was so heavy. I felt it so deep in my body. Heavy, shaky, with fear of what will happen to us. Although he knew everything, was aware of everything, he kept saying everything would be all right. Five minutes before they separated us, I turned around to see his eyes. Now I can say he was looking at death. He was speechless. His eyes were focused at one point. He wasn't saying anything. He held his jacket in his hands.

It took a long time for me to realize that the life stories of the survivors of Srebrenica are not only fragmented by the trauma of 1995, but also by the impossibility of telling the larger story. Because any narrative of the past is interwoven with a vision of the future, the confusion is aggravated. The women remember the multicultural society they originally came from, and they still think it is important to live together. They were raised on a brand of Yugoslav communism under Tito that suppressed any expression of cultural difference, but at the same time they internalized positive feelings toward the members of the other ethnic group. Despite the current nationalist myth that the region has always been rife with war and hostility, even illiterate women are able to describe the alliance between nationalism and state politics that was the origin of all the destruction and bloodshed. The loss of friendships mingles with a fundamental loss of trust in the world and the loss of loved ones. The survivors are left with unsettling grief, mourning, and conflicting emotions with no stable sense of normality to provide counterbalance.

CHAOTIC IMAGES DIFFICULT TO REMEMBER

The genocide in Srebrenica/Potočari was the conscious creation of chaos and panic through which the Serbs managed to dominate thousands of people. Remembering that situation seems impossible, though people have attempted to narrate in broken stories. There has hardly been a historical discourse they can refer to, and the events in Potočari have clearly not been integrated into personal life stories. These events stood apart, and were at the same time part of a more general confusion in memory. Trauma was the last element in a problematic interplay between not being able to remember and not wanting to remember.

Based on my interviews, I have concluded that the main problem is not how memories are constructed versus reality; the main problem is what cannot be remembered and put into words. To begin with, the women I interviewed were reluctant to talk about the atrocities and the pain they had gone through. At a deeper level betrayal—the betrayal of friends, neighbors, and loved ones in participating in murder and genocide—also prevents them from developing any vision of the future, for such a vision can only be based on feelings about what was perceived as "good" in the past.

LISTEN TO THEM

There is always that special, last moment engraved in the memory. A husband, a son, a father, a member of the family. A man and a woman embrace for the last time, their faces distorted, tears filling their eyes and rolling down their cheeks. A father embraces his daughter, and both know it is the last time. A child cries and calls the father, begging, "Daddy, please come back." A mother begs, "don't take my son away, he is so small." She tries to free him from the hands of Serb soldiers, in vain. Her life seems to be over.

Good memories of coexistence with Serbs have become problematic. It is easier not to talk about them, to deny past feelings and replace them with stronger emotions of hatred and disappointment. Memories of their previous lives are eclipsed by feelings of loss. This is why the women I interviewed can hardly imagine positive feelings when they think about the past. Everything that was normal has been disrupted. The moment of disruption is clearly grafted onto their memory, but it is precisely that moment that also conceals all positive feelings about the time before. Cruelty is present in abundance.

When emptiness replaces memory, connectedness, context, and a place in society, when there is no positive memory or positive future, it can be better to forget. Remembering the past requires the survivor to explore positive feelings that are bound to resurface, feelings that disrupt the negative paradigm and might prompt questions about past friendship and love.

TO RECONNECT?

I write history based on testimonies about the past. History presumes a kind of chronology, which is absent in the stories of most survivors. In *History beyond Trauma*, Francois Davoine and Jean-Max Gaudillière described how they in their practice as psychoanalysts search for times "when the time stands still."[23] Stories begin with the moment of trauma, and there does not seem to be time beyond that moment. Narratives of trauma are not straightforwardly referential; rather, they are what Cathy Caruth calls expressions of "a crisis of witnessing." She has dealt extensively with the ways trauma is sedimented in language and literature,[24] and considers any eyewitness account to be rooted in dislocations of history, which are imperative.[25] Anyone who has interviewed trauma cases knows that chronology fails, lapses occur, and confusion is normal.[26] Talking about trauma often means reliving it in all of its pain, difficulty, fear, confusion, and shame.

By not allowing the full truth of the stories in all their layered and unfinished forms, by dismissing them as outbursts of emotion, we deny their mediated authenticity and the way they might reconfigure or even remake the world for those who have lost their place in it.[27] In turn, we dislocate the meaning and place assigned to an event. In this entwinement between the legal truth and the victim's need to speak out, material compensation is merely one of many ways to reclaim a place in the world.[28]

To tell and to speak are at least as important as other agendas, such as depolarizing education systems, promoting tolerance, strengthening independent media, challenging dominant national narratives, granting privilege to other voices (such as women's groups), instituting truth-and-reconciliation commissions, finding a place for mourning, and, finally, prosecuting the criminals. But the creation of a collective story/memory is a first step for survivors to be reconnected to a fragmented world. While there are many expectations of the sporadic psychological help given to individual women, suffering seems individual but is collective. The organizations of survivors know this by experience, but no one knows how to start collective healing. Maybe only time can do so.

SELMA LEYDESDORFF is Professor of Oral History and Culture at the University of Amsterdam. She is author of *Surviving the Bosnian Genocide: The Women of Srebrenica Speak* and *Sasha Pechersky: Holocaust Hero, Sobibor Resistance Leader, and Hostage of History.*

NOTES

1. Selma Leydesdorff, *Surviving the Bosnian Genocide: The Women of Srebrenica Speak* (Bloomington: Indiana University Press, 2011).

2. It is common also in the stories of the women who survived the Rwanda genocide, though the genocide was far less gendered there. See Esther Mujawayo, *SurVivantes: Rwanda, dix ans après le genocide* (Paris: L'Aube, 2004).

3. NIOD, *Srebrenica, een "veilig gebied"; Reconstructie, Achtergronden, gevolgen en analyses van een Safe Area* (Amsterdam: Boom, 2002). There is a French report, several by Bosnian scholars, a United Nations report, and proceedings of the ICTY (International Criminal Tribunal for the former Yugoslavia).

4. Michel Foucault, *Society Must Be Defended: Lectures at the Collège de France, 1975–1976*, eds. Mauro Bertani and Alessandro Fontana, trans. David Macey (New York: Picador, 2003), 69. The first edition was published in 1997 by Editions de Seuil/Gallimard.

5. Edina Bećirević, *Genocide on the Drina River* (New Haven, CT: Yale University Press, 2014).

6. Lara J. Nettelfield and Sarah E. Wagner, *Srebrenica in the Aftermath of Genocide* (New York: Cambridge University Press, 2013).

7. Esmina Avdibegović and Osman Sinanović, "Consequences of Domestic Violence on Women's Mental Health in Bosnia and Herzegovina," *Croatian Medical Journal* 47, 5 (October 2006): 730–41. http://www.ncbi.nlm.nih.gov/pmc/articles/PMC2080462/.

8. Victor Turner, *Schism and Continuity in an African Society: A Study of Ndembu Village Life* (Manchester: Manchester University Press, 1957).

9. Dubravka Zarkov and Marlies Glasius, *Narratives of Justice in and out of the Courtroom: Former Yugoslavia and Beyond* (New York: Springer, 2014).

10. Nancy Fraser, "Rethinking Recognition," *New Left Review* 3 (2000): 107–20. See also Nancy Fraser and Axel Honneth, *Redistribution or Recognition? A Political-Philosophical Exchange* (London: Verso, 2003).

11. Alessandro Portelli, *The Order Has Been Carried Out: History, Memory, and Meaning of a Nazi Massacre in Rome* (New York: Palgrave Macmillan, 2003).

12. Portelli, *The Order*, 215.

13. Recently it has been possible for the first time to also discuss sexual aggression against men. See Olivera Simić, "Wartime Rape and Its Shunned Victims," in Amy E. Randall, *Genocide and Gender in the Twentieth Century: A Comparative Survey* (London: Bloomsbury Press, 2015), 237–58.

14. Irfan Ajanović, ed., *I Begged Them to Kill Me: Crimes against the Women of Bosnia-Herzegovina* (Sarajevo: CID, 2000). Amnesty International, "Whose Justice? Bosnia and Herzegovina's Women Still Waiting" (Amnesty International (Report). September 30, 2009.

15. Parliamentary Assembly of the Council of Europe. Resolution 1670 (2009), "Sexual violence against women in armed conflict." Adopted on May 29, 2009, paragraph 6. See also: Seada Vranić, *Breaking the Wall of Silence: The Voices of Raped in Bosnia* (Zagreb: Izdabja Antibarus, 1996), 239.

16. Albino Sorguc, "Srebrenica Anniversary: The Rape Victims' Testimonies," *Balkan Transitional Justice*, last accessed July 11, 2014, http://www.balkaninsight.com/en/article/srebrenica-anniversary-the-rape-victims-testimonies/1422/3.

17. Interview with anonymous, September 2004.

18. Interview in Tuzla with Edina, May 5, 2007.

19. Interview with Suhreta M. Sasse, 2004

20. Selma Leydesdorff, "When All Is Lost: Metanarrative in the Oral History of Hanifa, Survivor of Srebrenica," in Marc Cave and Stephen M. Sloan, *Listening on the Edge: Oral History in the Aftermath of Crisis* (New York: Oxford University Press, 2014), 17–33.

21. Interview with Nezira Sulejmanović, by Selma Leydesdorff, September 2005

22. Interview with Zumra Šehomerović, by Velma Sarić, 2006

23. Francois Davoine and Jean-Max Gaudilliére, *History beyond Trauma* (New York: Other Press, 2004), 163–207.

24. Cathy Caruth, *Unclaimed Experience, Trauma, Narrative and History* (Baltimore, MD: Johns Hopkins University Press, 1996).

25. Michael G. Levine, *The Belated Witness: Literature, Testimony and the Question of Holocaust Survival* (Redwood City, CA: Stanford University Press, 2006).

26. Kim Lacey Rogers, Selma Leydesdorff, and Graham Dawson, eds., *Trauma: The Life Stories of Survivors* (New Brunswick, NJ: Transaction Publishers, 2004).

27. Shoshana Felman and Dori Laub, *Testimony: Crises of Witnessing in Literature Psychoanalysis and History* (New York: Routledge, 1992); Dominick LaCapra, *Writing History, Writing Trauma* (Baltimore, MD: Johns Hopkins University Press, 2001).

28. Harmen Wilt, Jeroen Vervliet, Goran Sluiter, and Johannes. Th. M. Houwink ten Cate, eds., *The Genocide Convention: The Legacy of Sixty Years* (Den Haag, Netherlands: Martinus Nijhoff Publishers, 2012), 113.

13

The Plight and Fate of Females During and Following the Darfur Genocide

Samuel Totten

INTRODUCTION

During the course of the Darfur genocide (roughly 2003–09), sexual violence against black African females was as much a part of the horror as the sands on which the crimes were committed. Girls as young as seven years old and women as old as sixty-seven were subjected to horrific psychological and physical violence at the hands of Government of Sudan (GoS) troops and their allied militia, the "Janjaweed." Collectively, the females faced sexual taunts riddled with racism and violent threats, rape, gang rape, sexual mutilation, and death. They also faced potential arrest by local authorities and ostracism at the hands of their family and fellow villagers for having been raped.

Herein, I provide an overview of the genesis of the Darfur genocide, the main actors involved, how it was carried out, the international community's response, and a detailed examination of the plight and fate of the black African females of Darfur during and following the genocide.

THE DARFUR GENOCIDE

The genocide of the black Africans of Darfur (primarily those of the Fur, Massaliet, and Zaghawa, tribal groups) by GoS troops and the Janjaweed constituted the first acknowledged genocide of the twenty-first century. It is estimated that at least three hundred thousand people perished as a result of the genocide, either from being killed outright or dying as a result of dehydration, starvation, or unattended injuries.[1]

At the time, Darfur, a region in west Sudan, was comprised of three states: Northern Darfur, Western Darfur, and Southern Darfur.[2] The three-state region was roughly the size of Texas (or, for readers outside the US, the size of France), sharing borders with Libya, Chad, and the Central African Republic. The vast majority of the people of Darfur, both the so-called black Africans and the Arabs, are Muslim.

Darfur is one of the most underdeveloped regions of Sudan, and Sudan itself constitutes one of the twenty-five poorest countries in the world. More than 90 percent of Sudan's citizens live below the poverty line. While much of the Darfur region consists of large swaths of desert (except during the rainy season, when wadis, or dry riverbeds, swell with torrents of water), it also has lush grasslands where herds graze and areas where crops are cultivated. The most productive land was largely occupied by sedentary farmers and cattle owners who tended to be non-Arabs. Up through roughly the mid-1980s, at certain times of the year, the pasture land was shared with semi-nomadic and nomadic Arab groups. This resulted in a symbiotic and mutually appreciated relationship; while the Arabs' animals fed on the grasslands, they fertilized the ground owned by the black Africans, thus renewing the soil for subsequent growing seasons. Generally, when conflicts erupted at that time between individuals or groups (be it among individuals in the same village, different black African tribal groups, or between black Africans and Arabs), they were peacefully resolved by local leaders (umdas and/or sheiks) via mediation. While neither conflict nor violence was uncommon, it rarely resulted in wholesale violence that stretched on for months, let alone years. When deemed necessary, "blood money" was paid to the victim, whether for kin killed, animals stolen, or some other transgression. The exchange of blood money by the offending party to the victim generally settled the grievance.

The antecedents leading up to the outbreak of genocide in Darfur were many and complex. The main ones were the impact of extreme drought and desertification on both the sedentary (mainly black Africans) and nomadic (mainly Arabs) groups in Darfur; Arab supremacism, a rabid ideology that promotes ethnic, cultural, and racial ethnic superiority of Arabs, which arose as a reaction to European colonization; authoritarianism by the GoS; the disenfranchisement of black Africans at the hands of the Sudanese government; and the ever-increasing bellicosity in the region (within Sudan, Darfur, and beyond its borders).

Since the early 1970s, numerous droughts (including the "great drought" of 1984–85) resulted in ever-increasing desertification within the Darfur region. The desertification of the land resulted in a dramatic decline in the yield of produce and significant loss of pastureland. Along with famines (some caused by nature, others by man, and lasting much longer than in the past), the impact of the drought increased tensions between the sedentary and nomadic groups' over use and access to land and water. Ultimately, the latter resulted in increased conflict and violence between the seminomadic Arab groups and the sedentary, farming group of non-Arabs.[3]

Arab supremacism is an ideology that preaches and promotes the notion that Arab beliefs and way of life are superior to all others.[4] Essentially, it calls for Arab dominance in all aspects of life—culturally, economically, judicially, politically, religiously, and socially. Ultimately, it is an ideology that perceives all those who are not Arab as inferior. In Sudan, this has led to both the isolation and disenfranchisement (and in not a few cases, demonization) of certain groups, including the black Africans of Darfur. Major purveyors of Arab supremacism were Egypt's Gamal Abdel Nasser and Libya's Muammar Gaddafi. Gaddafi, in fact, dreamed of establishing an "Arab Belt" across the Sahel.

For more than twenty-five years (1989–present), Sudan has been under the authoritarian rule of Omar al-Bashir. His regime controls virtually every aspect of Sudanese life. Those living in what is commonly referred to as the peripheries in Sudan (that is, those areas far from Khartoum, the capital and so-called center in Sudan) were, and continue to be, perceived and treated as second-class citizens. To put this in perspective, North Sudan, where Khartoum is located, comprises only 5 percent of the country's population, yet it controls virtually all of Sudan. Every president and prime minister has come from the North, along with most of those who have held important positions dealing with the development, infrastructure, and economy of the country.

In May 2000, *The Black Book: Imbalance of Power and Wealth in Sudan* was produced and distributed by the Justice and Equality Movement (JEM), and was dedicated, in part, to "... the Sudanese people who have endured oppression, injustice and tyranny."[5] The authors of *The Black Book* duly noted that ever since Sudan's independence in 1956, those who have controlled both the political and economic power within the Sudanese government (variously referred to as "the elite" or "the ruling elite") and, by extension, the entire country, were from northern Sudan.[6]

For years on end, black Africans of Darfur had decried the hegemony of the North, along with the prejudice, discrimination, and disenfranchisement they had suffered at the hands of the North. Such complaints and calls for better government largely fell on deaf ears. Furthermore, the authors noted, development of the country—the construction of roads, bridges, water systems, hospitals, and schools—was largely limited to the North.

Beginning in the mid- to late-1980s, Arab herders began carrying out attacks against entire villages of sedentary black African farmers. Over time, such attacks began to involve both GoS troops and Arab herders working in tandem. While vicious, such attacks were certainly not as systematic as the scorched earth attacks that became increasingly common in 2003 and beyond. The initial increase in violent conflict within the region was due to a host of issues. First and foremost was conflict over the use of the land; also Arabs held most regional and local government positions, thus placing the black Africans of Darfur at a distinct disadvantage, since the authorities showed preferential treatment to their fellow Arabs.

Out of fear and anger over the constant assaults and attacks on their villages and farms, and the lack of protection from local and regional governmental authorities, along with the gradual realization that the Arab marauders had tacit approval from local government officials to do as they wished, the black Africans began to form self-defense groups "on a tribal basis as opposed to based on local communities."[7]

By the early 2000s, there was already ample evidence that the vast majority of attacks against black African villages were undertaken by GoS troops in tandem with the Janjaweed. In most cases, the attacks involved bombings by GoS aircraft, followed by a ground attack involving hundreds of Janjaweed on camels and horses, and then the entrance of both GoS troops and Janjaweed in four-wheel vehicles (some mounted with machine guns).

It is significant to note that the majority of the Arab tribes were not involved in the attacks, were not members of the Janjaweed, and did not necessarily support—and, in fact, may have looked askance at—the actions of the GoS and the Janjaweed. The only people who attempted to stave off the attacks and killing were fellow black Africans from other villages.

FEMALES IN SUDAN AT THE TIME OF THE GENOCIDE

Prior to discussing the plight and fate of Darfuri females during and following the genocide, it is essential to comment on the status of women in Sudan at the time of the genocide. While the black Africans of Darfur vehemently complained to their own leaders and local authorities (most of whom were Arab) that they were treated like second-class citizens by the GoS, females in Sudan were, by Western standards, treated as less than second-class citizens, a situation that has changed very little in subsequent years. This has been due to "discriminatory laws and legal provisions—particularly in the areas of criminal law and personal status law—which restrict women's ability to participate in many areas of life on an equal basis with men; and which prevent progress in ending harmful practices such as female genital mutilation, child marriage, and polygamy. Second, in addition to the harsh legal environment, women are subject to increasingly repressive, conservative religious practices which appear to be promoted by the regime."[8] In the report titled, "In Search of Confluence: Addressing Discrimination and Inequality in Sudan," the Equal Rights Trust quoted a female journalist (Liemia Abubakr) as asserting the following:

> When the current regime took over in 1989, it came with a specific
> ideology. In this ideology, women were viewed with great suspicion
> [purportedly resulting from, according to the authors, the beliefs inherent
> in fundamentalist Islamic belief]; women were targeted. This targeting was
> carried out through the law, such as the personal law, criminal law and the
> employment law. A specific dress code was imposed on women, in line with

this ideology.... This ideology and these policies created an environment where women experienced discrimination and violence. In addition, the conflicts and war which Sudan experienced in this period created an environment in which many violations of women's rights were carried out.[9]

In 1991, the Muslim Personal Status Act went into effect in Sudan, which essentially established "a strongly patriarchal system governing marriage, the marital relations and divorce."[10] The Act also resulted in "a hierarchy within marriage, whereby women are effectively subservient to their husbands, required to obey them in all matters."[11]

The report cited an academic who claimed, "There are 26 laws not in conformity with the constitution because of their explicit or implicit discrimination against women."[12] That said, Sudanese law, influenced by Sharia law, is predicated on the "assumption that husbands have an automatic right to control their wife's movements, body and property."[13]

There are even laws that allow for a female to be arrested, jailed, and whipped for having been raped. The latter comes under Section 145 of the Criminal Law Act of 1991, which criminalizes adultery (in Arabic, zina, or zena), and is defined as sexual intercourse "without there being a lawful bond between a man and a woman." The victim is liable to be charged with a criminal act if she is unable to prove, or at least convince the court, that the act of sex was nonconsensual. Furthermore, being unmarried and pregnant are, according to Sudan's Criminal Act of 1991, grounds for the court to prove adultery.

For a male to be prosecuted and held responsible for rape, he must confess, or four witnesses, all male adults, must testify to having witnessed the sexual act, stating that it was nonconsensual. This issue will be discussed in more detail below.

ATTACKS AGAINST BLACK AFRICAN FEMALES IN DARFUR

Brutal assaults against black African females in Darfur were, and continue to be, perpetrated at various times and in different places: during the course of attacks on black African villages by GoS troops and the Janjaweed; in the mountains and desert areas into which the victims of the aforementioned attacks fled; and, outside of both internally displaced persons (IDP) camps and refugee camps where black African females forage for wood. While Arab women certainly face rape in Sudan, sexual attacks against black African females are systematic, much more common, and greater in number.

The GoS troops and Janjaweed targeted women for many reasons, including but not limited to the following: for their own pleasure; because females are easy prey since the rapists are generally stronger than the women, and females generally are not armed; they perceive rape as part of the spoils of war; as a means to terrorize females and their families, with the aim of forcing the black Africans out of the region; as a way to dehumanize the black African females; to emasculate the females' male relatives; and, in some cases, because they seemed to believe that they were creating "tomatoes" (that is, red people as opposed to black), or "Baby Janjaweeds."

The females were subjected to a wide range of assaults, from verbal assaults and threats, to physical abuse, including rape, and abduction for purposes of sexual slavery. In many instances, black African females were also murdered by the perpetrators. As the situation in Darfur remains unresolved, black African females continue to face all of these types of attack.

SLURS AND THREATS

In almost every testimony provided by a black African female who was sexually assaulted by a GoS soldier or Janjaweed fighter, the victims commented on the slurs and threats directed at them. The slurs were often racial in nature and asserted that the black African females were godless. The threats were twofold. Perpetrators often threatened to impregnate the female so that she would have a "Janjaweed" or "Arab baby," and some rapists threatened to track their victims down in order to rape them again.

More often than not, rape terrorized females to such an extent that they fled their villages and homes, if not the region itself. In this regard, rape served as a weapon for ethnic cleansing.

The threats directed at the victims were diverse in nature. Some rapists referred to the race or blackness of the victims ("Black prostitute, whore— you are dirty blacks"[14]); some, as mentioned, taunted the victims that they would bear "Arab babies"[15]; and, some asserted that all females in Darfur were targeted for rape (for example, "We will kill all men and rape women. We want to change the color. Every woman will deliver red. Arabs [will be] the husbands of those women"[16]). Under Article II of the UN Convention on the Prevention and Punishment of the Crime of Genocide, two of the acts listed as constituting genocide (when there is the intent to destroy in whole or part, a group, as such in this case, an ethnic or racial one) are germane when it comes to rape: "(c) Deliberately inflicting on the group conditions of life calculated to bring about its physical destruction in whole or in part;" and "(d) Imposing measures intended to prevent births within the group."[17] This is not merely theory, for in 1998, a trial at the International Criminal Tribunal for Rwanda established, for the first time in international law, that rape could be tried as a component of genocide if committed with the intent to destroy a targeted group. In its findings, the Trial Chamber defined rape as "[…] a physical invasion of a sexual nature, committed on a person under circumstances which are coercive." The Chamber also stated that "[…] rape is a form of aggression and that the central elements of the crime of rape cannot be captured in a mechanical description of objects and body parts. This approach is more useful in international law."[18]

PHYSICAL ABUSE

During many of the sexual attacks against the females of Darfur, perpetrators beat their victims with whips, sticks, and other weapons. Some mutilated their victims' genitals and breasts. Some females were gang-raped—sometimes by up to six or more rapists—many times over. In other cases, females were sexually assaulted with knives, sticks, and other instruments. In a study conducted in 2005, Medecins Sans Frontieres found that "almost a third (28 percent) of the victims reported that they were raped more than one time, either by single or multiple assailants. In more than half of the cases, physical violence was inflicted beyond sexual violence; women are beaten with sticks, whips or axes."[19] Such brutal and sadistic attacks served various purposes, including expressing their hatred of the black Africans, degrading the females as a way of punishing the entire group of black Africans, humiliating the victims, and/or terrorizing them to the point where they are likely to flee the region.

RAPE

During the early years of the genocide (2004–07) almost every single major attack against various regions and villages in Darfur saw the perpetration of rape of black African females by GoS troops and the Janjaweed. Not infrequently, those females who were out fetching water or already tilling their fields were raped where they were caught. As the marauders reached the villages, females were often raped in their homes in front of their families. Those females who attempted to escape into the desert or up into the mountains were often caught and raped as well.

It is estimated that the number of females raped is in the tens of thousands. The latter estimate is based on the following report:

> UN workers say they registered 2,500 rapes in Darfur in 2006, but believe far more went unreported. The real figure is probably thousands a month, said a UN official.... Victims usually can't identify their aggressors, which makes prosecutions impossible.... Human rights activists in South Darfur who monitor violence in the refugee camps estimate more than 100 women are raped each month in and around Kalma alone.[20]

In its June 2007 report, "Laws Without Justice: An Assessment of Sudanese Laws Affecting Survivors of Rape," Refugees International asserted that "rape is an integral part of the pattern of violence that the GoS, [and through the actions of its proxies, the Janjaweed] is inflicting upon the targeted ethnic groups in Darfur.... The raping of Darfuri women is inexorably linked to the systematic destruction of their communities."[21]

In this regard, David Scheffer, a former US Ambassador at Large for War Crimes Issues from 1997 to 2001, and currently a law professor and the director of the Center for International Human Rights at Northwestern University School of Law, first comments on and then quotes a female rape victim: "'Janjaweed babies' born of the rapes rarely have a future in the mother's ethnic group. Infanticide and abandonment are common. [As one] victim explained: 'They kill our males and dilute our blood with rape. [They] ... want to finish us as a people, end our history.'"[22]

The sexual attacks were frequently laced with racial taunts, such as "You're going to have an Arab baby" and "No zuregs [a slur the equivalent of 'nigger'] belong here [within Sudan]." The intent to impregnate the black African females by Arab GoS soldiers and Janjaweed to create Arab babies constitutes a genocidal act under article 2b and 2c of the United Nations Convention on the Prevention and Punishment of the Crime of Genocide (UNCG). More specifically, as Scheffer notes, "mass rape can destroy a substantial part of a group and thus constitute genocide."[23]

Furthermore, assailants knew that any black African female who is raped will be considered a pariah within her own family and larger community, thus cutting off, especially for young females, the possibility of having children in the future with a man of her own people. When rape is carried out with that knowledge and intent it amounts to genocidal intent under Article 2d of the UNCG. Again, as Scheffer argues: "Imagine the collective horror if men and boys in these ethnic groups were raped and then castrated. Would anyone doubt that genocidal impulses were at work by depriving men of their ability to father children? In Darfur, raped women and girls are similarly crippled."[24]

Paradoxically, while the rapists of the black African females carry out their brutal and degrading deeds with impunity, the victims are the ones punished by the legal system. It is not uncommon for such females to be arrested, beaten, and jailed. Complicating and exacerbating matters is the commonly held belief by many Sudanese that nonconsensual sex cannot result in a pregnancy. Accordingly, it would be impossible for a female to become pregnant as a result of rape.[25]

In July 2005, the United Nations issued a report that accused the GoS of ignoring the mass rapes being perpetrated by their troops and the Janjaweed, and berated it for taking no action to either halt the rapes or bring the perpetrators to trial. Concomitantly, the UN report asserted that GoS officials both threatened and arrested rape victims in order to force them to recant their accusations or charges against the rapists. In its report, the UN called on the GoS to abolish all laws, rules, and regulations granting immunity from prosecution to those in the state's employ, and to provide in-depth training to police officials, prosecutors, and judges in regard to handling sexual assault cases. Some two years later, in 2007, Refugees International reported that Sudan's laws continued to grant immunity to members of the military, security services, police, and border guards; many Janjaweed members have been integrated into the Popular Defense Forces, which also makes them exempt from prosecution.[26]

In light of the fact that both their immediate family members and members of the larger community may treat them as pariahs for having been raped, many females refuse to inform loved ones or authorities about such attacks. This is true for several reasons: first, married women know there is a distinct possibility that their husbands might disown them; second, single women fear they will be marked forever and thus remain unmarriageable; third, if they end up pregnant as a result of the rape, their child will also be treated as a pariah. One woman who was raped and then rejected by her husband reported the following: "After six days some of the girls were released. But the others, as young as eight years old, were kept there. Five to six men would rape us in rounds, one after the other for hours during the six days, every night. My husband could not forgive me after this, he disowned me"—S. from Silaya.[27]

Wishing to keep their assaults a secret, many girls and women also purposely avoid seeking medical assistance following a rape. This, of course, can lead to additional and significant medical complications.

ABDUCTION AND SEXUAL SLAVERY

Females were often abducted by the GoS soldiers and/or Janjaweed. Sometimes they were held onto for days on end, sometimes for months, and other times for years. In its report *Sudan: Darfur: Rape as a Weapon of War*, Amnesty International quoted a Darfuri woman about this very issue:

> They took K.M., who is twelve years old in the open air. Her father was killed by the Janjawid in Um Baru, the rest of the family ran away and she was captured by the Janjawid who were on horseback. More than six people used her as a wife; she stayed with the Janjawid and the military more than ten days. K, another woman who is married, aged eighteen, ran away but was captured by the Janjawid who slept with her in the open place, all of them slept with her. She is still with them.[28]

Some were purportedly even flown to Khartoum where they served as chattel and sex slaves for members of the GoS military. Amnesty International reported that "girls as young as eight years old have been abducted and held in sexual slavery for many months."[29]

SUDANESE LAW AND RAPE

Black African females who were raped in Darfur and reported it (either to a local health organization or the police) were often arrested for either having engaged in extramarital or premarital sex. In an investigation carried out in Darfur in 2005, Medecins Sans Frontieres documented the fact of such arrests. One of the accounts included in the report was by a sixteen-year-old black African girl:

> When I was eight months pregnant from the rape [by three Janjaweed], the police came to my hut and forced me with their guns to go to the police station. They asked me questions, so I told them that I had been raped. They told me that as I was not married, I will deliver this baby illegally. They beat me with a whip on the chest and back and put me in jail.[30]

In 2005, UN High Commissioner for Human Rights Louise Arbour also reported that rape victims in Darfur could face criminal charges if and when courts ruled that they were unable to prove their case against the perpetrators, which ultimately discouraged victims from making accusations.[31] Adding insult to injury, in 2006, an analyst with the International Crisis Group, reported that "women [who reported they have been raped] are often ... accused by police of waging war on the central government."[32]

EFFORTS OF INTERNATIONAL HUMAN RIGHTS ORGANIZATIONS AND ACTIVISTS

Various international human rights organizations were on the forefront of addressing sexual assault of black African females by the GoS troops and the Janjaweed. Among those being the most vigilant were Human Rights Watch, Amnesty International, Refugees International, and Physicians for Human Rights. Such organizations conducted field investigations in the refugee camps in Chad and in the villages and IDP camps in Darfur; issued major reports; called on the international community to act in a speedy and efficient way to halt the sexual assaults and to provide assistance to those females who had already suffered attacks; testified before the US Congress; provided other activists and politicians with key information and statistics; wrote editorials for inclusion in newspapers across the globe; and, in certain cases, called on their constituents to apply pressure on the international community to act in a responsible manner relating to these issues.

The reports issued by these organizations were among the most detailed, hard-hitting, and widely distributed information on the sexual assaults perpetrated in Darfur. The titles alone provide one with a sense of the breadth of the issues they addressed: *Darfur: Rape as a Weapon of War: Sexual Violence and Its Consequences* (Amnesty International); *Sudan: Systematic Rape of Women and Girls* (Amnesty International); *Sudan: Security Forces Attacking Women Seeking Firewood* (Refugees International); "Darfur: Women Raped Even After Seeking Refuge" (Human Rights Watch); *Rape, Islam, and Darfur's Refugees and War Displaced* (Refugees International); *Laws Without Justice: An Assessment of Sudanese Laws Affecting Survivors of Rape* (Refugees International); and *Ending Sexual Violence in Darfur: An Advocacy Agenda* (Refugees International).

If it were not for such organizations, the international community, individual governments, and activists would be bereft of key information about the ongoing sexual assaults faced by the black African females of Darfur. It is also possible that much less assistance and support would have been provided to such victims. However, despite such efforts the international community was largely negligent in addressing the assaults in effective ways including, halting such attacks, applying real pressure on the GoS to rein in its troops and the Janjaweed, providing medical attention to those who have suffered the assaults, and bringing the perpetrators to trial.

THE AFTERMATH

Speaking about the various ramifications black African females face as a result of being raped, Amnesty International issued a report in which it stated the following:

> Rape will have a devastating and ongoing impact on the health of women and girls, and survivors now face a lifetime of stigma and marginalization from their own families and communities. Some who have become pregnant as a result of rape often suffer complications before, during and after giving birth, because of the physical injuries resulting from [sexual]

assault. When giving birth, women who have been raped are prone to fistula and lose control of the bladder or bowel functions. They become isolated as a result of their incontinence.[33]

Infections and injuries to the genital area and reproduction system can also result in the inability to have children. The latter could result in the rejection of the female victim by her husband (or, for that matter, her future husband). Of course, each victim who is raped is also in danger of contracting HIV/AIDS. Each infection and disease may also adversely impact the newborn child.

According to a 2006 report issued by UNICEF titled, "Children Born Out of Rape/Wedlock," no reliable social services exist in Darfur to care for children who are abandoned by their mothers. Many babies end up dying as a result of being abandoned, while others receive minimal care. That continues to be the case to this very day.

IMPUNITY

The UN Security Council (UNSC) initially referred the situation in Darfur to the International Criminal Court (ICC) on March 31, 2005. Subsequently, acting under the authority provided in Security Council Resolution 1593 (2005), the International Criminal Court (ICC) issued six arrest warrants for those allegedly in charge of planning, overseeing, and carrying out atrocities perpetrated in Darfur between 2003 and 2008.

On April 27, 2007, the ICC issued an arrest warrant for Ahmad Muhammad Haroun, the Sudanese minister for humanitarian affairs, charging him with twenty counts of crimes against humanity and twenty-two counts of war crimes, including rape. He is accused of recruiting, funding, and arming the Janjaweed militia. Currently, Haroun is the governor of North Kordofan State.

On May 2, 2007, the ICC issued an arrest warrant for Ali Kushayb, a Janjaweed leader, on fifty counts of crimes against humanity (i.e., deportation or forcible transfer of population, imprisonment or severe deprivation of physical liberty in violation of fundamental rules of international law, torture, persecution, and inhumane acts of inflicting serious bodily injury and suffering) and war crimes (i.e., violence to life and person, outrage on personal dignity in particular humiliating and degrading treatment), including rape, allegedly committed in Darfur in 2003 and 2004. To date, he has not been arrested.

On March 4, 2009, the ICC issued an arrest warrant for Sudanese President Omar Hassan Ahmad al-Bashir on seven counts of crimes against humanity and war crimes, including rape, allegedly committed in Darfur between 2004 and 2009. Then, on July 12, 2010, the ICC issued a second arrest warrant for al-Bashir for three counts of genocide allegedly committed against the Fur, Massaliet, and Zaghawa ethnic groups. Al-Bashir remains free as he continues to serve as president of Sudan.

On March 1, 2012, the ICC issued an arrest warrant for Sudanese Defense Minister Abdelrahim Mohamed Hussein on twenty counts of crimes against humanity, and twenty-one counts of war crimes, including rape, allegedly committed in Darfur. Since his indictment, Hussein has become governor of Khartoum (June 2015).

On June 29, 2015, Fatou Bensouda, the current Prosecutor of the International Criminal Court, asserted the following in her most recent report on the situation in Darfur to the United Nations Security Council: "without stronger action by the Security Council and States Parties, the situation in Sudan is unlikely to improve and the alleged perpetrators of serious crimes against the civilian population will not be brought to justice."[34] Unfortunately, she was absolutely correct. To date (December 2017), the situation in Darfur continues to degenerate into ever-increasing turmoil and violence.

CONCLUSION

For years on end, during the height of the Darfur genocide, journalists, activists, and scholars used such terms as "unspeakable," "unimaginable," and "unbelievable" to describe the sexual assaults suffered by the females of Darfur at the hands of GoS troops and the Janjaweed. In light of the brutality and the suffering involved in the rapes, one certainly appreciates why some would use such terms. The fact, though, is such atrocities were part and parcel of that genocide. They were everyday occurrences, in fact, not something in the realm of the unbelievable or the unimaginable. Indeed, sexual assaults were carried out during each and every major attack against the youngest of the young (girls as young as eight years old) and the oldest of the old (women as old as sixty and seventy). For the perpetrators, such crimes were neither unspeakable nor unimaginable, and for the victims the assaults they suffered were neither unimaginable nor unbelievable.

There are several messages inherent in the aforementioned facts. First, all of us—all of humanity—need to change the way we speak of such atrocities. By calling them unspeakable, unbelievable, and unimaginable, we almost shunt them aside, as if they cannot be dealt with in a concrete fashion, nor halted. But they can be.

The problem is that thus far in history (and I do mean history, for the perpetration of sexual assaults has been a part of warfare for ages) no one has really taken the time, put in the thought, or made the effort to alter, once and for all, the way such crimes are perceived or dealt with. The question, though, is this: Is anyone or any group willing to put their hearts, minds, and souls into bringing about such a paradigm change? Is it not past time?

SAMUEL TOTTEN is Professor Emeritus at the University of Arkansas, Fayetteville. Totten is author of many publications including, *An Oral and Documentary History of the Darfur Genocide*. His most recent coauthored and coedited publications include, Sudan's Nuba Mountains People Under Siege: Accounts by Humanitarians in the Battle Zone, and Dirty Hands and Vicious Deeds: The U.S. Government's Complicity in Crimes Against Humanity and Genocide.

NOTES

1. Violence continues unabated in Darfur but it now involves not only GoS attacks against the black Africans of Darfur, but scores of other actors, from various rebel groups to outlaws engaged in hijacking vehicles, attacking and plundering villages, raping, and killing at will).

2. In 2012, the GoS added two states—Central and East—to the region, for a total of five states.

3. The periods of drought and famine adversely affected other countries in the region as well, resulting in the migration of extremely large numbers of nomads from Chad and Libya to Darfur in search of grazing land, thus applying even more pressure on the scant resources available.

4. Beginning in fourteenth century, Arabs assumed control of the region, which resulted in the establishment of Islam. The latter fused with an growing sense of Arab nationalism. Together with their increase in power and a sense of superiority, Arabs looked down on blacks who often faced a life of slavery. As time passed, Arabs became slave masters, enslaving even more blacks, which, in turn, led to viewing blacks as lesser beings. Over time, Arab nationalism and the racist belief in the superiority of Arabs over indigenous blacks both contributed to, and drove the dream of, establishing a Pan-Arab empire.

5. Abdullahi El-Tom, "The Black Book: Imbalance of Power and Wealth in Sudan," *Journal of African National Affairs* 1 (2003): 25–35.

6. The authors of *The Black Book* also asserted that the vast majority of posts in the government, the judiciary, the military, and the police not only all came from the North but primarily from three tribal groups: the Shaygiyya, Ja'aliyiin, and Danagla, and were appointed by the ruling elite. Moreover, the authors reported that the "peripheries" of the country had been purposely denied fair representation in the government and had been forced to lead a life of impoverishment.

7. Abdul-Jabbar Fadul and Victor Tanner, "Darfur After Abuja: A View from the Ground," in *War in Darfur and the Search for Peace*, ed. Alex de Waal (Cambridge, MA: Harvard University, Global Equity Initiative, 2007), 301.

8. Equal Rights Trust, *In Search of Confluence: Addressing Discrimination and Inequality in Sudan* (London: Equal Rights Trust, 2014), 1.

9. Ibid., 108.

10. Ibid., 110.

11. Ibid., 113.

12. Ibid., 189n467.

13. Ibid., 113.

14. Kelly Dawn Askin, "Prosecuting Gender Crimes Committed in Darfur: Holding Leaders Accountable for Sexual Violence," in *Genocide in Darfur: Investigating Atrocities in the Sudan*, eds. Samuel Totten and Eric Markusen (New York: Routledge, 2006), 18.

15. Ibid., 19.

16. Ibid.

17. United Nations, *The United Nations Convention on the Prevention and Punishment of the Crime of Genocide* (New York: UN, 1948).

18. International Criminal Tribunal for Rwanda (1998), "Prosecutor v. Jean-Paul Akayesu" (Arusha, Tanzania: ICTR. 1998), 138.

19. Physicians for Human Rights, "The Use of Rape as a Weapon of War in the Conflict in Darfur, Sudan," (Cambridge, MA: Physicians for Human Rights, 2004), 3.

20. Alfred de Montesquiou, "Darfur Women Describe Gang Rape," *The Washington Post*, May 28, 2007, http://www.washingtonpost.com/wp-dyn/content/article /2007/05/27/AR2007052700634_pf.html

21. Adrienne Fricke and Amira Khair, *Laws Without Justice: An Assessment of Sudanese Laws Affecting Survivors of Rape* (Washington, DC: Refugees International, 2007), 4, 7.

22. David Scheffer, "Rape as Genocide in Darfur," *Los Angeles Times*, November 13, 2008, www.latimes.com/la-oe-scheffer13-2008nov13-story.html

23. Ibid. As Scheffer notes, "Prosecuting the rapes in Darfur as a crime against humanity would get at the crime's seriousness. But genocide is another order of destruction altogether. Elevating the mass-rape charges to that level indicates that Bashir intended not only to terrorize women or force a population out of a particular region but to end—or substantially imperil—the very existence of the three ethnic groups that dared to challenge his power." In many, if not most, cases, rape was perpetrated with the purpose of terrorizing the black African female population, shaming them, and making them pariahs and humiliating the black African men. Significantly, the rape of the black African females by the outsiders contributed to tearing apart the seams of the black African community, and, part and parcel of this was the calculated notion of creating "Arab babies."

24. Ibid.

25. Michele Lent Hirsch, "Darfur," *Women Under Siege*, Women's Media Center, February 8, 2012, www.womenundersiegeproject.org/conflicts/profile/darfur-sudan. While the origin of the belief amongst various tribal groups in Sudan that a woman cannot get pregnant if the sexual act was not consensual has been lost to history, it is worth noting the following: "Anthropologists in the 1960s supported the idea that the average woman could not be raped. Margaret Mead declared that 'by and large, within the same homogenous social setting an ordinarily strong man cannot rape an ordinarily strong healthy woman' (190). The beliefs also included the theory that a woman who became pregnant as a result of the claimed rape must have consented, regardless if she clearly refused, since a woman could only conceive as a result of experiencing lust and excitement (191). Another obstacle for victims of rape is a document known as "Form 8," which the government, between 1991 and 2005, required women to obtain from the police station to receive medical treatment after a sexual assault. Although the form is no longer required by law, doctors refuse to provide medical exams without the form for fear of reprisal.

26. Fricke and Khair, *Laws Without Justice*, 10–2.

27. Amnesty International, *Sudan: Darfur: Rape as a Weapon of War*. (London: Amnesty International, 2004), 10.

28. Ibid, 9.

29. Ibid, 10.

30. Medecins Sans Frontieres, *The Crushing Burden of Rape: Sexual Violence in Darfur. A Briefing Paper* (Paris: Medecins Sans Frontieres, 2005), 6.

31. BBC News, "UN Accuses Sudan Over Darfur Rape," July 29, 2005, news.bbc.co.uk /2/hi/africa/4728231.stm

32. Stephanie Nieuwoudt, "No Justice for Darfur Rape Victims." *Institute for War & Peace Reporting*, October 25, 2006.

33. Amnesty International, *Sudan: Darfur: Rape*, 15.

34. International Criminal Court, *Twentieth Report of the Prosecutor of the International Court to the UN Security Council Pursuant to UNSCR 1593 (2005)*, (The Hague, 2015), 9.

14

Grassroots Women's Participation in Addressing Conflict and Genocide

Case Studies from the Middle East North Africa Region and Latin America

Lisa Davis and Cassandra Atlas

INTRODUCTION

How does justice gain traction in countries afflicted by long histories of nearly intractable conflict-related violence that can lead to genocide and other mass atrocities? As governments seeking to end legacies of injustice and impunity take steps toward moral and material healing, they struggle to disrupt patterns of women's human rights violations.

A root cause of the persistence of injustice and impunity, and a major shortcoming of many transitional justice efforts, is the lack of attention to the voices and needs of grassroots women. They are the target of human rights violations at the hands of all armed actors during times of conflict. Women working to end conflict and achieve peace are critical as civil society representatives. Their work is often based on an analysis that bridges solutions for immediate violations with systemic root causes, producing a more lasting outcome. Conflict increases barriers that prevent these individuals and organizations from movement-building together—that is to say, coordinating their efforts to bring about long-term progressive social change. Conflict creates geographical divisions, fuels distrust, and increases competition for scarce resources within local civil society.

MADRE is an international women's human rights organization that partners with community-based women's groups worldwide facing war and disaster. Its longstanding strategy to empower women who are building peace in their countries helps position local women activists in leadership roles advocating for justice. Key stakeholders such as community-based organizations, local government members, national human rights institutes, first responders, the business community, and others at the national level and international NGOs, states, and UN agencies are often uncoordinated in their efforts and out of touch with the realities of ending violence and fostering peace on the ground. The voices of women-led civil society become deprioritized, which leads to their exclusion from international peace and reconstruction processes. Postconflict and post-genocide experiences teach that when women are excluded from such transitional processes, peace is more likely to collapse.[1]

This chapter discusses the critical need to empower women-led civil society in conflict, postconflict, and postgenocide settings in order to develop sustainable solutions for holistic redress and lasting peace. It explains MADRE's ground-up approach, which centers on building women's ability to advocate for human rights, strengthening women's networks, and championing women's strategies for change at the regional and international level. Case studies from Iraq and Syria, as well as Colombia and Guatemala, demonstrate MADRE's approach in action and provide replicable tactics for advocates.

BUILDING STRATEGIES FOR CHANGE: BRINGING TOGETHER IRAQI AND SYRIAN WOMEN'S RIGHTS ACTIVISTS FOR DIALOGUE AND EXCHANGE

Over the last five years, shocking patterns of sexual violence perpetrated by both regime and opposition forces have emerged in Syria. Numerous UN bodies and representatives, as well as NGOs, have documented widespread and systemic violence, as the conflict in Syria is increasingly marked by torture and sexual violence used "as a weapon of war to intimidate parties to the conflict, destroying identity, dignity and the social fabrics of families and communities."[2] Accordingly, the

UN Independent International Commission of Inquiry on the Syrian Arab Republic has consistently found the pattern and practice of sexual violence carried out in the conflict to meet the standard of crimes against humanity and war crimes.[3]

In June 2014, Iraq contended with the takeover of several major cities by the Islamic State of Iraq and Syria (ISIS), as well as a sharp increase in sectarian violence in Baghdad. In Iraq's North, ISIS immediately moved to impose its fundamentalist agenda directly on the bodies of women. Within days, credible reports began emerging of ISIS fighters abducting and raping women in the territories ISIS controls.[4] Several government officials and human rights bodies, including the Human Rights Council,[5] have named ISIS responsible for genocide against minority groups in areas under its control, including Christians, Shiite Muslims, and Yezidis.

Addressing both immediate needs and root causes of sexual- and gender-based violence (SGBV) in conflict demands cross-movement collaborations between international nongovernmental organizations (INGOs) and the community-based organizations (CBOs) they work with. Truly sustainable redress for and protection from SGBV (as opposed to the temporary solutions often pursued during conflict) can be achieved when direct service organizations work in collaboration with their policy advocacy counterparts. This two-pronged process effectively merges prevention and protection services with the human rights advocacy needed for long-term policy change.

Linking this imperative to the creation of lasting positive change requires strengthening the capacity of Iraqi citizens and local women's organizations committed to ending gender-based violence (GBV) and building a rights-based society in which democratic norms, including gender equality, can supplant sectarianism. In this moment of crisis in Iraq and Syria, it is precisely this approach to social change that will help weave solutions out of uncertainty and build more equitable foundations in the long term.

In Iraq and Syria, women's grassroots human rights groups play a critical role in addressing the impacts of conflict. They have mobilized to provide humanitarian aid and protect communities from armed groups, and thus have become the frontline of defense, sustaining community-based resilience against violence. In both countries, women's rights groups have unique knowledge of local needs and priorities; therefore, they are best positioned to devise strategies and develop solutions to critical issues based on analysis that often links solutions for immediate violations with systemic root causes, producing a more lasting outcome.

For this reason, MADRE, in partnership with the Women's International League for Peace and Freedom (WILPF), the Human Rights and Gender Justice (HRGJ) Clinic, and the Sorensen Center for International Peace and Justice at the City University of New York (CUNY) School of Law, and local Syrian and Iraqi women's organizations work to bring together dozens of grassroots women activists working on human rights issues in the context of the conflict to engage in dialogue and exchange. These gatherings are called the Strategies for Change convenings.

The Strategies for Change conference series provides an open and safe forum for Syrian and Iraqi women's rights advocates to share and discuss their narratives, feedback, and recommendations. Convenings are held two to three times a year in the Levant region, often in Beirut or Istanbul, where it is accessible for Iraqi and Syrian women's rights activists to travel. They serve as an important mechanism to capture the voices of grassroots women's rights advocates, highlighting the challenges these activists face. They also demonstrate the impact of defective policies at the international level on the reality of women at the local level, and help to catalyze solutions to overcome them and foster better-informed policy decisions. They provide a unique opportunity for activists to engage with one another, as well as with international experts, about root causes of gender-based violence and human rights abuses in Iraq and Syria, and to explore challenges in addressing women's rights violations in the context of the conflict. Perhaps most importantly, these convenings provide a space for participants to share practices and discuss ways in which their organizations can increase their security, networks, and ability to respond to all forms of gender-based violence.

Recognizing that, like the survivors they serve, women's human rights defenders are also often in need of psychosocial support, convenings include sessions on self-care that follow intense exchange and discussions on human rights abuses. Psychosocial trainers provide participants with concrete tools for self-care and psychosocial support for when they return to the demands of their work.

Each convening ends with participants building on the conclusions of the previous convening, identifying existing gaps in response to threats they face in conflict, and voicing recommendations for addressing sexual- and gender-based violence in Iraq and Syria. Each time, the consensus is clear: comprehensively addressing the rights and humanitarian needs of women and girls fleeing territories controlled by ISIS requires addressing preexisting threats embedded in Iraq's and Syria's laws and social norms. The strategies for change in addressing the continuum of harm exacerbated by conflict, which have been developed by Iraqi and Syrian women in the convenings, have become their roadmap for international advocacy; this reflects a ground-up approach that more accurately and practically provides solutions to conflict-related human rights abuses.

DISCRIMINATORY LAWS, PROCEDURE, AND PRACTICES: CHALLENGING PREEXISTING THREATS TO WOMEN IN CONFLICT

At convenings, both Iraqi and Syrian women's rights advocates raised concerns about preexisting discriminatory provisions within their national legislative frameworks and discussed how the impact of these provisions has grown exponentially worse in the context of the conflict.

Among the primary concerns in Iraq is the government's policy of prohibiting local NGOs from providing shelter to women. Women from Iraq also discussed how they are unable to replace legal identification in the absence of a male family member who can verify their identity. The sharp increase in rates of women fleeing violence and in need of new identification has become a crisis within the conflict. Without such documentation, women cannot travel, find housing, obtain employment, get health care services, or enroll into educational institutions. In such cases, women are at risk of becoming stateless and more vulnerable to violence and discrimination.

Similarly, in Syria, the Nationality Law[6] prevents women from passing their nationality on to their children. This discriminatory law has devastating impacts on the civil and economic rights of refugees. Lack of registration not only means no access to social services; it also leaves stateless individuals more vulnerable to abuse and exploitation including trafficking, forced labor, and sexual exploitation.[7] It is nearly impossible for these mothers to register their children's nationality.[8] The consequences are grave: children may be denied basic services such as education and healthcare, including vaccinations, and they may be unable to return to Syria.[9]

Syrian women advocates also recognize the links between the crisis of statelessness and the lack of reproductive justice for women. In the long term, in order to ensure that both the legal framework and the enforcement mechanisms to prevent and address statelessness are a priority in postconflict Syria, women must be actively involved now in the international peace and reconstruction planning processes.

ADDRESSING BARRIERS TO REPRODUCTIVE HEALTHCARE IN CONFLICT

In ISIS-controlled areas, women's reproductive healthcare services are minimal to nonexistent, mainly due to directives prohibiting male doctors from treating female patients, and imposing harsh restrictions on female doctors and medical professionals.[10] Participants attested to the dire situation of healthcare services in displacement camps. The medical centers in displacement camps are rudimentary, thus often inefficient in treating patients with more complicated health conditions and unable to provide adequate medication to camp residents. Furthermore, medical centers are incapable of offering psychosocial support, particularly to survivors of gender-based violence.

Iraqi and Syrian women's rights activists also remarked on how women's reproductive healthcare in particular has markedly worsened due to the conflict. In both countries, armed checkpoints, frequent roadblocks, and other severe mobility restrictions, coupled with a shortage of female doctors and soaring fuel prices has significantly impaired women's healthcare access. As a result, women often do not have access to gynecologists or prenatal healthcare. Doctors are hard to reach and are overwhelmed by treating casualties from the fighting and by severe shortages of drugs and medical supplies.

In Syria, women's rights advocates pointed out the deliberate and routine targeting and destruction of medical facilities by the regime. Ongoing fighting and bombardment have extensively damaged hospitals and other healthcare facilities. Intentional bombings of hospital and health care facilities as well as the targeted killing or imprisonment of medical professionals, who provide treatment to civilians,[11] are in clear violation of the Geneva Conventions. Doctors Without Borders reported numerous human rights violations affecting access to health care in the context of the conflict including, "targeting of medical personnel and health facilities; the non-issuance of work authorizations; increasing restrictions on delivery of aid; and attacks on humanitarian convoys."[12] Hospitals have been destroyed and local production of medicine has fallen by 90 percent.[13]

Attacks on hospitals and health facilities by both government and non-government forces further compound the consequences of sexual violence, limiting access to healthcare for entire vulnerable communities, including women and girls.[14] Women have been increasingly giving birth through cesarean sections in order to control the timing of their delivery and to avoid traveling in dangerous environments while in labor.[15]

With scarce availability of medical care and access to therapeutic abortion,[16] dozens of Syrian women activists underscored the need for contraception as a safety and survival issue. Even in times of peace, the ability to decide whether and when to become pregnant reinforces women's ability to exercise other human rights. Syrian women today are experiencing widespread hunger and malnutrition, severe stress, lack of medical care, forced displacement, and increased burdens of care for society's most vulnerable members. Under these adverse conditions, control over one's fertility becomes paramount.

During the convenings, Syrian advocates have also noted that a number of unidentified health problems have recently emerged, including infections, inflammations, and respiratory illnesses. Participants contended that the air pollution caused by the use of weapons and ongoing bombardment had had a detrimental effect on the health of the civilian population. Similarly, Iraqi women's rights advocates reported on the crisis that has ensued from the recent outbreak of cholera in at least five governorates and noted soaring rates of tuberculosis.

ADDRESSING GENDER-BASED VIOLENCE

Despite the shocking patterns of sexual violence and human rights abuses committed in the context of Syria's revolution,[17] with the rise of ISIS in June 2014, the international community's attention turned away from the war crimes committed by the Assad regime, and the human rights violations committed by all sides in the civil war started to fade from the public's attention. Syrian activists have noted that the international community has given less attention to the increased vulnerability of women refugees, which leaves them at greater risk of trafficking and forced marriage.

Regarding violations by ISIS, participants confirmed that the group continues to impose strict restrictions on women's dress, activities, professional work, and freedom of movement, which has had a devastating effect on their access to education and healthcare. In Iraq, an estimated three thousand people,[18] largely Yezidis, under ISIS captivity were subjected to rape and other sexual violence, and forced marriages, while at least a thousand more are still missing. In addition, the Organization of Women's Freedom in Iraq (OWFI) has documented the execution of over 150 women,[19] including women's rights activists who denounced and refused to adhere to the rules of the so-called Islamic State.

Additionally, ISIS has brutally murdered numerous individuals across Iraq and Syria based on their real or perceived sexual orientation, gender identity, or nonconformist social behavior.[20] Advocates described that individuals accused of "indecent" behavior, sodomy, adultery, and other so-called morality-based crimes have been beheaded or thrown off buildings. While militias across Syria and Iraq differ from each other, their patterns of gender-based violence are largely similar. Believing that the existence of lesbian, gay, bisexual, and transgendered (LGBT) people violates religious tenets, ISIS and other militia groups wage systematic campaigns of discrimination, violence, torture, and killing of real or perceived LGBT persons with near complete impunity.

ENGAGING WITH YEZIDI SURVIVORS
OF SEXUAL SLAVERY

Since the entry of ISIS into Iraq in June 2014, egregious human rights violations have been committed against the Yezidi community, as well as other minority groups including Christian, Shabak, Shia, and Turkmen populations. These abuses comprise murder, enslavement, forcible transfer, imprisonment, torture, rape, sexual slavery, and other forms of sexual violence and persecution,[21] and have been identified as forms of genocide. An Office of the High Commissioner for Human Rights (OHCHR) investigation into ISIS crimes carried out in fall 2014 found that the pattern of attacks committed against Yezidi community members in particular, signaled ISIS's intention to entirely eradicate the Yezidi population.[22]

While conflict rages on, activists have found that there is little means of engaging with Yezidi women in their struggle for redress and freedom. Strategies for Change convenings have thus provided a space for Iraqi and Syrian women's rights activists to engage with Yezidi women who have escaped captivity by ISIS fighters. Basma[23] stated that she attended the convening, with the objective of speaking on behalf of several Yezidi women who had survived abuse in captivity at the hands of ISIS militants. She described human rights abuses inflicted by ISIS on people in her community, including abduction of women and girls for sexual slavery, forced religious conversions, arbitrary detention, and summary killings.

Basma explained how Yezidi women who survived sexual slavery and the scourge of violence under ISIS continue to contend with serious challenges. The dearth of medical and psychosocial support services available in displacement camps and shelters where survivors are sent leaves them without help for the acute and prolonged physical and psychological trauma they have often suffered.[24]

Despite losing all of her family except for two siblings, Basma expressed hope for the future and felt inspired by all the advocates in the room, saying, "With you, I feel that I am strong... I would like to be an activist to talk about women's rights especially in areas that I was living, these are things that I have never heard about." Participants were deeply moved by her story, strength, and ambitions for the future. One participant encouraged her, stating, "You *are* a women's human rights activist here with the rest of us and this proves that we need to work together to make change."

CONVENING TAKEAWAYS

Overall, participants of these convenings have been extremely pleased with the substance and outcomes of the gatherings. They have commended these events as productive and highly useful to their work; they also note the long road to peace and redress ahead of them.

At the end of each convening, participants draw together their recommendations for change. These recommendations derive from their analysis of human rights abuses in the context of the ongoing conflicts in Syria and Iraq as well as root causes of gender-based violence and human rights violations in both countries. The grassroots women's groups in Iraq and Syria have unique knowledge of local needs and dynamics, putting them in the best position to offer solutions to challenges facing Iraqi and Syrian women and girls. These recommendations serve as guidelines for the international community on how to best support and strengthen women's rights and respond to human rights violations in these contexts.

Currently, there is a real danger that women who survive the rampant gender-based violence being committed in Iraq's and Syria's conflicts will continue to face gender-based violence once the conflict ends. Any government that is committed to addressing gender-based violence must include a ground-up approach to improve conditions for women, including passing measures to uphold all their human rights and to end discrimination based on gender. This means removing impediments to women's abilities to make autonomous decisions about their reproductive health and sexuality, by ending forced marriage, and by criminalizing all forms of rape, including spousal rape. It also means addressing and outlawing discrimination against women in property and inheritance laws, and in personal status laws that govern rights for families.

These are the types of measures that will be required in Syria and Iraq. UN Security Council Resolution 1325[25] provides guidance for, and obligates states to include women's active and meaningful participation in peace building as well as in postconflict reconstruction, so that initiatives to address gender-based violence are fully incorporated into Iraq's and Syria's governing structures.

A PERSISTENT PEACE

Guatemala's internal armed conflict lasted for thirty-six years, officially ending with the signing of the Peace Accords in 1996. The war resulted in approximately two hundred thousand deaths, three hundred thousand orphans, over one million internally displaced persons, and more than two hundred thousand refugees, the great majority being Indigenous peoples.[26] The Commission for Historical Clarification (CEH), a UN–sponsored truth and reconciliation commission, interviewed thousands of Guatemalans and established that the government was responsible for 93 percent of all human rights violations and acts of violence, and that the Guatemalan army, paramilitary, and police used violence against women as a weapon of war.[27] Indigenous women were specifically affected, with 9,411 reported female victims of human rights violations. Of these, 1,465 women reported sexual violence; some 89 percent of them were of Mayan descent.[28]

Impunity for past human rights violations and crimes still persist in Guatemala today. The historic trial of former dictator Efrain Ríos Montt, charged with genocide and crimes against humanity committed during his dictatorship in 1982–83, held the world's attention in the spring of 2013. However, the historic trial was annulled by Guatemala's Constitutional Court and thrown out on questionable legal grounds just ten days after it was announced. More recently, the Sepur Zarco trial, which charged two former military officers with sexual slavery and sentenced them to

360 years in prison, dealt a powerful blow against impunity. Yet, how this landmark ruling will inform future justice processes in Guatemala is still in question.

Similarly, until the signing of a landmark Peace Accord between the Colombian government and the Revolution Armed Forces of Colombia-People's Army (FARC-EP), the country's largest illegal armed group, in November 2017, Colombia remained mired in the Western Hemisphere's longest internal armed conflict. Violence committed by illegal armed groups, drug traffickers, and government security forces, coupled with displacement, rape, torture, disappearances, and other human rights violations, were, and are still everyday occurrences.

Women have borne the brunt of Colombia's conflict. Of the nearly four million Colombians who have been displaced as a result of war, over 70 percent are either women or children, and over 50 percent are women, the large majority of whom are Indigenous, or Afro-Colombian.[29] Women and girls are long-standing survivors of widespread and systematic campaigns of sexual- and gender-based violence.[30] They contend with broken social structures, rampant insecurity, and the responsibilities they bear to protect themselves and their families. Colombian women and girls who were, and continue to be targeted by illegal armed groups grapple with forced recruitment that leads to sexual servitude, exploitation, and often death.[31]

Despite past efforts at transitional justice, such as the Justice and Peace Law[32] and Victim's Law (Ley de Víctimas),[33] and recent legislative measures to end sexual violence, impunity remains rampant. Part of the problem is that Colombia has yet to implement the programs and policies mandated at the domestic level or by the many international human rights accords the government has ratified and signed.

The promise of a new peace, as implementation begins in earnest, must be informed by those who have been most affected by the decades of violence and displacement. For this reason, MADRE, in collaboration with the Guatemala Human Rights Commission and the Universidad de Los Andes School of Law in Colombia, partnered to bring representatives of grassroots women's groups from Guatemala and Colombia together for a series of exchanges, trainings, and network-building activities. The strategy was simple. As in the Strategies for Change model in the MENA (the

Middle East and North Africa) region, providing a space for local women's activists to share best practices and challenges in their work strengthens the design and implementation of local programs promoting healing, justice, and recovery from conflict and genocide.

Under the project, "A Persistent Peace: Creating Holistic Transitional Justice Programs Informed and Led by Grassroots Women in Guatemala and Colombia," through a series of joint convenings held between 2013 and 2015 in Bogotá, Colombia, and Guatemala City, Guatemala, MADRE brought together Colombian and Guatemalan women activists who worked to address the harm done by the conflicts in their countries and were involved in ongoing transitional justice and reconstruction processes. These convenings created a space where women from both countries could learn about grassroots transitional justice programs and initiatives in their countries and communities; discuss successes and challenges of their work; and offer recommendations and feedback on transitional justice strategies.

Activists also engaged in group exercises and in-depth discussions, which allowed for close listening, the creation of networks and solidarity among women within and across countries, and the establishment of trust among participants. Their discussions and analysis of the conflicts contribute to the foundation for creating sustainable postconflict redress.

IDENTIFYING OBSTACLES AND SOLUTIONS FOR INTERSECTIONAL AND HOLISTIC APPROACHES TO TRANSITIONAL JUSTICE

MADRE's project began with in-depth consultations with participants in both countries to identify shared concerns and potential strategies to improve transitional justice efforts. Both Guatemalan and Colombian women raised the concern that transitional justice had failed civil society, and women specifically, due to a lack of attention to gender-specific crimes committed during conflicts. Women went on to explain that state-led transitional justice efforts in both countries have also all but ignored other intersections that impact how women experience genocide and conflict, and how they transition into peace. Indigenous Guatemalan and Afro-Colombian women, in particular, noted their marked exclusion from national transitional justice processes, which do not take into account the double discrimination they face as a result of both their gender and ethnicity or race.

According to women in both countries, transitional justice has been dealt with through a myopic lens that takes a "one-size-fits-all" approach to peace, something problematic for sustainability and for reparations that have thus far reached very few people. Consequently, participants demanded a holistic methodology that achieves justice through diverse means, including, but not limited to, the recollection and recounting of distinct histories of violence, comprehensive psychosocial support to survivors, and access to criminal justice mechanisms for women to denounce crimes of sexual violence, break their silence, and hold perpetrators accountable. Transition, they all agreed, looks different from a ground-up approach, leads to the conditions that create sustainable peace, and builds the foundation for addressing widespread impunity.

Among the set of strategies identified by Guatemalan and Colombian women as integral to a holistic transitional justice was the need to create spaces where women can safely denounce crimes of sexual violence, and where perpetrators can be held accountable, such as domestic tribunals devoted to prosecuting gender-based violence. They noted the need for training on how to access legal justice at the domestic level and international legal remedies when domestic spaces are closed to them. For many Mayan women (and their family members) from Guatemala who served as witnesses, testifiers, and survivors seeking justice in the Ríos Montt genocide trial,[34] it was clear that legal justice is of central importance. "I want judges to say who is guilty," one woman noted. "I want to stand before a judge and ensure my voice is heard."[35]

Women further highlighted the dire need for psychosocial support and repair to be part of holistic transitional justice. There was unanimous agreement among Guatemalan and Colombian women that both psychological and spiritual healing must occur for women to emerge from legacies of violence and violation, let alone come forward and defend themselves in formal legal proceedings. As one Colombian woman explained, "We're talking about raising the voices of victims, but how can we do this without psychosocial support? Women have post-traumatic stress and this affects so many things. They have headaches, their menstruation is disrupted, but these are really pains of the soul that need to be healed."

A TOOL FOR REMEMBERING: CREATING HISTORICAL MEMORY

For women and communities who have experienced egregious and perpetual human rights violations as a result of conflict and genocide, justice and recovery often begin with remembering what has happened, and healing from it. The recollection and preservation of memory can take various forms, including oral histories, memoirs, monuments or murals that pay tribute to victims of conflict and genocide, and museums or art exhibitions.

Historical memory initiatives have the power to bring significance to the distinct suffering experienced by women and communities in the aftermath of conflict and genocide. They shed light on and preserve memories of violence, and help to ward off the stigma associated with sexual violence, which silences and degrades survivors of atrocities.[36] In the aftermath of conflict and genocide, memorializing these experiences can assist in restoring the dignity of survivors by ensuring that the truth of what they have endured is made visible and is recognized by their fellow communities, their countries, and internationally.[37] Such recognition helps prevent further human rights violations and the recurrence of conflict and genocide, by raising collective consciousness about the gravity of past abuses and their lasting impacts.[38]

Throughout the convenings, women recounted myriad ways in which they have employed historical memory as part of healing and justice processes at both the community and national level in Guatemala and Colombia. A Maya Ixil leader from Guatemala shared her experience working to construct La Casa de la Memoria, the first national historical memory museum. She described the museum as "a center for reflection where the people of Guatemala, and especially youth, can learn about the struggles and resistance of their ancestors, and teach people about how to build a country at peace, and without violence."[39] She noted in particular how government sponsorship of the museum has served as recognition that what happened to them was, in fact, genocide. Women from Putumayo, Colombia, recounted their experience working with Colombia's National Center for Historical Memory (Centro de memoria historica/CMH) on a documentary entitled, *Mujeres tras las huellas de la memoria* (Women in the footsteps of memory), which documents women's resistance and efforts to remember past atrocities and break down the stigmas that have marked their communities. Still others described small-scale efforts to transfer oral histories to community youth, and projects to construct murals naming and remembering the dead. One activist reflected that, "historical memory is a way to share what happened with our children and new generations, and a way to sensitize our communities. This is how we will create peace in the future."

WOMEN AND TRANSITIONAL JUSTICE BEFORE NATIONAL TRIBUNALS

The 1996 Peace Accords in Guatemala made way for the promise of accountability for nearly four decades of state-sponsored violence, yet their full potential is far from realization. Two Ixil women from El Quiche described their participation leading up to and during the genocide trial of Efraín Ríos Montt. They detailed a thirteen-year process of gathering witnesses and mounting testimonies that was wrought with challenges including fear, stigma, re-traumatization, and threats of retaliation for their efforts to expose the truth. "For most women," one of the panelists noted, "the trauma is still very present. So as part of the process, we worked as women to recuperate memory and to make spaces for women to organize, to share and to heal." These spaces, she explained, are places to generate healing through a return to Indigenous ancestry and traditional methods of physical and spiritual cleansing. Women remarked how such spaces play an essential role in assuring women and other witnesses that they are not alone in what they endured and in readying witnesses for their emotionally charged and arduous role at trial.

Although the conviction of Ríos Montt was ultimately overturned, both of the women from El Quiche agreed that the years-long process of organizing, documenting, healing, and pursuing legal justice for the crime of genocide in Guatemala was not lost. "We won a sentence," one woman stated. "We do not care that it was overturned. We will keep fighting, and we will keep working."[40] The other woman concurred, "I decided a long time ago that I am going to say what happened here, I am going to say what happened in Guatemala. I am so content to let go of what was in my mind and in my heart."[41]

An activist from Cali, Colombia, shared the experience of the mothers of twelve young Afro-Colombian boys who were massacred by paramilitaries in the area of Punta del Este district in Buenaventura, Colombia, in April 2005. She described the process by which these mothers sought justice for the massacre of their sons, and the many obstacles they faced, including delayed investigations by the police, overturned and reduced sentences for perpetrators, and a refusal to name paramilitary groups as the intellectual authors of these crimes. "The claims of these women have not been taken seriously because they are Afro-women," she noted. "Because they were Afro, the children who were murdered were accused during proceedings of being linked to common crime and drug trafficking, so they were never looked at as innocent victims."

She concluded by offering several measures to improve access to justice for Afro-Colombian women and community members, and others in Colombia and Guatemala facing similar obstacles. "The understanding of the conflict in this country by the government is one-dimensional" she noted, "but we as Afro-Colombians are multidimensional and so is our experience of conflict."

IMPROVING PSYCHOSOCIAL SUPPORT FOR
SURVIVORS OF CONFLICT AND GENOCIDE

Woven throughout the convenings was the theme of psychosocial support, highlighted by participants as essential not only for healing from the trauma of past injustice, but for readying survivors and activists to engage in transitional justice efforts in their current contexts. More formal conversations on psychosocial support and trauma healing were paired with exercises to offer relief and restoration to participants during the intense and emotional discussions that ensued throughout convenings.

To ensure that our process showed respect for the participants' culture and circumstances, we began each convening with an initiation ceremony. Many of the activists present at convenings, particularly the women activists from remote regions in Guatemala and Colombia, had never before left their home communities, let alone traveled internationally to interact and engage with women from other countries. Drawing on traditional practices, the ceremonies created a space in which the women could speak freely and openly, despite being in an unfamiliar place with new people. Respect for cultural values and traditions can be critical for success in creating justice, and the lack of such respect has the potential of leading to failed initiatives.[42] These ceremonies exemplified the kind of psychosocial support that empowers survivors and served to model the respect that must inform transitional justice initiatives if they are to have impact.

A Colombian psychosocial support specialist led self-healing sessions, drawing on her experience running a grassroots organization that helps survivors of Colombia's armed conflict heal from war and express themselves through art therapy. She taught women how to administer and apply this form of healing to others, explaining that meditative practices can be adopted by anyone and offer an accessible form of psychosocial rehabilitation for all. The psychosocial support specialist further discussed the importance of trauma healing not only for survivors of conflict and genocide, but also for those individuals and organizations working with trauma survivors.

Participants experienced comfort and felt encouraged as a result of interventions and instruction on psychosocial support and rehabilitation offered during convenings. Participants were given practical tools for healing and psychosocial support that can be used to improve their individual and collective community well-being. One participant noted, "The psychosocial strategy is a component that really complements the other measures of truth, justice, and reparation for victims."

CONVENING TAKEAWAYS

The ultimate goal of the convenings was to help support local women activists to build movements, share challenges and best practices, and develop recommendations that prioritize building sustainable peace within a human rights framework. This model of amplifying the voices of local women human rights leaders in postgenocide and postconflict transitional justice and peacebuilding processes bolsters justice efforts, capitalizes on the expertise of local women, and complements national and international processes with community and gender perspectives.

Women who participated in the A Persistent Peace project expressed great satisfaction with the process and its outcomes, and were grateful for the rare opportunity to come together to share strategies, tools, best practices, and lessons learned for advancing transitional justice. As one Guatemalan woman noted, "In spaces like these we learn as women to help other women. As leaders we have an obligation to do this. Today the war is over but as women we're still facing so many violations.... This is where we figure out together what we can do."

The project was equally effective for Colombian women. Given the potential at the time for peace accords to be signed after over fifty years of conflict, Colombian activists expressed that these convenings could not have been more timely or valuable. "The work done here is so valuable, undeniable. To have these discussions and arguments about transitional justice right now is integral, because whether we like it or not we have historic responsibility. If we don't contribute to the story, we're going to be left behind."

The groundwork laid under the A Persistent Peace project will not be left to sit on the shelf. It is critical for the innovative solutions elaborated and developed to take root and transform from paper into practice, making transitional justice a reality for grassroots women and their communities. Building on the robust foundation laid, MADRE is now embarking on follow-up programs with grassroots women's groups in Colombia and Guatemala to sustain the momentum for cultivating peace and justice at the community level. Through new ongoing consultations MADRE will continue to support grassroots women in their work to effect change.

CONCLUSION

History teaches that the process of healing from the legacy of conflict and genocide, building peace, and strengthening institutions and processes that slowly turn the wheels of justice is, quite simply, unsustainable and nearly impossible without consolidating and ensuring the meaningful participation of women.

Women who survive genocide, war, and conflict-related, gender-based violence will inevitably continue to face gender-based violence once the conflict ends, if it has not been adequately addressed in postconflict reconstruction. To address gendered violence, postwar conditions for women must be improved, from the creation or amendment of laws that prohibit human rights abuses and discrimination, to the enactment of those laws, to education around their implementation.

Addressing conflict-related, gender-based violence also requires guaranteeing women the right to make decisions about their reproductive health and sexuality, and providing protection and redress for when their rights are infringed. The case studies from Iraq, Syria, Colombia, and Guatemala all exemplify this common thread, yet the problem of gender-based violence and discrimination persists. Even after horrific wars and genocides, there often remains a lack of will and understanding of how to protect basic rights.

The answer lies in the full participation of women and other civil society members in peace processes. It is mandated under UN Security Council Resolution 1325[43] and has proven a critical component in achieving sustainable peace.[44] Women organizing in conflict and postconflict settings are the key to innovative models for peace and reconstruction, for implementing adequate transitional justice, and ultimately for preventing the repetition of conflict and genocide. Peace built with women's leadership from the ground up provides a stronger foundation for sustainability and redress in the long term.

To ensure that both the necessary legal framework and the enforcement mechanisms to prevent and address gender-based violence are a priority in postconflict environments, women must be involved in the processes that will lead to peace and rebuilding. There is no other party that will carry these issues forward and act on behalf of women in establishing new governance priorities.

Women from conflict countries have benefited immensely from the opportunity to share experiences across countries and conflict contexts, as well as sharing their solutions for change, projects, and collaborations.

Such exchanges have not just been *about* the roots of seeking justice and the means of healing from genocide and gross human rights violations; they are *themselves* effective justice initiatives that provide women a key opportunity to speak, to be heard, to act powerfully, and to win justice and peace for themselves, their communities, and their countries. Building sustainability in postconflict now is the only way to ensure sustainability in the future, and it begins with the women on the ground, who are working to truly achieve peace. Supporting grassroots women and their work to effect change is a vital part of cultivating peace and justice at the community level and ultimately builds long-lasting peace so that history does not repeat itself.

LISA DAVIS is Human Rights Advocacy Director for MADRE and a Clinical Professor of Law for the Human Rights and Gender Justice Clinic at the City University of New York School of Law.

CASSANDRA ATLAS is Director of Project Management for MADRE. She coordinates collaborations between MADRE's community organizing and advocacy efforts, and oversees project implementation, management, and monitoring and evaluation.

NOTES

The authors would like to thank Diana Duarte for her editorial assistance. Thanks to Afarin Dadkhah, Ramy Aqel, J.M. Kirby and Natalia Caruso for their contributions to this article and to MADRE's ongoing work with Iraqi and Syrian, and Colombian and Guatemalan women, and to the entire MADRE staff for their commitment to working on women's human rights issues worldwide. Lastly and most importantly the Authors would like to thank all of the activists who participated in our Iraq/Syria and Colombia/Guatemala convenings, and the many other men and women human rights activists in Iraq, Syria, Colombia, and Guatemala who put their lives at daily risk to protect and promote women's human rights. These individuals are true human rights defenders and unsung heroes, and we owe them the deepest gratitude.
    1. Pablo Castillo Diaz and Simon Tordjman, *Women's Participation in Peace Negotiations: Connections between Presence and Influence* (New York: UN Women, 2009).
    2. "Displacement in Syria giving way for serious gender-based crimes, warns UN official," UN.org, last modified February 26, 2013, Accessed January 30, 2017, http://www.un.org/apps/news/story.asp?NewsID=44230#.Vzoua_kgsdU.

3. UN General Assembly, Twenty-First Session, *Report of the Independent International Commission of Inquiry on the Syrian Arab Republic*, UN Doc. A/HRC/21/50 (2012); UN General Assembly, Twenty-Second Session, *Report of the Independent International Commission of Inquiry on the Syrian Arab Republic*, UN Doc. A/HRC/22/59 (2013); UN General Assembly, Twenty-Fourth Session, *Report of the Independent International Commission of Inquiry on the Syrian Arab Republic*, U.N. Doc. A/HRC/24/46 (2013).

4. Joint Written Statement: Human Rights Council, UN General Assembly, Twenty Second Special Session, September 1, 2014, 2, UN Doc. A/HRC/S-22/NGO/13 (August 31, 2014).

5. Human Rights Council, Report of the Office of the United Nations Commissioner for Human Rights on the Human Rights Situation in Iraq in the Light of the Abuses Committed by the So-called Islamic State in Iraq and the Levant and Associated Groups, 17, UN Doc. A/HRC/28/18 (March 13, 2015).

6. Legislative Decree 276—Nationality Law [Syrian Arab Republic], *Legislative Decree 276, 24*, at 20, 1969.

7. Lisa Davis, "Why Are So Many Syrian Children Being Left Stateless?" openDemocracy, July 1, 2015, accessed January 30, 2017, https://www.opendemocracy .net/5050/lisa-davis/why-are-so-many-syrian-children-being-left-stateless.

8. Ibid.

9. Ibid.

10. Adam Withnall, "Isis Shuts Down Women's Clinics in Raqqa to Prevent Male Gynecologists Treating Female Patients," *Independent* (October 29, 2015), http://www .independent.co.uk/news/world/middle-east/isis-shuts-down-womens-clinics-in-raqqa -to-prevent-male-gynaecologists-treating-female-patients-a6713266.html.; "Iraq: Women Suffer Under ISIS," Human Rights Watch, accessed January 30, 2017,https://www.hrw .org/news/2016/04/05/iraq-women-suffer-under-isis.

11. Alexandra Brosnan and Melissa Winkler, "Syria: A Regional Crisis: *The IRC Commission on Syrian Refugees.*" (London: International Rescue Committee UK, 2013).

12. Mego Terzian, "Speech Delivered to the United Nations Donor Conference on Syria on June 7," *Doctors Without Borders*, last modified June 5, 2013, accessed January 30, 2017, http://www.doctorswithoutborders.org/news-stories/speechopen-letter /speech-delivered-un-donor-conference-syria-june-7.

13. World Health Organization, "Health: Syrian Arab Republic 2013" (Geneva: World Health Organization, 2013).

14. UN General Assembly, Twenty-Fourth session, *Report of the Independent International Commission of Inquiry on the Syrian Arab Republic*, 136, 138 & 139, UN Doc. A/HRC/24/46 (2013).

15. Syria Integrated Needs Assessment: Syrian Arab Republic, December 2013.

16. Syria only allows for instances of abortion when the woman's life is in danger and only if her husband or father consents to the procedure. Penal Law, Art. 227–8, (1949).

17. Mohja Kahf, *Then and Now: The Syrian Revolution to Date: A Young Nonviolent Resistance and the Ensuing Armed Struggle* (St. Paul: Friends for a Nonviolent World, 2013).

18. "Iraq: ISIS Escapees Describe Systematic Rape," *hrw.org*, last modified April 14, 2015, accessed January 30, 2017, https://www.hrw.org/news/2015/04/14/iraq -isis-escapees-describe-systematic-rape.

19. For more information, see Ms. Yanar Mohammad statement at UN Security Council Open Debate on Women, Peace and Security, October 13, 2015.

20. For more information, see OutRight Action International, *Timeline of Publicized Executions for Alleged Sodomy by the Islamic State Militias*.

21. The Human Rights and Gender Justice Clinic (formerly the International Women's Human Rights Clinic) at CUNY School of Law, MADRE, The Organization of Women's Freedom in Iraq (OWFI) et al., *Seeking Accountability and Demanding Change: A Report on Women's Rights Violations in Iraq* (New York: MADRE, 2015).

22. Human Rights Council, Report on Iraq, 17.

23. This is a pseudonym used in place of the individual's real name for safety reasons.

24. Human Rights and Gender Justice Clinic et al., *Seeking Accountability*.

25. Security Council Resolution 1325 UN, Doc. S/RES/1325 (October 31, 2000).

26. La Comisión para el Esclarecimiento Histórico, *Guatemala: Memoria del Silencio* (Guatemala City: UNOPS, 1999).

27. Ibid., 23.

28. Guatemala Human Rights Commission, *Guatemala's Femicide Law: Progress Against Impunity?* (Washington, DC,: Guatemala Human Rights Commission, 2009).

29. US Office on Colombia, *The Impact of War on Women: Colombian Women's Struggle* (Washington, DC: USOC, 2004).

30. The International Women's Human Rights (IWHR) Clinic at CUNY School of Law, MADRE, Taller de Vida, et al., *Report on the Violations of the Convention Against Torture in Colombia* (New York: MADRE, 2010).

31. Ibid., 2.

32. Ibid.

33. Nicole Summers, "Colombia's Victim's Law: Transitional Justice in a Time of Violent Conflict?", *Harvard Human Rights Journal* 25, (2009): 220.

34. José Efraín Ríos Montt is a former Guatemalan army general and dictator who ruled Guatemala for seventeen months during 1982–83. In 2012, Ríos Montt, and his former military intelligence director, José Mauricio Rodríguez Sánchez, were charged with genocide and crimes against humanity. In May 2013, Ríos Montt was found guilty of masterminding and overseeing the massacre of 1,771 Ixil Mayans in the department of El Quiche, the forced displacement of twenty-nine thousand individuals, and 1,485 acts of sexual violence and acts of torture—all committed during his rule. He was sentenced to eighty years in prison; however, the guilty verdict was annulled just ten days later by Guatemala's Constitutional Court and thrown out on questionable legal grounds. A retrial was scheduled to begin on January 5, 2015, but after a series of delays by Ríos Montt's defense team was suspended before it even had a chance to begin. To date the trial has not restarted despite urgent calls from prosecutors and Ixil Mayans that the international community put pressure on the Guatemalan courts.

35. Interview with Guatemalan women's rights activist in Guatemala, City, Guatemala, February 27, 2014, on file with authors.

36. Emily Jastromb, "Facing History: Memory and Recovery in the Aftermath of Atrocity," *Penn State Journal of International Affairs* (2011), 18.

37. Ibid, 22.

38. "Truth and Memory," *International Center for Transitional Justice*, accessed January 30, 2017, https://www.ictj.org/our-work/transitional-justice-issues/truth-and-memory.

39. Interview with Guatemalan women's rights activist in Bogotá, Colombia, July 29, 2014, on file with authors.

40. Ibid.

41. Ibid.

42. Paige Arthur, *Identities in Transition: Developing Better Transitional Justice Initiatives in Divided Societies* (New York: International Center for Transitional Justice, 2009).

43. S/RES/1325.

44. Lisa Davis, "ISIL, Sexual Violence, the Syrian Conflict, and the Way Forward: Women's Inclusion in the Peace Process," New York University Journal of International Law and Politics 1, 47 (2016): 1167.

SELECTED BIBLIOGRAPHY: FURTHER READINGS

1. Indigenous Genocide

Arvin, Maile. *Pacifically Possessed*. La Jolla, CA: UC San Diego, 2013.

Beasely, Conger. "Dances with Garbage." *E Magazine*, November/December (1991): 40.

Danforth, Jessica. *Decolonizing Activist Practices*. Chicago: Critical Ethnic Studies Association, 2013.

Finley, Chris. "Decolonizing the Queer Native Body (and Recovering the Native Bull-Dyke): Bringing 'Sexy Back' and Out of the Native Studies Closet." In *Queer Indigenous Studies*, edited by Qwo-Li Driskill, Chris Finley, Brian Joseph Gilley, and Scott Morgensen, 31–42. Tucson: University of Arizona Press, 2011.

General Accounting Office. *Investigation of Allegations Concerning Indian Health Services B-164031(5); Hrd-77-3*. Washington, DC: General Accounting Office, 1976.

Hanania-Freeman, Debra. "Norplant: Freedom of Choice of a Plan for Genocide?" *EIR* 20, no. 19 (May 14 1993): 18–23.

Harjo, Suzan. "A Native Child Left Behind." *Indian Country Today*, July 2 (2004).

Hinkle, Jeff. "A Law's Hidden Failure." *American Indian Report* 19, no. 1 (2003): 12–14.

Honor the Earth. "Fossil Fuel Extraction Dangers: Native American and Women's Organizations Request UN Help on Sexual Violence." Indian Country Today, May 12 (2015). http://indiancountrytodaymedianetwork.com/2015/05/12/fossil-fuel-extraction-dangers-native-american-and-womens-organizations-request-un-help.

Incite! Women of Color Against Violence, ed. *The Color of Violence: Violence against Women of Color*. Cambridge, MA: South End Press, 2006.

———, ed. *The Revolution Will Not Be Funded: Beyond the Non-Profit Industrial Complex*. Cambridge, MA: South End Press, 2007.

Masterson, Mike, and Patricia Gutherie. "Taking the Shot," *Arizona Republic* (1986): n.p.

Million, Dian. *Therapeutic Nations: Healing in an Age of Indigenous Human Rights*. Phoenix: University of Arizona Press, 2013.

Minkin, Stephen. *Depo-Provera: A Critical Analysis*. San Francisco: Institute for Food and Development, n.d.

Morgensen, Scott Lauria. "Settler Homonationalism Theorizing Settler Colonialism within Queer Modernities." *GLQ: A Journal of Lesbian and Gay Studies* 16, no. 1/2 (2010): 105–31.

Richie, Beth. *Arrested Justice*. New York: NYU Press, 2012.

Roberts, Dorothy. *Killing the Black Body*. New York: Pantheon Books, 1997.

Robertson, Kimberly. "Rerighting the Historical Record: Violence against Native Women and the South Dakota Coalition against Domestic Violence and Sexual Assault." *Wicazo Sa Review* 27 (Fall 2012): 21–47.

Ross, Luana. *Inventing the Savage: The Social Construction of Native American Criminality.* Austin: University of Texas Press, 1998.

Smith, Andrea. *Conquest: Sexual Violence and American Indian Genocide*. Cambridge, MA: South End Press, 2005.

Sokoloff, Natalie, ed. *Domestic Violence at the Margins*. New Brunswick, NJ: Rutgers University Press, 2005.

Tallman, Valerie. "Toxic Waste of Indian Lives." *Covert Action* 17, Spring (1992): 16–22.

Trojan, Martha. "Sisters in Spirit? Nwac Hit by Division, Funding Crunch." Indigena. http://www.mediaindigena.com/martha-troian/issues-and-politics/sisters-in -spirit-nwac-hit-by-division-funding-crunch.

Wrone, David, and Russel Nelson, eds. *Who's the Savage?* Malabar, FL: Robert Krieger, 1982.

Yee, Jessica. "Native + Sex = Strong, Sexy, Powerful and Unapologetic." In *First Peoples Blog*, edited by Natasha Varner, 2010.

2. The Herero Genocide

Baranowski, Shelley. *Nazi Empire: German Colonialism from Bismarck to Hitler.* Cambridge, UK: Cambridge University Press, 2010.

Bechhaus-Gerst, Marianne and Mechthild Leutner. *Frauen in den deutschen Kolonien*. Berlin: Ch. Links Verlag, 2009.

Bridgman, Jon M. *The Revolt of the Hereros*. Berkeley: University of California Press, 1981.

Friedrichsmeyer, Sara L., Sara Lennox, and Susanne M. Zantop. *The Imperialist Imagination: German Colonialism and Its Legacy*. Ann Arbor: University of Michigan Press, 1998.

Goldenberg, Myrna. "Sex-Based Violence and the Politics and Ethics of Survival." In *Different Stories, Same Hell: Gender and the Holocaust*, edited by Myrna Goldenberg and Amy H. Shapiro, 99–127. Seattle: University of Washington Press, 2013.

von Joeden-Forgey, Elisa. "Gender and Genocide." In *The Oxford Handbook of Genocide Studies*, edited by Donald Bloxham and A. Dirk Moses, 61–80. New York: Oxford University Press, 2010.

MacKinnon, Catharine. "Genocide's Sexuality." *Nomos* 46 (2005): 313–56.

Mamdani, Mahmood. *When Victims Become Killers: Colonialism, Nativism, and the Genocide in Rwanda*. Princeton, NJ: Princeton University Press, 2001.

Moses, A. Dirk. ed. *Empire, Colony, Genocide: Conquest, Occupation and Subaltern Resistance in World History*. New York: Berghahn Books, 2008.

Schaller, Dominick J. *From Conquest to Genocide: Colonial Rule in German Southwest Africa and German East Africa*. New York: Berghahn Books, 2008.

Seifert, Ruth. "War and Rape: A Preliminary Analysis." In *Mass Rape: The War Against Women in Bosnia-Herzegovina*, edited by Alexandra Stiglmayer, 54–72. Lincoln: University of Nebraska Press, 1994.

Steinmetz, George. *The Devil's Handwriting: Precoloniality and the German Colonial State in Qingdao, Samoa, and Southwest Africa*. Chicago: Chicago University Press, 2007.

Walker, Cheryl. *Women and Gender in Southern Africa to 1945*. Cape Town, South Africa: D. Philip, 1990.

Zimmerer, Jürgen. *Deutsche Herrschaft über Afrikaner: staatlicher Machtanspruch und Wirklichkeit im kolonialen Namibia*. Münster, Germany: Lit, 2001.

———. *Völkermord in Deutshc-Südwestafrika: der Kolonialkrieg (1904–1908) in Namibia und seine Folgen*. Berlin: Links, 2003.

3. Armenia

Armaghanian, Arsha Louise. *Arsha's World and Yours*. New York: Vantage, 1977.

Armenian Genocide Museum-Institute. "'Auction of Souls,' or 'Memorial of Truth.'" Accessed April 11, 2016. http://www.genocide-museum.am/eng/online_exhibition_6.php.

———. "Becoming Someone Else: Genocide and Kidnapped Armenian Women." Online Exhibition. Accessed March 3, 2016. http://www.genocide-museum.am/eng/online _exhibition_2.php#sthash.VNaEE2Eq.dpuf.

Avakian, Asdghig. *Stranger No More: An Armenian Nurse from Lebanon Tells Her Story*. Beirut, Lebanon: Antelias, 1968.

Avakyan, Shushan. "Becoming Aurora: Translating the Story of Arshaluys Mardiganian." In *Dissidences: Hispanic Journal of Theory and Criticism* 4, no. 8 (2012). Accessed March 9, 2016. http://digitalcommons.bowdoin.edu/dissidences/vol4/iss8/13.

Azadian, Libarid. *Hay Orbere Mets Egherni (The Orphans of the Armenian Genocide.)* Los Angeles: Tparan, April 1995.

Balakian, Peter. *The Burning Tigress: The Armenian Genocide and America's Response*. New York: Harper Collins, 2003.

Bjørnlund, Matthias. "'A Fate Worse than Dying': Sexual Violence during the Armenian Genocide." In *Brutality and Desire: War and Sexuality in Europe's Twentieth Century*, edited by Dagmar Herzog, 16–58. Basingstoke, England: Palgrave Macmillan, 2009.

Caraman, Elizabeth and William Lytton Payne. *Daughter of the Euphrates*. New York: Harper & Bros, 1939.

Dadrian, Vahakn N. "Cultural and Social-Psychological Factors in the Study of Survivors of Genocide." *International Behavioral Scientist* 3, no. 2 (1971): 48–55.

Derderian, Katharine. "Common Fate, Different Experience: Gender-Specific Aspects of the Armenian Genocide, 1915–1917." *Holocaust Genocide Studies* 19, no. 1 (2005): 1–25.

Highgas, Dirouhi Kouymjian. *Refugee Girl*. Watertown, MA: Baikar Association, 1985.

Jafferian, Serpoohi Christine. *Winds of Destiny: An Immigrant Girl's Odyssey*. Belmont, MA: Armenian Heritage Press, 1993.

Kalajian, Hannah and Bernardine Sullivan. *Hannah's Story: Escape from Genocide in Turkey to Success in America*. Belmont, MA: Armenian Heritage Press, 1990.

Khardalian, Suzanne. *Grandma's Tattoos*. DVD. New York: Cinema Guild, 2011.

Kherdian, David. *The Road from Home: The Story of an Armenian Girl*. New York: Greenwillow Books, 1979.

League of Nations Assembly. Fifth Committee. *Deportation of Women and Children in Turkey, Asia Minor and the Neighboring Territories: Report.* Geneva, Switzerland, 1921 and 1922.

——. Fifth Committee. *Protection of Women and Children in the Near East: Report.* Geneva, 1923–1927.

Macartney, C.A. *Refugees: The Work of The League.* London: League of Nations Union, 1931.

Miller, Donald E. and Lorna Touryan. *Survivors: An Oral History of the Armenian Genocide.* Berkeley: University of California Press, 1993.

Matiossian, Vartan. "The Quest for Aurora: On 'Ravished Armenia' and its Surviving Fragment." *The Armenian Weekly*, April 15, 2014. Accessed March 12, 2016. http:// armenianweekly.com/2014/04/15/aurora/.

Morgenthau, Henry. *Ambassador Morgenthau's Story.* Garden City, N. Y.: Doubleday, 1918.

Okoomian, Janice. "Becoming White: Contested History, Armenian American Women, and Radicalized Bodies." *Melus* 27, no. 1 (2002): 213–37.

Rockwell, William W. *Ravished Armenia.* New York: ACASR, 1916.

——. *The Deportation of the Armenians: Described from Day to Day by a Kind Woman Somewhere in Turkey.* New York: ACASR, 1916.

Sarafian, Ara. "The Absorption of Armenian Women and Children into Muslim Households as a Structural Component of the Armenian Genocide." In *In God's Name: Genocide and Religion in the Twentieth Century*, edited by Omer Bartov and Phyllis Mack, 209–221. New York: Berghahn, 2001.

Slide, Anthony. *Ravished Armenia and the Story of Aurora Mardiganian.* Lanham, MD: Scarecrow, 1997.

Smith, Roger W. "Genocide and the Politics of Rape." In *Genocide Matters: Ongoing Issues and Emerging Perspectives*, edited by Joyce Apsel and Ernesto Verdeja, 82–105. New York: Routledge, 2013.

Tachjian Vahé. "Gender, Nationalism, Exclusion: The Reintegration Process of Female Survivors of the Armenian Genocide." *Nations and Nationalism* 15, no. 1 (2009): 60–80.

Tashjian, Alice A. *Silences: My Mother's Will to Survive.* Princeton, NJ: Blue Pansy, 1995.

Tavoukdjian, Serpouhi. *Exiled: Story of an Armenian Girl.* Takoma Park, MD: Review and Herald, 1933.

Torchin, Leshu. "Ravished Armenia: Visual Media, Humanitarian Advocacy, and the Formation of Witnessing Publics." *American Anthropologist* 108, no. 1 (2006): 214–21.

Watenpaugh, Keith David. "The League of Nations' Rescue of Armenian Genocide Survivors and the Making of Modern Humanitarianism, 1920–1927." *American Historical Review* 115, no. 5 (2010): 1315–39.

4. Holodomor

Avramescu, Catalin. *An Intellectual History of Cannibalism.* Translated by Alistair Ian Blyth. Princeton, NJ: Princeton University Press, 2009.

Bateson, Gregory. *Steps to an Ecology of Mind.* New York: Ballantine Books, 1972.

Dichter, Ernest. *Motivating Human Behavior.* New York: McGraw-Hill Book Company, 1971.

Dikötter, Frank. "The Great Leap Backward." *History Today*, November 2010.

——. *Mao's Great Famine: The History of Mao's Most Devastating Catastrophe.* New York: Walker, 2010.

Ernandes, Michele, Rita Cedrini, and Marco Giammanco. "Aztec Cannibalism and Maize Consumption: The Serotonin Deficiency Link." *Mankind Quarterly* 43, no. 1 (2002): 3–40.

Georges-Abeyie, Daniel A. "Women as Terrorists." In *Perspectives on Terrorism*, edited by Lawrence Zelic Freedman and Yonah Alexander, 71–84. Wilmington, DE: Scholarly Resources, 1983.

Graziosi, Andrea. "Lettres de Kharkov: La famine en Ukraine et dans le Caucase du Nord a travers les rapports des diplomates italiens, 1932–1934." *Cahiers du monde russe et sovietique* 30 (1989): 5–106.

———. *Lysty z Kharkova: Holod v Ukraini ta na Pivnichnomu Kavkazi v povidomplenniakh italiis'kykh dyplomativ. 1932–1933 roky*. Kharkiv: Folio, 2007.

———. "The Impact of the Holodomor Studies on the Understanding of the USSR." *East/West: Journal of Ukrainian Studies* 2, no. 1 (2015): 53–80.

———. "Why and in What Sense Was the Holodomor a Genocide?" In *Holodomor: Reflections on the Great Famine of 1932–1933 in Soviet Ukraine*, edited by Lubomyr Y. Luciuk, 139–57. Kingston, ON: Kashtan, 2008.

Graziosi, Andrea, Lubomyr A. Hajda, and Halyna Hryn. *After the Holodomor: The Enduring Impact of the Great Famine on Ukraine*. Cambridge, MA: Ukrainian Research Institute, 2013.

Grisard, Dominique. "History of Knowledge, Terrorism and Gender." *Historical Social Research* 39, no. 3 (2014): 82–99.

Kallen, Horace M. "Democracy versus the Melting Pot." *The Nation* 100, no. 2590 (1915): 190–94.

Kiss, Oksana. "National Femininity Used and Contested: Women's Participation in the Nationalist Underground in Western Ukraine in the 1940s–50s." *East/West: Journal of Ukrainian Studies* 2, no. 2 (2015): 53–82.

Kuśnierz, Robert. "The Impact of the Great Famine on Ukrainian Cities: Evidence from the Polish Archives." In *After the Holodomor: The Enduring Impact of the Great Famine on Ukraine*, edited by Andrea Graziosi, Lubomyr A. Hajda, and Halyna Hryn, 15–30. Cambridge, MA: Ukrainian Research Institute, 2013.

Lester, David, John White, and Giordano Brandi. "Cannibalism." *OMEGA-Journal of Death and Dying* 70, no. 4 (2015): 428–35.

Mace, James. "Is the Ukrainian Genocide a Myth?" In *Holodomor: Reflections on the Great Famine of 1932–1933 in Soviet Ukraine*, edited by Lubomyr Y. Luciuk, 49–60. Kingston, ON: Kashtan, 2008.

Marochko, Vasyl. "Kanibalizm v roky holodomoru." In *Holod 1932–1933 rokiv v Ukraini: prychyny ta naslidky*, edited by V. M. Lytvyn, 568–75. Kyiv: Naukova dumka, 2003.

Maslow, Abraham H. *Motivation and Personality*, Second edition. New York: Harper & Row, 1970.

Medina, Ortiz O., Galvis D. Contreras, N. Sánchez-Mora, and López C. Arango. "Cannibalism in Paranoid Schizophrenia: A Case Report." *Actas Esp Psiquiatr* 34, no. 2 (2006): 136–39.

Michael, Jack, and Lee Meyerson. "A Behavioral Approach to Human Control." In *Control of Human Behavior: Expanding the Behavioral Laboratory*, edited by Roger Ulrich, Thomas Stachnik, and John Mabry. Glenview, IL: Scott, Foresman and Company, 1966.

Pierpaoli Jr., Paul G. "Cannibalism in the Holodomor." In Vol. 4 of *Modern Genocide: The Definitive Resource and Document Collection*, ed. Paul R. Bartrop and Steven Leonard Jacobs, 1875–76. Santa Barbara, CA: ABC_CLIO, 2015.

Polishchuk, Tamara. *Stolytsia vidchaiu*. Kharkiv, Ukraine: Berezil, 2006.

Rummel, R. J. *Death by Government*. New Brunswick, NJ: Transaction, 2007.

Senninger, J., and A. Senninger. "Cannibalism, Schizophrenia and Cannabis Use." *European Psychiatry* 29, Sup. 1 (2014): 1 (an abstract of this study presented at the 22nd European Congress of Psychiatry).

Serbyn, Roman. "Photographic Evidence of the Ukrainian Famines of 1921–1923 and 1932–1933." *Holodomor Studies* 2, no. 1 (2010): 63–94.

Snyder, Timothy. *Bloodlands: Europe Between Hitler and Stalin*. New York: Basic Books, 2010.

Sorokin, Pitirim A. *Man and Society in Calamity: The Effects of War, Revolution, Famine, Pestilence upon Human Mind, Behavior, Social Organization and Cultural Life*. New York: E.P. Dutton, 1946.

Thaxton, Ralph. *Catastrophe and Contention in Rural China: Mao's Great Leap Forward Famine and the Origins of Righteous Resistance in Da Fo Village*. Cambridge, UK: Cambridge University Press, 2008.

Vardy, Steven Bela, and Agnes Huszar Vardy. "Cannibalism in Stalin's Russia and Mao's China." *East European Quarterly* 41, no. 2 (2007): 223–38.

Viola, Lynne. "*Bab'i bunty* and Peasant Women's Protest during Collectivization." *Russian Review* 45, no. 1 (1986): 189–205.

———. "Introduction." In *Contending with Stalinism: Soviet Power and Popular Resistance in the 1930s*, edited by Lynne Viola, 1–16. Ithaca, NY: Cornell University Press, 2002.

———. *Peasant Rebels Under Stalin: Collectivization and the Culture of Peasant Resistance*. New York: Oxford University Press, 1996.

Vossler, Ronald J., ed. *We'll Meet Again in Heaven: Germans in the Soviet Union Write Their Dakota Relatives, 1925–1937*. Fargo: North Dakota State University Libraries, 2003.

Weitz, Eric D. *A Century of Genocide: Utopias of Race and Nation*. Princeton, NJ: Princeton University Press, 2003.

Werth, Nicolas. *Cannibal Island: Death in a Siberian Gulag*. Princeton, NJ: Princeton University Press, 2007.

Zhou, Xun. *Forgotten Voices of Mao's Great Famine, 1958–1962: An Oral History*. New Haven, CT: Yale University Press, 2013.

5. The Holocaust

Baer, Elizabeth R., and Myrna Goldenberg, eds. *Experience and Expression: Women, the Nazis, and the Holocaust*. Detroit, MI: Wayne State University Press, 2003.

Baumel, Judith Tydor. *Double Jeopardy: Gender and the Holocaust*. London: Vallentine Mitchell, 1998.

Buber Agassi, Judith. *The Jewish Women Prisoners of Ravensbrück: Who Were They?* Oxford, UK: Oneworld Publications, 2007.

Choko, Isabelle, et al., *Stolen Youth: Five Women's Survival in the Holocaust*. New York: Holocaust Survivors' Memoirs Project, 2005.

Eibeschitz, Jehoshua, and Anna Eilenberg-Eibeshitz. *Women in the Holocaust: A Collection of Testimonies*. Brooklyn, NY: Remember, 1993.

Fuchs, Esther, ed. *Women and the Holocaust: Narrative and Representation.* Lanham, MD: University Press of America, 1999.

Goldenberg, Myrna. "Different Horrors, Same Hell: Women Remembering the Holocaust." In *Thinking the Unthinkable: Meanings of the Holocaust,* edited by Roger S. Gottlieb, 150–66. New York: Paulist, 1990.

———. "Lessons Learned from Gentle Heroism: Women's Holocaust Narratives." *Annals of the American Academy of Political and Social Science* 548 (November 1996): 78–93.

Gurewitsch, Brana, ed. *Mothers, Sisters, Resisters: Oral Histories of Women Who Survived the Holocaust.* Tuscaloosa: University of Alabama Press, 1998.

Helm, Sarah. *Ravensbrück: Life and Death in Hitler's Concentration Camp for Women.* New York: Nan A. Talese/Doubleday, 2015.

Mailander Koslov, Elissa. *Female SS Guards and Workaday Violence: The Majdanek Concentration Camp 1942–1944.* East Lansing: Michigan University Press, 2015.

Herz, Gabriele. *The Women's Camp in Moringen: A Memoir of Imprisonment in Germany, 1936–1937.* New York: Berghahn Books, 2006.

Karay, Felicja. *Hasag-Leipzig Slave Labour Camp for Women: The Struggle for Survival, Told by Women and their Poetry.* London: Vallentine Mitchell, 2002.

Katz, Esther, and Joan Miriam Ringelheim. *Proceedings of the Conference on Women Surviving: The Holocaust.* New York: Institute for Research in History, 1983.

Morrison, Jack G. *Ravensbrück: Everyday Life in a Women's Concentration Camp, 1939–45.* Princeton, NJ: Markus Wiener, 2000.

Ofer, Dalia, and Lenore J. Weitzman, eds. *Women in the Holocaust.* New Haven, CT: Yale University Press, 1998.

Ringelheim, Joan. "Thoughts about Women and the Holocaust." In *Thinking the Unthinkable: Meanings of the Holocaust,* edited by Roger S. Gottlieb, 141–49. New York: Paulist, 1990.

Rittner, Carol, and John K. Roth, eds. *Different Voices: Women and the Holocaust.* New York: Paragon House, 1993.

Saidel, Rochelle G. *The Jewish Women of Ravensbrück Concentration Camp.* Madison: University of Wisconsin Press, 2004.

Shelley, Lore, ed. *Auschwitz—the Nazi Civilization: Twenty-three Women Prisoners' Accounts.* Lanham, MD: University Press of America, 1992.

Tec, Nechama. *Resilience and Courage: Women, Men, and the Holocaust.* New Haven, CT: Yale University Press, 2003.

6. German Women and the Holocaust

Allen, Ann Taylor. "The Holocaust and the Modernization of Gender: A Historiographical Essay." *Central European History* 30, no. 3 (1997): 349–64.

Baer, Elizabeth, and Myrna Goldenberg. *Experience and Expression: Women, the Nazis and the Holocaust.* Detroit, MI: Wayne State University Press, 2003.

von Baumbach, Anna Luise. *Frauen an der Front: Krankenschwester im 2. Weltkreig,* 2010 (DVD).

Benedict, Susan. "Caring While Killing: Nursing in the 'Euthanasia' Centers." In *Experience and Expression: Women, the Nazis, and the Holocaust,* edited by Elizabeth R. Baer and Myrna Goldenberg. Detroit: Wayne State University Press, 2003.

Benedict, Susan, and Tessa Chelouche, "Meseritz-Obrawalde: A 'Wild Euthanasia' Hospital of Nazi Germany," *History of Psychiatry* 19 (2008): 68–76.

Bock, Gisela. "Ordinary Women in Nazi Germany: Perpetrators, Victims, Followers, and Bystanders." In *Women in the Holocaust*, edited by Dalia Ofer and Lenore J. Weitzman, 85–100. New Haven: Yale University Press, 1999.

Bourke, Joanna. *An Intimate History of Killing: Face-to-Face Killing in Twentieth-Century Warfare*, New York: Basic Books, 2000.

Bridenthal, Renate, Atina Grossmann, and Marion Kaplan, eds. *When Biology Became Destiny: Women in Weimar and Nazi Germany*. New York: Monthly Review Press, 1984.

Britton, Dana. *The Gender of Crime*. Lanham, MD: Rowman & Littlefield, 2011.

Brown, Daniel Patrick. *The Camp Women: The Female Auxiliaries Who Assisted the SS in Running the Nazi Concentration Camp System*. Atglen, PA: Schiffer, 2002.

Dörr, Margarete. *"Wer die Zeit nicht miterlebt hat ...": Frauenerfahrungen im Zweiten Weltkrieg und in den Jahren danach*, Vol. 2, *Kriegsalltag*. Frankfurt, New York: Campus Verlag, 1998.

Dombrowski, Nicole Ann. "Soldiers, Saints, or Sacrificial Lambs? Women's Relationship to Combat and the Fortification of the Home Front in the Twentieth Century." In *Women and War in the Twentieth Century: Enlisted with or without Consent*, edited by Nicole Ann Dombrowski. New York: Garland Publishing, 1999.

Eschenbach, Insa. "Gespaltene Frauenbilder: Geschechterdramaturgien im juristischen Diskurs ostdeutscher Gerichte." In *"Bestien" und "Befehlsempfänger": Frauen und Männer in NS-Prozessen nach 1945*, edited by Ulrike Weckel and Edgard Wolfrum. Göttingen, Germany: Vandenhoeck & Ruprecht, 2003.

Gaida, Ulrike. *Zwischen Pflegen und Töten: Krankenschwestern im Nationalsozialismus*. Frankfurt am Main: Mabuse Verlag, 2006.

Hagemann, Karen and Jean Quataert. *Gendering Modern German History: Rewriting Historiography*. New York and Oxford: Berghahn, 2007.

Harvey, Elizabeth. *Women and the Nazi East: Agents and Witnesses of Germanization*. New Haven, CT: Yale University Press, 2003.

Heineman, Elizabeth D. "Gender, Sexuality, and Coming to Terms with the Nazi Past." *Central European History* 38, no. 1 (2005): 41–74.

Hertzog, Esther, ed. *Life, Death and Sacrifice: Women and Family in the Holocaust*. Jerusalem and New York: Geffen, 2008.

Herzog, Dagmar, ed. *Brutality and Desire: War and Sexuality in Europe's Twentieth Century*, Basingstoke, England: Palgrave Macmillan, 2011.

Heschel, Susannah. "Does Atrocity Have a Gender? Feminist Interpretations of Women in the SS." In *Lessons and Legacies, Vol. 6: New Currents in Holocaust Research*, edited by Jeffrey Diefendorf, 300–21. Evanston, IL: Northwestern University Press, 2004.

Himmler, Katrin. "'Herrenmenschenpaare': Zwischen nationalsozialistischem Elitebewusstsein und rassenideologischer (Selbst-) Verpflichtung," In *Sie waren dabei: Mitläuferinnen, Nutzniesserinnen, Täterinnen im Nationalsozialismus*, edited by Marita Krauss. Göttingen, Germany: Wallstein Verlag, 2008.

Jones, Adam. "Gender and Genocide in Rwanda." In *Gendercide and Genocide*, edited by Adam Jones. Nashville, TN: Vanderbilt University Press, 2004.

Kellenbach, Katharina. "God's Love and Women's Love: Prison Chaplains Counsel the Wives of Nazi Perpetrators," *Journal of Feminist Studies in Religion* 20, no. 2 (Fall 2004): 7–24.

Kempner, Ruth, and Robert M. W. Kempner. *Women in Nazi Germany* [United States]: R. Kempner, 1944.

Killius, Rosemarie, ed. *Frauen für die Front: Gespräche mit Wehrmachtshelferinnen,* Leipzig: Militzke Verlag, 2003.

Kompisch, Kathrin. *Täterinnen: Frauen im Nationalsozialismus,* Koln, Weimar, Wien: Böhlau, 2008.

Koonz, Claudia. *Mothers in the Fatherland: Women, the Family, and Nazi Politics.* New York: St. Martin's Press, 1988.

————. *The Nazi Conscience.* Cambridge, MA: Harvard University Press, 2005.

————. "A Tributary and a Mainstream: Gender, Public Memory, and the Historiography of Nazi Germany." In *Gendering Modern German History: Rewriting Historiography,* edited by Karen Hagemann and Jean H. Quataert, 147–68. New York and Oxford: Berghahn, 2007.

Krauss, Marita, ed. *Sie waren dabei: Mitläuferinnen, Nutzniesserinnen, Täterinnen im Nationalsozialismus.* Göttingen: Wallstein Verlag, 2008.

Lower, Wendy. *Hitler's Furies: German Women in the Nazi Killing Fields.* Boston: Houghton Miflin Harcourt, 2013.

Reese, Dagmar. *Growing Up Female in Nazi Germany.* Translated by William Templer. Ann Arbor: University of Michigan Press, 2006.

Sayner, Joanne. *Women without a Past? German Autobiographical Writings and Fascism.* Amsterdam, Netherlands: Rodopi, 2007.

Schroeder, Christa. *He Was My Chief: The Memoirs of Adolf Hitler's Secretary.* London: Frontline Books, 2009.

Schwarz, Gudrun. *Eine Frau an seiner Seite: Ehefrauen in der "SS-Sippengemeinschaft,"* Hamburg: Verlag Hamburger Edition, 1997.

Sereny, Gitta. *Into That Darkness: An Examination of Conscience.* New York: Vintage Books, 1983.

Steinbacher, Sybille, ed. *Volksgenossinnen: Frauen in der NS-Volksgemeinschaft.* Göttingen Wallstein Verlag, 2007.

Stephenson, Jill. *Women in Nazi Germany.* New York: Routledge, 2001.

Thürmer-Rohr, Christina. "Frauen als Täterinnen und Mittäterinnen im NS-Deutschland." In *Frauen als Täterinnen und Mittäterinnen im Nationalsozialismus: Gestaltungsspielräume und Handlungsmöglichkeiten,* edited by Viola Schubert-Lehnhardt and Sylvia Korch. Halle: Martin Luther Universität Halle-Wittenberg, 2006.

Weckel, Ulrike, and Edgard Wolfrum, eds., *"Bestien" und "Befehlsempfänger": Frauen und Männer in NS-Prozessen nach 1945,* Gottingen: Vandenhoeck & Ruprecht, 2003.

Wobbe, Theresa, ed. *Nach Osten: Verdeckte Spuren nationalsozialistischer Verbrechen.* Frankfurt: Verlag Neue Kritik, 1992.

7. The Romani Genocide

Achim, Viorel. *The Roma in Romanian History.* Budapest: Central European University Press, 2004.

Ancel, Jean. "Tragedia romilor și tragedia evreilor din România: asemănări și deosebiri." In *Lacrimi rome,* edited by Luminița Mihai Cioabă, 3–32. București, Romania: Ro Media, 2006.

Bársony, János, and Ágnes Daróczi, eds. *Pharrajimos: The Fate of the Roma during the Holocaust*. Budapest: IDEA, 2008.

Blumer, Nadine. "From Victim Hierarchies to Memorial Networks: Berlin's Holocaust Memorial to Sinti and Roma Victims of National Socialism." PhD diss., University of Toronto, 2011.

Cioabă, Luminița, ed. *Lacrime Rome*. București, Romania: Ro Media, 2006.

Crowe, David M. "The Roma and the Burden of Holocaust Memory." *Zerstörer des Schweigens: Formen kuünstlerischer Erinnerung an die nationalsozialistische Rassen-und Vernichtungspolitik in Osteuropa* (2006): 3–16.

———. *The Holocaust: Roots, History and Aftermath*. Boulder: Westview, 2008.

Fings, Karola, Herbert Heuss, Frank Sparing, and Donald Kenrick. *From "Race Science" to the Camps*. Vol. 12. Hatfeld, England: University of Hertfordshire Press, 1997.

Kelso, Michelle. *Hidden Sorrows. The Persecution of Romanian Gypsies*. DVD. Austin, TX: In the Shadow Productions., 2005.

Ioanid, Radu. *Evreii sub regimul Antonescu*. București, Romania: Editura Hasefer, 1997.

———. *The Holocaust in Romania: The Destruction of Jews and Gypsies Under the Antonescu Regime, 1940–1944*. Chicago: Ivan R. Dee, 2008.

Ioanid, Radu, Michelle Kelso, and Luminița Cioabă, eds. *Tragedia romilor deportați in Transnistria, 1942–1945*. Iași, Romania: Polirom, 2009.

Ionescu, Ștefan Cristian. *Jewish Resistance to 'Romanianization,' 1940–44*. Basingstoke, England: Palgrave Macmillan, 2015.

Joskowicz, Ari. "Separate Suffering, Shared Archives: Jewish and Romani Histories of Nazi Persecution." *History & Memory* 28, no. 1 (2016): 110–40.

Kapralski, Slawomir. "Ritual of Memory in Constructing the Modern Identity of Eastern European Romanies." In *The Role of the Romanies: Images and Counter-Images of "Gypsies" Romanies in European Cultures*, edited by Nicholas Saul and Susan Tebbutt, 208–225. Liverpool: Liverpool University Press, 2004.

Kelso, Michelle. "The Deportation of Gypsies from Romania to Transnistria 1942–44." In *The Gypsies During the Second World War: In the Shadow of the Swastika*, edited by Donald Kenrick, 95–130. Hatfield, England: University of Hertfordshire Press, 1999.

Kovács, Éva Judit, András Lénárt, and Anna Lujza Szász. "Oral History Collections on the Holocaust in Hungary." *Shoah: Intervention Methods Documentation (Simon)* 1, no. 1 (2014): 1–19.

Milton, Sybil. "Hidden Lives: Sinti and Roma Women." In *Experience and Expression: Women, the Nazis, and the Holocaust*, edited by Elizabeth R. Baer and Myrna Goldenberg, 53–75. Detroit: Wayne State University Press, 2003.

———. "Holocaust: The Gypsies." *Century of Genocide: Critical Essays and Eyewitness Accounts* (2004): 161–204.

"Romani Women and the Holocaust: Testimonies of Sexual Violence in Romanian-controlled Transnistria." In *Women and Genocide: Gendered Experiences of Violence, Survival, and Resistance*, edited by JoAnn DiGeorgio-Lutz and Donna Gosbee, 37–72. Toronto, ON: Canadian Scholars' Press, 2016.

Sonneman, Toby. *Shared Sorrows: A Gypsy Family Remembers the Holocaust*. Hatfield, England: University of Hertfordshire Press, 2002.

Stewart, Michael. "Remembering without Commemoration: The Mnemonics and Politics of Holocaust Memories among European Roma." *Journal of the Royal Anthropological Institute* 10, no. 3 (2004): 561–82.

———. "Une catastrophe invisible. La Shoah des Tziganes." *Terrain. Revue d'ethnologie de l'Europe* 54 (2010): 100–21.

———. "The 'Gypsy Problem' An Invisible Genocide." In *Forgotten Genocides: Oblivion, Denial, and Memory*, edited by René Lemarchand, 137–56. Philadelphia: University of Pennsylvania Press, 2011.

Szász, Anna Lujza. *Is Survival Resistance? Experiences of Roma Women under the Holocaust.* Saarbrücken, Germany: Lambert Academic Publishing, 2012.

Tebbutt, Susan. "Stolen Childhood: Austrian Romany Ceija Stojka and Her Past." *Holocaust Studies* 11, no. 2 (2005): 38–61.

Weiss-Wendt, Anton, ed. *The Nazi Genocide of the Roma: Reassessment and Commemoration.* New York: Berghahn Books, 2013.

Wiesel, Elie, Tuvia Friling, Radu Ioanid, Mihail E. Ionescu, and L. Benjamin, eds. *Final Report.* Iaşi, Romania: Polirom, 2005.

Zimmermann, Michael. "The National Socialist 'Solution of the Gypsy Question': Central Decisions, Local Initiatives, and Their Interrelation." *Holocaust and Genocide Studies* 15, no. 3 (2001): 412–27.

8. Bangladesh

Anisuzzaman, M. "The Identity Question and Politics." In *Bangladesh: Promise and Performance*, edited by R. Jahan, 45–63. Dhaka, Bangladesh: University Press, 2000.

Begum, Suraya. "Masuda, elijan, duljan, momena: kushtiar charjon grihobodhu." In *Narir Ekattur o Judhyo Porobortee Kothyokahini*, edited by S. Akhter, S. Begum, H. Hossain, S. Kamal, and M. Guhathakurta, 80–107. Dhaka, Bangladesh: Ain-o-Shalish Kendro, 2001.

Brownmiller, Susan. *Against Our Will: Men, Women and Rape.* New York: Bantam Books, 1975.

Bunch, C. and N. Reilly. *Demanding Accountability: The Global Campaign and Vienna Tribunal for Women's Human Rights.* New York: Centre for Women's Global Leadership and UNIFEM, 1994.

Burke, S. M. "The Postwar Diplomacy of the Indo-Pakistani War of 1971." *Asian Survey* 13, no. 11 (1973): 1036–49.

Butalia, U. *The Other Side of Silence: Voices from the Partition of India.* New Delhi, India: Penguin Books India, 1998.

———. "Muslims and Hindus, Men and Women: Communal Stereotypes and the Partition of India." In *Women and Right-Wing Movements: Indian Experiences*, edited by Sarkar T. and U. Butalia, 58–81. London: Zed Books, 1995.

———. "A Question of Silence: Partition, Women and the State." In *Gender and Catastrophe*, edited by R. Lentin, 92–109. London: Zed Books, 1995.

Copelon, Rhonda. "Gendered War Crimes: Reconceptualising Rape in Time of War." In *Women's Rights Human Rights: International Feminist Perspectives*, edited by Julie Peters and Andrea Wolper, 197–214. New York: Routledge, 1995.

Das, Veena. "Moral Orientations to Suffering: Legitimation, Power, and Healing." In *Health and Social Change in International Perspective*, edited by L. C. Chen, A. Kleinman, and N. C. Ware, 139–70. Boston: Harvard School of Public Health, 1994.

———. *Critical Events: An Anthropological Perspective on Contemporary India.* Oxford: Oxford University Press, 1995.

D'Costa, Bina. "Coming to Terms with the Past in Bangladesh: Naming Women's Truths." In *Feminist Politics, Activism and Vision: Local and Global Challenges,* edited by Luciana Ricciutelli, Angela Miles and Margaret H. McFadden, 227–47. London: Zed Books, 2005.

——. *Nationbuilding, Gender and War Crimes in South Asia.* London: Routledge, 2011.

——. "Once Were Warriors: The Militarized State in Narrating the Past." *South Asian History and Culture.* 5, no. 4 (2014): 457–74.

D'Costa, Bina and Hossain, Sara. "Redress for Sexual Violence Before the International Crimes Tribunal in Bangladesh: Lessons from History and Hopes for the Future." *Criminal Law Forum,* 21 (2010): 331–59.

Gafur, M. A. *Shomaj Kolyan Porikroma.* Dhaka, Bangladesh: Pubali Prokashoni, 1979.

Ghosh, Partha. S. "Bangladesh at the Crossroads: Religion and Politics." *Asian Survey,* 33, no. 7 (1993): 697–710.

Hossain, Hameeda. "Overcoming the Trauma of War, Contesting Controls, the Struggle Beyond 1971." In *Freedom from Fear, Freedom from Want? Rethinking Security in Bangladesh,* 12–38. New Delhi, India: Rupa, 2010.

Ibrahim, Nilima. *Ami Birangana Bolchi.* Dhaka, Bangladesh: Jagriti Prokashoni, 1998.

Imam, Jahanara. *Ekatturer Dinguli.* Dhaka, Bangladesh: Sandhani, 1986.

Jahan, Rounaq. *Bangladeshi Politics: Problems and Issues.* Dhaka, Bangladesh: University Press, 1980.

——. *The Elusive Agenda: Mainstreaming Women in Development.* London: Zed Books, 1995.

Kabir, Shahriar. *Gonoadaloter Potobhumi,* Dhaka, Bangladesh: Dibyo Prokash, 1993.

——. "Introduction." *Ekatturer Dushoho Smriti,* edited by S. Kabir, 7–30. Dhaka, Bangladesh: Ekatturer Ghatok Dalal Nirmul Committee, 1999.

——. *Ekatturer Gonohotya, Nirjaton ebong Judhyaporadhider Bichar.* Dhaka, Bangladesh: Shomoy, 2000.

Kabeer, Naila. "Subordination and Struggle: Women in Bangladesh." *New Left Review,* no. 168 (March/April 1988): 95–121.

Kamal, Sultana. "Potobhumi." In *Narir Ekattur o Judhyo Porobortee Kothyokahini,* edited by S. Akhter, S. Begum, H. Hossain, S. Kamal, and M. Guhathakurta, 14–20. Dhaka, Bangladesh: Ain-o-Shalish Kendro, 2001.

Keck, Margaret E., and Kathryn Sikkink. *Activists Beyond Borders: Advocacy Networks in International Politics.* Ithaca, NY: Cornell University Press, 1998.

Khan, Naila. "War Crimes Against Bengali Women by Pakistani Army and their Collaborators in 1971: The Rape of a Nation." *The Daily Star* (12 December, 1997).

Kumar, Radha. *The History of Doing: An Illustrated Account of Movements for Women's Rights and Feminism in India, 1800–1990.* London: Verso, 1993.

LaPorte, R. "Pakistan in 1971: The Disintegration of a Nation." *Asian Survey* 12, no. 2 (1972): 97–108.

Manchanda, Rita. "Where Are the Women in South Asian Conflicts?" In *Women, War and Peace in South Asia: Beyond Victimhood to Agency,* edited by R. Manchanda, 9–41. New Delhi, India: Sage Publications, 2001.

Matsui, Y. "History Cannot Be Erased, Women Can No Longer Be Silenced." In *Common Grounds: Violence Against Women in War and Armed Conflict Situations,* edited by I. L. Sajor, 26–32. Philippines: Asian Center for Women's Human Rights (ASCENT), 1998.

Menon, R. "Reproducing the Legitimate Community: Secularity, Sexuality, and the State in Post-partition India." In *Appropriating Gender: Women's Activism and Politicized Religion in South Asia*, edited by P. Jeffrey and A. Basu, 15–32. New York: Routledge, 1998.

Menon, R., and K. Bhasin. *Borders and Boundaries: Women in India's Partition*. New Delhi, India: Kali for Women, 1998.

———. "Abducted Women, the State and Questions of Honor: Three Perspectives in the Recovery Operation in Post-partition India." In *Embodied Violence: Communalising Women's Sexuality in South Asia*, edited by Jayawardena Kumari and M. De Alwis, 1–31. London: Zed Books, 1996.

Menon-Sen, K. "Bridges Over Troubled Waters: South Asian Women's Movements Confronting Globalization." *Society for International Development*, 45, no. 1 (2002): 132–36.

Mookherjee, Nayanika. "Gendered Embodiments: Mapping the Body-Politic of the Raped Woman and the Nation in Bangladesh." *Feminist Review, Special Issue on War*, 88, no. 1 (2008): 36–53.

Pereira, F. *The Fractured Scales: The Search for a Uniform Personal Code*. Calcutta, India: Stree, 2002.

Puja, K. "Global Civil Society Remakes History: The Women's International War Crimes Tribunal 2000." *Positions: East Asia Cultures Critique* 9, no. 3 (2001): 611–20.

Puja, K. "Backlash Against the Comfort Women Issue: Moves Against History Textbook References." In *Common Grounds: Violence against Women in War and Armed Conflict Situations*, edited by I. L. Sajor, 198–204. Quezon City, Philippines: Asian Center for Women's Human Rights (ASCENT), 1998.

Rai, S. M. *Gender and the Political Economy of Development: From Nationalism to Globalization*, Cambridge, UK: Polity Press, 2002.

Saikia, Yasmin. *Women, War, and the Making of Bangladesh: Remembering 1971*. Durham, NC: Duke University Press, 2011.

Seifert, R. *War Rape: Analytical Approaches*, Geneva: Women's International League for Peace and Freedom, 1993.

Siddiqi, Dina. "Left Behind By The Nation: 'Stranded Pakistanis' on Bangladesh'." *Sites*, 10, no. 1 (2013): 1–33.

Sobhan, S. "The Women's Movement of Southern Asia." *Canadian Dimension*, 37 (Jan/Feb 2003): 1, 26.

Waylen, G. "Analysing Women in the Politics of the Third World." In *Women and Politics in the Third World*, edited by H. Afshar, 7–24. London: Routledge, 1996.

Women's International War Crimes Tribunal on Japan's Military Sexual Slavery. (2000). www1.jca.apc.prg/vaww-net-japan/e_new/judgement.html.

Ziauddin, Ahmed. "What Is to Be Done About the Pakistani War Criminals and Collaborators." *The Daily Star*, 3 December, 1999. http://www.bangladeshmariners .com/HmdrRprt/what.html

9. Cambodia

Brickell, Katherine. "'We Don't Forget the Old Rice Pot When We Get the New One': Gendered Discourses on Ideals and Practices of Women in Contemporary Cambodia." *Signs* 36, no. 2 (2011): 437–62.

Derks, Annuska. *Khmer Women on the Move: Exploring Work and Life in Urban Cambodia.* Honolulu: University of Hawai'i Press, 2008.

Ditmore, Melissa. "'Caught between the Tiger and the Crocodile': Cambodian Sex Workers' Experiences of Structural and Physical Violence." *Studies in Gender and Sexuality* 15, no. 1 (2014): 22–31.

Hoefinger, Heidi. "Professional Girlfriends," *Cultural Studies* 25, no. 2 (2011): 244–66.

Levine, Peg. *Love and Dread in Cambodia: Weddings, Births and Ritual Harm Under the Khmer Rouge.* Singapore: NUS Press, 2010.

So, Farina. *The Hijab of Cambodia: Memories of Cham Muslim Women After the Khmer Rouge.* Phnom Penh: Documentation Center of Cambodia, 2011.

Jacobsen, Trude. "'Riding a Buffalo to Cross a Muddy Field': Heuristic Approaches to Feminism in Cambodia." In *Women's Movements in Asia: Feminism and Transnational Activism,* edited by Mina Roces and Louise Edwards, 207–23. London: Routledge, 2010.

10. The Guatemalan Genocide

Aguilar, Yolanda, and Luz Mendez. *Rompiendo el Silencio: Justicia Para Las Mujeres Victimas de Violencia Sexual Durante el Conflicto Armado en Guatemala.* Guatemala: Consorcio Actoras de Cambio: Instituto de Estudios Comparados en Ciencias Penales de Guatemala, 2006.

Ball, Patrick, Paul Kobrak, and Herbert F. Spirer. *State Violence in Guatemala, 1960–1996: A Quantitative Reflection.* Washington, DC: American Association for the Advancement of Science, 1999.

Berger, Susan A. *Guatemaltecas: The Women's Movement, 1986–2003.* Austin: University of Texas Press, 2006.

Casaus Arzu, Marta. *Genocidio: ¿La Máxima Expresión del Racismo en Guatemala?* Guatemala City: F&G Editores, 2008.

———. *Guatemala: Linaje y Racismo.* Guatemala City: F&G Editores, 2010.

Chirix, Emma. *Cuerpos, Poderes y Politicas: Mujeres Mayas en un Internado Catolico.* Guatemala: Ediciones Maya' Na'oj, 2013.

Colom, Yolanda. *Mujeres en la Alborada. Guerilla y Participacion Femenina en Guatemala 1973–1978.* Cuarta edicion [1998]. Guatemala: Artemis and Edinter, 2013.

Crosby, A., and M. B. Lykes. "Mayan Women Survivors Speak: The Gendered Relations of Truth-Telling in Postwar Guatemala." *International Journal of Transitional Justice* 5, no. 3 (2011): 456–76.

Comisión para el Esclarecimiento Histórico. *Edicion Integra del Informe de la Comision para el Esclarecimiento Historico del las Violaciones a los Derechos Humanos y los Hechos de Violencia que han Causado Sufrimientos a la Poblacion Guatemalteca.* Guatemala, Primera Edicion, 1999.

Cosajay, Yoc. *Violencia Sexaul a Mujeres Indigenas Durante el Conflicto Armado Interno y el Genocidio en Guatemala.* Caravelle, 102 (2014): 157–62.

Drouin, Marc. *"Acabar Hasta Con la Semilla" Comprendiendo el Genocidio Guatemalteco de 1982.* Guatemala City: F&G Editores, 2011.

Dube, Dany, and Ruth Del Valle. *Genocidio.* Guatemala: Alianza contra la impunidad: Movimient Nacional por los Derechos Humanos, 2004.

Falla, Ricardo. *Massacres in the Jungle: Ixcán, Guatemala, 1975–1982.* Boulder, CO: Westview Press, 1994.

———. *Negreaba de Zopilotes: Masacre y Sobrevivencia, Finca San Francisco Nenton, Guatemala (1871 a 2010)*. Guatemala City: Asociacion para el Avance de las Ciencias Sociales en Guatemala (AVANCSO), 2011.

Green, Linda. *Fear as a Way of Life: Mayan Widows in Rural Guatemala*. New York: Columbia University Press, 1999.

Guatemala. Tribunal Primero de Sentencia Penal, Narcoactividad y Delitos contra el Ambiente. *Condenado por Genocidio. Sentencia Condenatoria en Contra de Jose Efrain Rios Montt*. Guatemala City: F&G Editores, 2013.

Jonas, Susanne, Ed McCaughan, and Elizabeth Sutherland Martínez. *Guatemala— Tyranny on Trial: Testimony of the Permanent People's Tribunal*. San Francisco: Synthesis, 1984.

Justicia por Genocidio: Las Denuncias Contra Ríos Montt y Lucas García en Guatemala (Justice for Genocide: Prosecuting Rios Montt and Lucas Garcia in Guatemala). Guatemala City: Programa de Justicia y Reconciliacion; Centro para Accion Legal en Derechos Humanos, 2003.

Konefal, Betsy. *For Every Indio Who Falls: A History of Maya Activism in Guatemala, 1960– 1990*. Albuquerque: University of New Mexico Press, 2010.

Menchu, Rigoberta. *I, Rigoberta Menchu: An Indian Woman in Guatemala*. Edited by Elisabeth Burgos-Debray. Translated by Ann Wright. London: Verso, 1984.

Osorio, Jesús Tecú, Rights Action. *The Rió Negro Massacres*. [Rabinal, Guatemala?]: Published by the author with assistance from Rights Action, 2003.

Por Favor, Nunca Mas: Testimonios de Mujeres, Victimas del Conflicto Armado en Guatemala. Guatemala: Ayuda de la Iglesia Noruega, 1997.

Ramirez, Chiqui. *La Guerra de los 36 Anos Vista Con Los Ojos de Mujer de Izquierda. III Edicion Corregida y Aumentada*. Guatemala: INGRAFIC, 2012.

Sanford, Victoria. *Buried Secrets: Truth and Human Rights in Guatemala*. New York: Palgrave Macmillan, 2003.

———. "From Genocide to Feminicide: Impunity and Human Rights in Twenty-First Century Guatemala." *Journal of Human Rights* 7, no. 2 (2008): 104–22.

———. *Guatemala: del Genocidio al Feminicidio*. Guatemala City: F&G Editores, 2008.

———. *La Masacre de Panzos: Etnicidad, Tierra y Violencia en Guatemala*. Guatemala City: F&G Editores, 2009.

———. *¡Si Hubo Genocidio en Guatemala! (Yes! There was Genocide in Guatemala!)*. Basingstoke, England: Palgrave Macmillan, 2008.

———. *Violencia y Genocidio en Guatemala*. Guatemala City: F&G Editores, 2003.

Stuesse, A., B. Manz,E. Oglesby, K. Olson, and V. Sanford. "Si Hubo Genocidio: Anthropologists and the Genocide Trail of Guatemala's Rios Montt." *American Anthropologists* 115, no. 4 (2013): 658–63.

Women's International Resource Exchange Service. *We Continue Forever: Sorrow and Strength of Guatemalan Women*. New York: Women's International Resource Exchange, 1983.

Zur, Judith N. *Violent Memories: Mayan War Widows in Guatemala*. Boulder, CO: Westview Press, 1998.

11. Rwanda

African Rights. *Death, Despair and Defiance*. London: African Rights, 1995.

———. *Rwanda Not So Innocent: When Women Become Killers*. London: African Rights, 1995.

Baines, Erin K. "Body Politics and the Rwanda Crises", *Third World Quarterly*, 24, 3 (2004): 479–93.

———. "Les femmes aux mille bras: Building Peace and Rwanda." In *Gender, Conflict, and Peacekeeping*, edited by Dyan Mazurana, Angeal Raven-Roberts, and Jane Partpart. Lanham, MD: Rowman & Littlefield, 2005.

Brounéus, Karen. "Truth-Telling as Talking Cure? Insecurity and Retraumatization in the Rwandan Gacaca Courts." *Security Dialogue* 39, no. 1 (March 2008): 55–76.

Burnet, Jennie. E. "Gender Balance and the Meanings of Women in Governance in Post-Genocide Rwanda." *African Affairs* 107, no. 428 (2008): 361–86.

———. *Genocide Lives in Us: Women, Memory and Silence in Rwanda*. Madison: The University of Wisconsin Press, 2012.

Clark, Phil. *The Gacaca Courts and Post-Genocide Justice and Reconciliation in Rwanda: Justice without Lawyers*. Cambridge, UK: Cambridge University Press, 2010.

Fein, Helen. "Genocide and Gender: The Uses of Women and Group Destiny." *Journal of Genocide Research* 1, no. 1 (1999): 43–63.

Holmes, Georgina. *Women and War in Rwanda: Gender, Media and the Representation of Genocide*. London: I.B Tauris, 2014.

———. "Gendering the Rwanda Defence Force: A Critical Assessment." *Journal of Intervention and Statebuilding* 8, no. 4 (2014): 321–33.

Jevremovas, Villia. *Brickyards to Graveyards: From Production to Genocide in Rwanda*. Albany: State University of New York Press, 2002.

Jones, Adam. *Gendercide and Genocide in Rwanda*. Nashville: Vanderbilt University Press, 2004.

Newbury, Catherine. "Ethnicity and the Politics of History in Rwanda." *Africa Today* 45, no. 1 (1996): 7–24.

Newbury, Catherine, and Hannah Baldwin. "Aftermath: Women in Postgenocide Rwanda." Washington, DC: Centre for Development Information and Evaluation, US Agency for International Development, 2000.

Newbury, David. "Understanding Genocide." *African Studies Review* 41, no. 1, (1998): 73–97.

Melvern, Linda. *A People Betrayed: The Role of the West in the Rwandan Genocide*, London: Zed Books, 2009.

Dallaire, Romeo. *Shake Hands with the Devil: The Failure of Humanity in Rwanda*. London: Arrow Books, 2003.

Prunier, Gerard. *The Rwandan Crisis: History of a Genocide*. London: Hurst, 1997.

———. *From Genocide to Continental War: The 'Congolese' Conflict and the Crisis in Contemporary Africa*. London: Hurst, 1997.

Taylor, Christopher C. *Sacrifice as Terror: The Rwandan Genocide of 1994*. Oxford, UK: Berg, 1999.

12. Bosnia

Delić, Amra., and Esmina Avdibegović. "Shame and Silence in the Aftermath of War Rape in Bosnia and Herzegovina: 22 Years Later." In *Interdisciplinary Perspectives on Children Born of War—From World War II to Current Conflict Settings*, edited by Glaesmer Heide and Lee Sabine, Conference, Hannover, Germany, 2015.

Ajanović, Irfan ed. *I Begged Them to Kill Me: Crimes against the Women of Bosnia-Herzegovina*. Sarajevo, Boxnia and Herzegovina: CID, 2000.

Amnesty International. "Whose Justice? Bosnia and Herzegovina's Women Still Waiting." *Amnesty International (Report)*. September 30, 2009.

Avdibegović, Esmina, and Osman Sinanović. "Consequences of Domestic Violence on Women's Mental Health in Bosnia and Herzegovina." *Croatian Medical Journal*, 47, 5 (October 2006): 730–41.

Bećirević, Edina. *Genocide on the Drina River*. New Haven, CT: Yale University Press, 2014.

Cloyes DioGuardi, Shirley. "Breaking the Protracted Silence about Genocidal Rape in Kosova." In *Women and Genocide, Gendered Experiences of Violence, Survival, and Resistance*, edited by JoAnn DiGeorgio-Lutz and Donna Gosbee. Toronto, ON: Women's Press, 2016.

Ensler, Eve. *Necessary Targets: A Story of Women and War*. New York: Villard, 2001.

Helms, Elissa. "Gendered Justice: Campaigning by and for Women War Survivors in Muslim Dominated Bosnia-Herzegovina." In *Peines de guerre: La justice internationale et l'ex-Yougoslavie*, edited by Isabelle Delpla and Magali Bessone. Paris: Editions de l'EHESS, 2010.

———. "Rejecting Angelina: Bosnian War Rape Survivors and the Ambiguities of Sex in War." *Slavic Review* 73, no. 3 (Fall 2014): 612–34.

Hatidža, Hren, and Nura Becgović. *Samrtno Srebreničko ljeto '95*. Tuzla, Boxnia and Herzegovina: Udruženje građana Zene Srebrenice, 1998.

Hunt, Swanee. *This Was Not Our War, Bosnian Women Reclaiming the Peace*. Durham, NC: Duke University Press, 2005.

von Joeden-Forgey, Elisa. "Gender and the Future of Genocide Studies and Prevention." In *Genocide and Gender in the Twentieth Century, A Comparative Survey*, edited by Amy E. Randall, 298–321. London: Bloomsbury Press.

Leydesdorff, Selma. *Prazninu ostaviti iza nas, Istorija Žene Srebrenice*. Sarajevo: Rabic, 2009.

———. "When Communities Fell Apart and Neighbors Became Enemies: Stories of Bewilderment in Srebrenica." In *Memories of Mass Repression, Narrating Stories in the Aftermath of Atrocity*, edited by Nanci Adler, Selma Leydesdorff et al., 21–41. New Brunswick, NJ: Transaction Publishers, 2009.

———. "How Shall we Remember Srebrenica?: Will the Language of Law Structure Our Memory?" In *Memory and the Future: Transnational Politics, Ethics and Society*, edited by Yifat Gutman, Adam D. Brown, and Amy Sodaro, 121–41. New York: Palgrave Macmillan, 2010.

———. *Surviving the Bosnian Genocide: The Women of Srebrenica Speak*. Bloomington: Indiana University Press, 2011.

———. "When all Is Lost: Metanarrative in the Oral History of Hanifa, Survivor of Srebrenica." In *Listening on the Edge: Oral History in the Aftermath of Crisis*, edited by Marc Cave and Stephen M. Sloan, 17–33. New York: Oxford University Press, 2014.

———. "Distortions in Survivors' Narratives from Srebrenica: The Impossibility of Conveying their Truth." In *Genocide and Gender in the Twentieth Century: A Comparative Survey*, edited by Amy E. Randall, 258–75. London: Bloomsbury.

Matton, Sylvie. *Srebrenica, Un Génocide annoncé*. Paris: Flammation, 2005.

Nettelfield, Lara J., and Sarah E. Wagner. *Srebrenica in the Aftermath of Genocide*. New York: Cambridge University Press, 2013.

Simic, Olivera. "Memorial Culture in the Former Yugoslavia: Mothers of Srebrenica and the Destruction of Artifacts by the ICTY." In *The Art of Transitional Justice: Culture, Activism and Memory after Atrocity*, edited by Peter Rush and Olivera Simic, 155–73. New York: Springer, 2013.

———. "'Pillar of Shame': Civil Society, the UN Responsibility, and Genocide in Srebrenica." In *Transitional Justice and Civil Society in the Balkans*, edited by Simic Olivera and Volcic Zlatko, 181–200. New York: Springer, 2013.

———. "Wartime Rape and Its Shunned Victims." In *Genocide and Gender in the Twentieth Century: A Comparative Survey*, edited by Amy E. Randall, 237–58. London: Bloomsbury, 2015.

Smith, Roger W. "Genocide and the Politics of Rape: Historical and Psychological Perspectives." In *Genocide Matters: Ongoing Issues and Emerging Perspectives*, edited by Joyce Apsel and Ernesto Verjeja, 83–85. London: Routledge, 2013.

Seada, Vranić. *Breaking the Wall of Silence. The Voices of Raped in Bosnia*. Zagreb, Croatia: Izdabja Antibarus, 1996.

Sorguc, Albino. "Srebrenica Anniversary: The Rape Victims Testimonies." *Balkan Transitional Justice*, last modified July 11, 2014. http://www.balkaninsight.com/en/article/srebrenica-anniversary-the-rape-victims-testimonies/1422/3.

Zarkov, Dubravka, and Glasius Marlies. *Narratives of Justice in and out of the Courtroom: Former Yugoslavia and Beyond*. New York: Springer, 2014.

13. Darfur

Abdel Halim, Asma. "Gendered Justice: Women and the Application of Penal Laws in the Sudan." In *Criminal Law Reform and Transitional Justice: Human Rights Perspectives for Sudan*, edited by Oette Lutz, 227–41. Farnham, UK: Ashgate, 2011.

Amnesty International. *Sudan: Darfur: Rape as a Weapon of War: Sexual Violence and Its Consequences*. London: Amnesty International, July 18, 2004.

Askin, Kelly. "Prosecuting Gender Crimes Committed in Darfur: Holding Leaders Accountable for Sexual Violence." In *Genocide in Darfur: Investigating the Atrocities in the Sudan*, edited Samuel Totten and Eric Markusen, 141–60. New York: Routledge, 2006.

Corcoran, Rebecca A. "Justice for the Forgotten: Saving the Women of Darfur." *Boston College Third World Law Journal* 28, no. 1 (January 2008): 203–38.

Gingerich, Tara, and Jennifer Leaning. *Rape as a Weapon of War in the Conflict in Darfur, Sudan*. Cambridge, MA: Physicians for Human Rights, 2004.

Hagan, John, Wenona Rymond-Richmond, and Alberto Palloni. "Racial Targeting of Sexual Violence in Darfur." *American Journal of Public Health* 99, no. 8 (August 2009): 1386–92.

Human Rights Watch. *Mass Rape in North Darfur: Sudanese Army Attacks Against Civilians in Tabit*. New York: Human Rights Watch, 2015.

———. *Men With No Mercy: Rapid Support Forces Attacks Against Civilians In Darfur, Sudan*. New York: Human Rights Watch, 2015.

———. *Sexual Violence and Its Consequences Among Displaced Persons in Darfur and Chad*. New York: Human Rights Watch, 2005.

Médecins Sans Frontières. "The Crushing Burden of Rape: Sexual Violence in Darfur." Geneva, Switzerland: Médecins Sans Frontières, March 8, 2005.

Physicians for Human Rights. *Nowhere to Turn: Failure to Protect, Support and Assure Justice for Darfuri Women*. Cambridge, MA: Physicians for Human Rights, 2009.

Redress. *Time for Change: Reforming Sudan's Legislation on Rape and Sexual Violence*. 2008. www.redress.org/downloads/.../Position%20Paper%20Rape.pdf

Tonnessen, Liv. "When Rape Becomes Politics: Negotiating Islamic Law Reform in Sudan." *Women's Studies International Forum* 44 (May–June 2014): 145–53.

Tonnessen, Liv, and Samia al-Nagar, eds. *Women and Girls Caught Between Rape and Adultery in Sudan: Criminal Law Reform, 2005–2015*. Bergen, Norway: Chr. Michelsen Institute (CMI), 2015.

Totten, Samuel. "The Darfur Genocide: The Mass Rape of Black African Girls and Women." In *Plight and Fate of Women During and Following Genocide*, edited by Samuel Totten, 47–66. New Brunswick, NJ: Transaction Publishers, 2009.

UNFPA/UNICEF. *The Effects of Conflict on Health and Well-Being of Women and Girls in Darfur: Situational Analysis Report: Conversations with the Community*. New York: United Nations, 2005.

Wagner, Justin. "The Systematic Use of Rape as a Tool of War in Darfur: A Blueprint for International War Crimes Prosecutions." *Georgetown Journal of International Law*, 37, 1 (Fall 2005).

14. Grassroots Women: From Iraq, Syria, and the Islamic State (ISIS) to Guatemala and Colombia

Al-Ali, N., and Nicola Pratt. *What Kind of Liberation? Women and the Occupation of Iraq*. Berkeley: University of California Press, 2009.

Bouvier, Virginia, ed. *Colombia: Building Peace in a Time of War*. Washington, DC: United States Institute of Peace, 2009.

Cockburn, Cynthia. *From Where We Stand: War, Women's Activism and Feminist Analysis*. London: Zed Books, 2007.

Christie, D. J., R. V. Wagner, and D. A. Winter, eds. *Peace, Conflict, and Violence: Peace Psychology for the 21st Century*. Englewood Cliffs, NJ: Prentice-Hall, 2001.

Davis, Lisa. "Iraqi Women Confronting ISIL: Protecting Women's Rights in the Context of Conflict." *Southwestern Journal of International Law* 22, no. 1 (Fall 2016): 27–78.

Ghazzawi, Razan, Afra Mohammed, and Oula Ramadan. *"Peacebuilding Defines Our Future Now": A Study of Women's Peace Activism in Syria*. Istanbul: Badael Foundation, 2015.

Kuehnast, Kathleen, Chantal de Jonge Oudraat, and Helga Hernes, eds. *Women & War: Power and Protection in the 21st Century*. Washington, DC: United States Institute of Peace, 2011.

MADRE, Taller De Vida, Women's Link Worldwide, et al. *Report on Violations of Women's Human Rights: In response to the Sixth Periodic Report of Colombia to the United Nations Human Rights Committee*. New York: MADRE, 2010.

Méndez Gutiérrez, Luz and Amanda Carrera Guerra. *Clamor for Justice: Sexual Violence, Armed Conflict and Violent Land Dispossession*. Guatemala City: Equipo de Estudios Comunitarios y Acción Psicosocial, 2015.

Human Rights and Gender Justice (HRGJ) Clinic at CUNY Law School (formerly known as The International Women's Human Rights (IWHR) Clinic), MADRE, The Organization of Women's Freedom in Iraq (OWFI). *Seeking Accountability and Demanding Change: A Report on Women's Rights Violations in Iraq Under the UN Convention Against Torture.* New York: MADRE, 2015.

Human Rights and Gender Justice (HRGJ) Clinic at CUNY Law School (formerly known as The International Women's Human Rights (IWHR) Clinic), MADRE, The Women's International League for Peace and Freedom (WILPF). *Human Rights Violations Against Women and Girls in Syria: Submission to the United Nations Universal Periodic Review of the Syrian Arab Republic.* New York: MADRE, 2016.

Meintjes, Sheila, Meredeth Turshen, and Anu Pillay, eds. *The Aftermath: Women in Post-Conflict Transformation.* London: Zed Books, 2001.

Stern, Maria. *Naming Security—Constructing Identity: 'Mayan-Women' in Guatemala on the Eve of 'Peace.'* Manchester, UK: Manchester University Press, 2005.

Susskind, Yifat. *Promising Democracy, Imposing Theocracy: Gender-Based Violence and the US War on Iraq.* New York: MADRE, 2007.

Svedberg, Barbro, L. Alodaat, M. Rees, and N. Porobic Isakovic. *Women Organising for Change in Syria and Bosnia.* Geneva, Switzerland: Women's International League for Peace and Freedom (WILPF), 2014.

UN Women. *A Window of Opportunity: Making Transitional Justice Work for Women.* New York: United Nations, 2010.

INDEX

CPSIA information can be obtained
at www.ICGtesting.com
Printed in the USA
BVHW081554190220
572800BV00003B/335